THE COMPLETE BOOK OF BIBLE LITERACY

MARK D. TAYLOR

**Tyndale House
Publishers, Inc.
Wheaton, Illinois**

Scripture Press, England
Anzea Publishers, Australia
Campus Crusade Asia Limited, Singapore

D1111975

Unless otherwise identified, all Scripture quotations are taken from the King James Version.

Scripture quotations marked NAB are taken from *The New American Bible*, copyright 1970 by Confraternity of Christian Doctrine.

Scripture quotations marked NIV are taken from The *Holy Bible, New International Version*, copyright 1973, 1978, 1984 by International Bible Society. Used by permission of Zondervan Publishing House.

Scripture quotations marked NKJV are taken from The *Holy Bible, New King James Version*, copyright 1982 by Thomas Nelson, Inc.

Scripture quotations marked TLB are taken from *The Living Bible*, copyright 1971 by Tyndale House Publishers.

"How Great Thou Art" by Stuart K. Hine, copyright 1953, renewed 1981 by MANNA MUSIC, INC., 25510 Avenue Stanford, Valencia, CA 91355. International Copyright Secured. All rights reserved. Used by permission.

Front cover illustration by Don Kueker. Maps copyright © 1986, 1988 by Tyndale House Publishers, Inc. All rights reserved.

Visual art in this book appears by permission or courtesy of:

V. Gilbert Beers, 100, 114, 129, 130 left, 135 left, 157, 159, 162, 177, 183, 185, 186, 199, 200 right, 203 left, 204, 205, 207, 212, 226, 230, 234, 265, 275, 277 left, 281, 285, 296, 298 left, 361

The Billy Graham Center Museum, 256, 260, 269, 271 right, 273, 279, 280 left, 283, 293, 298 right, 299, 357

Historical Pictures/Stock Montage, 355, 365

William Koechling, 274; William Koechling/Lois Rusch, 314

Oxford University Press, 336

Religious News Service, 277 right, 278, 287, 294, 309, 335, 352, 364, 365 left, 366

H. Armstrong Roberts, Inc., 363

Peter W. Taylor, Charts and Timeline designed by, 141, 153, 155, 156, 164

John C. Trever, 75, 79

Tyndale House Publishers, Inc.: Blas Gallego, 172; Michael Hackett, 91, 152; Richard and Frances Hook, 116, 135 right, 139, 142, 206, 224; Don L. Kueker, 119, 198 top, 201, 213, 215, 219; Joseph Miralles, 128, 133, 149 left, 178, 229; Joan Pelaez, 109, 138, 147, 151, 179

William Stephens, 258, 289, 297, 350, 353

Wade Collection of Wheaton College, Illinois, 280 (right)

Library of Congress Cataloging-in-Publication Data

Taylor, Mark D.
   The complete book of Bible literacy / Mark D. Taylor.
      p. cm.
   Includes index.
   ISBN 0-8423-1072-X
   1.Bible—Handbooks, manuals, etc. 2. Church history—Handbooks, manuals, etc.
3. Theology—Handbooks, manuals, etc. 4. Arts and religion—Handbooks, manuals, etc.
I. Title.
BS417.T39   1992
220.6'1—dc20   92-22170

Printed in the United States of America

99 98 97 96 95 94
10 9 8 7 6 5 4

This book is dedicated to my wife, Carol, and to our children, Jeremy, Kristen, Margaret, Rebecca, and Stephen. Carol and I have tried to help our children become biblically literate, but our deeper aspiration is that they continue to love God's Word as they grow and mature.

CONTENTS

INTRODUCTION

When people want to communicate with each other, they need a common language—be it English, Russian, or Swahili. But for meaningful interaction, they need more than just a common language. They need a shared body of common knowledge. *The Dictionary of Cultural Literacy* makes this point beautifully. The authors say that their dictionary "identifies and defines the names, phrases, events, and other items that are familiar to most literate Americans: the information that we call cultural literacy."

This book, *The Complete Book of Bible Literacy*, applies the same concept to the world of the Bible and Christianity. If, as most Christians believe, the Bible is God's inspired communication to mankind, the only infallible rule for faith and practice, we need to know the Bible. This book identifies and defines the names, phrases, events, stories, and terms from the Bible and CHURCH HISTORY that are familiar to most Christians: the information that I call biblical literacy.

The Bible has had a profound impact on English literature and on many aspects of daily life. When I was a student at Duke University, one of my professors devoted an entire class period to the proposition that educated Americans need to know the key people and stories from the Bible, whether or not they believe the Bible to be true. If all literate Americans need to know about the MOSAIC LAW, the TWENTY-THIRD PSALM, the NATIVITY, and the phrase TURN THE OTHER CHEEK, how much more should Christians know them?

But the literate Christian knows *more* than the average American knows about the Bible. Cultural literacy, for example, includes recognition of the term TEN COMMANDMENTS, but biblical literacy includes recognition of each of the commandments themselves (e.g., REMEMBER THE SABBATH DAY, TO KEEP IT HOLY, and THOU SHALT NOT COMMIT ADULTERY). This does not mean that every

Christian must be able to rattle off the Ten Commandments from memory, but most Christians recognize them when they see them.

Cultural literacy includes recognition of the names ABRAHAM and ISAAC and DANIEL and PETER, but biblical literacy also includes SARAH, LOT, RACHEL, LEAH, NEBUCHADNEZZAR, and ANDREW. These names may not be familiar to the average American, but they should be familiar to most Christians.

This book includes entries from several areas that are not specifically related to the Bible. For instance, the chapter "Church History" includes key names and events from the EARLY CHURCH right up through the impact of GLASNOST in the 1990s, as well as the names of the largest American DENOMINATIONS. The chapter "Church Life and Theology" includes terms one is likely to encounter in the church today. "The Bible and Christianity in the Fine Arts" includes popular HYMNS, great works of religious art, artists and sculptors, and so forth.

Most of the definitions in this book contain other key words or phrases that are also defined in the book. The first time such a key word is used in a definition, it appears in small capitals (though I have not used small capitals for terms such as God, Lord, Jesus, and Bible that are used frequently throughout the book).

If you want to look up a particular word or phrase, use the index. The index includes every key entry, and it is generously cross-referenced. For instance, if you want to look up the **Babylonian captivity**, the index directs you to **Exile**.

I have included fourteen self-grading quizzes in the book—one for each major subject area and three longer quizzes that cover subjects from all of the chapters. If you enjoy testing your knowledge, you'll enjoy the quizzes. Take them before you begin reading the book if you want to, or brush up on your knowledge first. You may want to go back later and take a quiz a second time. Key words or phrases are printed in small capitals to help you find the pertinent entries in the book. For your convenience the answers appear immediately after each quiz.

Just a word about the Bible quotations in this book. Although many people now use modern TRANSLATIONS, the biblical phrases that are embedded in our culture are from the KING JAMES VERSION. Unless I indicate otherwise, all Bible quotations in the book are from that venerable translation.

There are differing opinions among scholars as to who wrote the various BOOKS OF THE BIBLE. I have chosen to reflect the traditional view of authorship when I mention the author of a particular book.

This is not a book to read at one sitting. You'll enjoy browsing. And by the time you've mastered all these names and terms, you'll find that you have a common language with Christians in your own church and around the world.

I am deeply indebted to my editors, LaVonne Neff and Carla Whitacre, and to my professional reviewers, Timothy Bayly, Tom Cornman, Doug Gropp, Marvin Mayer, and Robert Patterson. They gave me valuable counsel and saved me from some embarrassing errors. In the end, of course, I am responsible for the mistakes that remain.

QUIZZES

This section of the book includes fourteen self-grading quizzes. There are eleven shorter quizzes and three longer quizzes.

The "pop quizzes" contain twenty multiple-choice questions. The last three quizzes are hardest. They each contain fifty questions, and two of them are fill-in-the-blank quizzes. One of the longer quizzes covers only the Bible itself, and two cover many aspects of the Bible and the church. My wife thinks the last quizzes are too hard, but I'll let you come to your own conclusion!

In all the quizzes, key words or phrases are printed in small capitals to help you look up the appropriate definitions in the book. The answers for each quiz appear immediately after that quiz.

The following list of scores is for the quizzes with twenty multiple-choice questions:

0–1 wrong	Outstanding; you are well versed in the subject area covered in that quiz
2 wrong	Excellent; you're well on your way to mastering this subject area
3–4 wrong	Good; you know this subject area better than the average person, but you could brush up a little bit
5–6 wrong	Fair; you definitely need to study
7 or more wrong	Oops!

These scores are for the quizzes with fifty questions:

0–3 wrong	Outstanding; you are well versed in biblical and Christian literacy
4–7 wrong	Excellent; you're well on your way to mastering these subjects
8–12 wrong	Good; you know these subjects better than the average person, but you could brush up a little bit
13–17 wrong	Fair; you definitely need to study
18 or more wrong	Oops!

Enjoy testing yourself!

QUIZ THE BIBLE

The B-I-B-L-E, Yes That's the Book for Me

Select one answer for each question.

1. APOCALYPSE is another name for which book of the Bible?

    a. ☐ GENESIS
    b. ☐ MALACHI
    c. ☐ MATTHEW
    d. ☐ REVELATION

2. Different parts of the Bible were originally written in several different languages. Which one of these languages is not one of the original languages?

    a. ☐ GREEK
    b. ☐ LATIN
    c. ☐ HEBREW
    d. ☐ ARAMAIC

3. Which term is used to refer to the first five books of the Old Testament?

    a. ☐ BOOKS OF MOSES
    b. ☐ PENTATEUCH
    c. ☐ TORAH
    d. ☐ all of the above

4. Who is generally considered to have written the book of ACTS?

    a. ☐ MATTHEW
    b. ☐ MARK
    c. ☐ LUKE
    d. ☐ none of the above

5. The books in the following lists contain portions of the history of the people of ISRAEL. Which list is in the proper chronological sequence?

   a. ☐ GENESIS, DANIEL, 1 SAMUEL, NEHEMIAH
   b. ☐ NUMBERS, JOSHUA, 2 KINGS, RUTH
   c. ☐ EXODUS, 2 SAMUEL, 1 KINGS, EZRA
   d. ☐ 1 CHRONICLES, 2 CHRONICLES, JUDGES, ESTHER

6. Which of the following books is one of the MINOR PROPHETS?

   a. ☐ ISAIAH
   b. ☐ EZEKIEL
   c. ☐ DANIEL
   d. ☐ AMOS

7. In which book do we read about the statue with the FEET OF CLAY, the FIERY FURNACE, and the HANDWRITING ON THE WALL?

   a. ☐ DANIEL
   b. ☐ EXODUS
   c. ☐ MATTHEW
   d. ☐ REVELATION

8. The book of DEUTERONOMY consists primarily of a long speech to the people of ISRAEL. Who gave the speech?

   a. ☐ ABRAHAM
   b. ☐ MOSES
   c. ☐ DAVID
   d. ☐ PAUL

9. Which book contains the story of MOSES leading the people of ISRAEL out of EGYPT?

   a. ☐ EXODUS
   b. ☐ JOSHUA
   c. ☐ JUDGES
   d. ☐ 1 KINGS

10. Which three books are generally considered to have been written by PAUL?

   a. ☐ ACTS, ROMANS, 1 CORINTHIANS
   b. ☐ GALATIANS, EPHESIANS, PHILIPPIANS
   c. ☐ HEBREWS, JAMES, 1 PETER
   d. ☐ 3 JOHN, JUDE, REVELATION

11. Which TRANSLATION of the Bible is sometimes called the AUTHORIZED VERSION?

    a. ☐ VULGATE

    b. ☐ KING JAMES VERSION

    c. ☐ REVISED STANDARD VERSION

    d. ☐ NEW INTERNATIONAL VERSION

12. Which is the first book in the Bible?

    a. ☐ MATTHEW

    b. ☐ JOHN

    c. ☐ GENESIS

    d. ☐ PSALMS

13. Which book of the Bible begins with the phrase "IN THE BEGINNING was the Word"?

    a. ☐ GENESIS

    b. ☐ PSALMS

    c. ☐ MATTHEW

    d. ☐ JOHN

14. Which of the following books did JEREMIAH write?

    a. ☐ GENESIS

    b. ☐ LAMENTATIONS

    c. ☐ PROVERBS

    d. ☐ ROMANS

15. The book of JUDGES contains the stories of:

    a. ☐ ABRAHAM, ISAAC, and JACOB

    b. ☐ MOSES, AARON, and MIRIAM

    c. ☐ DEBORAH, GIDEON, and SAMSON

    d. ☐ PETER, JAMES, JOHN

16. The books of 1 and 2 KINGS contain, for the most part:

    a. ☐ poetry

    b. ☐ PROPHECY

    c. ☐ THEOLOGY

    d. ☐ history

17. Matthew, Mark, Luke, and John are:

    a. ☐ Gospels
    b. ☐ Epistles
    c. ☐ books of prophecy
    d. ☐ part of the Pentateuch

18. Which of the following statements is true of the original manuscripts of the Old Testament?

    a. ☐ they are now in a museum in Jerusalem
    b. ☐ they are no longer in existence
    c. ☐ they are called the Dead Sea Scrolls
    d. ☐ none of the above

19. Who was the original recipient of the letter we now know as the book of Philemon?

    a. ☐ Philemon
    b. ☐ Onesimus
    c. ☐ Paul
    d. ☐ James

20. Romans, a letter that sets forth a theology of the Christian faith, was written by:

    a. ☐ Jesus
    b. ☐ Peter
    c. ☐ David
    d. ☐ Paul

ANSWERS

1. d	6. d	11. b	16. d
2. b	7. a	12. c	17. a
3. d	8. b	13. d	18. b
4. c	9. a	14. b	19. a
5. c	10. b	15. c	20. d

QUIZ FROM THE QUOTATIONS BIBLE

Quote, Unquote

Select one answer for each question.

1. Who said, "AM I MY BROTHER'S KEEPER?"

- a. ☐ JACOB
- b. ☐ JAMES
- c. ☐ CAIN
- d. ☐ MIRIAM

2. To whom did God say, "BE FRUITFUL AND MULTIPLY"?

- a. ☐ ABRAHAM
- b. ☐ NOAH
- c. ☐ DAVID
- d. ☐ SOLOMON

3. "BLESSED ARE THE MEEK, . . ."

- a. ☐ for they shall be called sons of God
- b. ☐ for theirs is the KINGDOM OF HEAVEN
- c. ☐ for they shall inherit the earth
- d. ☐ for they shall be comforted

4. When did Jesus say, "DO THIS IN REMEMBRANCE OF ME"?

- a. ☐ while he was hanging on the CROSS
- b. ☐ when he fed 5,000 people with a few LOAVES AND FISHES
- c. ☐ just before the ASCENSION
- d. ☐ at the LAST SUPPER

5. Who said, "COME UNTO ME, ALL YE THAT LABOR"?

- a. ☐ MOSES
- b. ☐ ISAIAH
- c. ☐ JESUS
- d. ☐ MARY MAGDALENE

6. Which of these quotations is found in the book of PSALMS?

a. ☐ BLESS THE LORD, O MY SOUL
b. ☐ MAKE A JOYFUL NOISE UNTO THE LORD
c. ☐ THE LORD IS MY SHEPHERD
d. ☐ all of the above

7. From what part of the SCRIPTURE was Jesus quoting when he said, "You have heard that it was said, 'EYE FOR AN EYE, TOOTH FOR A TOOTH'"?

a. ☐ BOOKS OF MOSES
b. ☐ books of history
c. ☐ PSALMS
d. ☐ Books of PROPHECY

8. Who or what had "FEET OF CLAY"?

a. ☐ the GOLDEN CALF
b. ☐ the statue in NEBUCHADNEZZAR's dream
c. ☐ the prophets of BAAL
d. ☐ LOT'S WIFE

9. What is the first phrase of JOHN 3:16?

a. ☐ BLESSED ARE THE PEACEMAKERS
b. ☐ FOR GOD SO LOVED THE WORLD
c. ☐ OUR FATHER, WHO ART IN HEAVEN
d. ☐ LOVE THY NEIGHBOR AS THYSELF

10. To whom did Jesus say, "GET THEE BEHIND ME, SATAN"?

a. ☐ the DEMON-possessed Gadarene
b. ☐ JUDAS ISCARIOT
c. ☐ PETER
d. ☐ Pontius PILATE

11. "GIVE US THIS DAY OUR DAILY BREAD" is a phrase from:

a. ☐ the LORD'S PRAYER
b. ☐ the APOSTLES' CREED
c. ☐ the MAGNIFICAT
d. ☐ the BEATITUDES

12. Which one of the following statements is not one of the TEN COMMANDMENTS?

    a. ☐ THOU SHALT LOVE THE LORD THY GOD WITH ALL THY HEART, AND WITH ALL THY MIND, AND WITH ALL THY SOUL

    b. ☐ REMEMBER THE SABBATH DAY, TO KEEP IT HOLY

    c. ☐ THOU SHALT NOT COMMIT ADULTERY

    d. ☐ HONOR THY FATHER AND THY MOTHER

13. Who said, "IF I PERISH, I PERISH"?

    a. ☐ CAIN

    b. ☐ JONATHAN

    c. ☐ ESTHER

    d. ☐ JESUS

14. In which book of the Bible do we find the phrase "LET THERE BE LIGHT"?

    a. ☐ GENESIS

    b. ☐ PSALMS

    c. ☐ MATTHEW

    d. ☐ JOHN

15. What is the opening phrase of the TWENTY-THIRD PSALM?

    a. ☐ MAKE A JOYFUL NOISE UNTO THE LORD

    b. ☐ BLESS THE LORD, O MY SOUL

    c. ☐ The LORD IS MY SHEPHERD

    d. ☐ THY WORD IS A LAMP UNTO MY FEET

16. Which of these is incorrectly quoted from the Bible?

    a. ☐ For ALL HAVE SINNED, AND COME SHORT OF THE GLORY OF GOD

    b. ☐ BLESSED ARE THE MEEK, FOR THEY SHALL INHERIT THE EARTH

    c. ☐ MANY ARE CALLED, BUT FEW ARE CHOSEN

    d. ☐ MONEY IS THE ROOT OF ALL EVIL

17. Which of the following phrases is not found in the Bible?

    a. ☐ There is NOTHING NEW UNDER THE SUN

    b. ☐ VANITY OF VANITIES, ALL IS VANITY

    c. ☐ EAT, DRINK, AND BE MERRY

    d. ☐ WE HAVE LEFT UNDONE THOSE THINGS WHICH WE OUGHT TO HAVE DONE

18. Who said, "A PROPHET IS NOT WITHOUT HONOR, SAVE IN HIS OWN COUNTRY"?

    a. ☐ MOSES
    b. ☐ ELIJAH
    c. ☐ DANIEL
    d. ☐ JESUS

19. When ISAIAH said, "They shall beat their SWORDS INTO PLOWSHARES," he meant:

    a. ☐ his listeners needed farm implements more than they needed swords
    b. ☐ the BABYLONIANS would come to JUDAH to help farm the land
    c. ☐ there will be no more war during the peaceful reign of the MESSIAH
    d. ☐ the people would use swords to dig up the ground

20. When Jesus said, "YE CANNOT SERVE GOD AND MAMMON," he meant:

    a. ☐ only members of MONASTIC orders can truly serve God
    b. ☐ a person cannot WORSHIP money and also pursue a right relationship with God
    c. ☐ TAX COLLECTORS could not hope to enter the KINGDOM OF HEAVEN
    d. ☐ none of the above

ANSWERS

1. c	6. d	11. a	16. d
2. b	7. a	12. a	17. d
3. c	8. b	13. c	18. d
4. d	9. b	14. a	19. c
5. c	10. c	15. c	20. b

What Is It? Where Is It?

Select one answer for each question.

1. Which of the following were TRIBES OF ISRAEL?

    a. ☐ Asher, Dan, Gad
    b. ☐ Issachar, MOSES, Naphtali
    c. ☐ ABRAHAM, JUDAH, BENJAMIN
    d. ☐ all of the above

2. The land of CANAAN was located:

    a. ☐ at the mouth of the NILE RIVER
    b. ☐ between the TIGRIS and EUPHRATES RIVERS
    c. ☐ at the eastern end of the MEDITERRANEAN SEA
    d. ☐ at the western end of the Mediterranean Sea

3. Which of the following is not another name for the ISRAELITES?

    a. ☐ CANAANITES
    b. ☐ the CHOSEN PEOPLE
    c. ☐ HEBREWS
    d. ☐ CHILDREN OF ISRAEL

4. The gold-plated chest that was kept in the HOLY OF HOLIES was called:

    a. ☐ the HOLY GRAIL
    b. ☐ the SANHEDRIN
    c. ☐ the ARK OF THE COVENANT
    d. ☐ the TORAH

5. What is a COVENANT?

    a. ☐ a SACRIFICE
    b. ☐ another name for the TABERNACLE
    c. ☐ a residence for NUNS
    d. ☐ a solemn agreement between two parties

6. The JORDAN RIVER:

    a. ☐ flows into the DEAD SEA
    b. ☐ was held back so the ISRAELITES could cross over on dry land
    c. ☐ is used as a metaphor for crossing over into HEAVEN
    d. ☐ all of the above

7. The land at the mouth of the NILE RIVER is called:

    a. ☐ ISRAEL
    b. ☐ EGYPT
    c. ☐ BABYLON
    d. ☐ GREECE

8. On what mountain did NOAH's ark come to rest after the FLOOD?

    a. ☐ Mount SINAI
    b. ☐ ARARAT
    c. ☐ Mount of OLIVES
    d. ☐ Mount ZION

9. Which of these bodies of water is essentially north of JERUSALEM?

    a. ☐ JORDAN RIVER
    b. ☐ DEAD SEA
    c. ☐ Sea of GALILEE
    d. ☐ NILE RIVER

10. The DAY OF ATONEMENT:

    a. ☐ is also called PASSOVER
    b. ☐ was the only day the HIGH PRIEST could enter the HOLY OF HOLIES
    c. ☐ is still celebrated by JEWS as HANUKKAH
    d. ☐ was the festival of the harvest

11. The ROMAN province of GALILEE was located:

    a. ☐ north of SAMARIA and JUDEA
    b. ☐ east of Judea
    c. ☐ south of Samaria
    d. ☐ west of Judea

12. What is a GENTILE?

    a. ☐ a Christian
    b. ☐ a descendant of JACOB
    c. ☐ a JEW
    d. ☐ a person who is not a Jew

13. What land was described in the Old Testament as a LAND FLOWING WITH MILK AND HONEY?

    a. ☐ EGYPT
    b. ☐ CANAAN
    c. ☐ GREECE
    d. ☐ BABYLON

14. What was the capital of ISRAEL during King SOLOMON's reign?

    a. ☐ JERICHO
    b. ☐ SAMARIA
    c. ☐ BETHLEHEM
    d. ☐ JERUSALEM

15. The term NORTHERN KINGDOM refers to:

    a. ☐ the ROMAN EMPIRE
    b. ☐ the Kingdom of ISRAEL
    c. ☐ the Kingdom of JUDAH
    d. ☐ GREECE

16. The MOSAIC LAW is found in:

    a. ☐ the PENTATEUCH
    b. ☐ the GOSPELS
    c. ☐ the PSALMS
    d. ☐ the EPISTLES

17. The Mount of OLIVES:

    a. ☐ was the site of the LAST SUPPER
    b. ☐ is where the Lord gave MOSES the TEN COMMANDMENTS
    c. ☐ is just east of JERUSALEM
    d. ☐ is next to the Sea of GALILEE

18. Who were the PHARISEES?

    a. ☐ a religious party within JUDAISM
    b. ☐ the nations driven out of CANAAN by JOSHUA
    c. ☐ the followers of Jesus
    d. ☐ the descendants of PHARAOH

19. Which of the following was not an Old Testament prophet?

   a. ☐ SAMUEL
   b. ☐ SOLOMON
   c. ☐ ISAIAH
   d. ☐ JONAH

20. Which empire controlled ISRAEL at the time of Jesus?

   a. ☐ ASSYRIA
   b. ☐ BABYLONIA
   c. ☐ GREECE
   d. ☐ ROME

ANSWERS

1. a	6. d	11. a	16. a
2. c	7. b	12. d	17. c
3. a	8. b	13. b	18. a
4. c	9. c	14. d	19. b
5. d	10. b	15. b	20. d

From Adam to Zerubbabel

Select one answer for each question.

1. Who was AARON's younger brother?

    a. ☐ JOSHUA
    b. ☐ CALEB
    c. ☐ DAVID
    d. ☐ MOSES

2. When the Lord wanted to test ABRAHAM's faith, what did he tell Abraham to do?

    a. ☐ lead the people of ISRAEL across the RED SEA
    b. ☐ SACRIFICE his son ISAAC
    c. ☐ lead the army of Israel around the walls of JERICHO
    d. ☐ send HAGAR and ISHMAEL into the WILDERNESS

3. Who were ABRAHAM's sons?

    a. ☐ JACOB and ESAU
    b. ☐ MOSES and JOSHUA
    c. ☐ ISAAC and ISHMAEL
    d. ☐ Isaac and JACOB

4. Which of the following is true of JACOB?

    a. ☐ he stole his brother's birthright
    b. ☐ his name was changed to ISRAEL
    c. ☐ he tricked ISAAC
    d. ☐ all of the above

5. Who was thrown into a lions' den?

    a. ☐ DAVID
    b. ☐ DANIEL
    c. ☐ SHADRACH, MESHACH, AND ABEDNEGO
    d. ☐ ISAIAH

6. To whom did the Lord give the TEN COMMANDMENTS on Mount SINAI?

  a. ☐ ADAM
  b. ☐ AARON
  c. ☐ ABRAHAM
  d. ☐ MOSES

7. Who was MOSES' sister?

  a. ☐ MIRIAM
  b. ☐ DEBORAH
  c. ☐ ELIZABETH
  d. ☐ RACHEL

8. Which of the following is true of NOAH?

  a. ☐ he received the TEN COMMANDMENTS on Mount SINAI
  b. ☐ the Lord told him to SACRIFICE his son
  c. ☐ he built an ARK and survived a great flood
  d. ☐ he built a tower at BABEL

9. Who were JUDAH and BENJAMIN?

  a. ☐ sons of ABRAHAM
  b. ☐ sons of ISAAC
  c. ☐ sons of JACOB
  d. ☐ sons of DAVID

10. To whom did RUTH say, "WHITHER THOU GOEST, I WILL GO; and where thou lodgest I will lodge"?

  a. ☐ BOAZ
  b. ☐ NAOMI
  c. ☐ SAMUEL
  d. ☐ DAVID

11. One of the low points of DAVID's life was:

  a. ☐ when he was thrown into the lions' den
  b. ☐ when he murdered his brother
  c. ☐ when he committed ADULTERY with BATHSHEBA
  d. ☐ when he WORSHIPED the GOLDEN CALF

12. Who killed ABEL?

    a. ☐ ADAM
    b. ☐ the SERPENT
    c. ☐ CAIN
    d. ☐ none of the above

13. Who was the second king of ISRAEL?

    a. ☐ SAUL
    b. ☐ DAVID
    c. ☐ SOLOMON
    d. ☐ REHOBOAM

14. Who was taken to HEAVEN in a CHARIOT OF FIRE?

    a. ☐ ADAM
    b. ☐ METHUSELAH
    c. ☐ ELIJAH
    d. ☐ ELISHA

15. Which list shows people in the correct chronological sequence?

    a. ☐ ADAM, DAVID, MOSES
    b. ☐ JOSHUA, ISAAC, JOSEPH
    c. ☐ ESTHER, RUTH, JEZEBEL
    d. ☐ SAMUEL, SOLOMON, JOASH

16. Who was HANNAH's son?

    a. ☐ CAIN
    b. ☐ ISAAC
    c. ☐ SAMUEL
    d. ☐ SOLOMON

17. HOSEA was a PROPHET in ISRAEL who:

    a. ☐ married a prostitute
    b. ☐ married a PHILISTINE
    c. ☐ called down FIRE FROM HEAVEN
    d. ☐ was swallowed by a great fish

18. REHOBOAM and JOASH were both:

    a. ☐ PROPHETS
    b. ☐ PRIESTS
    c. ☐ kings of ISRAEL
    d. ☐ kings of JUDAH

19. Who wrote many of the PSALMS?

    a. ☐ SAMUEL
    b. ☐ DAVID
    c. ☐ DEBORAH
    d. ☐ JEREMIAH

20. LEAH and RACHEL were:

    a. ☐ sisters
    b. ☐ wives of DAVID
    c. ☐ NAOMI's daughters-in-law
    d. ☐ married to twin brothers, ESAU and JACOB

ANSWERS

1. d	6. d	11. c	16. c
2. b	7. a	12. c	17. a
3. c	8. c	13. b	18. d
4. d	9. c	14. c	19. b
5. b	10. b	15. d	20. a

QUIZ HISTORY IN THE OLD TESTAMENT

What Happened When?

Select one answer for each question.

1. Which sequence of events is in the correct order?

    a. ☐ CREATION, UNITED KINGDOM, MOSES IN THE BULRUSHES
    b. ☐ HANDWRITING ON THE WALL, EXILE, DIVIDED KINGDOM
    c. ☐ fall of the Kingdom of ISRAEL, fall of the Kingdom of JUDAH, PERSIA conquers BABYLON
    d. ☐ all of the above

2. Who built a giant boat and was safe during the FLOOD?

    a. ☐ ADAM
    b. ☐ METHUSELAH
    c. ☐ NOAH
    d. ☐ ABRAHAM

3. What happened in the story of the Tower of BABEL?

    a. ☐ God confused the languages of the people
    b. ☐ the Lord sent FIRE FROM HEAVEN
    c. ☐ SODOM AND GOMORRAH were destroyed
    d. ☐ the tower fell down

4. What happened to SODOM AND GOMORRAH?

    a. ☐ their walls fell down
    b. ☐ they were destroyed by fire and brimstone
    c. ☐ they were destroyed in an earthquake
    d. ☐ they were captured by King DAVID

5. Who dreamed of a ladder stretching up to HEAVEN, with ANGELS ascending and descending?

    a. ☐ JACOB
    b. ☐ JOSEPH
    c. ☐ JOB
    d. ☐ PHARAOH

6. Who received a COAT OF MANY COLORS as a sign of favoritism from his father?

    a. ☐ ISAAC
    b. ☐ JACOB
    c. ☐ JOSEPH
    d. ☐ DAVID

7. In which country was JOSEPH first a slave and later prime minister?

    a. ☐ ISRAEL
    b. ☐ GREECE
    c. ☐ BABYLON
    d. ☐ EGYPT

8. Who saw a BURNING BUSH in the WILDERNESS?

    a. ☐ ABRAHAM
    b. ☐ MOSES
    c. ☐ DANIEL
    d. ☐ JOHN THE BAPTIST

9. What was the EXODUS?

    a. ☐ when ADAM and EVE were expelled from the Garden of EDEN
    b. ☐ when the inhabitants of ISRAEL were taken as captives to ASSYRIA
    c. ☐ when the inhabitants of JUDAH were taken as captives to BABYLON
    d. ☐ when the ISRAELITES left EGYPT

10. What annual celebration commemorates the EXODUS?

    a. ☐ PASSOVER
    b. ☐ EXODUS
    c. ☐ PURIM
    d. ☐ DAY OF ATONEMENT

11. Who created the GOLDEN CALF for the people of ISRAEL?

    a. ☐ AARON
    b. ☐ SAMSON
    c. ☐ AHAB
    d. ☐ the PHILISTINES

12. When did the ISRAELITES conquer JERICHO?

    a. ☐ before the EXODUS
    b. ☐ after the period of forty years in the WILDERNESS
    c. ☐ during the life of SAMSON
    d. ☐ during King DAVID's reign

13. When was the period of the JUDGES?

    a. ☐ before the EXODUS
    b. ☐ after the period of the DIVIDED KINGDOM
    c. ☐ after the ISRAELITES returned from EGYPT to the PROMISED LAND
    d. ☐ after the EXILE

14. The period of the DIVIDED KINGDOM:

    a. ☐ began during the reign of King SOLOMON
    b. ☐ means ISRAEL was divided by the JORDAN RIVER
    c. ☐ preceded the period of the UNITED KINGDOM
    d. ☐ began after the reign of King Solomon

15. Who spent three days and nights in the belly of a whale?

    a. ☐ JACOB
    b. ☐ JONAH
    c. ☐ JOASH
    d. ☐ JEHU

16. Who was the first king of the Kingdom of ISRAEL during the period of the DIVIDED KINGDOM?

    a. ☐ DAVID
    b. ☐ SOLOMON
    c. ☐ REHOBOAM
    d. ☐ JEROBOAM

17. Why were SHADRACH, MESHACH, AND ABEDNEGO thrown into the FIERY FURNACE?

    a. ☐ they insisted on praying to the God of ISRAEL
    b. ☐ they refused to bow down and worship NEBUCHADNEZZAR's gold statue
    c. ☐ they refused to eat the rich food offered to them
    d. ☐ they were unable to interpret the king's dream

18. Which nation overthrew the NORTHERN KINGDOM of ISRAEL in 722 B.C.?

    a. ☐ EGYPT
    b. ☐ ASSYRIA
    c. ☐ BABYLON
    d. ☐ GREECE

19. Which nation overthrew the SOUTHERN KINGDOM of JUDAH in 586 B.C.?

    a. ☐ GREECE
    b. ☐ ROME
    c. ☐ ASSYRIA
    d. ☐ BABYLON

20. Which kingdom fell immediately after the incident of the HANDWRITING ON THE WALL?

    a. ☐ ISRAEL
    b. ☐ JUDAH
    c. ☐ BABYLON
    d. ☐ ASSYRIA

ANSWERS

1. c	6. c	11. a	16. d
2. c	7. d	12. b	17. b
3. a	8. b	13. c	18. b
4. b	9. d	14. d	19. d
5. a	10. a	15. b	20. c

QUIZ — WHO'S WHO IN THE NEW TESTAMENT

From Andrew to Zacchaeus

Select one answer for each question.

1. What did Jesus say to NICODEMUS?

    a. ☐ Sell all you have and give the money to the poor
    b. ☐ This day you shall be with me in PARADISE
    c. ☐ No one can see the KINGDOM OF HEAVEN unless he is BORN AGAIN
    d. ☐ Arise, take up your bed, and walk

2. When JOHN was an old man, he had a VISION. In which book of the New Testament is his vision recorded?

    a. ☐ GOSPEL of JOHN
    b. ☐ REVELATION
    c. ☐ 1 JOHN
    d. ☐ ROMANS

3. What elderly woman recognized the infant Jesus as the MESSIAH when JOSEPH and MARY took him to the TEMPLE?

    a. ☐ ANNA
    b. ☐ ELIZABETH
    c. ☐ DORCAS
    d. ☐ PRISCILLA

4. Who was emperor in ROME at the time of the birth of Jesus?

    a. ☐ CAESAR Augustus
    b. ☐ Julius Caesar
    c. ☐ Nero
    d. ☐ HEROD

5. Who was the mother of JOHN THE BAPTIST?

   a. ☐ MARY
   b. ☐ MIRIAM
   c. ☐ ANNA
   d. ☐ ELIZABETH

6. What was CORNELIUS's occupation?

   a. ☐ tentmaker
   b. ☐ TAX COLLECTOR
   c. ☐ HIGH PRIEST
   d. ☐ Roman CENTURION

7. Who ordered that all boys in BETHLEHEM under the age of two be killed?

   a. ☐ HEROD the Great
   b. ☐ PHARAOH
   c. ☐ Pontius PILATE
   d. ☐ CAIAPHAS

8. Which two people were struck dead when they lied to PETER about some property they had sold?

   a. ☐ AQUILA AND PRISCILLA
   b. ☐ MARY MAGDALENE and LAZARUS
   c. ☐ ANANIAS AND SAPPHIRA
   d. ☐ JUDAS ISCARIOT and CAIAPHAS

9. When HEROD told SALOME she could have anything she requested, what did she ask for?

   a. ☐ that Herod marry her
   b. ☐ THIRTY PIECES OF SILVER
   c. ☐ the head of JOHN THE BAPTIST
   d. ☐ half the kingdom

10. Who was the brother of JAMES (SON OF ZEBEDEE)?

   a. ☐ PETER
   b. ☐ PAUL
   c. ☐ ANDREW
   d. ☐ JOHN

11. Which three DISCIPLES were closest to JESUS?

    a. ☐ PETER, ANDREW, and JAMES
    b. ☐ Peter, JOHN, and PAUL
    c. ☐ Peter, James, and John
    d. ☐ MATTHEW, MARK, and LUKE

12. After the WISE MEN visited the baby Jesus, an ANGEL appeared to JOSEPH in a dream. What did the angel tell him?

    a. ☐ to take MARY and Jesus to EGYPT
    b. ☐ to take Jesus to the TEMPLE
    c. ☐ that Jesus was the SON OF GOD
    d. ☐ that Joseph should marry Mary

13. Who was the HIGH PRIEST who presided at the trial of Jesus?

    a. ☐ CAIAPHAS
    b. ☐ AARON
    c. ☐ BARNABAS
    d. ☐ EZRA

14. What does the Bible tell us about JOSEPH OF ARIMATHEA?

    a. ☐ his father gave him a multicolored coat
    b. ☐ he was the husband of the VIRGIN MARY
    c. ☐ he carried Jesus' CROSS to GOLGOTHA
    d. ☐ he owned the tomb in which Jesus was buried

15. Who were four of JESUS' DISCIPLES?

    a. ☐ MATTHEW, MARK, LUKE, JOHN
    b. ☐ Matthew, Mark, PETER, John
    c. ☐ Matthew, JUDAS ISCARIOT, ANDREW, John
    d. ☐ Peter, JAMES, John, PAUL

16. The brother of MARY AND MARTHA died, but Jesus brought him back to life. What was his name?

    a. ☐ CORNELIUS
    b. ☐ SIMON
    c. ☐ ANANIAS
    d. ☐ LAZARUS

17. Who betrayed Jesus with a kiss?

    a. ☐ PONTIUS PILATE
    b. ☐ Simon the Sorcerer
    c. ☐ JUDAS ISCARIOT
    d. ☐ MARY MAGDALENE

18. Who was ONESIMUS?

    a. ☐ a centurion
    b. ☐ a slave
    c. ☐ a TAX COLLECTOR
    d. ☐ one of Jesus' DISCIPLES

19. SAUL of Tarsus was present when one of these men was stoned to death. Which one was it?

    a. ☐ PETER
    b. ☐ SAUL
    c. ☐ JOHN
    d. ☐ STEPHEN

20. THOMAS is sometimes called Doubting Thomas because he did not believe that:

    a. ☐ PETER had WALKED ON WATER
    b. ☐ Jesus had CALMED THE STORM
    c. ☐ Peter had been released from prison
    d. ☐ Jesus had come back to life

ANSWERS

1. c	6. d	11. c	16. d
2. b	7. a	12. a	17. c
3. a	8. c	13. a	18. b
4. a	9. c	14. d	19. d
5. d	10. d	15. c	20. d

King of Kings and Lord of Lords

Select one answer for each question.

1. Which event is called the ANNUNCIATION?

    a. ☐ When Jesus rose from the tomb on the third day

    b. ☐ When Jesus died on the CROSS

    c. ☐ When the ANGEL GABRIEL told the VIRGIN MARY that she would have a baby who would be the SON OF GOD

    d. ☐ When MOSES and ELIJAH appeared with Jesus on a mountaintop

2. What was the name of the hill where Jesus was CRUCIFIED?

    a. ☐ Mount SINAI

    b. ☐ Mount of OLIVES

    c. ☐ Mount of TRANSFIGURATION

    d. ☐ GOLGOTHA

3. What was the town on the Sea of GALILEE where much of Jesus' ministry took place?

    a. ☐ CAPERNAUM

    b. ☐ JERUSALEM

    c. ☐ BETHLEHEM

    d. ☐ JERICHO

4. The names *CHRIST,* from a GREEK word, and *MESSIAH,* from a HEBREW word, both mean the same thing. What do they mean?

    a. ☐ BREAD OF LIFE

    b. ☐ God with us

    c. ☐ Anointed One

    d. ☐ PROPHET

5. What term is used to describe Jesus' death on the CROSS?

    a. ☐ the Ascension
    b. ☐ the Crucifixion
    c. ☐ the Resurrection
    d. ☐ the Transfiguration

6. Where was Jesus born?

    a. ☐ Jerusalem
    b. ☐ Bethlehem
    c. ☐ Capernaum
    d. ☐ Nazareth

7. In the PARABLE of the SOWER, what does the seed represent?

    a. ☐ the plentiful harvest
    b. ☐ the cares of this world
    c. ☐ seven years of plenty
    d. ☐ the Good News

8. Where did Jesus go to pray with his DISCIPLES after the LAST SUPPER?

    a. ☐ Garden of Gethsemane
    b. ☐ Garden of Eden
    c. ☐ Bethlehem
    d. ☐ Capernaum

9. Who brought gifts of GOLD, FRANKINCENSE, AND MYRRH to the infant Jesus?

    a. ☐ the Shepherds
    b. ☐ the Angels
    c. ☐ the Wise Men
    d. ☐ King Herod

10. What PARABLE did Jesus tell in response to the question, "Who is my neighbor?"

    a. ☐ parable of the Good Samaritan
    b. ☐ parable of the Lost Sheep
    c. ☐ parable of the Prodigal Son
    d. ☐ parable of the Pearl of Great Price

11. What is the ASCENSION?

    a. ☐ When Jesus came back to life again on the third day
    b. ☐ When Jesus raised Jairus's daughter back to life
    c. ☐ When Jesus rose into HEAVEN after the RESURRECTION
    d. ☐ When the ANGEL GABRIEL appeared to the VIRGIN MARY to tell her that she would have a son

12. Which of these expressions is called the GREAT COMMISSION?

    a. ☐ I am ALPHA AND OMEGA
    b. ☐ Behold the LAMB OF GOD
    c. ☐ GO YE INTO ALL THE WORLD and preach the gospel to every creature
    d. ☐ TRAIN UP A CHILD IN THE WAY HE SHOULD GO

13. Who said, "Behold the LAMB OF GOD"?

    a. ☐ ISAIAH
    b. ☐ PETER
    c. ☐ PAUL
    d. ☐ JOHN THE BAPTIST

14. What were Jesus and his DISCIPLES celebrating when they ate the LAST SUPPER?

    a. ☐ the fall of ROME
    b. ☐ the PASSOVER
    c. ☐ the DAY OF ATONEMENT
    d. ☐ the Feast of Tabernacles

15. What is the NATIVITY?

    a. ☐ the birth of Jesus
    b. ☐ the MANGER where MARY laid the baby Jesus
    c. ☐ the death of Jesus
    d. ☐ the ANGELS' announcement to the SHEPHERDS that the SAVIOR had been born

16. Where did JOSEPH and MARY live before Jesus was born?

    a. ☐ JERUSALEM
    b. ☐ EGYPT
    c. ☐ NAZARETH
    d. ☐ BETHANY

17. Which term refers to Jesus' coming back to life after his death on the CROSS?

   a. ☐ the NATIVITY
   b. ☐ the CRUCIFIXION
   c. ☐ the RESURRECTION
   d. ☐ the SECOND COMING

18. According to the GOSPELS, what was Jesus' first MIRACLE?

   a. ☐ WALKING ON WATER
   b. ☐ healing a blind man
   c. ☐ multiplying the LOAVES AND FISHES
   d. ☐ TURNING WATER INTO WINE

19. Which quotation is not found in the SERMON ON THE MOUNT?

   a. ☐ GO YE INTO ALL THE WORLD, and preach the gospel to every creature
   b. ☐ BLESSED ARE THE POOR IN SPIRIT
   c. ☐ Ye are the LIGHT OF THE WORLD
   d. ☐ Go the SECOND MILE

20. On what day do Christians commemorate the TRIUMPHAL ENTRY?

   a. ☐ CHRISTMAS
   b. ☐ GOOD FRIDAY
   c. ☐ PALM SUNDAY
   d. ☐ PENTECOST Sunday

ANSWERS

1. c	6. b	11. c	16. c
2. d	7. d	12. c	17. c
3. a	8. a	13. d	18. d
4. c	9. c	14. b	19. a
5. b	10. a	15. a	20. c

QUIZ CHURCH HISTORY

Saints and Sinners, Past and Present

Select one answer for each question.

1. He is called the "Father of CHURCH HISTORY," and he wrote a biography of CONSTANTINE THE GREAT:

    a. ☐ ATHANASIUS
    b. ☐ AUGUSTINE OF HIPPO
    c. ☐ JEROME
    d. ☐ EUSEBIUS OF CAESAREA

2. What was the purpose of the Edict of MILAN, which was issued by CONSTANTINE THE GREAT in A.D. 313?

    a. ☐ to move the capital from ROME to Byzantium and rename it CONSTANTINOPLE
    b. ☐ to establish the NEW TESTAMENT CANON
    c. ☐ to legalize Christianity in the ROMAN EMPIRE
    d. ☐ to mandate that all Roman citizens had to become Christians

3. His autobiography, *CONFESSIONS*, is a classic account of a CONVERSION from paganism to Christianity:

    a. ☐ AUGUSTINE OF HIPPO
    b. ☐ Thomas AQUINAS
    c. ☐ THOMAS À KEMPIS
    d. ☐ C. S. LEWIS

4. Whose LATIN TRANSLATION of the Bible was called the VULGATE?

    a. ☐ EUSEBIUS OF CAESAREA
    b. ☐ JEROME
    c. ☐ Martin LUTHER
    d. ☐ ERASMUS

5. The result of the GREAT SCHISM of 1054 was:

    a. ☐ the establishment of PROTESTANTISM

    b. ☐ the separation of the ROMAN CATHOLIC CHURCH and the EASTERN ORTHODOX CHURCH

    c. ☐ that two competing POPES EXCOMMUNICATED each other

    d. ☐ the separation of the CHURCH OF ENGLAND from the Roman Catholic church

6. What was the purpose of the CRUSADES?

    a. ☐ to consolidate the power of the HOLY ROMAN EMPIRE

    b. ☐ to allow Germany to adopt PROTESTANTISM

    c. ☐ to wrest control of the HOLY LAND from the Muslims

    d. ☐ to stop the Muslims from advancing into Europe

7. This archbishop of CANTERBURY was murdered in the CATHEDRAL in 1170 because he resisted King Henry II's attempts to limit the authority of the church:

    a. ☐ AUGUSTINE OF CANTERBURY

    b. ☐ Thomas à BECKET

    c. ☐ THOMAS À KEMPIS

    d. ☐ Girolamo SAVONAROLA

8. This Czech reformer attacked abuses in the church a century before the start of the PROTESTANT REFORMATION:

    a. ☐ John WYCLIFFE

    b. ☐ Peter Waldo

    c. ☐ Ulrich ZWINGLI

    d. ☐ John HUS

9. This REFORMER announced his disagreements with the Roman authorities in the church by posting his NINETY-FIVE THESES on the door of the castle church in Wittenberg:

    a. ☐ William TYNDALE

    b. ☐ John CALVIN

    c. ☐ Martin LUTHER

    d. ☐ Ulrich ZWINGLI

10. Which British monarch established the CHURCH OF ENGLAND?

    a. ☐ King Henry II

    b. ☐ King HENRY VIII

    c. ☐ Queen Elizabeth I

    d. ☐ King JAMES I

11. Which of the following was not a MARTYR?

   a. ☐ William TYNDALE
   b. ☐ Thomas MORE
   c. ☐ Girolamo SAVONAROLA
   d. ☐ Tomás de TORQUEMADA

12. He was a leader of the REFORMATION in Switzerland and the author of *INSTITUTES OF THE CHRISTIAN RELIGION:*

   a. ☐ John CALVIN
   b. ☐ Martin LUTHER
   c. ☐ John KNOX
   d. ☐ John HUS

13. This sixteenth-century movement denounced INFANT BAPTISM and accepted only the BAPTISM of those old enough to understand the meaning of faith:

   a. ☐ METHODISM
   b. ☐ ANABAPTIST MOVEMENT
   c. ☐ GREAT AWAKENING
   d. ☐ SOUTHERN BAPTIST CONVENTION

14. Who was one of the founders of METHODISM?

   a. ☐ John KNOX
   b. ☐ John WESLEY
   c. ☐ John CALVIN
   d. ☐ Thomas CRANMER

15. Which pioneer MISSIONARY founded the CHINA INLAND MISSION in 1866?

   a. ☐ David LIVINGSTONE
   b. ☐ William CAREY
   c. ☐ J. Hudson TAYLOR
   d. ☐ Mother TERESA

16. A conservative theological movement that arose early in the twentieth century; among other essentials, it stressed the inerrancy of SCRIPTURE:

   a. ☐ GREAT AWAKENING
   b. ☐ NEOORTHODOXY
   c. ☐ METHODISM
   d. ☐ FUNDAMENTALISM

17. The twentieth-century movement that emphasizes BAPTISM IN THE HOLY SPIRIT as an individual experience:

a. ☐ PENTECOSTALISM
b. ☐ LUTHERANISM
c. ☐ ARMINIANISM
d. ☐ ANABAPTIST MOVEMENT

18. Dietrich BONHOEFFER is best known for:

a. ☐ his role in the development of NEOORTHODOXY
b. ☐ helping Martin LUTHER establish the LUTHERAN church
c. ☐ speaking out against Hitler and the Nazis during World War II
d. ☐ his role in the ECUMENICAL movement

19. A twentieth-century EVANGELIST who has preached to millions of people:

a. ☐ George WHITEFIELD
b. ☐ Billy GRAHAM
c. ☐ Martin LUTHER
d. ☐ Karl BARTH

20. Who was elected POPE in 1978?

a. ☐ PIUS XII
b. ☐ JOHN XXIII
c. ☐ PAUL VI
d. ☐ JOHN PAUL II

ANSWERS

1. d	6. c	11. d	16. d
2. c	7. b	12. a	17. a
3. a	8. d	13. b	18. c
4. b	9. c	14. b	19. b
5. b	10. b	15. c	20. d

QUIZ THE CHURCH TODAY

The Church at the End of the Twentieth Century

Select one answer for each question.

1. ADVENT is:

    a. ☐ a period of preparation before CHRISTMAS

    b. ☐ a Christian celebration derived from the celebration of PASSOVER

    c. ☐ the ANGEL GABRIEL's announcement to the VIRGIN MARY that she would have a son

    d. ☐ a period of preparation before EASTER

2. ALL SAINTS DAY is celebrated on:

    a. ☐ January 6

    b. ☐ EASTER

    c. ☐ October 31

    d. ☐ November 1

3. ANGLICAN refers to:

    a. ☐ ANGELS

    b. ☐ the EUCHARIST

    c. ☐ the CHURCH OF ENGLAND

    d. ☐ the AFRICAN METHODIST EPISCOPAL CHURCH

4. The ASSEMBLIES OF GOD is a DENOMINATION in which tradition?

    a. ☐ BAPTIST

    b. ☐ PENTECOSTAL

    c. ☐ EPISCOPAL

    d. ☐ PRESBYTERIAN

5. Which SACRAMENT is a public affirmation that an individual is a part of Christ's church?

   a. ☐ EUCHARIST
   b. ☐ MATRIMONY
   c. ☐ HOLY ORDERS
   d. ☐ BAPTISM

6. Which of these churches does not have BISHOPS?

   a. ☐ METHODIST
   b. ☐ EPISCOPAL
   c. ☐ CONGREGATIONAL
   d. ☐ ROMAN CATHOLIC

7. *The BOOK OF COMMON PRAYER contains:*

   a. ☐ prayers of CONFESSION
   b. ☐ the LITURGY of the ROMAN CATHOLIC CHURCH
   c. ☐ children's bedtime prayers
   d. ☐ all of the above

8. Members of the CHURCH OF JESUS CHRIST OF LATTER-DAY SAINTS are called:

   a. ☐ EPISCOPALIANS
   b. ☐ PENTECOSTALS
   c. ☐ MORMONS
   d. ☐ SEVENTH-DAY ADVENTISTS

9. When does the CHURCH YEAR begin?

   a. ☐ The first Sunday of ADVENT
   b. ☐ New Year's Day
   c. ☐ ASH WEDNESDAY
   d. ☐ EASTER

10. What is another name for the EUCHARIST?

   a. ☐ TRANSUBSTANTIATION
   b. ☐ the LORD'S SUPPER
   c. ☐ the LAST SUPPER
   d. ☐ all of the above

11. When would you most likely hear the expression, "DEARLY BELOVED, WE ARE GATHERED TOGETHER"?

   a. ☐ at a CHRISTENING
   b. ☐ at a CONFIRMATION
   c. ☐ at a wedding
   d. ☐ at a funeral

12. Which of the following constitutes one of the three major branches of Christianity?

   a. ☐ ROMAN CATHOLIC CHURCH
   b. ☐ PROTESTANTISM
   c. ☐ EASTERN ORTHODOX CHURCH
   d. ☐ all of the above

13. What is the "GLORIA PATRI"?

   a. ☐ a CATHEDRAL in ROME
   b. ☐ the song of the ANGELS who announced Jesus' birth to the SHEPHERDS
   c. ☐ the LATIN name of a HYMN still frequently sung in churches today
   d. ☐ the LATIN TRANSLATION of the Bible

14. JESUITS, DOMINICANS, and FRANCISCANS are all:

   a. ☐ NUNS
   b. ☐ members of RELIGIOUS ORDERS
   c. ☐ teachers
   d. ☐ MISSIONARIES

15. As a religious group, the AMISH are related to:

   a. ☐ SOUTHERN BAPTISTS
   b. ☐ MORMONS
   c. ☐ PRESBYTERIANS
   d. ☐ MENNONITES

16. Which of the following is primarily an African-American DENOMINATION?

   a. ☐ ASSEMBLIES OF GOD
   b. ☐ NATIONAL BAPTIST CONVENTION
   c. ☐ SOUTHERN BAPTIST CONVENTION
   d. ☐ PRESBYTERIAN CHURCH (USA)

17. PALM SUNDAY:

    a. ☐ commemorates Jesus' entry into JERUSALEM
    b. ☐ is celebrated primarily in the tropics
    c. ☐ is the beginning of the CHURCH YEAR
    d. ☐ celebrates the CREATION

18. According to ROMAN CATHOLIC tradition, who was the first POPE?

    a. ☐ JESUS
    b. ☐ PETER
    c. ☐ JOHN
    d. ☐ ATHANASIUS

19. What term has been defined as "an outward and visible sign of an inward and spiritual grace"?

    a. ☐ SACRAMENT
    b. ☐ BAPTISM
    c. ☐ CONFIRMATION
    d. ☐ LAST RITES

20. Where is the VATICAN?

    a. ☐ Paris
    b. ☐ CONSTANTINOPLE
    c. ☐ Athens
    d. ☐ ROME

ANSWERS

1. a	6. c	11. c	16. b
2. d	7. a	12. d	17. a
3. c	8. c	13. c	18. b
4. b	9. a	14. b	19. a
5. d	10. b	15. d	20. d

QUIZ · THEOLOGY IN EVERYDAY LIFE

A Few Sesquipedalian Words

Select one answer for each question.

1. What is an AGNOSTIC?

    a. ☐ a person who believes there is no God
    b. ☐ a person who does not know if there is a God
    c. ☐ a person who believes in God
    d. ☐ a person who commits ADULTERY

2. Which of these Bible verses best reflects the DOCTRINE of ORIGINAL SIN?

    a. ☐ The WAGES OF SIN IS DEATH; but the gift of God is ETERNAL LIFE through Jesus Christ our Lord (ROMANS 6:23)
    b. ☐ God demonstrates his LOVE for us in this: While we were still sinners, Christ died for us (Romans 5:8, NIV)
    c. ☐ Just as SIN entered the world through one man, and death through sin, and in this way death came to all men, because all sinned (Romans 5:12, NIV)
    d. ☐ FOR GOD SO LOVED THE WORLD that he gave his one and only SON, that whoever believes in him shall not perish but have ETERNAL LIFE (JOHN 3:16, NIV)

3. What is BLASPHEMY?

    a. ☐ turning away from the faith
    b. ☐ gossiping
    c. ☐ another term for ADULTERY
    d. ☐ insulting or mocking God

4. Assisted suicide and mercy killing are examples of:

    a. ☐ ECUMENISM
    b. ☐ EUTHANASIA
    c. ☐ POLYTHEISM
    d. ☐ HERESY

5. The OMNIPOTENCE OF GOD means:

    a. ☐ God is all-powerful
    b. ☐ God is present everywhere
    c. ☐ God is all-knowing
    d. ☐ God is unchangeable

6. What is CONVERSION?

    a. ☐ the process of being recognized as a SAINT
    b. ☐ moving from nonbelief or nominal belief to an active faith
    c. ☐ stubborn sinfulness
    d. ☐ the act of CONFESSION

7. Which term indicates the basis for reconciliation between God and sinners through the death of Christ?

    a. ☐ CANONIZATION
    b. ☐ SANCTIFICATION
    c. ☐ ATONEMENT
    d. ☐ TRANSUBSTANTIATION

8. The term *rapture* is related to:

    a. ☐ AGAPĒ love
    b. ☐ ESCHATOLOGY
    c. ☐ the TRANSFIGURATION of Christ
    d. ☐ the GLORY of God

9. What is the MARK OF THE BEAST?

    a. ☐ the MARK OF CAIN
    b. ☐ ORIGINAL SIN
    c. ☐ an ICON
    d. ☐ the number 666

10. Which statement most closely reflects the traditional PROTESTANT view of DOCTRINE?

    a. ☐ doctrine must be validated by SCRIPTURE
    b. ☐ doctrine is God's objective truth defined by the church
    c. ☐ the validity of doctrine is dependent on the historical and cultural context
    d. ☐ it does not matter what an individual believes as long as he is sincere

11. What is the FALL OF MAN?

    a. ☐ the first SIN committed by each person

    b. ☐ ORIGINAL SIN

    c. ☐ ADAM's disobedience by eating the FORBIDDEN FRUIT

    d. ☐ Jesus' descent into HELL after the CRUCIFIXION

12. Which of the following is a GIFT OF THE HOLY SPIRIT, as described in the New Testament?

    a. ☐ faith

    b. ☐ SPEAKING IN TONGUES

    c. ☐ teaching

    d. ☐ all of the above

13. YAHWEH is:

    a. ☐ the food that miraculously appeared each morning while the ISRAELITES were in the WILDERNESS

    b. ☐ a HEBREW name for God

    c. ☐ the community that created the DEAD SEA SCROLLS

    d. ☐ a GREEK word for 'love'

14. Which of the following relates to the DOCTRINE that God exists in three persons?

    a. ☐ the IMMACULATE CONCEPTION

    b. ☐ the TRINITY

    c. ☐ the INCARNATION

    d. ☐ the OMNIPOTENCE OF GOD, the OMNIPRESENCE OF GOD, and the OMNISCIENCE OF GOD

15. What is HERESY?

    a. ☐ detracting from God in any way, such as by mocking him

    b. ☐ a deliberate repudiation and abandonment of the faith

    c. ☐ adherence to a belief that is contrary to church DOGMA

    d. ☐ saying one thing but doing another

16. In the EUCHARIST, what does the wine signify?

    a. ☐ the fruit of our labor

    b. ☐ the BODY OF CHRIST

    c. ☐ the SINS of mankind

    d. ☐ the BLOOD OF CHRIST

17. JUSTIFICATION is God's action of declaring sinners righteous because of Christ. According to the New Testament, how are we justified?

a. ☐ through SACRIFICES
b. ☐ by the GRACE of God, through faith
c. ☐ by following the GOLDEN RULE
d. ☐ by meditating

18. What is SANCTIFICATION?

a. ☐ the ongoing development of holiness in the life of the Christian
b. ☐ the act of becoming a Christian
c. ☐ the inspiration of SCRIPTURE
d. ☐ SPEAKING IN TONGUES

19. According to ROMAN CATHOLIC DOGMA, what is PURGATORY?

a. ☐ the eternal resting place of the SOULS of unbaptized infants
b. ☐ a place where a person is purified of VENIAL SINS unforgiven on earth
c. ☐ a place of everlasting punishment for those who have committed MORTAL SINS
d. ☐ none of the above

20. Which term relates to the DOCTRINE that God chooses the people who will receive SALVATION?

a. ☐ FREE WILL
b. ☐ CONSUBSTANTIATION
c. ☐ filioque
d. ☐ ELECTION

ANSWERS

1. b	6. b	11. c	16. d
2. c	7. c	12. d	17. b
3. d	8. b	13. b	18. a
4. b	9. d	14. b	19. b
5. a	10. a	15. c	20. d

QUIZ — THE BIBLE & CHRISTIANITY IN THE FINE ARTS

Books, Cathedrals, Paintings, and Hymns

Select one answer for each question.

1. The term *a capella* refers to:

- a. ☐ singing without accompaniment
- b. ☐ the tradition that men do not wear hats in a church
- c. ☐ the central portion of a BASILICA
- d. ☐ paint applied to wet plaster

2. Who wrote the music for the ORATORIO *MESSIAH?*

- a. ☐ Johann Sebastian BACH
- b. ☐ Ludwig van Beethoven
- c. ☐ Wolfgang Amadeus Mozart
- d. ☐ George Frederick HANDEL

3. What book written by a Civil War general was made into a highly acclaimed motion picture in the 1950s?

- a. ☐ *MERE CHRISTIANITY*
- b. ☐ *IMITATION OF CHRIST*
- c. ☐ *IN HIS STEPS*
- d. ☐ *BEN-HUR*

4. Who wrote *The BOOK OF MARTYRS?*

- a. ☐ Martin LUTHER
- b. ☐ John Foxe
- c. ☐ Dietrich BONHOEFFER
- d. ☐ Thomas CRANMER

5. Which one of these books was written by AUGUSTINE OF HIPPO?

    a. ☐ *The CITY OF GOD*
    b. ☐ *IMITATION OF CHRIST*
    c. ☐ *INSTITUTES OF THE CHRISTIAN RELIGION*
    d. ☐ *SUMMA THEOLOGICA*

6. What is a CATHEDRAL?

    a. ☐ a church that contains the BISHOP's throne
    b. ☐ a church built in the Middle Ages
    c. ☐ an ornate church with high ceilings and flying buttresses
    d. ☐ a ROMAN CATHOLIC church

7. Who created the marble sculptures *DAVID* and *PIETÀ?*

    a. ☐ RAPHAEL
    b. ☐ LEONARDO DA VINCI
    c. ☐ MICHELANGELO
    d. ☐ Donatello

8. The English version of "ADESTE FIDELES" is called:

    a. ☐ "SILENT NIGHT"
    b. ☐ "O COME, ALL YE FAITHFUL"
    c. ☐ "HALLELUJAH CHORUS"
    d. ☐ *IMITATION OF CHRIST*

9. Which phrase is found in DANTE's *DIVINE COMEDY?*

    a. ☐ Happy families are all alike; every unhappy family is unhappy in its own way
    b. ☐ ABANDON HOPE, ALL YE WHO ENTER HERE
    c. ☐ JUSTIFY THE WAYS OF GOD TO MEN
    d. ☐ To be, or not to be: that is the question

10. The central church in the VATICAN is:

    a. ☐ SAINT PETER'S BASILICA
    b. ☐ SAINT PAUL'S CATHEDRAL
    c. ☐ Basilica of HAGIA SOPHIA
    d. ☐ NOTRE DAME DE PARIS

11. "GONNA LAY DOWN MY BURDEN" and "WHEN THE SAINTS GO MARCHING IN" are examples of:

    a. ☐ HYMNS
    b. ☐ GOSPEL SONGS
    c. ☐ SPIRITUALS
    d. ☐ ORATORIOS

12. What is an ICON?

    a. ☐ a BISHOP's hat
    b. ☐ an IDOL
    c. ☐ an image of Jesus or of a SAINT
    d. ☐ a ceremonial candle

13. "INFERNO," "Purgatorio," and "PARADISO" are the three sections of what literary work?

    a. ☐ *PARADISE LOST*
    b. ☐ *The DIVINE COMEDY*
    c. ☐ *SUMMA THEOLOGICA*
    d. ☐ *The PILGRIM'S PROGRESS*

14. Which of the following is not a book by C. S. LEWIS?

    a. ☐ *The LION, THE WITCH, AND THE WARDROBE*
    b. ☐ *MERE CHRISTIANITY*
    c. ☐ *Surprised by Joy*
    d. ☐ *The Power of Positive Thinking*

15. Which one of these works of art is by LEONARDO DA VINCI?

    a. ☐ *DAVID* (sculpture)
    b. ☐ *Moses* (sculpture)
    c. ☐ *The LAST SUPPER* (fresco)
    d. ☐ *The Last Judgment* (fresco)

16. Which of these HYMNS was written during the American Civil War?

    a. ☐ "AMAZING GRACE"
    b. ☐ "BATTLE HYMN OF THE REPUBLIC"
    c. ☐ "A MIGHTY FORTRESS"
    d. ☐ "PRAISE GOD, FROM WHOM ALL BLESSINGS FLOW"

17. Martin LUTHER wrote the words and music to which of these songs?

    a. ☐ "A MIGHTY FORTRESS"
    b. ☐ "We Shall Overcome"
    c. ☐ "JESUS LOVES ME"
    d. ☐ "HOW GREAT THOU ART"

18. What book written in the late 1800s is about people who ask themselves what Jesus would have done in their situation?

    a. ☐ *IN HIS STEPS*
    b. ☐ *IMITATION OF CHRIST*
    c. ☐ *Born Again*
    d. ☐ *MY UTMOST FOR HIS HIGHEST*

19. Which term is found in *The PILGRIM'S PROGRESS*?

    a. ☐ CELESTIAL CITY
    b. ☐ SLOUGH OF DESPOND
    c. ☐ City of Destruction
    d. ☐ all of the above

20. Where is the SISTINE CHAPEL?

    a. ☐ Athens
    b. ☐ ROME
    c. ☐ CONSTANTINOPLE
    d. ☐ St. Petersburg

ANSWERS

1. a	6. a	11. c	16. b
2. d	7. c	12. c	17. a
3. d	8. b	13. b	18. a
4. b	9. b	14. d	19. d
5. a	10. a	15. c	20. b

QUIZ THE BIBLE

Test Your Bible Literacy

Match each of the following books of the Bible to its content:

1. ____ GENESIS
2. ____ EXODUS
3. ____ LEVITICUS
4. ____ NUMBERS
5. ____ DEUTERONOMY
6. ____ JOSHUA
7. ____ JUDGES
8. ____ RUTH
9. ____ 1 SAMUEL
10. ____ 2 SAMUEL
11. ____ 1 KINGS
12. ____ 2 KINGS

a. Moses' speech to the people of ISRAEL before they entered into the PROMISED LAND

b. The story of NAOMI and her daughter-in-law

c. Histories of the PATRIARCHS of Israel

d. History of King SAUL's reign

e. History of King SOLOMON's reign and the early years of the DIVIDED KINGDOM

f. Details of the MOSAIC LAW

g. The years of wandering in the WILDERNESS

h. Stories of DEBORAH, GIDEON, and SAMSON

i. History of King DAVID's reign

j. The latter years of the DIVIDED KINGDOM

k. Moses leads the ISRAELITES out of EGYPT

l. The Israelites' conquest of the PROMISED LAND

13. Identify each of these books as being from the Old Testament (OT) or the New Testament (NT):
    ____ REVELATION
    ____ DEUTERONOMY
    ____ MALACHI
    ____ HEBREWS

14. List the five BOOKS OF MOSES:
    _____
    _____
    _____
    _____
    _____

15. In what language was the New Testament first written? _____

16. List the four GOSPELS in the order in which they are traditionally found in the New Testament:

_____

_____

_____

_____

17. Which BOOK OF THE BIBLE records the history of the first years of the EARLY CHURCH? _____

18. Who said, "LET THERE BE LIGHT"? _____

19. Who wrote, "CHILDREN, OBEY YOUR PARENTS"? _____

20. List three of the TEN COMMANDMENTS:

_____

_____

_____

21. List four of the nine FRUITS OF THE SPIRIT, as they are listed in the fifth chapter of GALATIANS:

_____

_____

_____

_____

22. About whom did JOHN THE BAPTIST say, "Behold, the LAMB OF GOD"?

_____

23. What is the first phrase of JOHN 3:16?

_____

24. Which two books of the Bible begin with the phrase, "IN THE BEGINNING"?

_____

_____

25. Which PSALM begins with the phrase, "The LORD IS MY SHEPHERD"?

_____

26. According to the APOSTLE PAUL, what is the root of all evil?

_____

27. How does the LORD'S PRAYER begin? _____

28. Name three of the TRIBES OF ISRAEL:

    _____

    _____

    _____

29. What annual celebration was established to commemorate the EXODUS of ISRAEL from EGYPT? _____

30. What city was the capital of the Kingdom of ISRAEL during most of King DAVID's reign? _____

31. After the death of SOLOMON, the Kingdom of ISRAEL was divided into two kingdoms. What were they called?

    _____

    _____

32. What is the name of the region between JUDEA and GALILEE?

    _____

33. Who was ABRAHAM's wife? _____

34. Who was AARON's younger brother? _____

35. Who was the third king of ISRAEL? _____

36. Which of SOLOMON's sons succeeded him as king? _____

37. What were the names of DANIEL's friends who were thrown into the FIERY FURNACE?

    _____

    _____

    _____

38. Indicate the sequence (1, 2, 3, 4) in which these events took place:
    ____ the EXILE to BABYLON
    ____ the period of the JUDGES
    ____ the DIVIDED KINGDOM
    ____ the EXODUS

39. List the correct order (1, 2, 3, 4) in which these people lived:
    ____ JOASH
    ____ REHOBOAM
    ____ EZRA
    ____ AARON

40. In what village was Jesus born? _____

41. List six of Jesus' twelve DISCIPLES:

_____

_____

_____

_____

_____

_____

42. Who was converted on the DAMASCUS ROAD? _____

43. Indicate the sequence (1, 2, 3, 4) in which these events took place:
   ____ the VIRGIN BIRTH
   ____ PENTECOST
   ____ MISSIONARY JOURNEYS OF PAUL
   ____ the HANDWRITING ON THE WALL

44. SAUL of Tarsus was later known by another name. What was his other name?

_____

45. Who was the first Christian MARTYR? _____

46. What was the relationship between the HEROD who killed the infants in BETHLEHEM and the Herod who killed JOHN THE BAPTIST?

_____

47. What primary issue was resolved at the Council at JERUSALEM in about A.D. 50?

_____

48. Who wrote 1 CORINTHIANS and 2 CORINTHIANS? _____

49. In what language was most of the Old Testament first written?

_____

50. On what special day was a SCAPEGOAT taken out into the WILDERNESS each year?

_____

ANSWERS

1. c	7. h
2. k	8. b
3. f	9. d
4. g	10. i
5. a	11. e
6. l	12. j

13. NT Revelation
    OT Deuteronomy
    OT Malachi
    NT Hebrews
14. Genesis
    Exodus
    Leviticus
    Numbers
    Deuteronomy
15. Greek
16. Matthew
    Mark
    Luke
    John
17. Acts
18. God (Genesis 1:3)
19. Paul (Ephesians 6:1, Colossians 3:20)
20. Any three of the following (this wording is from Exodus 20:1-17, King James Version):
    • Thou shalt have no other gods before me.
    • Thou shalt not make unto thee any graven image.
    • Thou shalt not take the name of the Lord thy God in vain.
    • Remember the Sabbath day, to keep it holy.
    • Honor thy father and thy mother.
    • Thou shalt not kill.
    • Thou shalt not commit adultery.
    • Thou shalt not steal.
    • Thou shalt not bear false witness against thy neighbor.
    • Thou shalt not covet . . .
21. Any four of the following (these terms are used in the NIV; wording from the King James Version, if it differs, is in parentheses):
    • love
    • joy
    • peace
    • patience (longsuffering)
    • kindness (gentleness)
    • goodness
    • faithfulness (faith)
    • gentleness (meekness)
    • self-control (temperance) (Galatians 5:22-23)

22. Jesus
23. "For God so loved the world . . ."
24. Genesis
    Gospel of John
25. Psalm 23
26. the love of money (not simply money)
27. "Our Father, who art in heaven . . ."
28. Any three of the following:
    • Asher
    • Benjamin
    • Dan
    • Ephraim
    • Gad
    • Issachar
    • Judah
    • Levi
    • Manasseh
    • Naphtali
    • Reuben
    • Simeon
    • Zebulun
29. Passover
30. Jerusalem
31. Israel (or northern kingdom)
    Judah (or southern kingdom)
32. Samaria
33. Sarah (or Sarai)
34. Moses
35. Solomon
36. Rehoboam
37. Shadrach (or Hananiah)
    Meshach (or Mishael)
    Abednego (or Azariah)
38. 4 the Exile to Babylon
    2 the period of the judges
    3 the Divided Kingdom
    1 the Exodus
39. 3 Joash
    2 Rehoboam
    4 Ezra
    1 Aaron
40. Bethlehem

41. Any six of the following:
    - Andrew
    - Bartholomew (also called Nathanael)
    - James (son of Alphaeus)
    - James (son of Zebedee)
    - John
    - Judas Iscariot
    - Matthew
    - Peter (also called Simon Peter)
    - Philip
    - Simon the Zealot
    - Thaddaeus (also called Judas, son of James)
    - Thomas
42. Saul of Tarsus (or Paul)

43. 2 the Virgin Birth
    3 Pentecost
    4 missionary journeys of Paul
    1 the handwriting on the wall

44. Paul

45. Stephen

46. Herod the Great killed the infants in Bethlehem; his son Herod Antipas killed John the Baptist.

47. Whether Gentile believers had to be circumcised and obey all the other laws of Moses. (Acts 15)

48. Paul

49. Hebrew

50. Day of Atonement

QUIZ ON ALL ASPECTS OF THE BIBLE AND THE CHURCH

Test your Christian Literacy

Select one answer for each question.

1. Who wrote many of the PSALMS?

    a. ☐ ISAIAH
    b. ☐ PAUL
    c. ☐ DAVID
    d. ☐ MOSES

2. Which of these is not a BOOK OF THE BIBLE?

    a. ☐ ISAIAH
    b. ☐ HEZEKIAH
    c. ☐ JUDE
    d. ☐ ZEPHANIAH

3. Which book contains stories of DAVID?

    a. ☐ 2 SAMUEL
    b. ☐ 1 KINGS
    c. ☐ 2 KINGS
    d. ☐ PSALMS

4. Who wrote the book of PHILEMON?

    a. ☐ PHILEMON
    b. ☐ ONESIMUS
    c. ☐ PAUL
    d. ☐ PETER

5. What is an EPISTLE?

    a. ☐ a theological discourse
    b. ☐ the wife of an APOSTLE
    c. ☐ a letter
    d. ☐ a GREEK MANUSCRIPT

6. Which TRANSLATION of the Bible was first published in 1611?

    a. ☐ NEW INTERNATIONAL VERSION

    b. ☐ SEPTUAGINT

    c. ☐ VULGATE

    d. ☐ KING JAMES VERSION

7. Who said, "AM I MY BROTHER'S KEEPER?"

    a. ☐ JACOB

    b. ☐ ESAU

    c. ☐ CAIN

    d. ☐ ABEL

8. Who first said, "ALL WE LIKE SHEEP HAVE GONE ASTRAY"?

    a. ☐ JESUS

    b. ☐ ISAIAH

    c. ☐ George Frederick HANDEL

    d. ☐ JOHN THE BAPTIST

9. Which expression is not found in the Bible?

    a. ☐ BE FRUITFUL, AND MULTIPLY

    b. ☐ EAT, DRINK, AND BE MERRY

    c. ☐ LORD, MAKE ME AN INSTRUMENT OF THY PEACE

    d. ☐ JUDGE NOT, THAT YE BE NOT JUDGED

10. Which of the following is not a saying of Jesus?

    a. ☐ BLESSED ARE THE MEEK, FOR THEY SHALL INHERIT THE EARTH

    b. ☐ DO THIS IN REMEMBRANCE OF ME

    c. ☐ THOU SHALT HAVE NO OTHER GODS BEFORE ME

    d. ☐ YE ARE THE LIGHT OF THE WORLD

11. When did Jesus say, "FATHER, FORGIVE THEM, FOR THEY KNOW NOT WHAT THEY DO"?

    a. ☐ when he threw the MONEY CHANGERS out of the TEMPLE

    b. ☐ in the Garden of GETHSEMANE

    c. ☐ in the SERMON ON THE MOUNT

    d. ☐ while he was hanging on the CROSS

12. "GIVE US THIS DAY OUR DAILY BREAD" is a phrase from:

    a. ☐ the TWENTY-THIRD PSALM

    b. ☐ the LORD'S PRAYER

    c. ☐ the BEATITUDES

    d. ☐ the APOSTLES' CREED

13. Where is the land of PALESTINE?

- a. ☐ at the mouth of the NILE RIVER
- b. ☐ at the eastern end of the MEDITERRANEAN SEA
- c. ☐ between the TIGRIS and EUPHRATES RIVERS
- d. ☐ between Italy and GREECE

14. The ARK OF THE COVENANT was:

- a. ☐ another name for NOAH's ark
- b. ☐ a gold-plated box kept in the HOLY OF HOLIES
- c. ☐ the stone tablet on which God wrote the TEN COMMANDMENTS
- d. ☐ another name for the TEMPLE

15. Which term does not refer to the CHILDREN OF ISRAEL?

- a. ☐ HEBREWS
- b. ☐ ISRAELITES
- c. ☐ CANAANITES
- d. ☐ God's CHOSEN PEOPLE

16. In what Roman province was the Mount of OLIVES located?

- a. ☐ GALILEE
- b. ☐ SAMARIA
- c. ☐ JUDEA
- d. ☐ ROME

17. Which of the following was not a Jewish religious and/or political party at the time of Jesus?

- a. ☐ ZEALOTS
- b. ☐ SADDUCEES
- c. ☐ PHARISEES
- d. ☐ PHILISTINES

18. Who was ABRAHAM's eldest son?

- a. ☐ ISAAC
- b. ☐ JACOB
- c. ☐ ISHMAEL
- d. ☐ CAIN

19. Who tried to seduce JOSEPH?

    a. ☐ POTIPHAR'S WIFE
    b. ☐ LOT'S WIFE
    c. ☐ JEZEBEL
    d. ☐ BATHSHEBA

20. Who was one of the spies that said God would help the ISRAELITES overcome the CANAANITES?

    a. ☐ CALEB
    b. ☐ JONATHAN
    c. ☐ DAVID
    d. ☐ BALAAM

21. Who was the first king of ISRAEL?

    a. ☐ HEROD
    b. ☐ MOSES
    c. ☐ DAVID
    d. ☐ SAUL

22. Who led the people in reconstructing the walls of JERUSALEM after the EXILE?

    a. ☐ EZRA
    b. ☐ NEHEMIAH
    c. ☐ ZECHARIAH
    d. ☐ DANIEL

23. Which event occurred first?

    a. ☐ the building of the Tower of BABEL
    b. ☐ the FLOOD
    c. ☐ the EXODUS
    d. ☐ the EXILE to BABYLON

24. Who defeated the prophets of BAAL on Mt. Carmel?

    a. ☐ ELIJAH
    b. ☐ ELISHA
    c. ☐ AHAB
    d. ☐ NEBUCHADNEZZAR

25. Which one of the following was never part of the ISRAELITE community living in EXILE?

   a. ☐ EZRA
   b. ☐ NEHEMIAH
   c. ☐ ESTHER
   d. ☐ JOB

26. Which event occurred last?

   a. ☐ SAMSON's captivity by the PHILISTINES
   b. ☐ The EXILE of the people of JUDAH to BABYLON
   c. ☐ The coronation of DAVID as king of ISRAEL
   d. ☐ The exile of the people of Israel to ASSYRIA

27. The ANGEL GABRIEL appeared to MARY and told her she would have a son. This event is called:

   a. ☐ the ASCENSION
   b. ☐ the ANNUNCIATION
   c. ☐ the TRANSFIGURATION
   d. ☐ the RESURRECTION

28. Which of these men was one of Jesus' twelve DISCIPLES?

   a. ☐ PAUL
   b. ☐ TIMOTHY
   c. ☐ LUKE
   d. ☐ MATTHEW

29. Which of these men did not become a follower of Jesus?

   a. ☐ CAIAPHAS
   b. ☐ NICODEMUS
   c. ☐ JOSEPH OF ARIMATHEA
   d. ☐ PETER

30. What prisoner did Pontius PILATE release?

   a. ☐ BARNABAS
   b. ☐ BARABBAS
   c. ☐ PETER
   d. ☐ SILAS

31. Who denied three times that he knew Jesus?

    a. ☐ MATTHEW
    b. ☐ JUDAS ISCARIOT
    c. ☐ JOHN
    d. ☐ PETER

32. Who traveled with PAUL on one of his MISSIONARY JOURNEYS?

    a. ☐ BARNABAS
    b. ☐ DORCAS
    c. ☐ PETER
    d. ☐ ANDREW

33. Which one of the following was not a Bible translator?

    a. ☐ William TYNDALE
    b. ☐ Martin LUTHER
    c. ☐ Johannes GUTENBERG
    d. ☐ JEROME

34. Which one of these was an influential black church leader?

    a. ☐ Martin LUTHER
    b. ☐ Richard ALLEN
    c. ☐ Jackie Robinson
    d. ☐ Harriet Beecher Stowe

35. Which of the following was a MISSIONARY in Africa?

    a. ☐ Mother TERESA
    b. ☐ John WESLEY
    c. ☐ JUSTIN MARTYR
    d. ☐ David LIVINGSTONE

36. What is a STATE CHURCH?

    a. ☐ the principal church in the capital city
    b. ☐ a CATHEDRAL
    c. ☐ a church established by civil authorities
    d. ☐ a small DENOMINATION located in only one state

37. Which of the following was an EVANGELIST?

    a. ☐ Roger WILLIAMS
    b. ☐ Karl BARTH
    c. ☐ William WILBERFORCE
    d. ☐ Dwight L. MOODY

38. Which POPE convened VATICAN II?

    a. ☐ PIUS XII
    b. ☐ JOHN XXIII
    c. ☐ PAUL VI
    d. ☐ JOHN PAUL II

39. Which ecclesiastical tradition has a hierarchy that includes BISHOPS?

    a. ☐ BAPTIST
    b. ☐ CONGREGATIONAL
    c. ☐ EPISCOPAL
    d. ☐ PRESBYTERIAN

40. Which of the following is most likely to come at the end of a WORSHIP service?

    a. ☐ BENEDICTION
    b. ☐ INVOCATION
    c. ☐ COLLECT
    d. ☐ CONFESSION

41. What is the official approval by the ROMAN CATHOLIC CHURCH that a book may be printed?

    a. ☐ "GLORIA PATRI"
    b. ☐ *Anno Domini*
    c. ☐ IMPRIMATUR
    d. ☐ KOINĒ

42. A PSALTER is:

    a. ☐ a musical instrument
    b. ☐ a book of PSALMS used for public or private WORSHIP
    c. ☐ the podium where the MINISTER stands
    d. ☐ the round window above the door in a gothic church

43. GRACE means:

    a. ☐ EVERLASTING LIFE
    b. ☐ unmerited favor
    c. ☐ peace
    d. ☐ JUSTICE

44. MONOTHEISM means:

    a. ☐ belief in one God
    b. ☐ belief in many gods
    c. ☐ belief that there is no God
    d. ☐ uncertainty about one's belief in God

45. PAPAL INFALLIBILITY means:

    a. ☐ the POPE is without ORIGINAL SIN
    b. ☐ the pope cannot be married
    c. ☐ the pope must live a sinless life
    d. ☐ the pope is without error when he speaks EX CATHEDRA

46. According to ORTHODOX Christian THEOLOGY, GOD THE SON:

    a. ☐ has always existed with GOD THE FATHER
    b. ☐ was created at the time MARY conceived the Christ child
    c. ☐ appeared to be human, but was not fully human
    d. ☐ none of the above

47. Who is believed to have written *IMITATION OF CHRIST*?

    a. ☐ Martin LUTHER
    b. ☐ Oswald Chambers
    c. ☐ IGNATIUS OF LOYOLA
    d. ☐ THOMAS À KEMPIS

48. Who painted the ceiling of the SISTINE CHAPEL?

    a. ☐ LEONARDO DA VINCI
    b. ☐ MICHELANGELO
    c. ☐ Johann Sebastian BACH
    d. ☐ Martin LUTHER

49. Who wrote *MERE CHRISTIANITY?*

    a. ☐ John BUNYAN
    b. ☐ John CALVIN
    c. ☐ C. S. LEWIS
    d. ☐ Martin Luther KING, Jr.

50. Which of the following HYMNS was written by John Newton, a former slave trader?

   a. ☐ "O COME, ALL YE FAITHFUL"
   b. ☐ "NEARER, MY GOD, TO THEE"
   c. ☐ "AMAZING GRACE"
   d. ☐ "HOW GREAT THOU ART"

ANSWERS

1. c	14. b	27. b	40. a
2. b	15. c	28. d	41. c
3. a	16. c	29. a	42. b
4. c	17. d	30. b	43. b
5. c	18. c	31. d	44. a
6. d	19. a	32. a	45. d
7. c	20. a	33. c	46. a
8. b	21. d	34. b	47. d
9. c	22. b	35. d	48. b
10. c	23. b	36. c	49. c
11. d	24. a	37. d	50. c
12. b	25. d	38. b	
13. b	26. b	39. c	

ON ALL ASPECTS OF THE BIBLE AND THE CHURCH

Test Your Christian Literacy

Match each of the following books of the Bible to its content:

1. ____ 1 CHRONICLES
2. ____ 2 CHRONICLES
3. ____ EZRA
4. ____ NEHEMIAH
5. ____ ESTHER
6. ____ JOB
7. ____ MATTHEW
8. ____ MARK
9. ____ ACTS
10. ____ ROMANS

a. The story of Jesus as told by an eyewitness who was not one of the DISCIPLES

b. The story of a queen who risked her life to save her people

c. History of the reign of King DAVID

d. An EPISTLE from the APOSTLE PAUL

e. The first return of the JEWS after the EXILE

f. History of JUDAH from the reign of SOLOMON to the EXILE

g. History of the first years of the EARLY CHURCH

h. The rebuilding of the walls of JERUSALEM

i. The story of Jesus written especially for a Jewish audience

j. The tribulations of a just man

Match each of the following books of the Bible to its content:

11. ____ PSALMS
12. ____ PROVERBS
13. ____ ECCLESIASTES
14. ____ SONG OF SOLOMON
15. ____ ISAIAH
16. ____ DANIEL
17. ____ LUKE
18. ____ JOHN
19. ____ 1 CORINTHIANS
20. ____ REVELATION

a. Shows the futility of life apart from God

b. A collection of HEBREW poems and songs

c. The story of Jesus as told by a GENTILE physician

d. The story of Jesus as told by one of Jesus' DISCIPLES

e. PROPHECIES to the Kingdom of JUDAH

f. An EPISTLE from the APOSTLE PAUL

g. A collection of wise and pithy sayings

h. A celebration of romantic love

i. A VISION about future events, including the NEW JERUSALEM

j. Stories from the EXILE in BABYLON

21. In which BOOK OF THE BIBLE can you find "The LORD IS MY SHEPHERD"?

_____

22. Who led the first group of JEWS that returned to JERUSALEM after the EXILE in BABYLON? _____

23. Why did the ANGEL tell JOSEPH to take MARY and the infant Jesus to EGYPT?

_____

24. Complete this saying of Jesus: "FOLLOW ME, and I will make you . . ."

_____

25. What Roman centurion was CONVERTED after he was told in a VISION to send for PETER? _____

26. Who was the "Father of the PROTESTANT REFORMATION"?

_____

27. What mission organization was founded by J. Hudson TAYLOR in 1866 for the evangelization of China?

_____

28. According to the WESTMINSTER SHORTER CATECHISM, what is the CHIEF END OF MAN?

_____

29. Two of the following are included in the SEVEN DEADLY SINS. Which ones are they?
_____adultery
_____divorce
_____gluttony
_____covetousness

30. What is a religious awakening that sweeps through a congregation or even an entire nation? _____

31. List the correct sequence (1, 2, 3, 4) in which these events took place:
_____VATICAN II
_____LUTHER's posting of the NINETY-FIVE THESES
_____Council of CHALCEDON
_____Council of TRENT

32. What is the name for the first day of LENT? _____

33. On what SUNDAY do Christians celebrate the RESURRECTION of JESUS?

_____

34. What term refers to a person who doesn't know if there is a God, and who may believe it is impossible ever to know? _____

35. Who are the three Persons of the TRINITY?

_____

_____

_____

36. What term means that God is all powerful? _____

37. Who wrote the ORATORIO *MESSIAH*? _____

38. What sculptor created *DAVID* and the *PIETÀ*? _____

39. Who wrote the words to 8,000 HYMNS and GOSPEL SONGS, including "BLESSED ASSURANCE"? _____

Match the author to his book:

40. ____ Thomas AQUINAS   a. The PILGRIM'S PROGRESS
41. ____ John BUNYAN   b. MERE CHRISTIANITY
42. ____ DANTE   c. PENSÉES
43. ____ John MILTON   d. INSTITUTES OF THE CHRISTIAN RELIGION
44. ____ C. S. LEWIS   e. SUMMA THEOLOGICA
45. ____ John CALVIN   f. The BOOK OF MARTYRS
46. ____ AUGUSTINE OF HIPPO g. MY UTMOST FOR HIS HIGHEST
47. ____ Oswald Chambers   h. The DIVINE COMEDY
48. ____ John Foxe   i. CONFESSIONS
49. ____ Charles Sheldon   j. PARADISE LOST
50. ____ Blaise PASCAL   k. IN HIS STEPS

ANSWERS

1. c
2. f
3. e
4. h
5. b
6. j
7. i
8. a
9. g
10. d
11. b
12. g
13. a

14. h
15. e
16. j
17. c
18. d
19. f
20. i
21. Psalms (Psalm 23)
22. Zerubbabel
23. to escape Herod the Great's massacre of the infants in Bethlehem
24. fishers of men
25. Cornelius

26. Martin Luther
27. China Inland Mission (now known as Overseas Missionary Fellowship, or OMF)
28. "The chief end of man is to love God and enjoy him forever."
29. gluttony
covetousness
30. revival
31. 4 Vatican II
2 Luther's posting of the Ninety-five Theses
1 Council of Chalcedon
3 Council of Trent
32. Ash Wednesday
33. Easter
34. agnostic
35. Father
Son
Holy Spirit (or Holy Ghost)

36. omnipotence of God
37. George Frederick Handel
38. Michelangelo
39. Fanny Crosby
40. e
41. a
42. h
43. j
44. b
45. d
46. i
47. g
48. f
49. k
50. c

THE BIBLE

While this entire book is about biblical literacy, this first chapter is about the Bible itself. It includes the name of every BOOK OF THE BIBLE, with a brief statement of the theme of the book. Each book of the Bible is identified as being from the Old Testament (OT) or the New Testament (NT).

Every literate person should know that the book of PSALMS is a collection of poems found in the Old Testament and that the GOSPELS are biographies of Jesus found in the New Testament. But literate Christians also recognize ZEPHANIAH as one of the MINOR PROPHETS in the Old Testament, and they know that 1 THESSALONIANS is a letter from the APOSTLE PAUL to one of the EARLY CHURCHES.

This chapter also includes a chart of the best-known English TRANSLATIONS of the Bible, such as the KING JAMES VERSION, the NEW INTERNATIONAL VERSION, and *The Living Bible*. The entry for each translation is immediately followed by the abbreviation most commonly used for that translation or version.

Also included in this chapter are descriptions of Bible study tools such as BIBLE DICTIONARY and BIBLE COMMENTARY. Finally, there are terms such as GREEK, HEBREW, *KOINĒ*, MANUSCRIPT, DEAD SEA SCROLLS, and TEXTUS RECEPTUS that relate to the manner in which the Bible was first written and has been handed down through the centuries.

Acts or **Acts of the Apostles** (NT) The book of Acts follows the Gospels and tells of the founding and growth of the Christian church in the first century A.D. It was written by Luke and starts where the narrative of the Gospel of Luke ends. In the second chapter, just ten days after Jesus' Ascension into heaven, we see the coming of the Holy Spirit at Pentecost. The main character in the first twelve chapters is Peter, who became one of the leaders in the emerging church in Jerusalem. The remaining chapters then follow Paul on his various missionary journeys. The time period covered by the book of Acts is approximately A.D. 30–65.

Amos (OT) One of the Minor Prophets, this book contains the messages of the prophet Amos. Amos was a shepherd who pronounced God's judgment upon the people of the Northern kingdom of Israel shortly be-fore Israel was taken into Exile by the Assyrians in 722 B.C.

Apocalypse Another name for the New Testament book of Revelation. The word *apocalypse* means 'disclosure' or 'revelation'.

Apocrypha Seven books in the Old Testament (plus additions to the books of Esther and Daniel) that are included in Roman Catholic Bibles but are not included in the Jewish Bible or in most Protestant Bibles. These books, usually called "Apocrypha" by Protestants, are called "Deuterocanonical books" by Catholics. When the Old Testament canon was being consolidated several centuries before Christ, the Apocryphal books were considered to be of lesser authority than the books that were accepted into the canon. For a list of books in the Apocrypha, see Old Testament.

❦ Although the word *Apocrypha*

comes from a GREEK word meaning 'hidden', the word *apocryphal* has generally come to mean spurious, or something that is probably not true.

Aramaic An ancient language closely related to HEBREW. Several portions of the Old Testament were originally written in Aramaic. The JEWS of Jesus' day spoke Aramaic, so presumably Jesus' own teachings were originally spoken in Aramaic, then later recorded in GREEK.

Bible The holy book of the Christian faith, containing the Old Testament and the New Testament. It is often called the Holy Bible. Most Christians believe the Bible to be the inspired WORD OF GOD. The BOOKS OF THE BIBLE were written by dozens of writers over a period of about 1,500 years.

The books that Christians call the Old Testament constitute the entirety of the Jewish Bible. The Old Testament tells of the CREATION, the FALL OF MAN, God's COVENANT with ABRAHAM, and the history of Abraham's descendants, the JEWS, till about 430 B.C. It also contains the MOSAIC LAW, HEBREW poetry (including the PSALMS and PROVERBS), and the messages of the PROPHETS.

The New Testament contains the four GOSPELS, which tell the stories of the life and ministry of Jesus, culminating in his suffering, CRUCIFIXION, and RESURRECTION. Next comes the book of ACTS, which tells of the EARLY CHURCH in the first century, and the EPISTLES, which are letters to the Christians of the first century.

For a complete list of the books of the Bible, see OLD TESTAMENT and NEW TESTAMENT.

❧ The Bible defines many concepts that are foundational to Western culture—concepts such as JUSTICE and MERCY, fair play, marriage, and family relationships.

❧ The Bible, particularly the KING JAMES VERSION, has had more impact on the literature of the English language than has any other single source.

Bible commentary A book that provides information and interpretation to help the reader understand the biblical text. Some commentaries cover the entire text of the Bible in one volume. Other commentary series devote an entire volume to each BOOK OF THE BIBLE.

Bible concordance A listing of key words in the Bible, along with the references where they are found. Many Bibles have abridged concordances printed at the end of the book. Complete concordances list every occurrence of every word in the Bible, usually with a phrase to show the context for the word.

Bible dictionary A dictionary that defines all the terms and names found in the Bible.

The Most Popular English Translations of the Bible

Amplified Bible, The The unique feature of this translation is the addition of thousands of alternate (amplified) readings in brackets to help the reader understand the text. It was published in 1964.

Authorized Version (AV) *See* KING JAMES VERSION.

Douay-Rheims Bible A ROMAN CATHOLIC translation produced in the early seventeenth century—about the same time as the KING JAMES VERSION. For the most part it was translated from the LATIN VULGATE. Until the 1970s, when the NEW AMERICAN BIBLE was completed, the Douay-Rheims Bible was the standard English translation of the Bible for the Roman Catholic church.

Good News Bible *See* TODAY'S ENGLISH VERSION.

King James Version (KJV) Until recently, the King James Version was the most widely used English translation of the Bible. It was first published in 1611 under the authorization of King JAMES I of England. In Britain it is called the Authorized Version (AV). Its stately language has had a great influence on spoken English and on English literature over nearly four centuries. Most biblical phrases and quotations that are popularly known (*see the entries under "Quotations from the Bible"*) are from the King James Version. In recent years, modern translations have replaced the King James Version in many churches.

Living Bible, The (TLB) A thought-for-thought translation of the Bible. It has been widely used since its initial publication in 1971. In the early 1970s it was the best-selling book in the United States.

New American Bible (NAB) A translation sponsored by the ROMAN CATHOLIC CHURCH. Sometimes called the Confraternity Bible, it was first published in 1970 and is the translation now most widely used by Catholics.

New American Standard Bible (NASB) A translation first published in 1971, it gained popularity among EVANGELICALS as an accurate word-for-word style of translation.

New English Bible (NEB) A thought-for-thought translation published in 1970, the New English Bible was more popular in Britain than in the United States. In 1989 a revision called the Revised English Bible (REB) was published.

New International Version (NIV) A popular translation that has been widely accepted by EVANGELICALS since its publication in 1978. It has recently surpassed the KING JAMES VERSION as the most widely-used English translation of the Bible.

New King James Version (NKJV) A popular revision of the KING JAMES VERSION, it was first published in 1982. Many difficult and archaic words have been updated, and the words THEE AND THOU have been replaced with the contemporary *you*.

New Revised Standard Version (NRSV) *See* REVISED STANDARD VERSION.

Revised Standard Version (RSV) The standard Bible used by most MAINLINE DENOMINATIONS. The translation was sponsored by the NATIONAL COUNCIL OF THE CHURCHES OF CHRIST IN THE USA and was first published in 1952. In 1990 a revised edition called the New Revised Standard Version (NRSV) was published to replace the former edition.

Today's English Version (TEV) This modern translation, published by the American Bible Society, has been quite popular since its publication in 1976. It uses simple English and tends to be a thought-for-thought style of translation. It is also called the *Good News Bible*.

biblical criticism The process of applying scientific methods in studying the text of the Bible. Biblical criticism is often divided into lower and higher criticism. Lower (or textual) criticism focuses exclusively on the text itself. Its objective is to determine as nearly as possible the exact wording of the original text. Higher criticism addresses issues such as date of writing, authorship, and the oral traditions assumed to lie behind the written text.

Higher critics have often been accused of starting with presuppositions that deny the supernatural or that assume that prophetic passages could not have been written before the occurrence of the event they foretell. Many higher critics doubt the historical accuracy of many parts of the Bible. Other scholars, who prefer to take the text at face value, feel that higher criticism is not a valid way of approaching the text.

books of the Bible The Bible is made up of sixty-six individual books (seventy-three books when the APOC-RYPHA are included). Each book is divided into CHAPTERS AND VERSES. The longest book in the Bible is PSALMS, with 150 chapters. Five books have only one chapter. The books of the Bible were written by many different authors over a long period—possibly as long as 1,500 years (1400 B.C. to A.D.

95). For a complete list of the books of the Bible, see OLD TESTAMENT and NEW TESTAMENT.

❧ The titles of books that start with a number (e.g., 1 SAMUEL, 2 SAMUEL) are usually pronounced *First* Samuel (rather than *One* Samuel) and *Second* Samuel (rather than *Two* Samuel).

❧ The word *Bible* comes from the GREEK word for 'book'.

Books of Moses The first five books of the Old Testament are called the Books of Moses, reflecting the traditional view that they were written by MOSES. They are also called the PENTATEUCH (GREEK for 'five books') and TORAH. The Books of Moses contain the stories of the CREATION, the FALL OF MAN, God's COVENANT with ABRA-HAM, the EXODUS of the ISRAELITES from EGYPT, the TEN COMMANDMENTS and the rest of the MOSAIC LAW, and the experiences of the ISRAELITES as they wandered in the WILDERNESS for forty years. (*See* GENESIS; EXODUS; LEVITICUS; NUM-BERS; DEUTERONOMY.)

canon The official list of books that are included in the Old Testament and the New Testament.

Since the books of the Old Testament were written over a period of 800 or more years, the development of the Old Testament canon was a gradual process. The earliest Old Testament writings were accepted as having unique significance early in the history of the nation of ISRAEL. For instance, the Lord was speaking of the MOSAIC LAW when he said to JOSHUA, "Do not let this Book of the Law depart from your mouth; meditate on it day and night, so that you may be careful to do everything written in it. Then you will be prosperous and successful" (Joshua 1:8, NIV). According to tradition, EZRA played a role in compiling the canon of the Jewish SCRIPTURE in the fifth century B.C. The Jewish canon contains the same books that comprise the Old Testament for PROTESTANTS.

The New Testament canon was recognized by the CHURCH FATHERS as early as A.D. 200 and was largely undisputed by the fourth century A.D. It is accepted by all Christian churches (*see* NEW TESTAMENT CANON ESTABLISHED *under "Church History"*).

Canticles *See* SONG OF SOLOMON.

chapter and verse Each BOOK OF THE BIBLE is divided into chapters, and each chapter is divided into verses. Passages in the Bible are identified by their chapter and verse. The longest and shortest chapters are both in the PSALMS. Psalm 119 has 176 verses; Psalm 117 has only 2 verses.

The original MANUSCRIPTS were not divided into chapters and verses. In fact, the New Testament was first divided into verses in the sixteenth century. (For a comment about other features that have been added to the Bible text, see the entry for RED-LETTER EDITIONS.)

❧ More broadly, to quote "chapter and verse" is to give the specific source of any quotation.

1 Chronicles (OT) The books of 1 & 2 Chronicles tell the story of the history of ISRAEL during the period from King DAVID to the fall of the Kingdom of JUDAH. They emphasize the role of the PRIESTS and the establishment of the pattern of WORSHIP in the TEMPLE. The book of 1 Chronicles begins with a GENEALOGY of Israel and then tells the story of the reign of King David. It covers much the same time period as is covered in the book of 2 SAMUEL.

2 Chronicles (OT) The book of 2 Chronicles begins where 1 CHRONICLES ends. It covers the period from the reign of King SOLOMON to the fall of Judah and the EXILE to BABYLON. It covers much the same period as is covered in the books of 1 & 2 KINGS.

Colossians (NT) PAUL's letter to the church in Colosse (an ancient city in present-day Turkey; see map on next page). This letter was written about A.D. 60 while Paul was in prison in ROME. (The letters to the EPHESIANS and the PHILIPPIANS may also have been written about the same time.) The purpose of this letter was to combat theological errors that had crept into the Colossian church. The primary theme is that the fullness of divinity and of the divine purpose is embodied in Christ, and that Christ is the head of the church. The letter then draws numerous conclusions as to how Christians should live.

1 Corinthians (NT) One of PAUL's letters to the church in Corinth (in GREECE). This letter was written about A.D. 55, while Paul was on his third MISSIONARY JOURNEY. The primary purpose of the letter was to offer solutions to problems in the Corinthian church. The thirteenth chapter is often called the LOVE CHAPTER. It begins, "Though I speak with the tongues of men and of angels, and have not charity [love], I am become as sounding brass, or a tinkling cymbal."

2 Corinthians (NT) Another of PAUL's letters to the church in Cor-

inth (in GREECE). This letter was written about A.D. 55–57, while Paul was on his third MISSIONARY JOURNEY. The primary purpose of the letter was to affirm Paul's own authority as an APOSTLE so he could continue refuting the false teachers in Corinth. This is an intensely personal letter.

cross references Notations in the margin or in a center column in a Bible to indicate other verses where a similar subject is found.

Daniel (OT) DANIEL and his friends SHADRACH, MESHACH, AND ABEDNEGO were among the group of ISRAELITES taken to BABYLON in the EXILE in 605 B.C., nineteen years before the fall of JERUSALEM. The first half of this book contains the familiar stories about Daniel—interpreting NEBUCHADNEZZAR's dream about the statue with the FEET OF CLAY, the FIERY FURNACE, the HAND-

CORINTH AND EPHESUS
Paul founded the churches in Corinth and Ephesus during his missionary journeys. The books we call 1 & 2 Corinthians and Ephesians were letters to those churches. The book of Colossians was a letter to the church in Colosse, a group Paul had never visited.

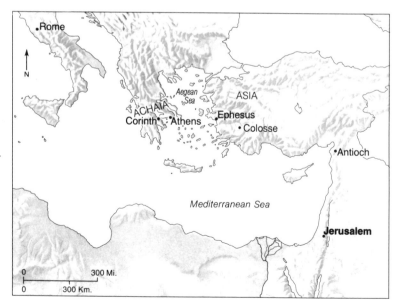

WRITING ON THE WALL, and DANIEL IN THE LIONS' DEN. In the book of Daniel we see the Babylonians defeated by King Darius, which marks the start of the PERSIAN Empire. The second half of the book of Daniel contains prophetic VISIONS about the future.

Dead Sea Scrolls A collection of SCROLLS, MANUSCRIPTS, and manuscript fragments dating from the third century B.C. to the first century A.D. Most of them were found in 1947–1952 in caves along the northern shore of the DEAD SEA. They include HEBREW, ARAMAIC, and GREEK manuscripts of parts of the Old Testament and are the oldest existing manuscripts of the Bible. The Dead Sea Scrolls include an entire text of the book of ISAIAH. Most of the scrolls are made of leather (some are papyrus) and

are believed to have been part of the library of a religious community of Essenes (an ASCETIC and communal sect within JUDAISM) at Qumran. They were stored (or perhaps hidden) in pottery jars, where they remained for 2,000 years.

Deuterocanonical books *See* APOCRYPHA.

Deuteronomy (OT) The fifth and last of the BOOKS OF MOSES. After having wandered in the WILDERNESS for forty years, the generation of ISRAELITES that left EGYPT in the EXODUS had now died, and their children were ready to enter the PROMISED LAND. Deuteronomy contains MOSES' speech in which he reminded this new, young generation of all that the Lord had done for his CHOSEN PEOPLE. Moses then reviewed the LAW for

DEAD SEA SCROLLS This scroll contains the "Manual of Discipline" from the Qumran community.

them and challenged them to commit themselves to the Lord.

Ecclesiastes (OT) This book shows the futility of life apart from God. The author, traditionally said to be SOLOMON, tells of his own search for meaning through wisdom, pleasure, work, success, and wealth. He says at various points along the way that everything is meaningless, "a chasing after the wind" (1:12, NIV). In the end he concludes, "Fear God, and keep his commandments: for this is the whole duty of man."

The book of Ecclesiastes (the name comes from the GREEK word for 'preacher') contains such well-known phrases as "VANITY OF VANITIES; ALL IS VANITY"; "There is NOTHING NEW UNDER THE SUN"; "EAT, DRINK, AND BE MERRY"; and "TO EVERYTHING THERE IS A SEASON."

Ephesians (NT) PAUL's letter to the church in Ephesus (see the map at the entry for 1 CORINTHIANS). Like PHILIPPIANS and COLOSSIANS, this letter was written about A.D. 60 while Paul was in prison in ROME. The primary purpose of the letter was to strengthen and encourage the Ephesian Christians, whom Paul knew very well. The letter to the Ephesians contains such well-known passages as "CHILDREN, OBEY YOUR PARENTS" and "Put on the whole armor of God."

Epistles An epistle is a letter, and the Epistles in the New Testament include letters written by PAUL, PETER, JOHN, JAMES (brother of Jesus), and Jude. This section of the Bible outlines various aspects of Christian DOCTRINE and contains practical exhortations for Christian living.

Esther (OT) This book tells the story of ESTHER, a young Jewish woman who had been selected because of her beauty to become a member of the harem of King Ahasuerus (Xerxes) of PERSIA. He later selected her to be queen. When Esther's cousin and foster father, Mordecai, heard that the prime minister, Haman, had launched a plan to kill all of the JEWS in the kingdom, he urged Esther to ask the king to countermand the plan. Although she was the queen, she was not permitted, on pain of death, to speak to the king without being called by him. Esther devised a plan to gain the attention and favor of the king. She succeeded, and the plan to exterminate the Jews was reversed. The Jewish holiday of PURIM commemorates this rescue of the Jews.

The story of Esther takes place about 474 B.C., sixty years after the first Jews had returned to JERUSALEM from the EXILE in BABYLON and PERSIA. Esther was in the Jewish community that stayed in Persia.

Exodus (OT) The second of the BOOKS OF MOSES. It contains the account of MOSES, the first PASSOVER, and the EXODUS from EGYPT. The Lord sent Moses to tell the PHARAOH, "LET MY PEOPLE GO." When Pharaoh refused, the Lord sent ten PLAGUES to convince him to heed the word of the Lord. The last plague was the death of the firstborn son and the firstborn of the livestock in every Egyptian home and barn. The Lord instructed the ISRAELITES to put blood on their doorposts; he would then pass over their houses as he killed the sons of Egypt. The Israelites were then allowed to leave Egypt, and God miraculously spared their lives in the parting of the RED SEA.

The Israelites did not trust God, so God told Moses the people would have to wander in the WILDERNESS for forty years. The remainder of the book tells of God's COVENANT with the people in giving them the LAW, including the TEN COMMANDMENTS. There are also long sections detailing the manner in which the TABERNACLE was to be constructed.

Ezekiel (OT) One of the MAJOR PROPHETS, this book contains the messages of the PROPHET EZEKIEL. Along with thousands of other JEWS, he was captured by the BABYLONIANS in 597 B.C., eleven years before the fall of JERUSALEM. His prophetic ministry took place in Babylon among his fellow captives, telling them that the EXILE was because of their sins. The PROPHECIES at the end of the book are

from the period after the fall of Jerusalem, and Ezekiel gives a message of hope to his people.

Ezra (OT) Like NEHEMIAH and ESTHER, this is one of the historical books from the period during and after the EXILE in BABYLON and PERSIA. King Cyrus of Persia conquered Babylon in 539 B.C. and issued a decree that permitted the captive JEWS to return to their homeland. In 538 B.C. the first group of about 42,000 Jews returned under ZERUBBABEL and began rebuilding the TEMPLE. Eighty years later, in 458 B.C., EZRA, a PRIEST and PROPHET, traveled to Jerusalem with another group of about 1,800 Jews. When Ezra arrived he found the Jews in Jerusalem living in a state of religious indifference because of their intermarriage with the heathen nations around them. Though the prophets ZECHARIAH and HAGGAI had urged the people to repent, it was not until Ezra's arrival that the people returned to God. The third and final contingent of Jews to return from Babylonia was led by NEHEMIAH in 445 B.C. Their story is recounted in the book bearing his name.

Galatians (NT) PAUL's letter to the churches in Galatia (an ancient region in present-day Turkey). The primary purpose of the letter (which may have been written about A.D. 49) was to refute the arguments of those who said GENTILE Christians had to obey the MOSAIC LAW in order to be saved. This issue was officially resolved in about A.D. 50 at the Council at JERUSALEM. The letter to the Galatians stresses the Christian's freedom in Christ.

Genesis (OT) The first book in the Bible and the first of the BOOKS OF MOSES. It contains the accounts of the CREATION, NOAH and the ark, the Tower of BABEL, and the PATRIARCHS of ISRAEL—ABRAHAM, ISAAC, JACOB, and JOSEPH and his brothers. The book begins with the Creation ("IN THE BEGINNING, God created the heaven and the earth") and ends with the death of Joseph in EGYPT. Genesis is interesting to read since it contains so many familiar Bible stories.

❧ The word *genesis* means beginning, or origin—a fitting title for a book that tells of the origin of all creation.

Gospels The first four books of the New Testament: MATTHEW, MARK, LUKE, and JOHN. Each of the Gospels (the word *gospel* means GOOD NEWS) tells the story of the life, death, and RESURRECTION of Jesus. There is much overlap of content between the four accounts, but each Gospel also has unique material not found in any of the others.

Greek The language of ancient GREECE, in which the books of the New Testament were first written. The New Testament was not written in classical Greek, but in KOINĒ Greek, the form of the language spread throughout the Near East by the conquests of Alexander the Great. This was the language of the marketplace at the time of the EARLY CHURCH. Since Greek was spoken as a trade language throughout much of the ROMAN EMPIRE, Christianity was able to spread from region to region without a language barrier.

Habakkuk (OT) One of the MINOR PROPHETS, this book contains the messages of the PROPHET Habakkuk to the people of the Kingdom of JUDAH. Like JEREMIAH, Habakkuk prophesied during the final years before the fall of JERUSALEM to the BABYLONIANS.

Haggai (OT) One of the MINOR PROPHETS from the period after the EXILE. This book contains the messages of the PROPHET Haggai to the ISRAELITES who had returned to JERUSALEM. It is a challenge to finish the rebuilding of the TEMPLE, which had been started twenty years earlier by ZERUBBABEL, but never completed. The messages of Haggai fall between the two events recorded in the book of EZRA—the return of Zerubbabel and the return of EZRA. *See also* ZECHARIAH; NEHEMIAH.

Hebrew The language of the ancient HEBREW people. Most of the Old Testament was written in Hebrew.

❧ Modern Hebrew, used in the modern state of Israel, is based on ancient Hebrew, but thousands of words have been added to the vocabulary to allow for communication in our present complex world. Hebrew is written from right to left.

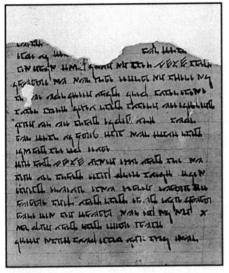

HEBREW Hebrew lettering on one of the Dead Sea Scrolls. The text is part of the "Habakkuk Commentary."

Hebrews (NT) A New Testament EPISTLE written to Jewish Christians during the first century A.D. The author is not identified. The primary theme of the letter is the superiority of Christ, including his superiority over MOSES and the Old Testament priesthood. Many quotations from the Old Testament are woven through the book of Hebrews.

higher criticism See BIBLICAL CRITICISM.

Holy Bible See BIBLE.

Holy Writ Another term for the BIBLE.

Hosea (OT) One of the MINOR PROPHETS, this book contains the messages of the PROPHET HOSEA to the people of the Kingdom of ISRAEL shortly before that nation fell to the ASSYRIANS in 722 B.C. At God's command, Hosea married GOMER, a prostitute. She and her children served as object lessons as Hosea preached about Israel's faithlessness and God's willingness to forgive them.

Isaiah (OT) The book that contains the messages of the PROPHET ISAIAH. It is one of the MAJOR PROPHETS. Isaiah's ministry was to the people of the Kingdom of JUDAH at the time that the Kingdom of ISRAEL fell to the ASSYRIANS (722 B.C.). The book of Isaiah contains many PROPHECIES regarding the coming of the MESSIAH, some of which were set to music in HANDEL'S *Messiah*. A familiar passage is this prophecy concerning the future Messiah: "Behold, a virgin shall conceive, and bear a son, and shall call his name IMMANUEL" (Isaiah 7:14).

James (NT) This EPISTLE was written by James (brother of Jesus) to Jewish Christians living outside PALESTINE. (For a comment about varying interpretations of who "Jesus' brothers" were, see the entry for JAMES (brother of Jesus) under "People and Events in the New Testament.") James is a practical letter that shows the importance of living out one's faith in day-to-day life.

❧ Since the book of James emphasizes the importance of works in proving one's SALVATION, Martin LUTHER did not believe it should be part of the CANON.

Jeremiah (OT) This book, one of the MAJOR PROPHETS, contains the messages of the PROPHET JEREMIAH. His ministry was to the Kingdom of JUDAH in the years just before it was conquered by BABYLON. He urged the people to repent of their SINS and turn back to God.

Job (OT) The story of Job (pronounced *Jōb*), the man who bore great suffering with great patience, is not placed at any particular time or place in history. The author of this book is unknown, but the purpose is to answer the perennial question, Why do good people suffer? See the entry for JOB under "People and Events in the Old Testament" for more details about Job and his trials.

Joel (OT) One of the MINOR PROPHETS, containing the messages of the PROPHET Joel to the people of the Kingdom of JUDAH. The people had become prosperous and had turned away from God. Joel called the people to REPENTANCE and predicted that a great plague of locusts would destroy their crops.

John, Gospel of (NT) This GOSPEL was written by JOHN, the DISCIPLE of Jesus. It opens with the familiar verse, "IN THE BEGINNING was the WORD, and the Word was with God, and the Word was God." John tells the stories of the life and ministry of Jesus, but he includes more of Jesus' discourses than are found in the other Gospels.

One of the most familiar verses in the Bible is JOHN 3:16: "For God so loved the world, that he gave his only begotten Son, that whosoever believeth in him should not perish, but have everlasting life."

1 John (NT) There are three EPISTLES in the New Testament written by John the Elder. There are various scholarly views as to the identity of John the Elder, but the traditional view is that JOHN the DISCIPLE of Jesus wrote these epistles late in his life. The first epistle of John was written to all the GENTILE churches. Its primary purpose was to reassure the BELIEVERS about their faith. John was perhaps the last surviving disciple by this time, so he wrote to the younger generations of believers as an eyewitness of Jesus' ministry.

2 John (NT) This is the second of the three EPISTLES written by JOHN late in his life. It is the shortest book in the Bible (just one chapter, comprising thirteen verses). It is written to "the elect lady and her children," which may be a reference to a specific person or to a church that is not otherwise identified. John warns against the false teachers that were prevalent in the EARLY CHURCH.

3 John (NT) This is the third of the three EPISTLES of JOHN. It is a personal letter to a man named Gaius, encouraging and affirming him in his practice of hospitality, especially to visiting teachers and MISSIONARIES.

Jonah (OT) This book, one of the MINOR PROPHETS, contains the familiar story of JONAH AND THE WHALE. JONAH tried to run away when God sent him to preach to Nineveh, the heathen capital of ASSYRIA. He was swallowed by a great fish and stayed in its belly for three days and three nights. After Jonah finally obeyed God and preached in Nineveh, the people of Nineveh repented and turned to God. God chose not to destroy the city when the people repented, but this made Jonah angry. He had been preaching that the city would be destroyed because of the people's wickedness, and he may have resented God's compassion for the wicked Assyrians.

Jesus referred to Jonah's experience in the belly of the whale as a picture of his own death and subsequent RESURRECTION (Matthew 12:40).

Joshua (OT) The book of Joshua begins where DEUTERONOMY leaves off. MOSES has died, and the people of ISRAEL are just about to enter the PROMISED LAND after having been in the WILDERNESS for forty years. The book of Joshua tells of the ISRAELITES' conquest of the land of CANAAN under the leadership of JOSHUA, who had been Moses' assistant. The Lord shows his care for the people by holding back the waters of the JORDAN RIVER so the entire nation can cross on dry ground. Then comes the story of RAHAB and the Battle of JERICHO, when the walls of the city come tumbling down. After the land is conquered, the TRIBES OF ISRAEL receive their allotted territories.

Jude (NT) This short EPISTLE was written by Jude, one of Jesus' brothers who became a leader in the EARLY CHURCH. (For a comment about varying interpretations of who "Jesus' brothers" were, see the entry for JAMES (brother of Jesus) under "People and Events in the New Testament.") Jude's letter was written to all the churches, and it reminds the BELIEVERS to stay away from false teachings.

Judges (OT) After the EXODUS, the ISRAELITES returned to the PROMISED LAND and conquered the land under JOSHUA's leadership. Then came a period of 200 or more years (some scholars believe it was as long as 325 years) during which ISRAEL had no king. Instead, the people were led by "judges." The book of Judges tells the history of this period and includes the stories of DEBORAH, GIDEON, and SAMSON, among others. *See* *also* JUDGES, PERIOD OF THE *under "People and Events in the Old Testament."*

1 Kings　(OT) This book contains the history of the reign of SOLOMON and then the first eighty years of the DIVIDED KINGDOM (JUDAH and ISRAEL). It includes stories of the great PROPHET ELIJAH, including his contest with the prophets of BAAL, when Elijah called down FIRE FROM HEAVEN. The books of 1 and 2 Kings were originally one book, and the book of 2 CHRONICLES covers the same time period from a different perspective.

2 Kings　(OT) This book begins where 1 KINGS ends. It contains the rest of the history of the Kingdoms of JUDAH and ISRAEL, until the fall of Israel to the ASSYRIANS in 722 B.C. and the fall of Judah to the BABYLONIANS in 586 B.C. It includes stories about the PROPHET ELISHA. The books of 1 and 2 Kings were originally one book, and the book of 2 CHRONICLES covers the same time period from a different perspective.

koinē　The New Testament was written in *koinē* GREEK, the language spoken throughout most of the ROMAN EMPIRE at the time of the EARLY CHURCH. Since *koinē* (Greek for 'common') was the common language of nearly the entire MEDITERRANEAN world, the GOSPEL was able to travel quickly without language barriers.

Lamentations　(OT) This book was written by the PROPHET JEREMIAH (the "weeping prophet") after JERUSALEM fell to the BABYLONIANS. It is a funeral dirge for the fallen city and its people.

Law, Books of　The first five books of the Old Testament are called the BOOKS OF MOSES, the Books of Law, or the PENTATEUCH. In addition to the early history of the HEBREW people, they contain the TEN COMMANDMENTS and the rest of the MOSAIC LAW.

Leviticus　(OT) This book contains a substantial portion of the MOSAIC LAW—detailed instructions for the PRIESTS as well as specific regulations for the people of ISRAEL. It is the third of the five BOOKS OF MOSES.

Luke, Gospel of　(NT) This GOSPEL was written by LUKE, a GENTILE physician who was a companion of PAUL's. Like the other Gospels, it contains an account of the life and ministry of Jesus, culminating in his suffering, CRUCIFIXION, and RESURRECTION. The most familiar account of the birth of Jesus is taken from the second chapter of Luke's Gospel (*see* NATIVITY *under "People and Events in the New Testament"*).

Maccabees　The books of 1 & 2 Maccabees are included in the APOCRYPHA. They tell of the history of IS-RAEL during the second century B.C., which is in the 400-year period between the Old Testament and the New Testament. One of the Jewish leaders of that period was Judas Maccabaeus, who led a revolt against the tyranny of Antiochus, the Syrian king.

MACCABEES "He [Antiochus] was thrown from the chariot, with the result that he was bruised all over his body.... Maggots swarmed out of the body of this man, and while he still lived in grief and pain, his flesh rotted away, and the stench of his decay made his army sick" (2 Maccabees 9:7, 9, TLB).

❧ HANUKKAH (Chanukah) is the Jewish holiday that commemorates the cleansing of the TEMPLE during the days of the Maccabees.

❧ One of HANDEL'S ORATORIOS is titled *Judas Maccabaeus.*

Major Prophets The Old Testament books of ISAIAH, JEREMIAH, and EZEKIEL. They are called the Major Prophets because of their length. *See also* MINOR PROPHETS; PROPHECY, BOOKS OF.

Malachi (OT) The last book in the Old Testament, it contains the messages of the PROPHET Malachi. After the EXILE, many JEWS returned to JERUSALEM. The TEMPLE had now been rebuilt (*see* EZRA), and the wall of the city had been rebuilt (*see* NEHEMIAH), but the people again neglected the Lord. Malachi called them to REPENTANCE and held out the promise of God's FORGIVENESS and GRACE.

BIBLICAL MANUSCRIPTS The original manuscripts of the Bible were written by hand, and until the fifteenth century all copies were also made by hand.

manuscripts, biblical The word *manuscript* literally means 'written by hand'. Originally, each of the BOOKS OF THE BIBLE was written by hand, and for many centuries all copies were also written by hand. None of the original manuscripts of the Bible is still in existence, but thousands of handwritten HEBREW and GREEK manuscripts or manuscript fragments have been found (e.g., the DEAD SEA SCROLLS). For the most part, the oldest manuscripts are deemed to be closest to the exact wording of the original manuscripts. There are minor variations in wording among the various manuscripts—due primarily to scribal errors when the manuscripts were being copied—but overall the manuscripts show an amazing degree of accuracy and faithfulness.

Mark, Gospel of (NT) This is the shortest of the GOSPELS, and the action is fast. Like the other Gospels, it contains an account of the life and ministry of Jesus, culminating in his suffering, CRUCIFIXION, and RESURRECTION. It was written by MARK; he was not one of the twelve DISCIPLES, but he was an eyewitness of Jesus' ministry. Mark's Gospel was written for a GENTILE audience. Many scholars believe it was the first of the Gospels to be written.

Matthew, Gospel of (NT) This GOSPEL was written by MATTHEW, one of Jesus' DISCIPLES. It was written primarily for a Jewish audience, so it emphasizes the ways in which Jesus fulfilled Old Testament PROPHECIES. It begins with a GENEALOGY that shows that Jesus was a descendant of King DAVID.

Micah (OT) One of the MINOR PROPHETS, this book contains the messages of the PROPHET Micah to the people of both ISRAEL and JUDAH. He describes God's hatred of the SINS of his CHOSEN PEOPLE. The NORTHERN KINGDOM fell to the ASSYRIANS during Micah's ministry. This book includes the PROPHECY that the insignificant village of BETHLEHEM would be the birthplace of a future king. Hundreds of years later, this prophecy led the WISE MEN to Bethlehem.

Minor Prophets The twelve short books of PROPHECY found at the end of the Old Testament. They are called Minor Prophets because they are short books. The PROPHETS whose messages are recorded in these books lived and prophesied over a period of about 400 years. Some preached in the NORTHERN KINGDOM of ISRAEL, and some preached in the SOUTHERN KINGDOM of JUDAH. *See also* MAJOR PROPHETS; PROPHECY, BOOKS OF.

Nahum (OT) One of the MINOR PROPHETS, this book contains the messages of the PROPHET Nahum. His ministry was to the people of the Kingdom of JUDAH, but this book contains a pronouncement of God's judgment on Nineveh, the capital city of ASSYRIA, the world power that had already defeated the Kingdom of ISRAEL. (JONAH had preached to the people of Nineveh more than 120 years earlier.) Assyria was indeed defeated—by the BABYLONIANS—before many years passed.

Nehemiah (OT) The events in this historical book took place long after the JEWS had begun returning to JERUSALEM from the EXILE in BABYLON (*see* EZRA). NEHEMIAH was a cupbearer to King Artaxerxes of PERSIA, but he went to Jerusalem in 445 B.C. to lead the people there in rebuilding their city wall. After the wall had been built, Nehemiah and EZRA led the people into a renewed relationship with God.

New Testament The portion of the Christian Bible that contains the record of the life and ministry of Jesus and of the spread of the GOSPEL and the establishment of the church. The GREEK word that is translated 'testament' is also commonly translated 'covenant', so the New Testament tells of the NEW COVENANT between God and mankind made possible by the life, death, and RESURRECTION of Jesus Christ.

The New Testament contains twenty-seven books—four GOSPELS, the ACTS of the Apostles, twenty-one letters (or EPISTLES), and the REVELATION. The various books were written over a period of about fifty years, from A.D. 40 to A.D. 90, by nine or ten different authors. Although none of the original MANUSCRIPTS has sur-

vived, thousands of New Testament fragments and manuscripts have been found, one dating from as early as about A.D. 125.

The New Testament CANON in its present form was largely in place by about A.D. 200, but the first exact list of the twenty-seven books we now know as the New Testament is found in a letter of ATHANASIUS in A.D. 367. Thirty years later the same canon was listed by a CHURCH COUNCIL, at which time it seemed to be undisputed.

Books of the New Testament

Matthew	1 Timothy
Mark	2 Timothy
Luke	Titus
John	Philemon
Acts	Hebrews
Romans	James
1 Corinthians	1 Peter
2 Corinthians	2 Peter
Galatians	1 John
Ephesians	2 John
Philippians	3 John
Colossians	Jude
1 Thessalonians	Revelation
2 Thessalonians	

Numbers (OT) This book contains the stories of the people of ISRAEL during their forty years in the WILDERNESS—after the EXODUS and before they entered the PROMISED LAND. The first portion of the book contains data about a census (hence the name of the book) of the nation. On their first approach to the land of CANAAN, the people grew rebellious when they heard the reports of the spies MOSES had sent into the land. (JOSHUA and CALEB were the only spies who came back expressing confidence that God would help them defeat the Canaanites.) As a result, the Lord told Moses that the people would not be able to enter the Promised Land until that entire generation of adults (except for Joshua and Caleb) had died in the wilderness. Numbers is the fourth of the five BOOKS OF MOSES.

Obadiah (OT) One of the MINOR PROPHETS, this is the shortest book in the Old Testament (just one chapter, comprising twenty-one verses). It contains a prophetic VISION of the destruction of Edom, a country southeast of ISRAEL. The Edomites were descendants of ABRAHAM and ISAAC through Isaac's son ESAU.

Old Testament The GREEK word that is translated 'testament' is also translated 'covenant'. The Old Testament, which is the same for both JEWS and Christians, is the record of God's covenants with the ISRAELITES—his CHOSEN PEOPLE—and the history of the Israelite people.

The Old Testament contains thirty-nine books—five BOOKS OF MOSES (the PENTATEUCH), twelve books of history, seven poetic books, and fifteen Books of PROPHECY. The various books were written over a period of hundreds of years by numerous authors. All of them were written before the birth of Jesus. Although none of the original MANUSCRIPTS has survived, hundreds of Old Testament fragments and manuscripts have been found, some dating from slightly earlier than 200 B.C. (*see* DEAD SEA SCROLLS).

For Jesus and his Jewish contemporaries, as for the EARLY CHURCH, what we now call the Old Testament was the entire SCRIPTURE.

ROMAN CATHOLICS and some PROTESTANTS include the DEUTEROCANONICAL BOOKS in the Old Testament, in which case there are forty-six Old Testament books. See the list of books of the Old Testament.

Pentateuch The first five books of the Old Testament. They are also called the BOOKS OF MOSES. The word *Pentateuch* comes from two GREEK words meaning 'five books'. For JEWS, the Pentateuch is called the TORAH. (*See* GENESIS; EXODUS; LEVITICUS; NUMBERS; DEUTERONOMY.)

1 Peter (NT) The first of two EPISTLES written by PETER. This letter was written to Jewish Christians scattered across Asia Minor (present-day Turkey). Its purpose was to encourage these Christians, who were facing increasing persecution under the heavy hand of the ROMAN EMPIRE.

2 Peter (NT) The second of two EPISTLES written by PETER. This letter was written to the church at large. Its purpose was to warn Christians about false teachers and to encourage them in their faith.

Philemon (NT) A short and tender letter from the APOSTLE PAUL to PHILEMON. It was hand carried to Philemon by ONESIMUS, a slave who had run away from Philemon but was now a BELIEVER and was returning to his master. Paul appeals to Philemon to treat Onesimus as a brother.

Philippians (NT) A letter from PAUL and TIMOTHY to the church in Philippi (in GREECE). Paul had started the church at Philippi on his second MISSIONARY JOURNEY. He was now in prison in ROME, and the Philippians had sent a gift to him there. In this letter, he thanks them for their gift and reminds them that true joy comes only from Jesus Christ.

Prophecy, Books of The Books of Prophecy in the Old Testament include the three MAJOR PROPHETS and the twelve MINOR PROPHETS. In the HEBREW Bible, the grouping of books called "The Prophets" includes some of the historical books as well as the Major and Minor Prophets. After Jesus gave the two greatest commandments (*see* THOU SHALT LOVE THE LORD THY GOD WITH ALL THY HEART *and* LOVE THY NEIGHBOR AS THYSELF), he said, "On these two commandments hang all the law and the prophets" (Matthew 22:40). By "all the law" he meant the Books of LAW, and "the prophets" meant the Books of Prophecy and the historical books.

Books of the Old Testament

Genesis	Ezra	*Wisdom (of*	Jonah
Exodus	Nehemiah	*Solomon)*	Micah
Leviticus	*Tobit*	*Sirach* (or	Nahum
Numbers	*Judith*	*Ecclesiasticus)*	Habakkuk
Deuteronomy	Esther	Isaiah	Zephaniah
Joshua	*1 Maccabees*	Jeremiah	Haggai
Judges	*2 Maccabees*	Lamentations	Zechariah
Ruth	Job	*Baruch*	Malachi
1 Samuel	Psalms	Ezekiel	
2 Samuel	Proverbs	Daniel	
1 Kings	Ecclesiastes	Hosea	
2 Kings	Song of Solomon	Joel	
1 Chronicles	(*or* Song of Songs,	Amos	
2 Chronicles	*or* Canticles)	Obadiah	

Note: DEUTEROCANONICAL BOOKS (the APOCRYPHA) are listed in italics.

Proverbs (OT) An Old Testament book of poetry that contains a collection of wise and often pithy sayings. The first several chapters contain advice to young men about the importance of wisdom and of pure living. Many of the Proverbs were written by SOLOMON.

Psalms (OT) A collection of 150 HEBREW poems and songs that express a full range of human emotion in relation to God. Many of the Psalms were written by King DAVID. The book of Psalms contains a treasury of well-loved passages.

red-letter editions Bibles in which all the words spoken by Jesus are printed in red. Red-letter editions are a twentieth-century in-novation in Bible publishing. The original MANUSCRIPTS of the Bible did not highlight the words of Christ in any way. Other features that have been added to the Bible text for ease of readability include para-graphs, quotation marks, parenthe-ses, and the division of the text into CHAPTERS AND VERSES.

Revelation (NT) Also called the APOCALYPSE, it is the last book in the Bible. It is presumed to have been written by JOHN (the disciple). It is his description of a VISION in which he saw future events: the persecution of the church, the coming of the AN-TICHRIST, the triumph of God over EVIL at a great battle (ARMAGEDDON), the MILLENNIUM, when SATAN is bound for

---

Selections from Proverbs (New International Version)

Trust in the Lord with all your heart
and lean not on your own understanding;
in all your ways acknowledge him,
and he shall make your paths straight. Proverbs 3:5-6

Can a man scoop fire into his lap
without his clothes being burned?
Can a man walk on hot coals
without his feet being scorched?
So is he who sleeps with another man's wife;
no one who touches her will go unpunished. Proverbs 6:27-29

The fear of the Lord is the beginning of wisdom,
and knowledge of the Holy One is understanding. Proverbs 9:10

Like a gold ring in a pig's snout
is a beautiful woman who shows no discretion. Proverbs 11:22

A gentle answer turns away wrath,
but a harsh word stirs up anger. Proverbs 15:1

Train a child in the way he should go,
and when he is old he will not turn from it. Proverbs 22:6

A wife of noble character who can find?
She is worth far more than rubies. Proverbs 31:10

Selections from the Psalms (King James Version)

Blessed is the man that walketh not in the counsel of the ungodly,
nor standeth in the way of sinners,
nor sitteth in the seat of the scornful. Psalm 1:1

O Lord our Lord,
how excellent is thy name in all the earth! Psalm 8:1

The heavens declare the glory of God;
and the firmament showeth his handywork.
Day unto day uttereth speech,
and night unto night showeth knowledge. Psalm 19:1-2

The Lord is my shepherd;
I shall not want. Psalm 23:1
(*For the complete text, see* TWENTY-THIRD PSALM.)

The Lord is my light and my salvation;
whom shall I fear?
The Lord is the strength of my life;
of whom shall I be afraid? Psalm 27:1

As the hart [deer] panteth after the water brooks,
so panteth my soul after thee, O God. Psalm 42:1

God is our refuge and strength,
a very present help in trouble. Psalm 46:1

Make a joyful noise unto the Lord,
all ye lands.
Serve the Lord with gladness:
come before his presence with singing. Psalm 100:1-2

Bless the Lord, O my soul:
and all that is within me, bless his holy name. Psalm 103:1

Thy word is a lamp unto my feet,
and a light unto my path. Psalm 119:105

I will lift up mine eyes unto the hills,
from whence cometh my help.
My help cometh from the Lord,
which made heaven and earth. Psalm 121:1

Except the Lord build the house,
they labor in vain that build it. Psalm 127:1

O give thanks unto the Lord;
for he is good:
for his mercy endureth for ever. Psalm 136:1

I will praise thee;
for I am fearfully and wonderfully made:
marvellous are thy works;
and that my soul knoweth right well. Psalm 139:14

Search me, O God, and know my heart:
try me and know my thoughts:
And see if there be any wicked way in me,
and lead me in the way everlasting. Psalm 139:23-24

1,000 years, the final judgment (JUDGMENT DAY), and the NEW JERU- SALEM. The vision ends with the promise that Jesus is coming again soon (the SECOND COMING).

Many popular descriptions of HEAVEN come from Revelation: ANGELS sing- ing, white robes, PEARLY GATES, streets of gold. John's vision also includes the FOUR HORSEMEN OF THE APOCALYPSE, representing judgment to come upon the earth because of people's wickedness.

❦ Revelation should not be pro- nounced *Revelations*, a common er- ror.

Romans (NT) An EPISTLE in which the APOSTLE PAUL sets forth an exten- sive THEOLOGY of the Christian faith. It emphasizes JUSTIFICATION BY GRACE, THROUGH FAITH. Martin LUTHER's study of Romans led him to the conclusion that the prevalent teachings of the sixteenth-century church were not consistent with SCRIPTURE.

Ruth (OT) The book that tells the story of RUTH, NAOMI, and BOAZ. Ruth was a poor widow from the land of Moab (east of the DEAD SEA) whose husband had been an ISRAELITE. When her widowed mother-in-law, Naomi, returned to ISRAEL, she en- couraged Ruth to stay with her own people in Moab. But Ruth re- sponded, "WHITHER THOU GOEST, I WILL GO; and where thou lodgest, I will lodge: thy people shall be my people, and thy God my God" (Ruth 1:16). When they arrived in Naomi's hometown, Ruth gathered food in the fields of Boaz, a wealthy relative of her deceased husband. Boaz no- ticed Ruth because of her generos- ity to her mother-in-law, and he soon married her. Their great-grandson was DAVID, the great king of Israel.

1 Samuel (OT) The book that tells the stories of SAMUEL, the great PROPHET, and SAUL, the first king of ISRAEL. There are also stories about DAVID before he succeeded Saul as king. This book includes the story of the friendship of David and JONA- THAN, the story of David and GOLIATH, and accounts of Saul's jealousy of David. The book of 2 SAMUEL begins where 1 Samuel ends.

2 Samuel (OT) This book contin- ues the history of ISRAEL where 1 SAMUEL ends—with the death of King SAUL and the accession of DAVID to the throne of ISRAEL. It recounts the history of David's many con- quests in battle as well as his per- sonal struggles, including his ADULTERY with BATHSHEBA. Much of the latter part of the book revolves around the rivalry between David's sons (including ABSALOM and SOLO- MON) and the problem of succession to the throne. The time period cov- ered by 2 Samuel is presented from a different perspective in the book of 1 CHRONICLES.

Scripture The term *Scripture* (from the LATIN word for 'writings') is often used to mean the Bible, or a passage from the Bible. There are frequent references to "the Scriptures" in the New Testament, and in that context the writers meant the HEBREW Scriptures, which Christians now call the Old Testament.

scroll A long strip of paper or leather rolled up on two sticks. The text of the SCRIPTURE was written on scrolls. Even today, ornamental TORAHS are scrolls.

Septuagint A GREEK TRANSLATION of the Old Testament, parts of which date from the third century B.C. At the time of Christ and in the EARLY CHURCH, the SCRIPTURES (i.e., the Old Testament) were known both in the original HEBREW and in this Greek translation. The word *Septuagint* comes from the LATIN for 'seventy', because seventy scholars are said to have worked on the translation. It is

often abbreviated LXX, the Roman numeral for seventy.

Song of Solomon (OT) This book of poetry celebrates romantic love and the sexual relationship between husband and wife. On another level, it is also an allegory of God's love for ISRAEL and for the church. Traditionally said to have been written by SOLOMON, this book is also called Canticles or Song of Songs.

Popular Study Bibles

> **Harper Study Bible**
> **Life Application Bible**
> **NIV Study Bible**
> **Open Bible, The**
> **Oxford Annotated Bible**
> **Ryrie Study Bible**
> **Scofield Reference Bible**
> **Thompson Chain-Reference**
>   **Study Bible**

Song of Songs *See* SONG OF SOLOMON.

study Bible A Bible with notes that help the reader understand the text. The notes of some study Bibles are largely technical in nature, dealing with the original HEBREW or GREEK text. Other study Bibles help the reader apply the truth of SCRIPTURE to contemporary life.

❦ Readers of study Bibles must take care to distinguish between the text of Scripture, which is the WORD OF GOD, and the text of the study notes.

SCROLL The books of the Old Testament were originally written and copied on scrolls.

The notes, however wise, are still only the words of man.

synoptic Gospels The GOSPELS of MATTHEW, MARK, and LUKE. *Synoptic* means seeing things from the same point of view, and the first three Gospels are similar in their approach to the life of Jesus. The Gospel of John also tells of the life and ministry of Jesus, but it gives fewer details and presents longer passages of Jesus' discourses.

Textus Receptus A GREEK text of the New Testament that was compiled in 1550. It was based on Greek MANUSCRIPTS that were known in the sixteenth century but are now considered less accurate than older manuscripts discovered in the last 150 years. The KING JAMES VERSION of 1611 was translated from the Textus Receptus (LATIN for 'received text').

thee* and *thou Many contemporary readers are frustrated by the archaic English of the KING JAMES VERSION, which includes frequent use of *thee* and *thou* and the verb suffix *-est* (example: "The eyes of all wait upon thee; and thou givest them their meat in due season," Psalm 145:15). Just as there are singular and plural forms of the second-person pronoun in French (*tu* and *vous*), there used to be a distinction in English between singular pronouns (thou, thee) and plural pronouns (ye, you). In the King James Version, the singular pronouns in HEBREW and GREEK were translated 'thou' (nominative) and 'thee' (objective), and the plural pronouns

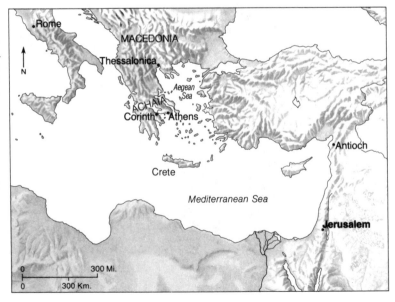

LETTERS TO THESSALO-NICA
When Paul and Silas visited Thessalonica, many people became believers as a result of Paul's preaching. The books we call 1 & 2 Thessalonians were letters to the church there. The book of Titus was a letter written to Titus, a church leader on the island of Crete.

were translated 'ye' (nominative) and 'you' (objective). In conformity with modern English, most modern TRANSLATIONS simply use 'you' for all four cases.

❧ Since God was always addressed as *thou* (singular) in the King James Version, the terms *thou* and *thee* took on a special sense of dignity and reverence. Many people still use those terms when they pray.

1 Thessalonians (NT) The first of the APOSTLE PAUL'S letters to the church in Thessalonica, GREECE, and one of Paul's earliest letters. It was written to encourage the Christians in Thessalonica and to assure them of Christ's return (the SECOND COMING). It also answers their questions about the state of BELIEVERS who had already died.

2 Thessalonians (NT) PAUL'S second letter to the church in Thessalonica, GREECE. It was written shortly after 1 THESSALONIANS and again contains information about Christ's SECOND COMING.

1 Timothy (NT) The first of the APOSTLE PAUL'S letters to his friend TIMOTHY, who was a young PASTOR. It is a very practical letter, addressing such issues as qualifications for church leaders and the care of different groups of people within the church.

2 Timothy (NT) The second of the APOSTLE PAUL'S letters to TIMOTHY.

Written shortly before Paul's death, it includes instructions and encouragement to the younger PASTOR. It includes the familiar statement about the authenticity and value of SCRIPTURE: "All scripture is given by inspiration of God, and is profitable for doctrine, for reproof, for correction, for instruction in RIGHTEOUSNESS" (2 Timothy 3:16).

Titus (NT) A letter from the APOSTLE PAUL to Titus, who was supervising the churches on the island of Crete (see map on page 92). It is a very practical letter about various aspects of church leadership and how Christians ought to live.

Torah A SCROLL containing the HEBREW text of the PENTATEUCH. The text of the books, whether or not on a scroll, is also called the Torah. More broadly, the Hebrew SCRIPTURE in its entirety (i.e., the Old Testament) is sometimes called Torah.

translation The BOOKS OF THE BIBLE were originally written in HEBREW and ARAMAIC (Old Testament) and GREEK (New Testament). Accordingly, all English Bibles are translations from the original languages. There are various methods of translation, from a strict word-for-word style to a thought-for-thought style. Word-for-word translations are helpful for understanding the syntax of the original language, but thought-for-thought translations are easier to read and understand. See the chart "How Bible Translations Differ" (below) for a comparison of wording between several popular translations.

The Bible has been translated into thousands of languages by MISSIONARIES and organizations such as Wycliffe Bible Translators and the United Bible Societies.

verse See CHAPTER AND VERSE.

Vulgate A LATIN TRANSLATION of the Bible prepared by JEROME in the fourth century A.D. It was called the *Vulgate* (from the Latin for 'common' or 'popular') because it was written in the "vulgar," or common, language. It was the predominant translation used by the church for the next 1,100 years. As the REFORMERS began to stress the value of vernacular translations (such as LUTHER's in German and TYNDALE's in English), the Council of TRENT confirmed the Vulgate in 1546 as the official translation of the ROMAN CATHOLIC CHURCH, a position it held until the twentieth century. The DOUAY-RHEIMS BIBLE is an English text

How Bible Translations Differ

The following translations of 1 Corinthians 13:4-7 show the difference in style of TRANSLATION between *The LIVING BIBLE*, the NEW INTERNATIONAL VERSION, and the KING JAMES VERSION. Just for fun, I've also included the same verses as they were translated by William TYNDALE in 1534.

Love is very patient and kind, never jealous or envious, never boastful or proud, never haughty or selfish or rude. Love does not demand its own way. It is not irritable or touchy. It does not hold grudges and will hardly even notice when others do it wrong. It is never glad about injustice, but rejoices whenever truth wins out. If you love someone, you will be loyal to him no matter what the cost. You will always believe in him, always expect the best of him, and always stand your ground in defending him. (TLB, 1971)

Love is patient, love is kind. It does not envy, it does not boast, it is not proud. It is not rude, it is not self-seeking, it is not easily angered, it keeps no record of wrongs. Love does not delight in evil but rejoices with the truth. It always protects, always trusts, always hopes, always perseveres. (NIV, 1978)

Charity suffereth long, and is kind; charity envieth not; charity vaunteth not itself, is not puffed up, Doth not behave itself unseemly, seeketh not her own, is not easily provoked, thinketh no evil; Rejoiceth not in iniquity, but rejoiceth in the truth; Beareth all things, believeth all things, hopeth all things, endureth all things. (KJV, 1611)

Love suffreth longe, and is corteous. Love envieth not. Love doth not frowardly, swelleth not dealeth not dishonestly, seketh not her awne, is not provoked to anger, thynketh not evyll, reioyseth not in iniquite: but reioyseth in the trueth, suffreth all thynge, beleveth all thynges, hopeth all thynges, endureth in all thynges. (TYNDALE, 1534)

translated for the most part from the Vulgate.

Word of God Another name for the Bible. It is called the Word of God because of the belief by most Christians that the Bible is God's written revelation to mankind.

❧ In John 1:1, Jesus is called the WORD.

Zechariah (OT) One of the MINOR PROPHETS, this book contains the messages of the PROPHET Zechariah (not to be confused with ZECHARIAH, the father of JOHN THE BAPTIST). Zechariah's ministry was to the people of ISRAEL while the TEMPLE was being rebuilt after the EXILE (the details of which are included in the first half of EZRA). The book of Zechariah contains many PROPHECIES regarding the coming MESSIAH.

Zephaniah (OT) One of the MINOR PROPHETS, this book contains the messages of the PROPHET Zephaniah. He preached to the Kingdom of JUDAH during the reign of King JOSIAH, a good king who led the people away from IDOL worship back to the Lord. The last years of Zephaniah's ministry coincided with the early years of JEREMIAH's ministry.

QUOTATIONS FROM THE BIBLE

English literature is filled with biblical quotations and allusions. Shakespeare, Milton, Donne, Wordsworth, Dickens, Emerson, and even Mark Twain used many biblical quotations or allusions to biblical characters. One can scarcely pick up *Time* magazine or the *New York Times* without finding phrases or words from the Bible. Everyday speech is peppered with phrases (EAT, DRINK, AND BE MERRY; go the SECOND MILE; be a GOOD SAMARITAN) that are biblical quotations or allusions. The titles of many books (e.g., Steinbeck's *East of Eden*) contain biblical allusions.

This chapter contains many well-known quotations from the Bible. Unless otherwise indicated, the quotations are from the KING JAMES VERSION. This is not because the King James Version is easy to read. It's not. But the phraseology of that stately TRANSLATION is a mainstay of literary English, and the biblical phrases we instantly recognize tend still to be in King James language, even in this day of modern translations.

All have sinned, and come short of the glory of God This verse, Romans 3:23, means that none of us measures up to God's standard of perfection. We are all sinners. But see the promise at the end of Romans 6:23: "For the WAGES OF SIN IS DEATH, but the gift of God is ETERNAL LIFE through Jesus Christ our Lord."

all things to all men When the APOSTLE PAUL said in 1 Corinthians 9:22 that he was "all things to all men," he meant that he wanted to find common ground with each person he met so he could tell others about Christ. Perhaps this is the biblical equivalent of "When in Rome, do as the Romans do," except that Paul had a specific purpose in mind. Today the phrase is often used disparagingly, suggesting that a person is wishy-washy.

all things work together for good The complete verse (Romans 8:28) reads as follows in the KING JAMES VERSION: "And we know that all things work together for good to them that love God, to them who are the called according to his purpose." It does not mean that only good things will happen to those who love God, but that God will use every circumstance in their lives and turn it into something for their good.

All we like sheep have gone astray A phrase from Isaiah 53, in which ISAIAH described the people of ISRAEL as having wandered away from God, just as SHEEP tend to wander away from the SHEPHERD.

Am I my brother's keeper? After CAIN had killed his brother ABEL, God asked Cain where Abel was. Cain retorted, "Am I my brother's keeper?" (Genesis 4:9). The expression has come to be used in any situation in which a person is disclaiming responsibility for another person.

Ask, and it shall be given you
One of the teachings of Jesus from the SERMON ON THE MOUNT (Matthew 7:7). He was teaching that God wants to give good gifts to anyone who asks him for them. The entire quotation is: "Ask and it will be given to you; seek and you will find; knock and the door will be opened to you" (NIV).

BEHOLD, I STAND AT THE DOOR AND KNOCK Jesus knocks at a door, symbolizing his desire to enter each person's life.

Be fruitful, and multiply God's instruction to ADAM and EVE (Genesis 1:28), telling them to populate the earth. God gave the same instruction to NOAH and his family after the Flood.

Beatitudes Eight pithy teachings of Jesus, found in the SERMON ON THE MOUNT. The word *beatitude* is from the LATIN word meaning 'blessed', and each of the Beatitudes begins with the word *blessed*. In most of these statements, Jesus took common wisdom and turned it upside down to show that man's natural perspective is usually different from God's perspective. The entire text (Matthew 5:3-10, NIV) is:

Blessed are the poor in spirit,
    for theirs is the kingdom of heaven.
Blessed are those who mourn,
    for they will be comforted.
Blessed are the meek,
    for they will inherit the earth.
Blessed are those who hunger and thirst
        for righteousness,
    for they will be filled.
Blessed are the merciful,
    for they will be shown mercy.
Blessed are the pure in heart,
    for they will see God.
Blessed are the peacemakers,
    for they will be called sons of God.
Blessed are those who are persecuted
        because of righteousness,
    for theirs is the kingdom of heaven.

Behold, I stand at the door and knock The complete verse (Revelation 3:20) reads as follows in the KING JAMES VERSION: "Behold, I stand at the door, and knock: if any man hear my voice, and open the door, I will come in to him, and I will sup with him, and he with me." The rendering in *The LIVING BIBLE* is more contemporary: "Look! I have been standing at the door, and I am constantly knocking. If anyone hears me calling him and opens the door, I will come in and fellowship with him and he with me." The door is a metaphor for a person's life. Jesus wants to enter into each person's life and have fellowship with him or her.

Bless the Lord, O my soul A phrase found in several of the PSALMS (the NIV translates it 'Praise the Lord, O my soul'). A very familiar passage is found in the opening verses of Psalm 103:

Bless the Lord, O my soul,
and all that is within me, bless his holy
    name.
Bless the Lord, O my soul,
and forget not all his benefits.

Blessed are the meek: for they shall inherit the earth One of the BEATITUDES of Jesus (Matthew 5:5). People who are meek are usually shoved aside by those who are powerful, but Jesus was teaching that meekness is a higher value than worldly power.

Blessed are the peacemakers: for they shall be called sons of God One of the BEATITUDES of Jesus (Matthew 5:9). Great warriors and generals have always captured the respect and admiration of people, but Jesus was pointing out that peacemaking is one of the highest of virtues.

blind leading the blind Jesus said the PHARISEES were blind guides, meaning that they were spiritually

blind. He also said, "Can a blind man lead a blind man? Will they not both fall into a pit?" (Luke 6:39, NIV). He meant that we should be careful not to choose as teachers and leaders people who are themselves spiritually blind.

But as many as received him, to them gave he power to become the sons of God From John 1:12, this means that anyone, JEW or GENTILE, who receives Jesus becomes a child of God.

By their fruits ye shall know them A saying of Jesus from the SERMON ON THE MOUNT (Matthew 7:20). He was giving a warning about false PROPHETS and said people are like fruit trees. Bad trees yield bad fruit and good trees yield good fruit. We can judge the motives of people by observing their actions. *See also* WOLF IN SHEEP'S CLOTHING.

cast the first stone The PHARISEES tried to trick Jesus by bringing to him a woman who had been caught in the act of ADULTERY. (One wonders where the man went!) According to the MOSAIC LAW, the woman should have been stoned to death. The Pharisees asked Jesus what they should do. If he said not to stone her, they would accuse Jesus of breaking the law. If he said they should stone her, he would be breaking the law of ROME, under which the JEWS were not allowed to pronounce their own death penalty.

Jesus saw the trap, and he also had compassion for the woman. He responded, "He that is without SIN among you, let him first cast a stone at her" (John 8:7). One by one her accusers slipped away, for they all recognized sin in their own lives. When Jesus saw that her accusers had all left, he said to the woman, "Neither do I condemn thee; go, and sin no more" (John 8:11). In saying this, he was not condoning her sin, for he told her to sin no more. Instead, he offered a promise of FORGIVENESS for sin.

❧ The story of the adulterous woman is not included in the earliest and most reliable MANUSCRIPTS of John's GOSPEL. This does not necessarily mean that the event never happened. It simply means that JOHN probably did not write the verses (John 7:53–8:11) that tell about it.

Cast thy bread upon the waters An expression in the book of ECCLESIASTES (11:1). The entire verse in the KING JAMES VERSION says, "Cast thy bread upon the waters: for thou shalt find it after many days." It is an admonition to faith and to generosity. This verse is paraphrased in *The Living Bible*, "Give generously, for your gifts will return to you later."

Children, obey your parents An admonition from the APOSTLE PAUL in his letters to the Ephesians (6:1) and the Colossians (3:20). This statement is a paraphrase of one of the TEN COMMANDMENTS: "HONOR THY FATHER AND THY MOTHER."

Come unto me, all ye that labor Jesus said, "Come unto me, all ye that labor and are heavy laden, and I will give you rest" (Matthew 11:28). He meant that he wanted to provide peace of mind and the confidence that comes from doing the will of God. He also meant that it was no longer necessary to work at keeping the MOSAIC LAW to achieve SALVATION. Through Jesus, there was going to be a new way for people to be reconciled with God.

Consider the lilies *See* LILIES OF THE FIELD, CONSIDER THE.

cup of cold water Jesus said, "If, as my representatives, you give even a cup of cold water to a little child, you will surely be rewarded" (Matthew 10:42, TLB).

Do this in remembrance of me Jesus said this at the LAST SUPPER (Luke 22:19). He was instructing his DISCIPLES—and all Christians—to observe the LORD'S SUPPER as a reminder of his death. Nearly 2,000 years later, Christians around the world do so every time they take COMMUNION. These words are often carved on tables used for Communion in PROTESTANT churches.

Do unto others as you would have them do unto you This is a common paraphrase of one of Jesus' teachings in the SERMON ON THE MOUNT. As translated in the KING JAMES VERSION, he said in Matthew 7:12, "All things whatsoever ye would that men should do to you, do ye even so to them." Also called the GOLDEN RULE, this teaching is central to much of what is considered civilized behavior in Western cultures.

DO THIS IN REMEMBRANCE OF ME
Jesus and his disciples at the Last Supper.

Dust thou art, and unto dust shalt thou return When ADAM and EVE SINNED, God banished them from the Garden of EDEN and pronounced a curse upon the earth. He said to Adam, "Dust thou art, and unto dust shalt thou return" (Genesis 3:19). He was reminding Adam that he had been created from "the dust of the ground," and he was telling Adam that he and his descen-dants would all die because of their sin.

❧ In the traditional Christian funeral service, the MINISTER sprinkles soil (dust) on the casket before it is buried and quotes, "Earth to earth, ASHES TO ASHES, dust to dust." This is a reminder to all who are present that all of us will die and will "return to dust."

earth was without form, and void The first two verses of Genesis read as follows in the KING JAMES VERSION: "IN THE BEGINNING, God created the heaven and the earth. And the earth was without form, and void; and darkness was upon the face of the deep." The account then goes on to describe the CREATION.

eat, drink, and be merry In Ecclesiastes 8:15, SOLOMON used this phrase in advising his readers to seek out and enjoy the good things in life as they carry out their daily responsibilities. Jesus also used the phrase in his PARABLE of the rich farmer. The self-sufficient farmer built large barns and said, "I will say to my SOUL, 'Soul, you have many goods laid up for many years; take your ease; eat, drink, and be merry.' But God said to him, 'Fool! This night your soul will be required of you'" (Luke 12:19-20, NKJV).

eye for an eye, tooth for a tooth According to the MOSAIC LAW (Deuteronomy 19:21), the penalty for gouging out a person's eye was that the offender's eye was to be gouged out. Similarly, knocking out a tooth resulted in loss of a tooth for the offender. This concept of JUSTICE called for a penalty equal to—but not greater than—the offense.

Jesus made reference to this law when he said, "You have heard that it was said, 'Eye for eye, and tooth for tooth.' But I tell you, Do not resist an evil person. If someone strikes you on the right cheek, turn to him the other also" (Matthew 5:38-39, NIV). *See also* TURN THE OTHER CHEEK; *also* HEAP COALS OF FIRE ON HIS HEAD.

eye of a needle A rich man asked Jesus what he could do to get ETERNAL LIFE. Jesus told him to sell his possessions and give to the poor and follow him, and the man went away sad, because he had great wealth. "Jesus said to his DISCIPLES, 'I tell you the truth, it is hard for a rich man to enter the KINGDOM OF HEAVEN. Again I tell you, it is easier for a CAMEL to go through the eye of a needle than for a rich man to enter the kingdom of God.' When the disciples heard this, they were greatly astonished and asked, 'Who then can be saved?' Jesus looked at them and said, 'With man this is impossible, but with God all things are possible'" (Matthew 19:23-26, NIV). Even rich people can get into heaven if God brings them in, but wealth is a liability, not an asset, in one's spiritual journey.

❦ This "eye of a needle" has often been defined as a small doorway that a camel could get through only with great difficulty. There is no historical evidence that such doors were called eyes of a needle, and such an interpretation seems contrary to the intent of Jesus' teaching.

faith, hope, charity The beautiful thirteenth chapter of 1 Corinthians (the LOVE CHAPTER) stresses the importance of LOVE (it is translated CHARITY in the KING JAMES VERSION). The chapter ends with the statement, "And now abideth faith, hope, charity, these three; but the greatest of these is charity."

Father, forgive them; for they know not what they do One of the SEVEN LAST WORDS OF CHRIST—spoken while he was hanging on the CROSS (Luke 23:34). He was referring to those who were responsible for his CRUCIFIXION.

fatted calf, kill the A fatted calf is a calf that is ready to be slaughtered and eaten as part of a special feast. In Jesus' PARABLE of the PRODIGAL SON (Luke 15), the father tells his servants to "kill the fatted calf" and prepare a feast in honor of his son who has returned. The expression can be used of any preparation for a gala event.

first shall be last One of the teachings of Jesus (Matthew 19:30). He meant that those who are not powerful or wealthy in this life will be greatest in the KINGDOM OF HEAVEN if they have followed him. Those who are wealthy and powerful will be the least in the kingdom of heaven (if they get there at all) if they have put worldly concerns first in this life. *See also* EYE OF A NEEDLE.

fishers of men Jesus' first DISCIPLES were ANDREW and PETER, JAMES and JOHN, all of whom were commercial fishermen on the Sea of GALILEE. Jesus said to them, "FOLLOW ME, and I will make you fishers of men" (Matthew 4:19). He meant that they would be able to spread the GOOD NEWS of SALVATION to other people rather than simply catching fish.

Follow me Jesus said this to PETER and ANDREW and JAMES and JOHN when he invited them to be his DISCIPLES. Since they were all fishermen, he also said, "I will make you FISHERS OF MEN" (Matthew 4:19).

For God so loved the world The beginning of JOHN 3:16, one of the best-known and best-loved verses in the Bible. The complete text, as found in the KING JAMES VERSION: "For God so loved the world, that he gave his only begotten SON, that whosoever believeth in him should not perish, but have EVERLASTING LIFE."

for such a time as this ESTHER was a Jewish woman who had been selected because of her beauty to become a wife of King Ahasuerus (Xerxes) of PERSIA. When her older cousin and foster father, Mordecai, heard that the prime minister, Haman, had launched a plan to kill all of the JEWS in the kingdom, he urged Esther to ask the king to countermand the plan. Mordecai sent her a message that said, "Who knows but that you have come to royal position for such a time as this?" (Esther 4:14, NIV). The entire story is told in the book of ESTHER.

Forgive us our trespasses This is a phrase from the LORD'S PRAYER, as it is printed in *The Book of Common Prayer*. The complete sentence is, "FORGIVE us our trespasses, as we forgive those who trespass against us." An alternate reading, often used in public WORSHIP, is, "Forgive us our debts, as we forgive our debtors" (Matthew 6:12). It is a request that God forgive us for having SINNED against him, just as we forgive those who sin against us. But it is also a challenge to us to be forgiving, for the converse of this request is that God will forgive us only a little if we forgive others only a little.

Get thee behind me, Satan Jesus said these words on two different occasions. During the TEMPTATION OF JESUS, SATAN took Jesus to the top of a high mountain and showed him all the kingdoms of the world. Then Satan said he would give all this to Jesus if Jesus would bow down and WORSHIP him. Jesus responded, "Get thee behind me, Satan. For it is written, Thou shalt worship the Lord thy God, and him only shalt thou serve" (Luke 4:8). He was quoting from the sixth chapter of DEUTERONOMY.

Toward the end of his ministry on earth, Jesus told his DISCIPLES that he would be killed, but that he would come back to life again three days later. PETER took him aside and told him he should not say such things. Jesus rebuked Peter by saying, "Get thee behind me, Satan" (Matthew 16:23). He meant that Peter was being used as Satan's instrument. Jesus went on to say that Peter was looking at the situation only from a human point of view, not a divine point of view.

GET THEE BEHIND ME, SATAN Jesus said this both to Satan and to Peter.

Give us this day our daily bread A phrase from the LORD'S PRAYER. It is a request that God provide us with daily food. The Lord's Prayer is found in Matthew 6:9-13.

Gloria in excelsis Deo LATIN for 'GLORY TO GOD IN THE HIGHEST'. This was the chorus of the ANGELS who appeared to the SHEPHERDS outside BETHLEHEM on the night of Jesus' birth (Luke 2:14).

Glory to God in the highest, and on earth peace, good will toward men The chorus of the ANGELS who announced the birth of Jesus to the SHEPHERDS in the fields outside BETHLEHEM (Luke 2:14). The LATIN text is also familiar from CHRISTMAS carols: *GLORIA IN EXCELSIS DEO*. The familiar Christmas narrative from the Gospel of Luke is presented at the entry for NATIVITY in the chapter "People and Events in the New Testament."

Go, and sin no more *See* CAST THE FIRST STONE.

Go ye into all the world The first phrase of the GREAT COMMISSION, in which Jesus instructed his DISCIPLES to preach the GOSPEL throughout the world (Mark 16:15).

God created man in his own image The account of the CREATION in GENESIS includes this poetic description of the creation of the first man and woman (Genesis 1:27):

So God created man in his own image, in the image of God created he him; male and female created he them.

This does not mean that God is human in form. ADAM and EVE were created in the image of God in the sense that they had intelligence and FREE WILL and were capable of loving God and each other.

God is love In a passage from the fourth chapter of 1 John, we are told, "Dear friends, let us love one another, for love comes from God. Everyone who loves has been born of God and knows God. Whoever does not love does not know God, because God is love" (NIV).

good tidings of great joy When the ANGEL appeared to the SHEPHERDS to announce the birth of Jesus, he said, "Fear not: for behold I bring you good tidings of great joy, which shall be to all people. For unto you is born this day in the city of DAVID a SAVIOR, which is Christ the Lord" (Luke 2:10-11).

He that is not with me is against me Jesus said this to show that there is no middle ground—either a person believes in Jesus or is his enemy. The quotation is found in Matthew 12:30.

heap coals of fire on his head In Romans 12:20, PAUL quoted from Proverbs 25 in teaching that we are not to avenge ourselves: "If thine enemy hunger, feed him; if he thirst, give him drink: for in so doing thou shalt heap coals of fire on his head." In other words, he will feel ashamed

of himself for what he has done. The expression is used in any situation in which a person will feel ashamed because of kindness done to him after he has been unkind.

Hear, O Israel: the Lord our God is one Lord This great declaration of MONOTHEISM is found in Deuteronomy 6:4. Belief in one God was one feature that distinguished the people of ISRAEL from the nations around them.

heavens declare the glory of God, The This beautiful passage from Psalm 19 reminds us that all of CREATION shows us God's splendor.

Honor thy father and thy mother One of the TEN COMMANDMENTS (Exodus 20:12). It does not require explanation—except to children!

house divided against itself cannot stand, A Once when Jesus cast out a DEMON, the SCRIBES said he was possessed by Beelzebub (SATAN). Jesus responded, "How can Satan cast out Satan? And if a kingdom be divided against itself, that kingdom cannot stand. And if a house be divided against itself, that house cannot stand" (Mark 3:23-25).

❦ Abraham Lincoln quoted Jesus when he said in 1858, three years before the start of the Civil War, "'A house divided against itself cannot stand.' I believe this government cannot endure permanently half slave and half free. I do not expect the Union to be dissolved—I do not expect the house to fall—but I do expect it will cease to be divided."

I am the light of the world As recorded in the GOSPEL of JOHN, Jesus frequently used light as a metaphor for his role in the world. Jesus said, "I am the light of the world. Whoever follows me will never walk in darkness, but will have the light of life" (John 8:12, NIV). *See also* LIGHT OF THE WORLD, YE ARE THE; *and* THY WORD IS A LAMP UNTO MY FEET.

I am the resurrection and the life After LAZARUS had died, Jesus went to BETHANY. He said to MARTHA, "Your brother will rise again." She responded, "I know he will rise again in the resurrection at the last day."

Jesus then said, "I am the resurrection and the life. He who believes in me will live, even though he dies; and whoever lives and believes in me will never die" (John 11:25-26, NIV). Jesus was predicting his own death and RESURRECTION, and he meant that anyone who believed in him would be raised again to ETERNAL LIFE. Jesus then went to Lazarus's tomb and raised him back to physical life.

I am the way, the truth, and the life Jesus told his DISCIPLES he was going to his FATHER's house (by which he meant HEAVEN), and that they would join him there. THOMAS said, "Lord, we don't know where you are going, so how can we know the way?" Jesus answered, "I am the way and the truth and the life. No one comes to the Father except through me" (John 14:5-6, NIV).

I will never leave thee, nor forsake thee The book of HEBREWS (13:5) makes this statement, quoting from DEUTERONOMY. MOSES was preparing the people of ISRAEL for their entrance into the PROMISED LAND, where they would fight the CANAANITES. Moses said, "Be strong and courageous. Do not be afraid or terrified because of them, for the Lord your God goes with you; he will never leave you nor forsake you" (Deuteronomy 31:6, NIV).

If I perish, I perish ESTHER was a Jewish woman who had been selected because of her beauty to become a member of the harem of King Ahasuerus (Xerxes) of PERSIA. She later became queen. When her cousin and foster father, Mordecai, heard that Haman had launched a plan to kill all of the JEWS in the kingdom, he urged Esther to ask the king to countermand the plan. Although she was the queen, she could be put to death for speaking to the king without being bidden to do so. Before going in to see the king, she said, "If I perish, I perish" (Esther 4:16). The king granted her an audience, and the plan to exterminate the Jews was reversed.

The entire story is told in the book of ESTHER. The Jewish holiday of PURIM commemorates this rescue of the Jews.

If ye love me, keep my commandments Jesus was speaking to his DISCIPLES when he said this (John 14:15). It is part of a lengthy discourse that, according to the Gospel of JOHN, occurred after the LAST SUPPER while they were still together in the Upper Room.

IF I PERISH, I PERISH King Ahasuerus holds out his scepter to show that Esther may speak to him.

In my father's house are many mansions Jesus spoke these words in telling his DISCIPLES that he would soon be returning to his FATHER in HEAVEN and that he would prepare a place for them there (John 14:1-4). Modern TRANSLATIONS use the word *rooms* rather than *mansions*, but the size of our abode there is not significant. The important point is that we will be with God in heaven.

In the beginning The opening words of GENESIS and of the Gospel of JOHN.

The first verse of Genesis reads: "In the beginning, God created the heaven and the earth."

JOHN purposely began his GOSPEL with a parallel statement: "In the beginning was the WORD, and the Word was with God, and the Word was God." John meant that Jesus, the Word, had existed in the very beginning with God.

Into thy hands I commend my spirit One of the SEVEN LAST WORDS OF CHRIST as he hung on the CROSS (Luke 23:46). He was speaking to his FATHER, God.

It is finished Jesus' last words before he died on the CROSS, as recorded in John 19:30. *See* SEVEN LAST WORDS OF CHRIST *under "People and Events in the New Testament."*

John 3:16 If a person has memorized only one verse from the Bible, it is probably John 3:16. "FOR GOD SO LOVED THE WORLD, that he gave his only begotten SON, that whosoever believeth in him should not perish, but have EVERLASTING LIFE."

Jubilate Deo LATIN for 'O be joyful in the Lord'. This is a translation of the opening phrase of the hundredth Psalm. *See also* MAKE A JOYFUL NOISE UNTO THE LORD.

Judge not, that ye be not judged A saying of Jesus, from the SERMON ON THE MOUNT (Matthew 7:1). He was reminding his listeners that we are all sinners, and if we point out the SIN in others, we will have our own sins pointed out. *See also* CAST THE FIRST STONE.

just shall live by faith This statement, found several times in the New Testament (e.g., Romans 1:17), is a quotation from Habakkuk 2:4. It was one of the verses that helped Martin LUTHER understand the concept of JUSTIFICATION BY GRACE, THROUGH FAITH.

last shall be first, and the first last *See* FIRST SHALL BE LAST.

Lay not up for yourselves treasures upon earth This is part of Jesus' teaching from the SERMON ON THE MOUNT. The NIV translates it, "Do not store up for yourselves treasures on earth, where moth and rust destroy, and where thieves break in and steal. But store up for yourselves treasures in HEAVEN, where moth and rust do not destroy, and where thieves do not break in and steal. For where your treasure is, there your heart will be also" (Matthew 6:19-21).

Lead us not into temptation A phrase from The LORD'S PRAYER. It is a request that God protect the BELIEVER from falling into temptation. The Lord's Prayer is found in Matthew 6:9-13.

Let my people go When MOSES went to the PHARAOH to demand that he release the ISRAELITES from slav-ery, he said, "Let my people go" (Exodus 5:1). God sent PLAGUES upon EGYPT to encourage Pharaoh to respond, but Pharaoh steadfastly refused. He finally relented when God sent the final plague, the death of the firstborn in every household in Egypt. The Israelites then left Egypt, an event called the EXODUS.

❦ The slavery of blacks in America has often been compared to the Israelites' slavery in Egypt. For that reason, Abraham Lincoln, the Great Emancipator, is sometimes likened to Moses.

Let the dead bury their dead One of Jesus' followers said he wanted to bury his father before following Jesus. Jesus responded, "Follow me, and let the dead bury their dead" (Matthew 8:22). He meant that those who were spiritually dead could care for their own dead, but he expected his followers to put obedience to him above earthly concerns.

Let there be light In the GENESIS account of the CREATION, God created light with the command, "Let there be light" (Genesis 1:3).

Letter killeth, but the spirit giveth life A phrase from 2 Corinthians 3:6, in which PAUL was contrasting the old COVENANT of the law and the NEW COVENANT of GRACE. He meant that trying to follow the MOSAIC LAW "to the letter" will only result in death, but to follow the HOLY SPIRIT will result in ETERNAL LIFE.

light of the world, Ye are the A saying of Jesus in the SERMON ON THE MOUNT (Matthew 5:14). He used light as a metaphor for all that is good in the world. He was telling his followers that they were to bring GOOD NEWS and goodness to people around them—indeed, to the whole world. *See also* I AM THE LIGHT OF THE WORLD.

LET THERE BE LIGHT God's first command as he creates the world.

lilies of the field, Consider the In the SERMON ON THE MOUNT, Jesus taught his followers not to worry about things such as food, drink, or clothing. God would take care of their physical needs. Instead, they should seek the KINGDOM OF HEAVEN. He said, "And why do you worry about clothes? See how the lilies of the field grow. They do not labor or spin. Yet I tell you that not even SOLOMON in all his splendor was dressed like one of these. If that is how God clothes the grass of the field, . . . will

he not much more clothe you, O you of little faith?" (Matthew 6:28-30, NIV).

live by the sword shall die by the sword, All who A paraphrase of Jesus' statement to PETER in the Garden of GETHSEMANE when Peter cut off the ear of the HIGH PRIEST's servant (Matthew 26:52). Jesus then touched the man's ear and healed it.

Lord bless thee, and keep thee The Lord told MOSES that AARON was to bless the people of ISRAEL with this blessing:

The Lord bless thee, and keep thee:
The Lord make his face shine upon thee, and be gracious unto thee:
The Lord lift up his countenance upon thee, and give thee peace. Numbers 6:24-26

This blessing is frequently used as a BENEDICTION in PROTESTANT churches today.

Lord is my shepherd, The The opening line of the twenty-third Psalm, the best-known of all the PSALMS. For the complete text, see TWENTY-THIRD PSALM.

Lord's Prayer When Jesus' DISCIPLES asked him how they should pray, he taught them a prayer that is recorded in Matthew 6:9-13 (compare Luke 11:2-4). It is recited regularly in many PROTESTANT and ROMAN CATHOLIC churches. Some churches say "debts," and some say "trespasses." Catholics do not usually include the last two lines. Some churches use modern translations. Here is one form of the prayer:

Our Father, who art in heaven,
Hallowed be thy name.
Thy kingdom come.
Thy will be done on earth as it is in heaven.
Give us this day our daily bread,
And forgive us our debts as we forgive our debtors.
Lead us not into temptation,
But deliver us from evil.
For thine is the kingdom, and the power, and the glory, for ever. Amen.

love chapter (1 Corinthians 13) In the KING JAMES VERSION, this beautiful chapter begins, "Though I speak with the tongues of men and of angels, and have not charity [love], I am become as sounding brass, or a tinkling cymbal." The last verse reads, "And now abideth FAITH, HOPE, CHARITY, these three; but the greatest of these is charity." (A passage from the love chapter is presented in four different translations at the entry for TRANSLATION under "The Bible.")

love of money is the root of all evil, For the The APOSTLE PAUL was warning TIMOTHY (1 Timothy 6:10) that a person who wants to be wealthy will be tempted to SIN in order to gain the wealth. This expression is commonly misquoted as, "Money is the root of all evil."

Love the Lord thy God with all thy heart, soul, and mind *See* THOU SHALT LOVE THE LORD THY GOD WITH ALL THY HEART, AND WITH ALL THY SOUL, AND WITH ALL THY MIND.

Love thy neighbor as thyself When a PHARISEE asked Jesus which of the commandments in the MOSAIC LAW was the greatest, Jesus responded, "THOU SHALT LOVE THE LORD THY GOD WITH ALL THY HEART, AND WITH ALL THY SOUL, AND WITH ALL THY MIND. This is the first and great commandment. And the second is like unto it, Thou shalt love thy neighbor as thyself. On these two commandments hang all the LAW and the PROPHETS" (Matthew 22:37-40). Jesus was not quoting directly from the TEN COMMANDMENTS; rather, he was quoting from Deuteronomy 6:5 and Leviticus 19:8. When the man then asked, "Who is my neighbor?" Jesus responded by telling the PARABLE of the GOOD SAMARITAN.

Love your enemies As in the BEATITUDES, here Jesus takes common wisdom and turns it upside down to show that man's wisdom is often contrary to God's wisdom (Matthew 5:44). *See also* TURN THE OTHER CHEEK; *also* HEAP COALS OF FIRE ON HIS HEAD.

Make a joyful noise unto the Lord The opening phrase of the hundredth Psalm. *See also* JUBILATE DEO.

Make a joyful noise unto the Lord, all ye lands.
Serve the Lord with gladness:
come before his presence with singing.

Man shall not live by bread alone During the TEMPTATION OF JESUS in the WILDERNESS, when he was very hungry after FASTING for forty days and nights, SATAN tempted him to turn stones into bread. Jesus responded by quoting from the eighth chapter of Deuteronomy: "It is written, Man shall not live by bread alone, but by every word that proceedeth out of the mouth of God" (Matthew 4:4). The phrase is sometimes used today to refer to a person's need for emotional and spiritual sustenance.

Many are called, but few are chosen Jesus said this to illustrate that God calls all people to respond to him, but relatively few choose to follow him (Matthew 22:14). *See also* WIDE IS THE GATE, AND BROAD IS THE WAY, THAT LEADETH TO DESTRUCTION.

Money is the root of all evil A common misquotation of the APOSTLE PAUL's warning that "the LOVE OF MONEY IS THE ROOT OF ALL EVIL" (1 Timothy 6:10).

more blessed to give than to receive, It is In one of PAUL's sermons in the book of Acts (20:35), this saying is quoted as being a saying of Jesus, although it is not recorded as such in any of the GOSPELS.

mustard seed, faith as small as a Jesus used a mustard seed, which is tiny, as an example of the power of even a small amount of faith. He said, "If you have faith as small as a mustard seed, you can say to this mountain, 'Move from here to there'

and it will move. Nothing will be impossible for you" (Matthew 17:20, NIV).

My cup runneth over A line from the twenty-third Psalm. DAVID, the psalmist, used this metaphor to mean that he was filled with joy. For the complete text of the psalm, see TWENTY-THIRD PSALM.

My God, my God, why hast thou forsaken me? One of the SEVEN LAST WORDS OF CHRIST—spoken while he was hanging on the CROSS (Matthew 27:46). He was quoting the first verse of Psalm 22. Jesus had never SINNED, yet he was dying as a SACRIFICE to make ATONEMENT for all people. For a brief period of time (until the RESURRECTION), he was separated from the presence of GOD THE FATHER. That was more painful to him than the excruciating physical pain of hanging on the cross.

No man can serve two masters A teaching of Jesus from the SERMON ON THE MOUNT (Matthew 6:24). He went on to say, "YE CANNOT SERVE GOD AND MAMMON." He meant that a person cannot WORSHIP money and also pursue a right relationship with God. One or the other will win out as "master" in our lives.

nothing new under the sun, There is An expression from the book of ECCLESIASTES (1:9, NIV).

Of making many books there is no end If this was true in SOLO-

MON's day (Ecclesiastes 12:12), how much more is it true today!

Our Father, who art in heaven The beginning of the Lord's Prayer. For the complete text, see LORD'S PRAYER.

pearls before swine, Cast not Jesus said this as part of the SERMON ON THE MOUNT (Matthew 7:6). He meant that it is useless to try to teach holy things to unholy or unbelieving people.

Physician, heal thyself When Jesus returned to his hometown of NAZARETH after performing many MIRACLES in other towns, he anticipated that his friends and neighbors would quote this proverb as a means of demanding that he perform miracles for them also (Luke 4:23). He went on to say that a PROPHET IS NOT WITHOUT HONOR, SAVE IN HIS OWN COUNTRY.

Prophet is not without honor, save in his own country Jesus said this when he was rejected in his hometown of NAZARETH after having received great acclaim in other parts of the country (Matthew 13:57). *See also* PHYSICIAN, HEAL THYSELF.

Remember the sabbath day, to keep it holy One of the TEN COMMANDMENTS (Exodus 20:8). By the time of Jesus, the PHARISEES had added hundreds of laws to the MOSAIC LAW, including many laws concerning the SABBATH. Jesus said, "The Sabbath was made to benefit man,

and not man to benefit the Sabbath" (Mark 2:27, TLB).

Render to Caesar the things that are Caesar's, and to God the things that are God's The PHARISEES wanted to trap Jesus, so they asked him whether it was right to pay taxes to ROME. Jesus perceived their trick, so he took a coin and asked whose image was on it. When they responded that it was CAESAR's, he said, "Render to Caesar the things that are Caesar's, and to God the things that are God's" (Mark 12:17). He meant that we can pay earthly possessions to earthly governments, but our very lives belong to God, so we should submit ourselves to God.

RENDER TO CAESAR THE THINGS THAT ARE CAESAR'S Jesus may have been holding a coin like this, showing a likeness of Caesar Augustus.

salt of the earth, Ye are the A saying of Jesus in the SERMON ON THE MOUNT (Matthew 5:13). He used salt as a metaphor to mean that his followers are to influence the world around them, just as salt adds flavor whenever it is added to food.

❧ The expression *salt of the earth* is now used to refer to a good, decent, hardworking person—the sort of person one would want as a neighbor.

second mile, go the In the days of Jesus, ROMAN soldiers could compel citizens to carry their gear for them. In the SERMON ON THE MOUNT (Matthew 5:41), Jesus taught his listeners to go an extra mile if a soldier compelled them to go one mile. The expression can be applied to any situation in which a person willingly goes beyond what is required.

Seek, and ye shall find *See* ASK, AND IT SHALL BE GIVEN YOU.

sheep from the goats, separating the Jesus once described the JUDGMENT DAY as a time when God will separate the sheep from the goats. The SHEEP, representing people who showed God's love to others, will receive an eternal reward. The GOATS, representing those who did not show God's love to others, will receive an eternal punishment. Another frequent interpretation is that the sheep represent BELIEVERS and the goats represent nonbelievers. The PARABLE is found in Matthew 25:31-46.

skin of my teeth An expression from the book of Job. JOB said, "I am nothing but skin and bones; I have escaped with only the skin of my teeth" (Job 19:20, NIV). To escape "by the skin of my teeth" means I have

just barely escaped death or some other calamity.

soft answer turneth away wrath, A The complete proverb reads:

A soft answer turneth away wrath:
But grievous words stir up anger.
    Proverbs 15:1

spirit indeed is willing, but the flesh is weak In the Garden of GETHSEMANE, shortly before he was betrayed by JUDAS ISCARIOT, Jesus asked PETER, JAMES, and JOHN to pray with him. They fell asleep while they were praying, and Jesus said, "The SPIRIT indeed is willing, but the flesh is weak" (Matthew 26:41). He meant that it is sometimes hard to follow through even when we have the best of intentions.

straight and narrow A popular term that is actually a misquotation of Jesus' statement, "Strait [narrow] is the gate, and narrow is the way, which leadeth unto life, and few there be that find it" (Matthew 7:14). To "stay on the straight and narrow" is to try to do what is right, particularly in the face of temptation to SIN. (*See* WIDE IS THE GATE, AND BROAD IS THE WAY, THAT LEADETH TO DESTRUCTION.)

strain at a gnat and swallow a camel Jesus said this of the SCRIBES and PHARISEES as a metaphor for their HYPOCRISY (Matthew 23:24). They followed some of the tiny details of the MOSAIC LAW (e.g., they strained their water so as not to swallow a gnat, which was an UNCLEAN ANIMAL), but they neglected far weightier aspects of the law (e.g., caring for widows and orphans).

Suffer the little children to come unto me This quotation from the KING JAMES VERSION is confusing because we no longer use the word *suffer* to mean allow. One day some mothers brought their children to Jesus so he could bless them, but the DISCIPLES told them Jesus was too busy. When Jesus saw what was happening, he was indignant. He said, "Let the little children come to me, and do not hinder them, for the KINGDOM OF GOD belongs to such as these. I tell you the truth, anyone who will not receive the kingdom of God like a little child will never enter it" (Mark 10:14-15, NIV). Then he took the children in his arms and blessed them.

swords into plowshares This description of "the last days" is found in Isaiah 2:4 and Micah 4:3: "They will beat their swords into plowshares and their spears into pruning hooks. Nation will not take up sword against nation, nor will they train for war anymore" (NIV). This means that implements of war will no longer be needed; they will be changed into implements of peaceful life.

In Joel 3:10, the phrase is turned

around. The nations of the world are warned about the coming judgment of the Lord, and they are told, "Beat your plowshares into swords and your pruninghooks into spears." In other words, prepare yourselves; don't be complacent; prepare to meet God.

SUFFER THE LITTLE CHILDREN TO COME UNTO ME Jesus blesses a child.

This is my beloved Son, in whom I am well pleased A voice from HEAVEN made this proclamation on two different occasions—when Jesus was BAPTIZED by JOHN THE BAPTIST (Matthew 3:17) and at the TRANSFIGURATION (Matthew 17:5). GOD THE FATHER was identifying Jesus as his SON.

This is my body, which is broken for you Jesus said this at the LAST

SUPPER as he broke the bread and shared it with his DISCIPLES (1 Corinthians 11:24). He meant that he would soon die, and that his death was for their benefit (as an ATONEMENT for the SINS of mankind). This phrase is usually repeated as part of the COMMUNION service.

❦ It has long been suggested that the pretend incantation *hocus-pocus* was originally a parody of the LATIN phrase *hoc est corpus meum* ('this is my body') used in the ROMAN CATHOLIC MASS.

This is the day the Lord has made A popular verse from Psalm 118: "This is the day the Lord has made, let us rejoice and be glad in it."

Thou art the Christ, the Son of the living God One day Jesus asked his DISCIPLES, "Who do people say I am?" They answered, "JOHN THE BAPTIST, ELIJAH, or JEREMIAH." Jesus then asked, "Who do you say I am?" PETER answered, "Thou art the Christ, the Son of the living God" (Matthew 16:16). Jesus then warned them not to tell anyone that he was the Christ.

Thou shalt have no other gods before me The first of the TEN COMMANDMENTS (Exodus 20:3). The people of ISRAEL regularly broke this commandment by WORSHIPING BAAL and other gods of the neighboring nations.

Thou shalt love the Lord thy God with all thy heart, and with all thy soul, and with all thy mind This was Jesus' response when someone asked him which of the commandments in the MOSAIC LAW was the greatest. Jesus went on to say, "This is the first and great commandment. And the second is like unto it, Thou shalt LOVE THY NEIGHBOR AS THYSELF. On these two commandments hang all the LAW and the PROPHETS" (Matthew 22:37-40). Jesus was not quoting directly from the TEN COMMANDMENTS; rather, he was quoting from Deuteronomy 6:5 and Leviticus 19:18.

THOU SHALT HAVE NO OTHER GODS BEFORE ME Moses breaks the tablets containing the Ten Commandments when he finds the people worshiping the golden calf.

Thou shalt not bear false witness against thy neighbor One of the TEN COMMANDMENTS (Exodus 20:16).

This commandment relates both to formal judicial proceedings (e.g., lying on the witness stand) and to everyday life (e.g., lying to or about another person).

Thou shalt not commit adultery One of the TEN COMMANDMENTS (Exodus 20:14). Jesus expanded on the meaning of this commandment when he taught, as part of the SERMON ON THE MOUNT, "Anyone who even looks at a woman with lust in his eye has already committed ADULTERY with her in his heart" (Matthew 5:28, TLB).

Thou shalt not covet The last of the TEN COMMANDMENTS; it reads, "Thou shalt not covet thy neighbor's house, thou shalt not covet thy neighbor's wife . . . nor any thing that is thy neighbor's" (Exodus 20:17). In the ROMAN CATHOLIC and LUTHERAN traditions, this verse constitutes two separate commandments.

Thou shalt not kill One of the TEN COMMANDMENTS (Exodus 20:13). Jesus expanded on the meaning of this commandment when he taught, as part of the SERMON ON THE MOUNT, "Whosoever is angry with his brother without a cause shall be in danger of the judgment" (Matthew 5:22).

Thou shalt not make unto thee any graven image The second of the TEN COMMANDMENTS (Exodus 20:4). In the ROMAN CATHOLIC and LUTHERAN traditions, the first two commandments (*see also* THOU SHALT HAVE NO OTHER GODS BEFORE ME) are treated together as the first commandment. Whether it is one or two commandments, it is clear that the people of ISRAEL were to have no carved images that they might be tempted to worship.

Thou shalt not steal One of the TEN COMMANDMENTS (Exodus 20:15).

Thou shalt not take the name of the Lord thy God in vain One of the TEN COMMANDMENTS (Exodus 20:7). This commandment relates both to taking an oath (e.g., don't lie when you take an oath in court) and to cursing (don't do it).

through a glass, darkly In the thirteenth chapter of 1 Corinthians (the LOVE CHAPTER), PAUL used the metaphor of looking into a clouded glass (a mirror) to show that we cannot presently understand much of God. But eventually we will see God face to face, and then we will know him more fully. *See also* FAITH, HOPE, CHARITY.

Thy will be done Jesus used this expression in two different contexts. First, it is a phrase from the LORD'S PRAYER: "Thy will be done on earth as it is in HEAVEN" (Matthew 6:10). At the end of his ministry, when he was praying in the Garden of GETHSEMANE, Jesus was in deep anguish. He prayed, "FATHER, if you are willing, take this cup from me; yet not my will, but yours be done" (Luke 22:42, NIV). The "cup" is a metaphor for the terrible agony that lay ahead, but in spite of it all, Jesus wanted to fulfill the will of GOD THE FATHER.

Thy word is a lamp unto my feet Psalm 119 is the longest chapter in the Bible. The entire psalm is about the wonderful attributes of the WORD OF GOD. Verse 105 reads, "Thy word is a lamp unto my feet, and a light unto my path."

THY WILL BE DONE Jesus is in agony as he prays in the Garden of Gethsemane.

Time to be born, and a time to die One of the cycles of life mentioned in the third chapter of Ecclesiastes, which begins, "TO EVERYTHING THERE IS A SEASON, and a time to every purpose under HEAVEN."

To every thing there is a season In the third chapter of Ecclesiastes,

SOLOMON wrote, "To every thing there is a season, and a time to every purpose under HEAVEN." Then follows a long and poetic list of opposites, including "a TIME TO BE BORN, AND A TIME TO DIE . . . a time to mourn, and a time to dance . . . a time of war, and a time of peace."

Train up a child in the way he should go The entire quotation from Proverbs 22:6 is: "Train up a child in the way he should go: and when he is old, he will not depart from it." It is a reminder that a child's early training affects the rest of his or her life.

turn the other cheek In the SERMON ON THE MOUNT, Jesus taught his followers not to resist violence. He said, "Do not resist an evil person. If someone strikes you on the right cheek, turn to him the other also" (Matthew 5:39, NIV). The expression can be used in any situation in which a person whose rights are violated refuses to retaliate. *See also* SECOND MILE, GO THE; *also* HEAP COALS OF FIRE ON HIS HEAD.

❦ This teaching of Jesus was one of the bases for the nonviolent resistance advocated by Mahatma Gandhi and Martin Luther KING, Jr.

Twenty-third Psalm The best-known and best-loved of all the PSALMS of the Old Testament. The complete text, as found in the KING JAMES VERSION, is shown on page 120.

two shall be one flesh In the GENESIS account of the CREATION, the woman was created from ADAM's rib, and Adam said, "This is now bone of my bones, and flesh of my flesh" (Genesis 2:24). The text goes on to say, "Therefore shall a man leave his father and his mother, and shall cleave [cling] unto his wife: and they shall be one flesh."

In answer to a question about divorce, Jesus quoted this passage of SCRIPTURE and went on to say, "What therefore God hath joined together, let not man put asunder [divide]" (Matthew 19:6).

Unto us a child is born The ninth chapter of Isaiah contains this beautiful and familiar description of the coming MESSIAH:

For unto us a child is born,
unto us a son is given;
and the government shall be upon his
    shoulder:
and his name shall be called Wonderful,
Counsellor, The mighty God,
The everlasting Father,
The Prince of Peace.

valley of the shadow of death A phrase from the twenty-third Psalm. DAVID, the psalmist, used this metaphor to mean situations in which he had been near death. For the complete text of the psalm, see TWENTY-THIRD PSALM.

❦ The phrase has come to mean any situation in which one encounters the perils of life, especially a close brush with death.

Vanity of vanities; all is vanity The book of ECCLESIASTES begins with this gloomy statement. SOLOMON meant that everything is futile. He goes on to describe the futility of work, wisdom, pleasure, wealth, and knowledge, but in the end he concludes, "Fear God, and keep his commandments: for this is the whole duty of man."

voice of one crying in the wilderness When the Jewish leaders

Twenty-third Psalm (King James Version)

The Lord is my shepherd; I shall not want.
He maketh me to lie down in green pastures:
he leadeth me beside the still waters.
He restoreth my soul:
he leadeth me in the paths of righteousness for his name's sake.
Yea, though I walk through the valley of the shadow of death,
I will fear no evil:
for thou art with me;
thy rod and thy staff, they comfort me.
Thou preparest a table before me in the presence of mine enemies;
thou anointest my head with oil; my cup runneth over.
Surely goodness and mercy shall follow me all the days of my life:
and I will dwell in the house of the Lord for ever.

asked JOHN THE BAPTIST if he was the Christ, he said he was not. He went on to say, "I am the voice of one crying in the WILDERNESS, Make straight the way of the Lord" (John 1:23). He was quoting Isaiah 40:3, and he meant that he was the spokesman whose role was to announce the coming of the MESSIAH.

❧ The expression is sometimes used today if a person has an important message but can't get anyone to listen.

THE VOICE OF ONE CRYING IN THE WILDERNESS John the Baptist preaches in the wilderness.

wages of sin is death, For the The first phrase of a well-known verse from PAUL'S EPISTLE to the Romans: "For the wages of SIN is death; but the gift of God is ETERNAL LIFE through Jesus Christ our Lord" (Romans 6:23). It means that all people deserve to die because of their sin, but God has provided eternal life in HEAVEN for anyone who believes in Jesus Christ.

What God hath joined together, let not man put asunder When Jesus was asked a question about divorce, he quoted the passage from the account of the CREATION in GENESIS that says, "Therefore shall a man leave his father and his mother, and shall cleave [cling] unto his wife: and they shall be one flesh" (Genesis 2:24). Jesus went on to say, "What therefore God hath joined together, let not man put asunder" (Matthew 19:6). This quotation, slightly paraphrased, is part of the traditional wedding ceremony.

When I was a child, I spake as a child A phrase from the thirteenth chapter of 1 Corinthians (the LOVE CHAPTER). PAUL goes on to say that when he became a man he put away childish things. In the same way, we can only partially know God now, but eventually we will know him more fully. *See also* THROUGH A GLASS, DARKLY.

Whither thou goest, I will go In the story of RUTH and NAOMI, Naomi urged Ruth to return to her own people. Ruth responded, "Whither thou goest, I will go; . . . thy people shall be my people, and thy God my

God" (Ruth 1:16). This expression of commitment is sometimes quoted today in weddings.

Wide is the gate, and broad is the way, that leadeth to destruction Jesus said this in the SERMON ON THE MOUNT (Matthew 7:13-14). He meant that it is easy to live a life that will result in destruction—eternal separation from God. In contrast, he said, "Strait [narrow] is the gate, and narrow is the way, which leadeth unto life, and few there be that find it." This teaching is popularly alluded to by the expression, "staying on the STRAIGHT AND NARROW."

wolf also shall dwell with the lamb An example of the peace that will prevail at the coming of the MESSIAH. This phrase is from a prophetic passage in the book of Isaiah (11:6).

wolf in sheep's clothing An expression taken from Jesus' warning about false PROPHETS. He said, "Beware of false prophets, which come to you in SHEEP's clothing, but inwardly they are ravening wolves" (Matthew 7:15). *See also* BY THEIR FRUITS YE SHALL KNOW THEM.

❧ A wolf in sheep's clothing is anyone who appears benign or innocent but has wicked or harmful motives.

Ye cannot serve God and mammon A teaching of Jesus in the SERMON ON THE MOUNT. He said, "NO MAN CAN SERVE TWO MASTERS. . . . Ye cannot serve God and MAMMON" (Matthew 6:24). He meant that a person cannot WORSHIP money and also pursue a right relationship with God. Either God or money will emerge as the guiding force in our life.

100 KEY EVENTS IN THE OLD TESTAMENT

1. God creates the world, *Genesis 1*
2. God creates ADAM and EVE, *Genesis 2*
3. Adam and Eve sin—the FALL OF MAN, *Genesis 3*
4. Adam and Eve are expelled from the GARDEN OF EDEN, *Genesis 3*
5. CAIN kills his brother, ABEL, *Genesis 4*
6. NOAH AND THE ARK survive the Flood, *Genesis 6–9*
7. Noah's descendants build the TOWER OF BABEL, *Genesis 11*
8. God tests JOB, *Job*
9. God calls ABRAM to move to CANAAN, *Genesis 12*
10. Abram and LOT separate, *Genesis 13*
11. God promises a son to Abram, *Genesis 15*
12. ISHMAEL is born to Abraham and HAGAR, *Genesis 16*
13. God destroys SODOM AND GOMORRAH, *Genesis 18–19*
14. ISAAC is born to Abraham and SARAH, *Genesis 21*
15. Abraham is willing to SACRIFICE Isaac, *Genesis 22*
16. Isaac marries REBEKAH, *Genesis 24*
17. ESAU sells his birthright to JACOB, *Genesis 25*
18. Jacob steals Isaac's blessing, *Genesis 27*
19. Jacob flees and has a dream—JACOB'S LADDER, *Genesis 28*
20. Jacob marries LEAH and RACHEL, *Genesis 29*
21. Jacob wrestles with God, *Genesis 32*
22. Jacob gives JOSEPH a COAT OF MANY COLORS, *Genesis 37*
23. Joseph's dreams alienate his family, *Genesis 37*
24. Joseph's brothers sell him into slavery in EGYPT, *Genesis 37*
25. POTIPHAR'S WIFE tries to seduce Joseph, *Genesis 39*
26. Joseph interprets PHARAOH's dreams, becomes prime minister, *Genesis 41*
27. Joseph is kind to his brothers, *Genesis 45*
28. Jacob and his sons move to Egypt, *Genesis 46*
29. Joseph dies, *Genesis 50*
30. The ISRAELITES become slaves in Egypt, *Exodus 1*
31. MOSES is born; MOSES IN THE BULRUSHES, *Exodus 2*
32. Moses kills an Egyptian and flees from Egypt, *Exodus 2*
33. Moses meets the Lord at the BURNING BUSH, *Exodus 3*
34. God afflicts the Egyptians with PLAGUES, *Exodus 7–11*
35. The first PASSOVER; the EXODUS, *Exodus 12*
36. The Israelites cross the RED SEA, *Exodus 14*
37. God provides MANNA and quails for his people, *Exodus 16*
38. Water gushes from the rock, *Exodus 17*
39. God gives Moses the TEN COMMANDMENTS, *Exodus 20*
40. The Israelites WORSHIP the GOLDEN CALF, *Exodus 32*
41. The TABERNACLE is constructed, *Exodus 35–40*
42. God gives Moses the laws regarding sacrifices, *Leviticus*
43. God leads through the PILLAR OF CLOUD and PILLAR OF FIRE, *Numbers 9*
44. The twelve spies go into Canaan, *Numbers 13*
45. The Israelites are in the WILDERNESS forty years, *Numbers 14–36*
46. Moses makes a bronze snake to save the people, *Numbers 21*
47. BALAAM's donkey speaks; ISRAEL's army is saved, *Numbers 22*
48. JOSHUA is commissioned; the death of Moses, *Deuteronomy 34*
49. The Israelites cross the JORDAN RIVER into Canaan, *Joshua 3*

50. The Canaanites are subdued by Joshua, *Joshua 6–24*
51. Israel is victorious at the BATTLE OF JERICHO, *Joshua 6*
52. The army of Israel is defeated at Ai, *Joshua 8*
53. DEBORAH is a judge over Israel, *Judges 4–5*
54. GIDEON and his small army defeat the Midianites, *Judges 6–7*
55. RUTH follows NAOMI to Israel, *Ruth*
56. SAMSON is deceived by DELILAH, *Judges 16*
57. SAMUEL hears a message from God, *1 Samuel 3*
58. The ARK OF THE COVENANT is captured; ELI dies, *1 Samuel 4*
59. SAUL becomes first king of Israel, *1 Samuel 10*
60. Samuel anoints DAVID as future king of Israel, *1 Samuel 16*
61. David kills GOLIATH, *1 Samuel 17*
62. David and JONATHAN become close friends, *1 Samuel 18*
63. Saul is jealous of David, *1 Samuel 18–31*
64. Saul and Jonathan die in battle, *1 Samuel 31*
65. David is crowned king of JUDAH, then of all Israel, *2 Samuel 1,5*
66. The ark of the covenant is returned to JERUSALEM, *2 Samuel 6*
67. David commits ADULTERY with BATHSHEBA, *2 Samuel 11*
68. David writes many of the PSALMS, *Psalms*
69. ABSALOM leads a revolt against David; Absalom's death, *2 Samuel 15–18*
70. SOLOMON succeeds David as king of Israel, *1 Kings 1*
71. Solomon builds the TEMPLE in Jerusalem, *1 Kings 6–8*
72. Solomon falls into IDOL worship, *1 Kings 11*
73. JEROBOAM leads revolt against REHOBOAM; Israel is divided, *1 Kings 12*
74. The PROPHETS proclaim God's judgment on Israel, *1 Kings, 2 Kings*
75. The prophets proclaim God's judgment on JUDAH, *1 Kings, 2 Kings*
76. Ravens feed ELIJAH at Cherith Brook, *1 Kings 17*
77. Elijah defeats the PRIESTS of BAAL on Mount Carmel, *1 Kings 18*
78. Elijah is taken to HEAVEN in a CHARIOT OF FIRE, *2 Kings 2*
79. ELISHA succeeds Elijah and ministers to Israel, *2 Kings 2–13*
80. JOASH reigns as a good king in Judah, *2 Kings 11–12*
81. JONAH is swallowed by a big fish, *Jonah*
82. ISAIAH sees a vision in the temple, *Isaiah 6*
83. Isaiah prophesies about the coming MESSIAH, *Isaiah 7, 53*
84. Israel—the NORTHERN KINGDOM—falls to ASSYRIA, *2 Kings 17*
85. JEREMIAH prophesies and is persecuted, *Jeremiah*
86. BABYLON conquers Assyria, *secular history*
87. NEBUCHADNEZZAR takes DANIEL and others to Babylon, *Daniel 1*
88. Nebuchadnezzar dreams of a statue with FEET OF CLAY, *Daniel 2*
89. Daniel's friends are thrown into the FIERY FURNACE, *Daniel 3*
90. EZEKIEL prophesies to Judah, *Ezekiel*
91. Judah—the SOUTHERN KINGDOM—falls to Babylon, *2 Kings 25*
92. The people of Judah are exiled to Babylon, *2 Kings 25*
93. Daniel prophesies about the end of the world, *Daniel 7–12*
94. Daniel interprets the HANDWRITING ON THE WALL; Babylon falls to PERSIA, *Daniel 5*
95. Daniel is thrown into the lions' den, *Daniel 6*
96. Exiles begin returning to Jerusalem with ZERUBBABEL, *Ezra 1–2*
97. The temple in Jerusalem is rebuilt, *Ezra 3–6*
98. Various prophets appeal to Judah after the EXILE, *Haggai, Zechariah*
99. ESTHER saves the JEWS in Persia from destruction, *Esther*
100. NEHEMIAH builds the walls of Jerusalem, *Nehemiah*

PEOPLE AND EVENTS IN THE OLD TESTAMENT

The Old Testament is the account of God's dealings with his CHOSEN PEOPLE, the ISRAELITES. Many Old Testament names are familiar to anyone who is culturally literate—names such as ADAM and EVE, NOAH, ABRAHAM, MOSES, and DAVID. But there are many others whose names we need to know if we are to understand the full scope of the Old Testament story. And since the Old Testament was "the SCRIPTURES" for Jesus and his contemporaries, we need to know the people and events of the Old Testament to understand fully the teachings of the New Testament. For instance, the eleventh chapter of HEBREWS lists by name nineteen people from the Old Testament, sixteen of whom are included in this chapter.

The Old Testament begins with the words "IN THE BEGINNING God created the heaven and the earth." The account of the CREATION is followed by the FALL OF MAN, then the story of Noah and the ark. Next come the stories of Abraham and SARAH, ISAAC and REBEKAH, JACOB and ESAU, and JOSEPH and his COAT OF MANY COLORS. Four hundred and thirty years after Joseph is the story of Moses and the EXODUS, followed by the forty years in which the Israelites wandered in the WILDERNESS. JOSHUA leads the people in conquering the PROMISED LAND. After Joshua comes the period of the JUDGES, then the UNITED KINGDOM and the DIVIDED KINGDOM. ASSYRIA conquers ISRAEL, and BABYLON conquers

Judah. God's people are taken into exile. The Old Testament finally ends with the return of the people of Judah from the Exile.

We get a little bit of insight into the 400 years between the Old Testament and the New Testament by reading the Apocrypha. Otherwise, the Bible is silent about that time period.

There are many terms that are equally important in understanding the Old Testament and the New Testament—terms such as Jordan River, Jerusalem, circumcision, Passover, the Law, and temple. For the sake of consistency, terms that could have been listed either in this chapter or under "People and Events in the New Testament" are listed here.

Aaron Moses' older brother. Aaron plays a key role in the events related in the books of EXODUS and NUMBERS. When God told Moses to lead the ISRAELITES to freedom from slavery in EGYPT, Moses said he was not an eloquent speaker. God responded that Aaron could be Moses' spokesman. Moses and Aaron delivered God's message to PHARAOH: "LET MY PEOPLE GO."

After the EXODUS from Egypt, while the Israelites were wandering in the WILDERNESS, Moses met with God on Mount SINAI. In Moses' absence, Aaron gave in to the demands of the people and made a GOLDEN CALF for them to worship. Aaron later became the first HIGH PRIEST of ISRAEL, and all subsequent PRIESTS were descendants of Aaron.

Abel ADAM and EVE's second son (Genesis 4). Abel was a SHEPHERD and brought portions of a lamb to the Lord as a SACRIFICE. His brother, CAIN, was a farmer and brought some of his crops as a sacrifice to the Lord. The Lord accepted Abel's sacrifice, but he did not accept Cain's sacrifice. Cain became angry and murdered Abel.

Abraham Originally called ABRAM, he was the first of the PATRIARCHS of ISRAEL (Genesis 12–25). The Lord spoke to him in Ur of the Chaldeans (in present-day Iraq) and told him to move to CANAAN (present-day Israel). The Bible says that Abraham's faith in God was counted as RIGHTEOUSNESS (Genesis 15:6).

The Lord made a COVENANT with Abraham. Although Abraham and his wife, SARAH, were both too old to have a child, the Lord promised they would have a son and that their descendants would be "as numerous as the sands upon the seashore." When Sarah did not conceive, she gave Abraham her servant HAGAR to be his CONCUBINE and to bear him a son. Hagar did have a son, ISHMAEL. The Arabs regard themselves as descendants of Ishmael and consider Abraham the father of their race.

Finally, at age ninety, Sarah had a son named ISAAC. When Isaac was still a boy, the Lord tested Abraham's faith by asking him to SACRIFICE Isaac. Abraham was in the process of doing so when the Lord saw his faith and told him to stop. Through the descendants of Isaac, Abraham is also the father of the Jewish people.

ABRAHAM Abraham prepares to offer his son Isaac as a sacrifice.

Abram   ABRAHAM's name prior to receiving God's promise that he and SARAH would have a son. Abram means 'exalted father'; Abraham means 'father of many'.

Absalom   King DAVID's son, who led a rebellion against his father (2 Samuel 15–18). When his donkey ran under a low-hanging branch, his long hair became tangled in the tree. He was left hanging there, and JOAB, David's general, killed him. When David heard about Absalom's death, he mourned, "O my son Absalom, my son, my son Absalom!"

Adam   The first person created by God. He was created "in the image of God" (Genesis 1:27). His wife was EVE. According to the GENESIS account of the CREATION, God created Eve from one of Adam's ribs. Adam and Eve lived in the Garden of EDEN in a state of perfect communion with God. Adam tended the Garden and named all the animals God had created.

The SERPENT, identified in Revelation 20:2 as SATAN, tempted Eve to disobey God by eating the FORBIDDEN FRUIT from the TREE OF THE KNOWLEDGE OF GOOD AND EVIL. She ate the fruit and gave some to Adam to eat. This is called the FALL OF MAN. As a result of their disobedience, they were expelled from the Garden of Eden (*see* EXPULSION). God cursed the ground so it would produce thorns and thistles, and God told Adam he would now have to toil by the sweat of his brow. God told Eve she would have pain in childbirth. God also told Adam, "DUST THOU ART, AND UNTO DUST SHALT THOU RETURN" (Genesis 3:19).

Adam and Eve's sons included CAIN and ABEL.

adultery Any act of sexual intercourse between a married person and someone other than his or her spouse. In the Old Testament, adultery was punishable by death (Leviticus 20:10). One of the TEN COMMANDMENTS is THOU SHALT NOT COMMIT ADULTERY. Jesus expanded on this commandment by saying in the SERMON ON THE MOUNT, "Anyone who even looks at a woman with lust in his eye has already committed adultery with her in his heart" (Matthew 5:28, TLB). *See also* FORNICATION.

Ahab One of the most wicked of the kings of ISRAEL (1 Kings 16–22). He and his wife, JEZEBEL, promoted the worship of BAAL. It was during their reign that ELIJAH had his famous contest with the priests of Baal and called down FIRE FROM HEAVEN.

alleluia An alternate form of the word HALLELUJAH. It comes from the HEBREW and means 'praise YAHWEH', or 'praise the Lord'.

altar A stone or wood or earthen structure on which SACRIFICES are offered in worship. When the MOSAIC LAW was instituted, God instructed MOSES to construct an altar at the TABERNACLE for all the people to use in offering their sacrifices.

The CANAANITES also had altars to their gods, and the ISRAELITES were ordered to destroy those heathen altars as they took possession of the PROMISED LAND. The Israelites never fully obeyed that command, and they were continually drawn into worship of the foreign gods.

In churches today, the table at the front of the sanctuary where the EUCHARIST is blessed is often called an altar.

Ararat The mountain range where NOAH's ark came to rest after the Flood. Ararat is believed to be in present-day Turkey.

ALTAR This altar for burning sacrifices was used first at the tabernacle, later at the temple.

ark *See* ARK OF THE COVENANT *or* NOAH.

ark of the covenant A gold-plated box that was kept in the HOLY OF HOLIES, first in the TABERNACLE, then in the TEMPLE. Above it were two carved CHERUBIM. The ark (not to be confused with NOAH's ark) was the most sacred article in ISRAEL. Only the HIGH PRIEST could approach the ark, and then only once a year. It symbolized God's presence among the people of Israel. The ark contained the stone tablets on which God had inscribed the TEN COMMANDMENTS for MOSES, a jar of MANNA, and the rod with which AARON had performed MIRACLES at the time of the EXODUS. At one point the ark was captured by the PHILISTINES, but it brought a curse to them, so they returned it to Israel. The ark is described in Exodus 25.

❦ Notwithstanding the story in the popular film *Raiders of the Lost Ark*, it is safe to assume that the ark was destroyed during the destruction of JERUSALEM by the BABYLONIANS in 586 B.C. There was no ark in the second temple (built by ZERUBBABEL) or the third temple (built by HEROD the Great).

ARK OF THE COVENANT The high priest bows before the ark in the Holy of Holies.

Assyria, Assyrians Assyria was an ancient country in what is now northern Iraq and western Turkey. The Assyrians attained prominence in the Near East during the ninth century B.C. JONAH went to Nineveh, the capital of Assyria, to call the people to repentance (*see* JONAH AND THE WHALE). The Assyrians laid siege to SAMARIA, the capital of ISRAEL (the NORTHERN KINGDOM), for three years. Samaria finally fell in 722 B.C., and many of the ISRAELITES were taken as captives to Assyria (2 Kings 17). This marked the end of the Kingdom of Israel. We know from secular history that Assyria later fell to BABYLON (in 612 B.C.), the world power that destroyed JERUSALEM in 586 B.C.

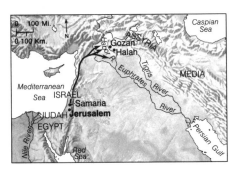

ASSYRIA TAKES ISRAEL CAPTIVE Samaria, the capital of the northern kindgom of Israel, was destroyed by the Assyrians. The people of Israel were led into captivity, swallowed up by the mighty, evil Assyrian empire. This marked the end of the northern kingdom, as the Israelites never returned.

Baal The most important of the many gods of the CANAANITES. He represented the harvest and fertility, and worship of Baal often included prostitution. The people of ISRAEL were repeatedly warned not to worship Baal, but they repeatedly fell into such worship. During the reign of King AHAB and Queen JEZEBEL, ELIJAH challenged the PRIESTS of Baal to a contest to show whether the God of Israel was stronger than Baal. The priests of Baal were unable to send FIRE FROM HEAVEN, but God sent fire that burned up the ALTAR itself in addition to the SACRIFICE.

Babel, Tower of A great tower built by the descendants of NOAH. In their pride, they intended to build the tower all the way to HEAVEN. It was located in the area that later became the city of BABYLON. To confound their efforts and to keep them from completing the tower, God confused their language so that they no longer understood one another. According to Genesis 11, where this story is told, this is the beginning of the multiplicity of languages in the world.

❦ A "Babel" is any scene of confusion, especially a confusion of multiple languages.

Babylon, Babylonians Babylon was the capital of the Babylonian Empire, which flourished in the region of present-day Iraq during the sixth century B.C. Secular history tells us that the Babylonians defeated the ASSYRIANS (the empire that had earlier defeated the NORTHERN KINGDOM of ISRAEL) in 612 B.C. Twenty-six years later, in 586 B.C., the Babylonians destroyed JERUSALEM (2 Kings 25). Many of the inhabitants were taken as captives to Babylon (*see* EXILE). About fifty years later the Babylonians were defeated by the PERSIANS (Daniel 5). The stories in the book of DANIEL take place in Babylon during the time of the JEWS' captivity there. Babylon is frequently mentioned in the Bible as a place of sin. It was the location of the Tower of BABEL, and in Revelation 14:8 Babylon is symbolic of ultimate evil.

TOWER OF BABEL The people cry out in despair when God confuses their languages at the Tower of Babel.

BABYLON TAKES JUDAH CAPTIVE Evil permeated Judah, and God's anger flared against his rebellious people. Babylon conquered Assyria and became the new world power. The Babylonian army marched into Jerusalem, burned the temple, tore down the city's massive walls, and carried the people off into captivity.

❧ During the 1980s, Saddam Hussein, the president of Iraq who fancied himself to be a latter-day NEBUCHADNEZZAR, began rebuilding the ancient city of Babylon.

❧ A "Babylon" is any place of sin and corruption.

Babylonian captivity   *See* EXILE.

Balaam   Before the conquest of CANAAN by JOSHUA, Balaam was hired by Balak, an enemy of ISRAEL, to curse Israel and its army (Numbers 22). While Balaam was on his way to curse Israel, an ANGEL blocked his path. He could not see the angel, but his donkey could, and the donkey spoke to Balaam. The angel then instructed Balaam to bless Israel instead of cursing it.

Bathsheba   The wife of Uriah, a soldier in King DAVID's army. David committed ADULTERY with Bathsheba while her husband was away at war, and she became pregnant (2 Samuel 11). David wanted to marry Bathsheba, but there was an obstacle— Uriah. So David arranged for Uriah to be killed in battle. David did then marry Bathsheba. David repented of his SIN, but their first child died. Bathsheba later became the mother of SOLOMON, who succeeded David as king of ISRAEL. Bathsheba is included in MATTHEW's GENEALOGY of Jesus, where she is referred to as the widow of Uriah.

behemoth   The book of JOB (chapter 40) contains a lengthy description of the behemoth, a large and very strong creature, perhaps an elephant or hippopotamus. God was showing JOB his great power in creating such an awesome animal. *See also* LEVIATHAN.

❧ The word *behemoth* has come to mean any person or animal that is huge.

Benjamin   The youngest son of JACOB and RACHEL, and JOSEPH's brother. When Joseph was prime minister of EGYPT, all of his brothers except Benjamin went to Egypt to buy grain (Genesis 42). The brothers did not recognize Joseph, and he accused them of being spies. Then, to test their sincerity, he insisted that they bring Benjamin to Egypt, and he kept Simeon as a hostage. Jacob did not want to let Benjamin go, but the brothers knew they could not return to Egypt for more food without Benjamin. When they did return to Egypt, Joseph finally revealed his identity to them. Benjamin became the PATRIARCH of the TRIBE of BENJAMIN.

Benjamin, tribe of   The descendants of BENJAMIN, JACOB's youngest son, became the tribe of Benjamin. King SAUL and the APOSTLE PAUL were from the tribe of Benjamin. During the period of the DIVIDED KINGDOM, the tribes of Benjamin and JUDAH constituted the Kingdom of JUDAH.

blessings and curses When the Lord made a COVENANT with a person or nation in the Old Testament, the covenant included both obligations and consequences. The consequences were blessings for those who obeyed the Lord and were faithful to the covenant, but curses for those who disobeyed the Lord. Although the people of ISRAEL disobeyed more than they obeyed, the Lord offered blessings far greater than the curses. When the Lord gave MOSES the TEN COMMANDMENTS, he said, "I, the Lord your God, am a jealous God, punishing the children for the SIN of the fathers to the third and fourth generation of those who hate me, but showing love to a thousand generations of those who love me and keep my commandments" (Exodus 20:5-6, NIV).

An important part of HEBREW culture was the blessing that a father bestowed on his children. The oldest son, in particular, received a special blessing. JACOB tricked his aged father, ISAAC, into blessing him with the blessing that would normally have gone to Jacob's older brother, ESAU.

Boaz A wealthy farmer who befriended and then married RUTH. Their great-grandson was DAVID. The story of Ruth and Boaz is told in the book of RUTH.

burning bush When MOSES was a SHEPHERD, he saw in the WILDERNESS a bush that "burned with fire, and the bush was not consumed" (Exodus 3:2). Moses went to investigate, and the Lord spoke to him from the fire. The Lord told him to return to EGYPT and to tell PHARAOH to release the ISRA-

BURNING BUSH The Lord speaks to Moses from the burning bush.

ELITES from slavery—to "LET MY PEOPLE GO." Moses was then to lead the ISRAELITES to the PROMISED LAND. Moses asked the Lord what his name was, and the Lord replied, "I AM THAT I AM." Moses did return to Egypt, and he and his brother, AARON, led the Israelites out of Egypt (see EXODUS, THE).

❦A "burning bush" experience is an experience with God that significantly changes the course of a person's life.

Cain The eldest son of ADAM and EVE (Genesis 4). Cain's brother, ABEL, was a SHEPHERD and brought portions of a lamb to the Lord as a SACRIFICE. Cain was a farmer and brought some of his crops as a sacrifice to the Lord. The Lord accepted Abel's sacrifice, but he did not accept Cain's sacrifice. This made Cain angry, and he murdered Abel. When the Lord asked Cain where Abel was, Cain responded, "AM I MY BROTHER'S KEEPER?" Cain was then banished from the Lord's presence, to become a wanderer upon the earth. He told the Lord that he was fearful he himself would be murdered because of his crime, so the Lord put a mark upon him (see MARK OF CAIN) as a warning to others not to harm him. Cain settled in the land of Nod, east of EDEN.

❦ To "raise Cain" is to make a disturbance or generally cause trouble. John Steinbeck's novel *East of Eden*

contains many allusions to the story of Cain.

Caleb With JOSHUA, Caleb was one of the twelve ISRAELITE spies sent into CANAAN after the EXODUS (Numbers 13). Caleb and Joshua were the only two who reported that with God's help the Israelites could overcome the CANAANITES. Because the people did not believe the Lord would help them conquer the land, they were condemned to stay in the WILDERNESS for forty years—until that generation of adults had died. Joshua and Caleb were the only ones of their generation who did eventually enter the PROMISED LAND.

camel The camel was an important means of transportation during Bible times and was often a measure of personal wealth. The description of JOB as a wealthy man includes the fact that he owned 3,000 camels.

Canaan The land at the eastern edge of the MEDITERRANEAN SEA, encompassing present-day Israel and parts of Lebanon, Syria, and Jordan. When ABRAM left his home in Ur of the Chaldeans (in what is now Iraq), God guided him to Canaan. God promised Abram that his descendants would receive the entire land of Canaan as an inheritance. Several generations later, when JACOB and his family moved to EGYPT, their descendants never forgot that God had promised Canaan to their ancestor

Abram. Accordingly, when MOSES led the people of ISRAEL out of Egypt 430 years later (*see* EXODUS, THE), they saw Canaan as the PROMISED LAND.

CAMEL Camels can still be seen in the Middle East.

Canaanites   The inhabitants of CANAAN. They were wicked, idolatrous people. After the EXODUS, God instructed the ISRAELITES to destroy the Canaanites and their gods (Deuteronomy 7:1-6). He gave this seemingly bloodthirsty command both to punish the Canaanites for their wickedness (Leviticus 18) and to keep the Israelites from being influenced by the EVIL of the Canaanites. During the conquest of Canaan under JOSHUA, many Canaanite cities were destroyed, but ISRAEL never fully obeyed God's command to destroy the Canaanites. As a result, they had problems with their Canaanite neighbors for centuries.

Captivity   *See* EXILE.

chariot   A two-wheeled vehicle pulled by one or more horses. Char-

iots were important in warfare both in Old Testament and New Testament times. In the story of DEBORAH, for example, the CANAANITES were a formidable foe because they had 900 iron chariots. ISAIAH warned the people of JUDAH not to trust in chariots, but to seek their help from the Lord (Isaiah 31:1).

chariot of fire   At the end of ELIJAH's life, he was taken up into HEAVEN in a CHARIOT that was made of fire and drawn by horses of fire (2 Kings 2:11).

❦ The title of the popular movie *Chariots of Fire* comes from a phrase in a HYMN by William Blake, which in turn is an allusion to Elijah's chariot of fire.

CHARIOT OF FIRE Elisha watches as Elijah is taken to heaven in a chariot of fire.

cherubim and seraphim Types of ANGELS. When the Lord drove ADAM and EVE out of the Garden of EDEN, cherubim with flaming swords guarded the way to the TREE OF LIFE (Genesis 3). Two gold-plated, carved cherubim formed part of the cover of the ARK OF THE COVENANT. In SOLOMON'S TEMPLE, two larger gold-plated cherubim spread their wings above the ark of the covenant, stretching from wall to wall within the HOLY OF HOLIES.

When ISAIAH saw the Lord in a VISION, he also saw seraphim worshiping the Lord (Isaiah 6). They were human in form, but with six wings.

children of Israel Another name for the HEBREWS or ISRAELITES, the descendants of ABRAHAM through ISAAC and JACOB.

chosen people The descendants of ABRAHAM, through ISAAC and JACOB, were God's "chosen people." He chose them to receive his COVENANT. They are also called HEBREWS, ISRAELITES, and the CHILDREN OF ISRAEL. During and after the EXILE, the term *Jews* is used in referring to members of the TRIBES of JUDAH and BENJAMIN.

coat of many colors A special coat that JACOB gave to his favorite son, JOSEPH. Joseph flaunted his position of privilege, and his brothers took revenge by selling him into slavery in EGYPT. Then they spilled goat blood on the coat and brought it back to their father, saying that Joseph had been killed by a wild animal (Genesis 37).

concubine A woman who was not a free wife but was a legitimate sexual partner of a man, who was responsible for her support. The most famous concubine in the Bible is HAGAR, the servant girl whom SARAH gave to her husband, ABRAHAM. She bore Abraham a son, ISHMAEL. SOLOMON had 700 wives and 300 concubines.

Creation, the The creation of the universe and of mankind by God, as described in the first two chapters of the book of GENESIS. The first chapter of Genesis begins, "IN THE BEGINNING, God created the heaven and the earth." The account goes on to describe God's creation of light, sky and water, sea and earth, sun, moon, and stars, fish and birds, animals, and man and woman (ADAM and EVE) during a six-day period. On the seventh day, God rested from his labors (*see* SABBATH).

❦ In the nineteenth century, Charles DARWIN devised the theory of EVOLUTION, which explains the diversity of species (including mankind) through mutation, natural selection, and the survival of the fittest. In the twentieth century, physicists and astronomers have explained the existence of the sun, the earth, the stars, and all celestial matter (i.e., the entire universe) as having emanated from a single explosion—a big bang. The big bang theory and the theory of evolution have come to be accepted by most scientists as logical explanations for the present existence of the universe and the diversity of species. Most scientists who accept these theories do not accept the biblical explanation that the Creation was the act of an all-powerful, pre-existent God.

❦ There is much debate today over the appropriate teaching in public schools of the origin of the universe and the origin of life on earth. Some Christians argue that evolution should be presented as a theory rather than as fact, and that Creation should also be presented as an alternate explanation for the origin of life. For the most part, however, the biblical account of Creation is not presented at all in the public schools.

crossing of the Red Sea *See* RED SEA, PARTING OF THE.

Daniel An ISRAELITE who was taken to BABYLON as a captive in 605 B.C., nineteen years before the fall of JERUSALEM. Various stories are told in the book of DANIEL about Daniel's faithfulness to God in a heathen culture. His friends SHADRACH, MESHACH, AND ABEDNEGO were thrown into a FIERY FURNACE when they refused to worship a golden statue, but an AN-GEL kept them safe. Some of Daniel's enemies, knowing he prayed to his God three times a day, tried to have him destroyed by convincing King Darius to pass a law requiring everyone to pray only to the king. Daniel was thrown into a den of lions when he insisted on praying to God rather than to the king, but an ANGEL kept him from harm (*see* DANIEL IN THE LIONS' DEN).

Daniel's PROPHECIES included the interpretation of NEBUCHADNEZZAR's dream about the statue with the FEET OF CLAY, and the interpretation of the HANDWRITING ON THE WALL. He also had VISIONS about future events, including events at the end of time.

Daniel in the lions' den DANIEL was a JEW, but he was a powerful official in the government of Darius, the king who took over the kingdom when the PERSIANS defeated the BAB-YLONIANS. Some of Daniel's adversaries wanted to get rid of him, and they saw their chance when they found that he prayed to the Lord three times a day. They convinced the king to pass an edict that his subjects could pray only to the king for a period of thirty days or be THROWN TO THE LIONS. When Daniel continued to pray to the Lord, his enemies triumphantly brought him to the king and accused him of breaking the law. The king was sorrowful, but he had to comply with his own law.

Before Daniel was thrown in with the lions, Darius said he hoped Daniel's God would be able to rescue him. Darius then spent a sleepless night, worrying about Daniel. Early the next morning, Darius went to the lions' den to see what had happened to Daniel. He was overjoyed to find that Daniel was safe—an ANGEL having kept the lions from harming him. He ordered Daniel pulled out of the lions' den, and he had Daniel's enemies thrown to the lions, who hungrily devoured them. Darius then issued an edict throughout the land that the people were to fear Daniel's God. The story is found in the sixth chapter of DANIEL.

❦ If you are "in the lions' den," you are in a situation where you are surrounded by adversaries.

David   The second and greatest king of ISRAEL, whom God called "a man after mine own heart" (Acts 13:22). His story is told in 1 Samuel 16–31 and 2 Samuel.

When David was a young SHEPHERD living in BETHLEHEM, SAMUEL anointed him as King SAUL's successor. While still a lad, David visited the army of Israel, which was engaged in warfare with the PHILISTINES. The Philistine giant, GOLIATH, had been terrorizing the ISRAELITES. David asked Saul's permission to fight the giant, but he turned down Saul's of-

fer of armor. Instead, David prayed and used a stone and a sling, with which he killed Goliath. This enabled the Israelite army to defeat the Philistines.

DANIEL IN THE LIONS' DEN King Darius finds that Daniel has been kept safe from the hungry lions.

Saul's son JONATHAN became David's closest friend. Saul was jealous because of David's great popularity with the people, and he tried to kill David on several occasions. David had several opportunities to kill Saul, but he refused to harm the one who had been anointed by God. After Saul and Jonathan were killed by the Philistines, David was crowned king, first of the TRIBE of JUDAH, then of the entire nation of Israel. He was a great warrior, a musician, and a poet. He wrote many of the PSALMS.

David had numerous wives, including Saul's daughter, Michal, and Bathsheba (for the story of David and Bathsheba, see BATHSHEBA.) David's sons included ABSALOM and SOLOMON. David was king of Israel for forty years, and his descendants ruled Israel for another 373 years. Jesus was a descendant of David and was called the SON OF DAVID. Bethlehem, where Jesus was born, was known at that time as the "city of David."

DAVID David uses a stone from a sling to kill Goliath.

Day of Atonement The word *ATONEMENT* refers to the reconciliation between God and sinners. Under the MOSAIC LAW of the Old Testament, the HIGH PRIEST made a special SACRIFICE once a year as an atonement for the SINS of the entire nation of ISRAEL (Leviticus 16). On that same day, the Day of Atonement, the sins of the people were placed symbolically on the head of a GOAT who became the SCAPEGOAT and carried the people's sins away into the desert. It was only on the Day of Atonement that the high priest could enter the HOLY OF HOLIES. JEWS still observe the Day of Atonement (YOM KIPPUR) as their holiest day of the year.

❦ The Day of Atonement was a reminder that the sacrifices made on a daily, weekly, and monthly basis were able to atone for sins only temporarily. For Christians under the NEW COVENANT, the death of Jesus, the perfect LAMB OF GOD, replaces all sacrifices as the perfect atonement for sins.

Dead Sea A very salty body of water at the southeastern corner of the land of ISRAEL. The JORDAN RIVER flows into the Dead Sea, but the Dead Sea has no outlet. It is called the Dead Sea because fish cannot survive in water with such a high salt content. The Dead Sea is not very large—400 square miles, or about one-sixth the size of Utah's Great Salt Lake. The surface of the Dead Sea lies about 1,300 feet below sea level in the geological rift that includes the Great

Rift Valley in East Africa. Its surface is the lowest elevation on the surface of the earth.

SODOM AND GOMORRAH may have been located in an area now covered by the Dead Sea. The Qumran community that created most of the DEAD SEA SCROLLS was located on the northeastern shore of the Dead Sea.

Deborah A judge over ISRAEL during the period of the JUDGES. She instructed Barak to take 10,000 soldiers to do battle with Sisera, a CANAANITE general. Barak said he would go only if Deborah went with him. She agreed to go, but she told Barak he would not receive the honor, for Sisera would be killed by a woman. The ISRAELITE army defeated Sisera's army, even though the Canaanites had 900 CHARIOTS. Sisera escaped, however, and hid in the tent of Jael. He asked her to keep a lookout for him while he slept. Instead, she killed him by hammering a tent peg through his temples as he slept. After Israel's victory, Deborah sang the "Song of Deborah," which is found in the fifth chapter of the book of JUDGES.

Delilah One of SAMSON's lovers (Judges 16). She was a PHILISTINE woman who tricked Samson into divulging the secret that his great strength would disappear if his hair were cut. She then arranged for his hair to be cut while he slept so that his Philistine enemies could capture him.

❦ A Delilah is a woman who cunningly entices a man and then deceives or betrays him.

Divided Kingdom The 200-year period (930–722 B.C.) from the death of King SOLOMON till the fall of the Kingdom of ISRAEL. Solomon's son REHOBOAM succeeded him as king of Israel. The ten northern TRIBES OF ISRAEL refused to submit to his authority, however, and they established their own kingdom (still called the Kingdom of Israel) with JEROBOAM as king (1 Kings 12). One of the key cities (and the capital during part of this period) was SAMARIA. The two southern tribes, JUDAH and BENJAMIN, made up the Kingdom of JUDAH, whose capital was JERUSALEM. The Kingdoms of Judah and Israel coexisted side by side until Israel (the NORTHERN KINGDOM) fell to the Assyrians in 722 B.C. The Kingdom of Judah (the SOUTHERN KINGDOM) fell to the BABYLONIANS in 586 B.C.

Eden, Garden of The garden where God placed ADAM and EVE after the CREATION. Before the FALL OF MAN, the Garden of Eden was a perfect environment. There was no SIN, and Adam and Eve lived in perfect harmony with one another and with God. God told Adam he could eat of the fruit of any tree in the Garden except the fruit of the TREE OF THE

KNOWLEDGE OF GOOD AND EVIL in the center of the Garden (the FORBIDDEN FRUIT). After the Fall, Adam and Eve were expelled from the Garden (*see* EXPULSION), lest they also eat the fruit of the TREE OF LIFE. CHERUBIM with flaming swords were placed at the entrance to the Garden to ensure that Adam and Eve would not return.

❦Figuratively, "Eden" is any perfect or idyllic spot.

Egypt The country in northeastern Africa, at the mouth of the NILE RIVER. Egypt plays a major role in biblical history, from the time of ABRAHAM all the way to the FLIGHT TO EGYPT in the New Testament. Abraham and SARAH journeyed to Egypt to escape a famine in CANAAN. JOSEPH, JACOB's favorite son, was sold by his brothers into slavery in Egypt. He later became prime minister of Egypt and oversaw a food storage program that saved the land from seven years of famine (Genesis 41). At that time Jacob and his sons and their families all moved to Egypt. Their descendants lived there for 430 years and became a mighty nation.

With the passage of time, Joseph's role in saving Egypt from famine was forgotten. The first chapter of EXODUS says the ISRAELITES were eventually enslaved by a PHARAOH "who knew not Joseph" (there may have been a new dynasty), and the Israelites were allowed to leave (*see* EXODUS, THE) only after the PLAGUES OF EGYPT. At various times in the history of the Kingdom of ISRAEL, Egypt was either an ally or an enemy of Israel.

Eli A judge over ISRAEL during the period of the JUDGES. He was the HIGH PRIEST at Shiloh, where the TABERNACLE

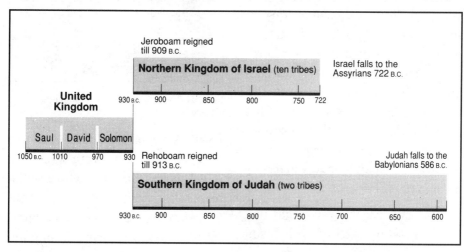

DIVIDED KINGDOM The Kingdom of Israel was divided after Solomon's death.

was located (1 Samuel 1–4). When SAMUEL was a child, he was taken to Shiloh to work and live with Eli. Eli's sons were wicked, and Eli died when he heard that the ARK OF THE COVENANT had been captured by the PHILISTINES and that his sons had been killed in the battle. Samuel then succeeded Eli as a PROPHET and the last judge during the period of the judges.

Elijah One of the great PROPHETS of the Old Testament (1 Kings 17–22 and 2 Kings 1–2). During the reign of King AHAB and Queen JEZEBEL of ISRAEL, Elijah prophesied that there would be no rain in Israel for three years. Elijah went into the WILDERNESS to hide from Ahab, and the Lord sent ravens to bring him food. At the end of that time, Elijah challenged the prophets of BAAL to a contest on Mt. Carmel. He built an ALTAR on the mountain and told the prophets of Baal to call upon their god to send fire to light the SACRIFICE. When they failed, Elijah called upon the Lord, who sent FIRE FROM HEAVEN that consumed the sacrifice and even the stones of the altar. At the end of his life, Elijah left his mantle (representing his prophetic power) to ELISHA and was taken up to HEAVEN in a CHARIOT OF FIRE.

MOSES and Elijah were the two prophets who appeared with Jesus on the Mount of TRANSFIGURATION.

❦ A leader "passes the mantle" by formally handing over leadership to his or her successor.

Elisha One of the great PROPHETS of the Old Testament (2 Kings 2–13). He was a disciple and then the successor of ELIJAH. Before Elijah was taken to HEAVEN in a CHARIOT OF FIRE, he gave his mantle to Elisha, symbolizing the transfer of his leadership and authority. Elisha performed many MIRACLES, including raising back to life a boy who had died.

ELIJAH Ravens bring food to Elijah in the wilderness.

Esau One of ISAAC and REBEKAH's sons, and the twin brother of JACOB (Genesis 25–33). Esau, who was the older of the twins, sold his birthright to Jacob for "a mess of pottage" (stew) when he returned from hunting one day and was famished. Later, when Isaac was old and blind, Jacob tricked Isaac into blessing him (*see* BLESSINGS AND CURSES) rather than Esau by wearing goatskins on his arms and neck so Isaac would think he was the hairy Esau. Esau's descendants, the Edomites, were a perennial enemy of the people of ISRAEL.

🦃 By extension, to "sell one's birthright" is to give up something of great value for a paltry price, especially if it is done as an act of desperation.

Esther   A Jewish woman who was part of the exiled community of Israel in PERSIA (*see* EXILE). Because of her beauty, Esther was selected to become a member of the harem of King Ahasuerus (Xerxes) of Persia. She later became queen. When Esther's older cousin and foster father, Mordecai, heard that Haman, the prime minister, had launched a plan to kill all the JEWS in the kingdom, he urged Esther to ask the king to countermand the plan. He sent her a message that said, "Perhaps you have come to royal position FOR SUCH A TIME AS THIS" (Esther 4:14, NIV). Although she was the queen, she could have been put to death for speaking to the king without being bidden to do so. Before going in to see the king she said, "IF I PERISH, I PERISH." The king granted her an audience, and the plan to exterminate the Jews was reversed.

The story of Esther is told in the book of ESTHER. The Jewish holiday of PURIM commemorates Esther's rescue of the Jews.

Euphrates River   A river that flows from present-day Turkey through Iraq to the Persian Gulf. It is the largest river in western Asia. The basins of the Euphrates River and TIGRIS RIVER formed part of the Fertile Crescent of the ancient world. The region of the Tigris and the Euphrates was called Mesopotamia in the Bible (the name comes from the GREEK for 'between the two rivers'). The city of BABYLON was located on the banks of the Euphrates.

EVE "She shall be called Woman, because she was taken out of Man" (Genesis 2:23).

Eve   The first woman, and ADAM's wife (Genesis 2–4). According to the GENESIS account of the CREATION, God created Eve from one of Adam's ribs. Adam and Eve lived in sinless harmony in the Garden of EDEN until the SERPENT (identified in Revelation 20:2 as SATAN) came to tempt Eve to eat the FORBIDDEN FRUIT—the fruit from the TREE OF THE KNOWLEDGE OF GOOD AND EVIL. Eve ate the fruit, then she gave some to Adam and he ate it. This is called the FALL OF MAN.

God told Eve that she would bear children in great pain and suffering as a result of her sin. Adam and Eve were expelled from the Garden (*see* EXPULSION) lest they also eat the fruit of the TREE OF LIFE. Adam and Eve's first sons were CAIN and ABEL.

Exile Two exiles are described in the Old Testament. When the NORTHERN KINGDOM of ISRAEL was defeated by ASSYRIA in 722 B.C., many of the people of those ten TRIBES OF ISRAEL were deported, or exiled, to Assyria. They never returned to ISRAEL, and for the most part they were assimilated into other cultures (2 Kings 17). These are the LOST TRIBES OF ISRAEL. Those who were not exiled intermarried with the nations around them, and their descendants became the SAMARITANS of the New Testament period.

More than 100 years after the fall of the northern kingdom, King NEBUCHADNEZZAR of BABYLON took some captives (including DANIEL) from the SOUTHERN KINGDOM of JUDAH (Daniel 1). This first invasion took place in 605

B.C., and the Kingdom of Judah was finally defeated in 586 B.C., when JERUSALEM and the TEMPLE were destroyed by the Babylonians (2 Kings 25). Many of the surviving residents of Jerusalem were taken to Babylon as captives. This is called the Exile, the Captivity, or the Babylonian captivity. PSALM 137 begins, "By the rivers of Babylon, there we sat down, yea, we wept when we remembered ZION." The stories in the book of DANIEL take place in Babylon during the Exile.

ZERUBBABEL led a group of JEWS back to Jerusalem in 538 B.C. (Ezra 1–6). They reconstructed the temple, though not to the same grandeur as SOLOMON's temple had been. This return to Jerusalem marked the end of the Exile, but some JEWS remained in Babylon and PERSIA. EZRA returned to Jerusalem about eighty years later (Ezra 7–10) in 458 B.C., and NEHEMIAH rebuilt the walls of Jerusalem in 445 B.C. ESTHER was part of the post-Exilic Jewish community still in Persia.

ISRAEL AND JUDAH IN EXILE The northern kingdom of Israel was taken captive by the Assyrians. Babylon later conquered Assyria and became the new world power. The Babylonian army marched into Jerusalem, burned the temple, tore down the city's massive walls, and carried the people of Judah off into captivity.

Exodus, the The Exodus is the mass departure of the ISRAELITES from EGYPT, as related in the book of EXODUS. The Israelites had been in Egypt for 430 years, ever since JACOB and his sons moved there to be with JOSEPH (Exodus 12:40). As the years went by, the Israelites grew to be a large nation, and they were enslaved by PHARAOH. After they had been slaves for many years, the Lord appeared to MOSES in a BURNING BUSH and told him to lead his people out of Egypt and back to CANAAN—the PROMISED LAND. Moses and his brother, AARON, told Pharaoh, "LET MY PEOPLE GO," but Pharaoh refused.

The Lord then sent PLAGUES upon the land of Egypt to convince the pharaoh to cooperate. The final plague was the death of the firstborn son in each family of Egypt. The Israelites, however, followed the Lord's instructions to put the blood of a lamb or a goat on the doorposts of their houses so the Lord would pass over their houses (*see* PASSOVER). This last plague convinced Pharaoh that the Israelites should be allowed to leave. As soon as they left, however, Pharaoh changed his mind. His army pursued the Israelites, but the Egyptian army was drowned in the RED SEA.

Expulsion, the When ADAM and EVE sinned in the Garden of EDEN by eating the FORBIDDEN FRUIT from the TREE OF THE KNOWLEDGE OF GOOD AND EVIL

(*see* FALL OF MAN), God sent them out of the Garden lest they also eat the fruit of the TREE OF LIFE (Genesis 3). This is often called the Expulsion. CHERUBIM with flaming swords kept Adam and Eve from returning to the Garden.

Ezekiel A PROPHET to the JEWS during the EXILE in BABYLON. His PROPHECIES, recorded in the book of EZEKIEL, include a VISION of a valley filled with dry bones that come back to life again. It was a prophecy that the captives would one day "come back to life again" by returning to their homeland.

THE EXPULSION Adam and Eve are expelled from the Garden of Eden.

Ezra A PRIEST and SCRIBE who led a contingent of JEWS back to JERUSALEM from the EXILE in BABYLON while NEHEMIAH was governor in Jerusalem. His messages to the people of Jerusalem are contained in the book of EZRA.

fall of man (the Fall) God created ADAM and EVE as sinless beings, HOLY and happy. When the SERPENT tempted Eve and she and ADAM disobeyed God by eating the FORBIDDEN FRUIT, they became sinful and miserable (Genesis 3). This is called the fall of man, or simply the Fall. As a result of the Fall, all humans are born in a state of SIN and misery, inheriting from Adam what is called ORIGINAL SIN.

❧ John MILTON's epic poem, *PARADISE LOST*, is about the fall of man.

feet of clay In the second chapter of the book of Daniel, NEBUCHADNEZZAR has a dream about a large statue of a man. Its head is of GOLD, its chest and arms are of silver, its belly and thighs are of brass, its legs are of iron, and its feet are made of a mixture of iron and clay. A rock hurtles down the mountainside and hits the feet of the statue, crushing them and causing the entire statue to collapse. DANIEL interprets the dream for the king, telling him that the different parts of the statue represent successive world powers, beginning with Nebuchadnezzar himself (the head of gold). The feet of mixed iron and clay represent a split kingdom, some parts of which would be strong and some weak. Some bibli-

cal scholars interpret the last stage (the mixture of iron and clay) to be the breakup of the ROMAN EMPIRE, when its territory became a mixture of strong and weak nations. Others see it as interethnic marriage after Alexander the Great's conquest of the region.

❧ The expression *feet of clay* is used to describe the weak point in an otherwise strong person.

fiery furnace When SHADRACH, MESHACH, AND ABEDNEGO refused to bow down and worship King NEBUCHADNEZZAR's huge statue, they were thrown into a fiery furnace (Daniel 3). Before they were sent to the furnace, however, they assured the king that their God was capable of keeping them safe. The king ordered that the furnace be heated seven times hotter than usual, then the three men were bound and thrown in. But when Nebuchadnezzar looked in, he saw *four* men walking around in the fire, unbound and unharmed. Nebuchadnezzar said that the fourth man looked "like a son of the gods" (NIV). The king then called Shadrach, Meshach, and Abednego out of the furnace and declared that no one in the kingdom was to speak against their powerful God.

fire and brimstone The KING JAMES VERSION says "brimstone and fire from the Lord" fell from the sky when SODOM AND GOMORRAH were destroyed. The NEW INTERNATIONAL VERSION calls it "burning sulfur." *Brimstone* is another word for *sulfur*, a flammable element that occurs naturally in the vicinity of the DEAD SEA, where Sodom and Gomorrah were located. This burning sulfur may have been a natural volcanic phenomenon, or it may simply have been a miraculous act of God.

❦ A "fire and brimstone" sermon contains dire warnings about HELL.

fire from heaven When ELIJAH challenged the PROPHETS of BAAL on Mount Carmel (1 Kings 18), he told them to ask their god to send fire from heaven to light a SACRIFICE that had been prepared. When Baal failed to respond, Elijah prayed to the Lord, who sent fire from heaven that consumed not only the sacrifice, but also the stones of the ALTAR and the water that Elijah had poured over the sacrifice. Elijah then killed all the prophets of Baal.

On another occasion, Elijah called down fire from heaven on two different contingents of fifty soldiers each (2 Kings 1).

❦ The expression "fire from heaven" can be used to describe any instance in which God responds supernaturally to a BELIEVER's prayer.

Flood, the *See* NOAH.

forbidden fruit When ADAM and EVE were in the Garden of EDEN, God told them they could eat the fruit of any tree in the Garden—except the fruit from the TREE OF THE KNOWLEDGE OF GOOD AND EVIL. When the SERPENT came, he tempted Eve to eat this forbidden fruit. He told her, "Your eyes will be opened, and you will be like God, knowing good and evil" (Genesis 3:5, NIV). Eve went ahead and ate the forbidden fruit and also gave some to Adam. This is called the FALL OF MAN.

❦ *Forbidden fruit* has come to mean anything that is attractive but is not allowed.

FORBIDDEN FRUIT The serpent tempts Eve to eat the forbidden fruit.

fornication The act of sexual intercourse outside of marriage. Fornication is clearly and specifically forbidden in the Bible, both in the MOSAIC LAW (Deuteronomy 22) and in the New Testament. The GREEK word that is translated 'fornication' is also translated more broadly as 'immorality' in some contexts. Paul said in 1 CORINTHIANS 6:18 (NIV), "Flee from sexual immorality." *See also* ADULTERY.

Garden of Eden   *See* EDEN, GARDEN OF.

Gentile   Any person who is not a JEW. In the Old Testament, the ISRAELITES were commanded to treat foreigners (Gentiles) in their midst with kindness, but God also strictly forbade the worship of the gods of the nations around them. Partly to protect the Israelites from worshiping other gods, the Lord also gave strict instructions that his people were not to intermarry with the Gentiles around them.

In the New Testament, there was a dispute among the early Christians as to whether Gentiles had to become Jews first in order to become Christians. This dispute was resolved at the Council at JERUSALEM, where the conclusion was that Gentile BELIEVERS did not need to convert to JUDAISM.

Gideon   A judge and military leader in ISRAEL during the period of the JUDGES. When God told him to fight the Midianites (Judges 6–7), he wanted to confirm that he had really received a message from God. He put out a fleece (a sheepskin) overnight and prayed that the fleece would be wet with dew but that the ground around it would be dry. After this happened, he wanted further confirmation and prayed that the next night the fleece would be dry but the ground around it would be wet. When this also happened, he was convinced that God had spoken to him. He wanted to take an army of thousands, but God told him to take only 300 so he would know that the Midianites were defeated by the power of God rather than by Israel's own military might.

❧ If a person "puts out a fleece," he is looking for a sign from God to confirm his plans.

goats   Important domestic animals both in Old Testament and New Testament times. They were used to provide food and milk, skins for tents and bottles (e.g., wineskins), and wool for clothing. They were frequently used as SACRIFICES (*see* SCAPEGOAT).

Because of the goat's independent nature, biblical writers sometimes used goats to symbolize the waywardness of God's people. Jesus described the JUDGMENT DAY as a time when God will separate the SHEEP FROM THE GOATS (Matthew 25). The SHEEP, representing people who showed God's love to others, will receive an eternal reward. The goats, representing those who did not show God's love to others, will receive an eternal punishment.

gold   As in our world today, gold was a precious metal and a sign of wealth in both Old Testament and New Testament times. The instruments in the TABERNACLE and the

TEMPLE were made of gold to symbolize their purity. Gold was one of the gifts the WISE MEN brought to the infant Jesus.

GOLDEN CALF Moses finds the people worshiping a golden calf.

golden calf After the EXODUS, the people of ISRAEL went to Mount SINAI, where the Lord met with MOSES and gave him the LAW. Moses was on the mountain for forty days, so the people thought he had died. They asked AARON to make a god for them, so he made a golden calf. The people said, "O Israel, this is the god that brought you out of EGYPT" (Exodus 32:4, TLB), and then they worshiped the golden calf.

When Moses came down from the mountain, he was so angry he threw down and broke the stone tablets on which God had inscribed the TEN COMMANDMENTS. Moses then ground up the golden calf and made the people drink it. He instructed the LEVITES to go among the people and kill many of them because of their SIN.

Goliath A PHILISTINE giant who was over nine feet tall (1 Samuel 17). Goliath had been taunting the army of ISRAEL for forty days, challenging their best warrior to fight him one on one. None of the ISRAELITES was willing to take the challenge. When young DAVID heard about it, he declared that God would give him the power to defeat Goliath. David picked up five smooth stones and killed Goliath with his sling. Then, using Goliath's

GOLIATH David used the giant Goliath's own sword to cut off his head.

own sword, he cut off the giant's head. At this, the Israelite army routed the Philistine army.

❧ A "David and Goliath" contest is any situation in which the smaller or weaker opponent beats a vastly superior opponent.

Gomer A prostitute who became the wife of HOSEA the PROPHET. She continued to commit ADULTERY, but Hosea kept forgiving her and inviting her to return home. Hosea used this as an object lesson to show God's patience and FORGIVENESS. He said the ISRAELITES were like prostitutes. They kept going after foreign gods as a prostitute goes after other men. But God kept offering to forgive the people of ISRAEL and welcome them back to himself.

Hagar When SARAH was unable to conceive a child, she gave her servant Hagar to ABRAHAM as his CONCUBINE (Genesis 16). Hagar then had a son named ISHMAEL. Fifteen years later, in fulfillment of God's promise, Sarah finally had a son, ISAAC. Sarah became so jealous of Hagar and Ishmael that she forced Abraham to send them away. The Arabs regard themselves as descendants of Ishmael.

hallelujah A HEBREW word that means 'praise the Lord'. It is used frequently in the Old Testament as an expression of praise. Some English TRANSLATIONS simply use the word *hallelujah*, while others translate it 'praise the Lord'.

❧ One of the best-known pieces of SACRED MUSIC is the "HALLELUJAH CHORUS" from HANDEL's *MESSIAH*.

handwriting on the wall Several years after NEBUCHADNEZZAR's death, Belshazzar became king of BABYLON. During a huge banquet in the palace, a hand appeared and wrote words on the plaster wall (Daniel 5). Belshazzar was terrified and called for his astrologers, but none of them could read the words or tell their meaning. Then DANIEL was called, and he interpreted the words for the king. The message was that God had numbered the days of the king's reign, that God had weighed the king in the balances and found him wanting, and that his kingdom would be divided and given to the Medes and the Persians. That very night Belshazzar was killed and the PERSIANS took control of the kingdom (539 B.C.).

❧ Today the phrase "handwriting on the wall" is used to mean that the outcome to a situation is obvious, though perhaps not to the person who will be most affected by it.

Hannah A devout woman who prayed for years that God would give her a son (1 Samuel 1–2). She promised that if she had a son she would give him back to the Lord. When she finally did have a son, SAM-

UEL, she took him to the TABERNACLE as a young child to be an assistant to ELI, the HIGH PRIEST. Samuel became a great PROPHET and the last of the judges of ISRAEL during the period of the JUDGES.

Hebrews (the people) The descendants of ABRAHAM through ISAAC and JACOB—the ISRAELITES—are sometimes called Hebrews. Their ancient language, still spoken today in the state of Israel, was HEBREW. The Old Testament was written in Hebrew.

THE HANDWRITING ON THE WALL King Belshazzar is terrified as a hand appears and writes on the wall.

Hezekiah The king of JUDAH at the time that the Kingdom of ISRAEL fell to the ASSYRIANS in 722 B.C. He was a good king, and he destroyed the pagan IDOLS and ALTARS in Judah and reopened the TEMPLE in JERUSALEM (2 Kings 18–20). Once when he was deathly ill he prayed that the Lord would spare his life. Through the PROPHET ISAIAH, the Lord promised Hezekiah that he would live for fifteen more years.

high priest In the Old Testament, the descendants of AARON, the older brother of MOSES, were the PRIESTS in ISRAEL. Aaron was the first high priest, the chief among the priests. This was a position that was passed from father to son. The high priest was the one who went into the HOLY OF HOLIES on the DAY OF ATONEMENT to make a SACRIFICE for the people.

In New Testament times, the high priest was the president of the SANHEDRIN—the highest office among the priests of Israel. CAIAPHAS was the high priest during the time of Jesus' ministry. Caiaphas's father-in-law, Annas, is also called the high priest in the GOSPEL accounts. He had actually been deposed by the Romans, but he was still honored by the people as though he were high priest.

Holy Land A name often used today for the land of ISRAEL.

Holy of Holies Also called the Most Holy Place, this was the innermost room of the TABERNACLE and of the TEMPLE (Exodus 26). It was here that the presence of the Lord dwelt among the people of ISRAEL. The ARK OF THE COVENANT and the CHERUBIM were the only objects in the Holy of Holies. The cover of the ark—called the mercy seat, or atonement cover—had gold-plated cherubim attached at each end. Only the HIGH PRIEST could enter the

Holy of Holies, and even he could enter only once a year—on the DAY OF ATONEMENT.

homosexuality Sexual relations between two people of the same sex. The Bible is quite clear in condemning homosexual acts as sinful (Leviticus 20:13; Romans 1:26-27). As with all SINS, however, God loves the sinner while hating the sin.

Hosea A PROPHET in the Kingdom of ISRAEL; his PROPHECIES are recorded in the book of HOSEA. The Lord told him to marry a prostitute to show that Israel was like an unfaithful wife. Hosea's wife, GOMER, continued to commit ADULTERY, and Hosea continued to FORGIVE her and invite her to return to their home. This became an object lesson of God's patience with the people of Israel.

hyssop An aromatic shrub. In preparation for the first PASSOVER at the time of the EXODUS from EGYPT, the ISRAELITES used hyssop branches to spread blood on the doorposts of their houses. When Jesus was on the CROSS, a sponge with WINE was put on a stalk of hyssop and lifted up to him.

idol Any man-made image that is worshiped. The second of the TEN COMMANDMENTS (THOU SHALT NOT MAKE UNTO THEE ANY GRAVEN IMAGE) is very explicit that the ISRAELITES were not to make or worship idols. Nonetheless, starting with AARON'S GOLDEN CALF, the people of ISRAEL repeatedly turned to idol worship, often borrowing the gods of the nations around them.

MAKING AN IDOL Idols can be made of wood or stone.

Isaac The son who was promised to ABRAHAM and SARAH and who was born in their old age. When Isaac was just a lad, God tested Abraham's faith by telling him to SACRIFICE Isaac on an ALTAR (Genesis 22). Sorrowfully, Abraham prepared to do so. At the last moment, just before Abraham would have killed Isaac, an ANGEL stopped him and showed him a ram caught in a thicket. Abraham sacrificed the ram in place of Isaac. Many years later, Isaac and his wife, REBEKAH, had twin sons, ESAU and

JACOB. Isaac was one of the great PA-TRIARCHS of ISRAEL.

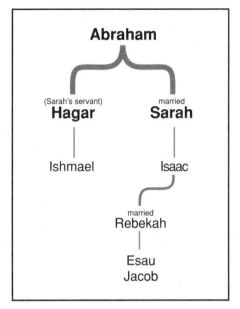

Abraham

(Sarah's servant)
Hagar

married
Sarah

Ishmael

Isaac

married
Rebekah

Esau
Jacob

ISAAC and ISHMAEL Isaac and Ishmael, Abraham's sons, were half brothers.

Isaiah One of the great PROPHETS in the Kingdom of JUDAH. Isaiah's ministry began when he saw a VISION of the Lord in the TEMPLE. He records in the sixth chapter of the book of Isaiah, "In the year that king Uzziah died, I saw also the Lord." The Lord asked, "Whom shall I send, and who will go for us?" Isaiah responded, "Here am I; send me."

Isaiah's messages include PROPHECIES of the coming MESSIAH: "Behold, a virgin shall conceive, and bear a son, and shall call his name IMMAN-UEL" (Isaiah 7:14). Also, "For UNTO US A CHILD IS BORN, unto us a son is given: and the government shall be upon

his shoulder; and his name shall be called Wonderful, Counsellor, The mighty God, The everlasting FATHER, The PRINCE OF PEACE" (Isaiah 9:6).

Another prophecy was, "He is despised, and rejected of men; a man of sorrows and acquainted with grief. . . . Surely he hath borne our griefs, and carried our sorrows. . . . He was wounded for our transgressions, he was bruised for our iniquities: the chastisement of our peace was upon him; and with his stripes we are healed. ALL WE LIKE SHEEP HAVE GONE ASTRAY; we have turned every one to his own way; and the Lord hath laid on him the iniquity of us all" (Isaiah 53:3-6). *See also MESSIAH under "The Bible and Christianity in the Fine Arts."*

Ishmael The son of ABRAHAM and his CONCUBINE, HAGAR (Genesis 16). ISAAC was born to Abraham and SARAH when Ishmael was about fifteen years old. Sarah had always been jealous of Hagar, but now that she had a son of her own she couldn't stand to have Hagar and Ishmael around. She forced Abraham to send them away. The Lord cared for Hagar and Ishmael in the WILDERNESS, and Ishmael grew up to be a great hunter.

❧ The Arabs, who regard themselves as descendants of Ishmael, are still at enmity with the JEWS, the descendants of Isaac.

Israel (the land) Ancient Israel was the region on the southeastern shore of the MEDITERRANEAN SEA. Also called PALESTINE, it included all of the territory in the modern state of Israel (including the West Bank) and part of what is now Lebanon, Syria, and Jordan. It was bounded by the Mediterranean on the west, Syria on the north, the Arabian Desert on the

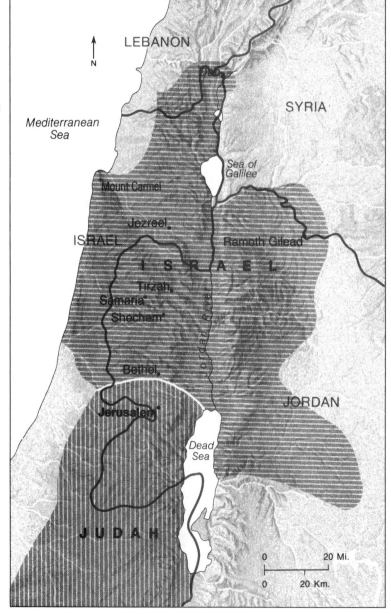

THE LAND OF ISRAEL
In Bible times, as today, Israel was at the southeastern edge of the Mediterranean Sea. All of Israel was under one government during the reigns of Saul, David, and Solomon. The kingdom was then divided into the Kingdoms of Israel and Judah. Modern country names are shown in gray.

LEBANON

N

SYRIA

Mediterranean
Sea

Sea of
Galilee

Mount Carmel

Jezreel

ISRAEL

Ramoth Gilead

I S R A E L

Tirzah

Samaria

Shechem

Bethel

JORDAN

Jerusalem

Dead
Sea

J U D A H

0   20 Mi.

0   20 Km.

East, and EGYPT on the south. It is a dry and hilly land, though it is described in the Old Testament as a LAND FLOWING WITH MILK AND HONEY. *See also* ISRAEL, ISRAELITES (the people) *and* ISRAEL, KINGDOM OF.

Israel (the man) When JACOB wrestled with God, God changed Jacob's name to Israel, which means 'he struggles with God' (Genesis 32). His sons were the PATRIARCHS of the twelve TRIBES OF ISRAEL. The name Israel was later used for the entire nation, then for the NORTHERN KINGDOM. Even later, *Israel* was used to represent the idealized fullness of God's people.

Israel, Israelites (the people) The descendants of ABRAHAM through ISAAC and JACOB (who was later called ISRAEL) are called the Israelites, or simply Israel. They are also called the CHILDREN OF ISRAEL, the CHOSEN PEOPLE, or HEBREWS. *See also* ISRAEL, KINGDOM OF.

Israel, Kingdom of After the period of the JUDGES, the people of ISRAEL demanded that they have a king, as the nations around them had. The PROPHET SAMUEL told them they needed no king but God, but the people insisted. God then told Samuel to anoint SAUL as king (1 Samuel 9). Saul ruled over the Kingdom of Israel for forty years, but he SINNED and God told him his descendants would not succeed him. Instead, God chose DAVID as king, and David's son SOLOMON after him. These three monarchs reigned for a total of 120 years. This period is often called the UNITED KINGDOM, in contrast to the DIVIDED KINGDOM that followed.

After Solomon's death in 930 B.C., his son REHOBOAM became king of Israel (1 Kings 12). The ten northern TRIBES OF ISRAEL refused to submit to his au-

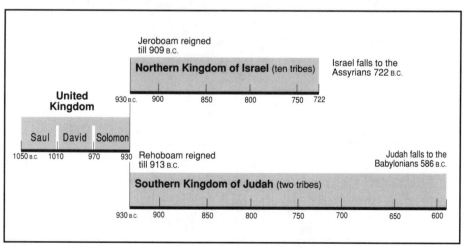

KINGDOM OF ISRAEL After Solomon's reign, the Kingdom of Israel was divided and became Israel and Judah.

thority, however, and they established their own kingdom (called the Kingdom of Israel) with JEROBOAM as king. The two southern tribes, JUDAH and BENJAMIN, became the Kingdom of JUDAH (the SOUTHERN KINGDOM), under Rehoboam. The Kingdom of Israel (also called the NORTHERN KINGDOM) survived as an independent nation until 722 B.C., when it fell to ASSYRIA.

Jacob ESAU and Jacob were the twin sons of ISAAC and REBEKAH. Once when Esau, who was the older of the two, had been out hunting and was famished, he sold his birthright to Jacob for a "mess of pottage" (stew). When Isaac was old and blind, he was ready to give Esau his blessing. While Esau, who was very hairy, was out hunting so he could prepare Isaac's favorite meal, Jacob tricked his father by wearing goatskins on his arms and neck so Isaac would think he was Esau. So Isaac blessed Jacob with the blessing of the firstborn.

Jacob had four wives and twelve sons and one daughter. His sons became the patriarchs of the TRIBES OF ISRAEL. His favorite sons were JOSEPH and BENJAMIN, from his favorite wife,

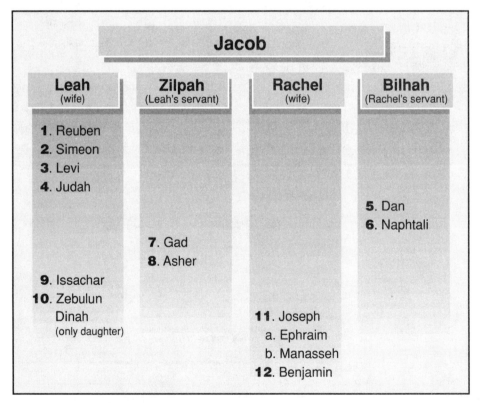

JACOB'S WIVES AND CHILDREN The numbers show birth order. Jacob's sons (and his grandsons Ephraim and Manasseh) became the patriarchs of the tribes of Israel.

RACHEL. Jacob gave Joseph a COAT OF MANY COLORS as a sign of his favoritism. Joseph's brothers were offended by Joseph, so they sold him into slavery in EGYPT and reported to their father that Joseph had been killed by a wild animal. Years later, when Joseph was prime minister of Egypt, Jacob and his other sons went to Egypt to live. The stories of Jacob are found in Genesis 25–47.

Jacob's ladder After JACOB tricked his father, ISAAC, and stole the blessing that should have gone to ESAU, Jacob left home to escape his brother's wrath (Genesis 28). While en route to live with his uncle Laban, he had a dream. He saw a ladder (stairway) stretching from HEAVEN to earth, with ANGELS going up and down. The Lord was at the top of the stairway and promised to bless Jacob and his descendants—just as he had promised to bless ABRAHAM and Isaac. Jacob named the place Bethel, which means 'House of God'.

Jehu An army commander who was made king of ISRAEL (2 Kings 9–10). He was responsible for the death of the wicked queen JEZEBEL. He tricked all the priests of BAAL into coming together in the temple of Baal—and he slaughtered them there.

🐦 Jehu was renowned for driving his CHARIOT fast, so a "Jehu" is a fast and wild driver.

Jeremiah One of the great PROPHETS in the Kingdom of JUDAH. He is known as the "weeping prophet." His PROPHECIES are recorded in the book of JEREMIAH, where he predicted the destruction of JERUSALEM. Later, looking back, he wrote LAMENTATIONS, which is a lament about the destruction of Jerusalem.

🐦 Because much of the book of Jeremiah is a prophecy of the doom of Jerusalem and of the Kingdom of Judah, the word *jeremiad* means a long lamentation or complaint.

Jericho A walled city east of JERUSALEM, near the JORDAN RIVER. It is one of the oldest cities in the world. When JOSHUA led the ISRAELITES into the PROMISED LAND, their first conquest was Jericho (*see* JERICHO, BATTLE OF). The treacherous road between Jerusalem and Jericho was the setting for Jesus' PARABLE of the GOOD SAMARITAN.

JERICHO Extensive archaeological digs have exposed the foundations of the ancient city of Jericho.

Jericho, Battle of When JOSHUA led the ISRAELITES into the PROMISED LAND, their first conquest was the walled city of JERICHO (Joshua 6). Joshua had earlier sent spies into Jericho, who had been assisted by RAHAB, a prostitute. Because of her bravery, the spies assured her that she and her family would not be killed when Jericho was attacked. Following instructions from an AN-GEL, Joshua told his army to march around the walled city of Jericho each day for six days. On the seventh day they marched around the city seven times. The Lord then caused the walls of the city to fall down, and the Israelite army went in and destroyed all the inhabitants of the city except RAHAB and her family. The Negro SPIRITUAL "JOSHUA FIT THE BATTLE OF JERICHO" is an allusion to this Old Testament event.

Jeroboam After SOLOMON's death, his son REHOBOAM succeeded him as king of ISRAEL. The people of the ten northern TRIBES rebelled against Rehoboam, however, and crowned Jeroboam as their king (1 Kings 12). Only the tribes of JUDAH and BENJAMIN remained loyal to Rehoboam. This was the start of the DIVIDED KINGDOM. Jeroboam was a wicked king who set up new centers of worship to rival JERUSALEM, and he led his people into IDOL worship.

Jerusalem The capital city of IS-RAEL from the time of King DAVID to the time of the New Testament. It is located on hills between the MEDI-TERRANEAN SEA and the JORDAN RIVER. SOLOMON built the TEMPLE in Jerusalem on the spot where ABRAHAM was thought to have taken his son ISAAC to SACRIFICE him. So Jerusalem, in addition to its political significance, was the central place of worship for the ISRAELITES. Many key events in the Bible took place in and around Jerusalem, including the CRUCIFIXION and RESURRECTION of Jesus. In A.D. 70 Jerusalem was destroyed by the Romans.

In a theological sense, Jerusalem is frequently used in the Bible as a symbol of God's JUSTICE and MERCY, just as BABYLON is often used as a symbol of human wickedness. The New Testament refers to the "NEW JERUSALEM" (Revelation 21), a heavenly and holy city.

❦ Today Jerusalem is a holy city for JEWS, Christians, and Muslims. The Temple Mount is sacred to Jews, but it has for centuries been the site of a Muslim holy place, the Dome of the Rock. The Western Wall (Wailing Wall), all that remains of HEROD's temple, is the most sacred spot of all for Jews. Jerusalem contains many spots sacred to Christians, including the Garden of GETHSEMANE, the Church of the Holy Sepulchre (an ancient church on the traditional sites of Jesus' crucifixion and resurrection), and the Garden Tomb (an alternate site of the Resurrection).

❦ Jerusalem was divided from 1948 to 1967. The eastern part of Jerusalem (the walled "old city") was controlled by the Kingdom of Jordan, and the western part of the city (the "new city") was controlled by the state of Israel. Following the Six-Day War of 1967, the two parts of the city were united under the control of Israel. Jerusalem is still a source of great conflict and tension between Israelis and Arabs. Jerusalem is the capital of modern Israel, but for political reasons the United States and many other countries do not recognize it as the capital.

Jews The descendants of ABRAHAM through ISAAC and JACOB. More specifically, the Jews are the descendants from the tribes of JUDAH and BENJAMIN, which comprised the Kingdom of JUDAH (the word *Jew* is derived from the name *Judah*). Jesus and his DISCIPLES were Jews, as were the APOSTLE PAUL and most of the earliest Christians.

Jews today fall into four main categories: Orthodox, Conservative, Reform, and those who characterize themselves as cultural Jews but without religious affiliation.

❦ Unfortunately, although the Christian church has its roots in JUDAISM, Jews have suffered greatly at the hands of Christians since the time of Christ. Jews have been persecuted and killed in the "Christian" nations of Europe for centuries, the most atrocious example of which was the Holocaust during World War II.

JERUSALEM This view of Jerusalem is from the Mount of Olives. The Dome of the Rock is situated where the temple once stood.

Jezebel Daughter of a Phoenician king and wife of King AHAB of ISRAEL, Jezebel ranks as the most wicked woman mentioned in the Bible (1 Kings 16–22). A wicked woman in the book of REVELATION is also called Jezebel—an allusion to the Jezebel of the Old Testament. Jezebel promoted the worship of BAAL and persecuted the PROPHETS of God. During her reign ELIJAH defeated the prophets of Baal by calling down FIRE FROM HEAVEN. At JEHU's instigation, Jezebel was thrown out a window and trampled to death by horses (2 Kings 9). Then dogs ate her body, as had been PROPHESIED by Elijah.

THE DEATH OF JEZEBEL Jezebel is thrown out the window, where horses trampled her to death.

Joab The general of King DAVID's army, he was a brilliant military leader. He murdered Abner, King SAUL's general, and later he murdered King David's son ABSALOM when Absalom led a revolt against David (2 Samuel 18).

Joash One of the kings of the Kingdom of JUDAH (2 Kings 11–12). His father died when Joash was an infant, and his wicked grandmother tried to kill all of the royal line. But Joash was saved by a loyal aunt and hidden in the TEMPLE for six years. He was crowned king when he was seven years old. He had a long and good reign, during which he renovated the temple, but he allowed the reintroduction of pagan practices. He sent the temple treasures to Syria as a bribe to keep Syria from invading Judah.

Job (pronounced *Jōb*) A righteous and wealthy man who lost all his possessions, his children, and his own health—but refused to curse God. According to the story in the book of JOB, God pointed to Job as a particularly good and God-fearing man. SATAN responded that Job would curse God if Job's wealth were taken away. God told Satan he could attack Job's wealth and his family, but he could not kill Job himself. So Satan arranged for Job's wealth to be destroyed and for his ten children to be killed. But Job still said, "Blessed be the name of the Lord."

When Satan then caused Job to break out with boils all over his body, his wife told him to "curse God and die" (Job 2:9), and three of Job's friends (*see* JOB'S COMFORTERS) told him that his misfortunes were the result of SIN in his life. When Job stayed true to God through it all, God rewarded him with ten more children, and twice as much wealth as he had had before.

❦ The "patience of Job" is proverbial (it is even mentioned as a proverb in James 5:11) because Job trusted God despite all the tragedy in his life.

JOB AND HIS COMFORTERS "The three men refused to reply further to Job because he kept insisting on his innocence" (Job 32:1, TLB).

Job's comforters The book of JOB (*Jōb*) tells the story of JOB, a righteous man who was tormented by SATAN. Three of Job's friends came to comfort him in his distress, but they told him that his problems were the result of SIN in his life.

❦ People may be called "Job's comforters" if they purport to give comfort but really bring blame upon the person they are "comforting."

Jonah A PROPHET to the Kingdom of ISRAEL who was also sent to preach to the people of Nineveh, the capital of ASSYRIA. Jonah was afraid to go to Nineveh and tried to run away, but God intercepted him (*see* JONAH AND THE WHALE) and sent him to Nineveh anyway. Jonah's message in Nineveh was that God would destroy the city if the people did not repent from their wicked ways. The people of Nineveh responded to Jonah's message and did repent of their SINS, so God relented and did not destroy the city. Jonah was angry that God did not destroy Nineveh, but God showed Jonah that he felt compassion for the many inhabitants of Nineveh.

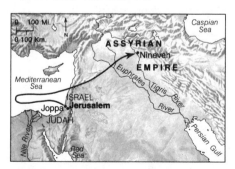

JONAH'S ROUNDABOUT JOURNEY God told Jonah to go to Nineveh, the capital of the Assyrian empire. Many of Jonah's countrymen had experienced the atrocities of these fierce people. The last place Jonah wanted to go on a missionary journey was Nineveh! So he went in the opposite direction. He boarded a ship in Joppa that was headed for Tarshish. But Jonah could not run from God.

Jonah and the whale   When JONAH was sent to preach in Nineveh, the heathen capital of ASSYRIA, he rebelled and tried to run away from God. He boarded a ship on the MEDITERRANEAN SEA and sailed westward. A great storm arose, and Jonah realized that the storm had been sent by God because of his SIN, so he convinced the sailors the storm would abate only if they threw him overboard. They did so and the storm stopped, and Jonah was swallowed by "a great fish." He was in the fish's belly for three days, which gave him an opportunity to reflect on his situation and to repent. The fish then spit Jonah out onto the land, and Jonah went and preached in Nineveh as he had been directed. His story is told in the book of JONAH.

🦃 Biblical critics have said this story could never have happened because a person could not live to tell about it if he were swallowed by a whale. In 1891, James Bartley, a sailor on a whaling ship, was swept overboard and was swallowed by a sperm whale. The whale was subsequently harpooned and killed. As the whale was being butchered the next day, Bartley's fellow whalers found him in the whale's stomach and rescued him.

Jonathan   The son of King SAUL, and DAVID's close friend (1 Samuel 18). Saul was very jealous of David, and on several occasions Jonathan protected David from Saul. Jonathan was a brave soldier, but he and Saul died in a battle with the PHILISTINES. David was then crowned king of ISRAEL.

Jordan River   The primary river that runs through the land of ISRAEL. Its headwaters are on Mount Hermon, from which it flows into the Sea of GALILEE, then south to the DEAD SEA, where it ends. Although it is only about 70 miles long, it drops more than 1,500 feet during its brief course. Most of the river is below sea level.

The Jordan River plays a significant role in both Old Testament and New Testament history. When JOSHUA led the ISRAELITES into the PROMISED LAND, they had to cross the Jordan River. The Lord performed a miracle for them, however, and the water of the river was held back so they could cross on dry land. JOHN THE BAPTIST BAPTIZED Jesus in the Jordan River.

🦃 Crossing the Jordan River has frequently been used as a metaphor for dying, as in the SPIRITUALS "GONNA LAY

JORDAN RIVER This is a typical view along the Jordan River, which now separates Israel and Jordan.

Down My Burden" and "Michael, Row the Boat Ashore."

Joseph Joseph and BENJAMIN were the sons of JACOB and RACHEL (Genesis 37–50). Jacob gave Joseph a COAT OF MANY COLORS, which made Joseph's brothers jealous. His brothers wanted to kill him, but JUDAH persuaded the others not to do it. Instead, they sold Joseph as a slave.

Joseph was taken as a slave to EGYPT, where he became chief steward in the household of Potiphar. POTIPHAR'S WIFE tried to seduce him, then she accused him of raping her when he would not yield to her seduction. He was thrown into prison, where he interpreted dreams for several of PHARAOH's staff who were also in prison. Joseph was released from prison when Pharaoh needed someone to interpret a dream. Joseph told him the dream meant that there would be seven years of plenty followed by seven years of famine. He recommended that Pharaoh institute a plan of food storage during the years of good harvests in preparation for the years of famine. Joseph was put in charge of this program and was second only to Pharaoh in power.

The famine affected the land of CANAAN also, so Jacob sent his ten older sons to Egypt to buy grain. Joseph recognized his brothers, but they did not recognize him. When Joseph found that they were sorry for what they had done to their brother, he identified himself. Jacob and his sons and their families all moved to Egypt, where their descendants lived for 430 years until the time of the EXODUS.

Joshua MOSES' assistant, who succeeded him as the leader of the ISRAELITES. Joshua's story is told in the books of EXODUS, NUMBERS, and JOSHUA. He was both a military leader and a spiritual leader. When it was time for Joshua to lead the people into the PROMISED LAND, the Lord held back the water of the JORDAN RIVER so the entire nation could cross over on dry ground. Joshua's first victory in CANAAN was in the Battle of JERICHO, and he led the people of ISRAEL in a systematic conquest of the land. When he was an old man he again challenged the people to follow the Lord. He said to all the people, "Choose for yourselves this day whom you will serve. . . . But as for me and my household, we will serve the Lord" (Joshua 24:15, NIV). *See also* CALEB.

Josiah Became king of JUDAH at the age of eight (2 Kings 22–23). The people of Judah had drifted away from worshiping the Lord and no longer remembered the MOSAIC LAW. When a SCROLL containing the LAW was found in the TEMPLE, Josiah led the nation into REPENTANCE and then back into vibrant WORSHIP of the

Lord. Because of this, the Lord promised Josiah he would not destroy Judah until after Josiah's death. It was twenty-three years after his death that the BABYLONIANS destroyed JERUSALEM (586 B.C.) and took the people to Babylon as captives.

Judah One of JACOB's sons (Genesis 38) and the PATRIARCH of the tribe of JUDAH. King DAVID was a descendant of Judah, as was Jesus.

Judah, Kingdom of After SOLOMON's death in 930 B.C., his son REHOBOAM became king of ISRAEL. The ten northern TRIBES OF ISRAEL refused to submit to his authority, however, and they established their own kingdom (called the Kingdom of Israel) with JEROBOAM as king. The two southern tribes, JUDAH and BENJAMIN, became the Kingdom of Judah (1 Kings 12), with JERUSALEM as its capital. The Kingdoms of Judah and

Israel coexisted side by side until Israel (the NORTHERN KINGDOM) fell to AsSYRIA in 722 B.C. Judah (the SOUTHERN KINGDOM) survived as an independent nation until it fell to the BABYLONIANS in 586 B.C. (2 Kings 25). *See also* IsRAEL, KINGDOM OF *and* DIVIDED KINGDOM.

Judah, tribe of The descendants of JACOB's son JUDAH became the tribe of Judah. DAVID and his royal descendants were from the tribe of Judah. Judah and BENJAMIN were the two TRIBES that remained loyal to SOLOMON's son REHOBOAM, forming the Kingdom of JUDAH. Jesus was a descendant of Judah and of David. The English word *Jew* is derived from *Judah*.

Judaism The religion of the JEWS, particularly as it developed from the time of the EXILE. Judaism came to include a complex system of regulations to help the Jews keep the 613

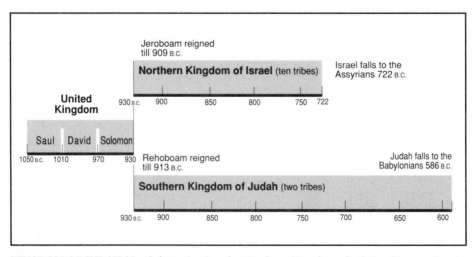

KINGDOM OF JUDAH After Solomon's reign, the Kingdom of Israel was divided and became Israel and Judah.

commandments in the PENTATEUCH. These additional regulations, codified in the Talmud, "make a hedge about the TORAH." If the people obeyed all the regulations, they would automatically be obeying the laws in the Torah.

judges, period of the After the death of MOSES, JOSHUA led the ISRAELITES into the PROMISED LAND. Joshua was the military and religious leader of the nation during the conquest of CANAAN. After his death, there was a period of about 200–325 years (there are varying scholarly opinions) called the period of the judges. There was no central government, and it was a time of anarchy in ISRAEL, for "every man did that which was right in his own eyes" (Judges 21:25). The neighboring nations, particularly the PHILISTINES, raided Israelite cities and generally made life difficult for Israel. Occasional leaders, called judges, arose to lead the people against their enemies. Several of these judges were DEBORAH, GIDEON, and SAMSON, whose stories are told in the book of JUDGES.

The period of the judges came to an end when the people told SAMUEL they wanted a king—just like the nations around them (1 Samuel 8). Samuel knew this was a mistake, but the Lord let the people have their way and instructed Samuel to anoint SAUL to be the first king of Israel.

land flowing with milk and honey This is a description of CANAAN, the PROMISED LAND. It means that the land was fruitful and pleasant. When JOSHUA and CALEB and the other spies returned from spying out the land after the EXODUS, they reported, "It is indeed a magnificent country—a land 'flowing with milk and honey'" (Numbers 13:27, TLB).

❦ Visitors to Israel today wonder at this description of a lush and fruitful land, because the land now is arid and rocky. The land has never had a very moderate climate, but evidently there were substantial areas of forest at the time of the Exodus. The land has since been deforested, and tremendous amounts of erosion have washed away much of the topsoil.

Law, the In the Bible, the term *the Law* refers to the Mosaic law or to the Books of Law in their entirety (*see* TORAH *and* LAW, BOOKS OF *under "The Bible"*). For a more complete explanation of the Law, see MOSAIC LAW.

After Jesus gave the two greatest commandments (THOU SHALT LOVE THE LORD THY GOD WITH ALL THY HEART ... and LOVE THY NEIGHBOR AS THYSELF), he said, "On these two commandments hang all the Law and the Prophets" (Matthew 22:40). By "all the Law" he meant the Books of Law, and "the

Prophets" meant the books of history and the Books of PROPHECY.

Leah   Leah and her sister, RACHEL, were both wives of JACOB (Genesis 29–30). Jacob worked for seven years to earn the right to marry Rachel, but her father tricked Jacob and gave him Leah instead. Jacob was then allowed to marry Rachel also by promising to work another seven years! Leah bore six of Jacob's twelve sons, including JUDAH and LEVI.

leaven   Another name for yeast, the agent that causes bread to rise. In the Bible, leaven was often used as a metaphor for evil and its corrupting power. *See also* UNLEAVENED BREAD.

leper, leprosy   An infectious disease that was dreaded in Bible times because there was no cure for it. The disease deadens nerve endings, so a leper (a person with leprosy) could cut or burn himself without even realizing it. Lepers were quarantined outside the camp or village and became social outcasts. Jesus broke the social custom by talking to and even touching lepers as he healed them.

❦ Leprosy is now called Hansen's disease, and it still afflicts millions of people in parts of Africa, India, and South America. It is unclear, however, whether this is the same "leprosy" mentioned so frequently in the Bible.

Levi   One of JACOB's sons and the PATRIARCH of the tribe of LEVI. His descendants were called LEVITES, and they became PRIESTS and TEMPLE workers. MOSES and AARON and MIRIAM were descendants of Levi.

leviathan   There is a lengthy description of the leviathan, a very fierce sea creature, in Job 41. It may have been a crocodile. God was rebuking JOB by showing his great power in creating such an awesome animal. *See also* BEHEMOTH.

LEVIATHAN "In that day the Lord will take his terrible, swift sword and punish leviathan . . . the dragon of the sea" (Isaiah 27:1, TLB).

Levites   The members of the TRIBE of Levi (the descendants of LEVI, one of the sons of JACOB) were called the Levites. They were given special responsibility for the care of the TABERNACLE and then the TEMPLE. The

Levites did not receive any land of their own when the ISRAELITES entered the PROMISED LAND. Instead, the other tribes were to support the Levites through their TITHES. The descendants of AARON, who constituted one branch of the Levites, were the PRIESTS.

In Jesus' PARABLE of the GOOD SAMARITAN, the two men who passed by without helping the man who had been robbed and beaten were a priest and a Levite.

lost tribes of Israel When the NORTHERN KINGDOM of ISRAEL was defeated by the ASSYRIANS in 722 B.C., many of the people of those ten TRIBES OF ISRAEL were deported to Assyria (*see* EXILE). They never returned to their own land (2 Kings 17). They were assimilated into the cultures of the people around them and ceased to exist as a distinct people. Those who were not taken into exile in Assyria also intermarried with the nations around them, and they lost their distinctives as ISRAELITES. Their descendants became the SAMARITANS of the New Testament period. They too eventually lost their distinctiveness and nearly ceased to exist as a separate people. There is a very small community of Samaritans, however, still living in Israel.

The ten northern tribes are the lost tribes of Israel. From the fall of the Kingdom of Israel onward (including the entire New Testament period), "the JEWS" are primarily members of the tribes of JUDAH or BENJAMIN, the two tribes that made up the Kingdom of JUDAH.

❧ There has been much speculation as to what happened to the lost tribes of Israel, including fanciful conclusions that they migrated to the British Isles or to America.

Lot ABRAHAM's nephew, who traveled with Abraham from Ur to CANAAN. When the land became too crowded for both of them and their vast flocks, Abraham allowed Lot to choose which part of the land he wanted for himself, and Abraham took the other portion. Lot moved toward SODOM AND GOMORRAH, where he barely escaped with his life when the cities were destroyed (Genesis 18–19). LOT'S WIFE turned into a pillar of salt when she looked back as they fled from the fiery destruction of the cities.

Lot's wife Her name is not given in the Bible, but she is well known because of the way she died. When she and her family were fleeing from the destruction of SODOM AND GOMORRAH, the ANGEL who was leading them told them not to look back. LOT's wife disobeyed, and she was turned into a pillar of salt (Genesis 19).

manna When the ISRAELITES were in the WILDERNESS after the EXODUS, they soon ran out of food. God miraculously provided for them by sending manna, a white substance that fell on the ground each morning (Exodus 16). The people gathered it and ate it. God provided food for them in this way each day (except on the SABBATH) for forty years. We're not sure exactly what it was, but neither did the Israelites know what it was. They called it *manna*, which means 'what is it?'.

Manna provided spiritual lessons as well as physical sustenance. When MOSES gave his farewell address to the people before he died, he reminded them that God had provided manna for them, "to teach you that man does not live on bread alone but on every word that comes from the mouth of the Lord" (Deuteronomy 8:3, NIV). When Jesus was tempted by SATAN in the wilderness, he quoted this passage of SCRIPTURE.

mark of Cain When CAIN murdered ABEL and was banished from his land and from God, he was fearful that he himself would be killed. To protect him, God put a mark upon Cain to identify him, so others would not harm him (Genesis 4:15).

❦ The phrase is sometimes used today to suggest that a person has a physical characteristic that identifies him as a criminal.

Mediterranean Sea The great sea between Europe and Africa and Asia. Most of the events in the Bible take place in the lands immediately surrounding the eastern end of the Mediterranean Sea. The story of JONAH AND THE WHALE takes place in the Mediterranean Sea, and the APOSTLE PAUL traveled the Mediterranean on each of his MISSIONARY JOURNEYS. The land of ISRAEL is at the southeastern end of the Mediterranean Sea.

Melchizedek He was the king of Salem (probably JERUSALEM) and the PRIEST of "God Most High" when ABRAM moved to CANAAN. Abram gave Melchizedek one-tenth of the spoils he had gotten in a battle (Genesis 14). This is all the information the Bible gives us about Melchizedek, but in Psalm 110 and the book of HEBREWS he is seen as superior to all subsequent priests of ISRAEL. He is an Old Testament person who points the way to Christ.

Methuselah The grandfather of NOAH, he is the oldest person listed in the Bible. He lived to the age of 969 years. According to the data in the GENEALOGY in Genesis 5, it appears that Methuselah died in the year of the FLOOD.

Miriam The sister of MOSES and AARON. When the infant Moses was found by the PHARAOH's daughter, big sister Miriam offered to find a HEBREW woman (the baby's own mother!) to care for him (*see* MOSES IN THE BULRUSHES). With her brothers,

Miriam was a leader of the people through the entire event of the Exodus and the years the ISRAELITES were in the WILDERNESS (Exodus and NUMBERS). After the parting of the RED SEA, Miriam led all the women of Israel in singing and dancing their praise to the Lord. Later, Miriam and Aaron were jealous of Moses' unique position of leadership, and God punished Miriam by inflicting her with LEPROSY for seven days.

Mosaic law After the Exodus, when the ISRAELITES left EGYPT, the Lord gave MOSES the TEN COMMANDMENTS and numerous other laws (Exodus 19–40). This entire system of laws, called the Mosaic law or simply the LAW, provided the framework for the Israelites' relationships with God, with one another, and with the nations around them. It includes the laws regarding the SACRIFICES, by which the people of Israel could WORSHIP God and make ATONEMENT for their SINS.

The Mosaic law is a central theme of the BOOKS OF MOSES, or TORAH. After the EXILE the JEWS developed the Talmud, a complex system of additional laws to "build a hedge about the Torah." A person could be certain of keeping the Torah by strictly observing all these additional regulations.

Christian teaching, particularly as developed by the APOSTLE PAUL, shows that we can never keep the Law to God's satisfaction. Instead of the sacrifices required under the Mosaic law, Jesus' death serves as the ultimate sacrifice to provide atonement for our sins once and for all.

❦ Many people are confused as to why Christians have traditionally kept some but not all of the Old Testament laws or regulations. The distinction is between the *ceremonial law,* which no longer applies to Christians under the NEW COVENANT, and the *moral law* (e.g., the Ten Commandments), which is still God's standard for right living.

Moses One of the greatest leaders in the history of ISRAEL. His story is told in the books of Exodus and NUMBERS. His parents were slaves in EGYPT when he was born, but through unusual circumstances (*see* MOSES IN THE BULRUSHES) he grew up in the household of PHARAOH. When he became an adult he recognized his heritage and killed an Egyptian while trying to help a fellow ISRAELITE. He fled to Midian (in present-day Saudi Arabia), where he was a SHEPHERD for forty years. There he met the Lord at the BURNING BUSH. The Lord told him to tell Pharaoh, "LET MY PEOPLE GO."

Moses and his brother, AARON, asked Pharaoh to let the Israelites leave Egypt. Pharaoh refused, and the

Lord sent a series of PLAGUES upon the land of Egypt. Finally, after the death of the oldest son in each family of Egypt, Moses was able to lead the people out of Egypt (*see* EXODUS, THE). Moses led the people all during the forty years they "wandered" in the WILDERNESS. During that time Moses received the TEN COMMANDMENTS and the rest of the LAW (*see* MOSAIC LAW) from the Lord at Mount SINAI.

Moses wrote the BOOKS OF MOSES, the first five books of the Old Testament. He is revered to this day as the great lawgiver for ISRAEL.

MOSES Moses comes down from Mount Sinai with the Ten Commandments.

Moses in the bulrushes MOSES was born in EGYPT at a time when the HEBREWS (the descendants of JACOB's twelve sons) had become a large na-

tion and were a threat to the Egyptians. To keep the Hebrews from becoming an even greater threat, the PHARAOH decreed that all boys born to Hebrew women were to be thrown into the NILE RIVER and drowned (Exodus 1). Moses' parents did not obey this command, but as their infant grew they were fearful he would be found. They prayed, and then consigned their baby to God's protection. They made a little basket of rushes and waterproofed it with tar. Then they put Moses in the basket and set the basket adrift on the river, while his older sister, MIRIAM, hid in the bulrushes to see what would happen.

One of the daughters of the Pharaoh came to the river to bathe and saw the little basket. When she saw the baby, she decided to keep him and raise him as her own son. Miriam stepped out and offered to find a Hebrew nurse for the baby—and ran home to get her own mother! As a result, Moses spent his first several years with his own parents, then lived in the royal household as a son of the princess.

Mount Sinai *See* SINAI, MOUNT.

Naomi RUTH's mother-in-law. Naomi was from ISRAEL, but she and her husband moved to Moab (east of the DEAD SEA) to escape a famine in the land of ISRAEL. Her two sons married women from Moab. When her husband and her sons died, she returned to ISRAEL. She urged her Moabite daughters-in-law, Ruth and Orpah, to stay in Moab, but Ruth insisted on staying with Naomi. Ruth said, "WHITHER THOU GOEST, I WILL GO; . . . thy people shall be my people, and thy God my God" (Ruth 1:16).

Nazirite A person specially dedicated by a vow to service to God, usually for a specified period of time. Nazirites could not drink wine or other intoxicating drinks, they could not cut their hair, and they were not allowed to touch dead bodies (Numbers 6). SAMSON was a Nazirite for life, and JOHN THE BAPTIST is thought to have been one. *Nazirite* should not be confused with *Nazarene*, which means simply a native of NAZARETH. Jesus was a Nazarene (he grew up in Nazareth), but he was not a Nazirite.

Nebuchadnezzar The king of BABYLON who defeated the Kingdom of JUDAH in 586 B.C. (2 Kings 24–25). He took many captives from Judah to Babylon (*see* EXILE), both before and after the final defeat of Judah. DANIEL was among an earlier group of captives. When Nebuchadnezzar had a dream about a statue with FEET OF CLAY, Daniel interpreted it for him. Nebuchadnezzar later threw Daniel's friends SHADRACH, MESHACH, AND ABEDNEGO into the FIERY FURNACE when they refused to bow down before a great statue he had constructed.

Later in life he was insane for seven years and lived "with the beasts of the field." This was a judgment of God on his pride, but he later regained his throne.

❦ The Hanging Gardens of Babylon, constructed by Nebuchadnezzar, were one of the Seven Wonders of the Ancient World.

❦ In the 1980s, Saddam Hussein, president of Iraq (the land that was once Babylon), rebuilt portions of the ancient city of Babylon. He styled himself as a modern-day Nebuchadnezzar.

Nehemiah A PROPHET and political leader in JERUSALEM after the EXILE; his story is told in the book of NEHEMIAH. He was a cupbearer to King Artaxerxes of PERSIA, but he went to Jerusalem to lead the people there in rebuilding their city wall. After the wall had been built, Nehemiah and EZRA led the people into a renewed relationship with God.

Nile River The longest river in the world, it flows north through EGYPT and empties into the MEDITERRANEAN SEA. In the KING JAMES VERSION it is called the River of Egypt. The Nile River played an important part in biblical history. It has always provided water for Egypt, and the annual flooding irrigates the fields. If there was a famine in the land of CANAAN, there was usually food available in Egypt (*see* JOSEPH). In the story of Moses and the bulrushes (Exodus 2), the baby's basket was placed in the Nile River.

Noah The story of Noah and the ark is one of the best-known stories in the Bible (Genesis 6–9). Noah lived at a time when people had become so wicked that God decided to destroy all mankind with a great flood. The only exception was Noah and his family, for "Noah found grace in the eyes of the Lord" (Genesis 6:8). God told Noah to build a great boat—an ark—450 feet long and 75 feet wide. Then he was to put a male and female of every kind of animal on the ark. When the ark was finished and the animals and Noah and his family were all on board, the Lord shut the door and the rain started. It rained for forty days and forty nights, and the floods covered all the land and drowned all the people. Eventually the water began to recede, and the ark came to rest on the mountains of Ararat (possibly in present-day Turkey). God promised never again to destroy all people with a flood, and he gave the rainbow as a sign of his covenant.

Noah lived in the time before recorded history. Since he and his family were the only survivors of the Flood, all people on earth are his descendants.

☙ Other ancient civilizations (e.g., the Sumerians and Babylonians) had similar flood stories. Some scholars have taken this as evidence that the Genesis story was simply borrowed from another culture. Others see it as corroboration that indeed all peoples on earth were descendants of Noah and his sons; as a result, many ancient people groups would have their own oral history of the great Flood their ancestors had survived.

NOAH Noah and his family build the ark.

northern kingdom When the Kingdom of ISRAEL split apart after SOLOMON's death (1 Kings 12), the ten northern TRIBES were still called the Kingdom of Israel. It is sometimes called the northern kingdom, in contrast to the SOUTHERN KINGDOM of JUDAH.

Palestine The entire region of ISRAEL, located between the MEDITERRANEAN SEA and the JORDAN RIVER, is called Palestine. It includes the regions that in New Testament times were called GALILEE, SAMARIA, and JUDEA. Today it is often called the HOLY LAND.

❦ Many Arabs from Palestine were made homeless when the modern state of Israel was formed in 1948. More than forty years later, there are still thousands of Palestinians living in refugee camps in Lebanon and Jordan. The avowed aim of the Palestine Liberation Organization and other Arab groups is to drive the JEWS out of Palestine altogether, or at least out of the West Bank (the region between JERUSALEM and the Jordan River).

Passover One of the most important festivals of the year for the people of ISRAEL, both in Old Testament and New Testament times. The first Passover took place at the time of the EXODUS, when the people of ISRAEL were finally able to leave EGYPT after their long captivity there

(Exodus 11–12). MOSES and AARON had said to PHARAOH, "LET MY PEOPLE GO." Pharaoh had refused, despite the nine PLAGUES that had afflicted the Egyptians. The Lord then told Moses he would send a final plague to convince Pharaoh. The Lord would go through the land and kill the oldest son in each family of Egypt. The ISRAELITES were to kill lambs and paint blood from the lambs on the door frames and above the doors of their houses. When the Lord saw the blood, he "passed over" those houses. That very night, while all Egypt was in mourning, the Pharaoh finally told the Israelites to leave.

The Lord commanded Moses and the people to celebrate the Passover each year as a reminder of the way the Lord had rescued them. Immediately after Passover came a week-long celebration of the Feast of Unleavened Bread (because the people ate UNLEAVENED BREAD on the night before the Exodus). The Lord gave very specific instructions as to how the Passover and the Feast of Unleavened Bread were to be celebrated. These annual celebrations would remind the people of the Lord's protection and PROVIDENCE for them. Through the rest of the Bible, the Israelites did observe these great feasts.

Jesus and his DISCIPLES were celebrating the Passover when they ate the

LAST SUPPER together. The next day Jesus was CRUCIFIED. In 1 Corinthians 5:7, the APOSTLE PAUL refers to Jesus as our Passover Lamb. He meant that Jesus was the perfect SACRIFICE to save us from the wrath of God, just as the Passover lambs were sacrificed to save the oldest sons of the Israelite families from death.

❦ The Passover is still celebrated today by JEWS around the world. It occurs in the spring, about the same time as EASTER.

patriarchs The patriarchs ('fathers') of ISRAEL were ABRAHAM, ISAAC, JACOB, and Jacob's twelve sons, the progenitors of the twelve TRIBES OF ISRAEL.

Persia, Persians Persia was an ancient empire that flourished in the region of present-day Iran from the sixth to the fourth centuries B.C. The Persians defeated the BABYLONIANS in 539 B.C., during the time that the people of the Kingdom of JUDAH were in EXILE in Babylon. The events in the first five chapters of the book of DANIEL took place during the rule of the Babylonian kings NEBUCHADNEZZAR and Belshazzar. After the HANDWRITING ON THE WALL, Belshazzar was killed by the Persians, and the rest of the events in the book of Daniel took place under the reigns of the Persian kings Darius (who had DANIEL thrown into the lions' den) and Cyrus. Secular history tells us that Persia was eventually defeated by Alexander the Great.

Pharaoh The ancient kings of EGYPT were known as pharaohs. Several pharaohs are mentioned in the Old Testament, the most infamous being the pharaoh at the time of the EXODUS (Exodus 1–14). The HEBREWS were slaves in Egypt, and MOSES and AARON told Pharaoh, "LET MY PEOPLE GO." Pharaoh refused to consider their request, so the Lord sent ten PLAGUES upon the Egyptians. Pharaoh finally consented to let the Hebrews leave after the last plague, when the Lord killed the firstborn son and firstborn of the livestock in every Egyptian household. Even then, Pharaoh retracted his permission and chased after the Hebrews with a great army. The Lord miraculously parted the waters of the RED SEA, and Moses led the people across on dry land. Pharaoh and his army chased them, but the waters engulfed them and they all drowned.

Philistines Perennial enemies of the ISRAELITES during the period of the JUDGES and during the reigns of SAUL and DAVID. The Philistines were a heathen nation, and they frequently influenced the Israelites to worship heathen gods.

❦ Today the term *philistine* means uncouth, or more interested in material goods than in intellectual or spiritual pursuits.

pillar of cloud, pillar of fire When the HEBREW people left EGYPT (*see* EXODUS, THE), the Lord caused a great cloud—the text calls it a pillar of cloud—to come between them and the Egyptian army that was pursuing them. This afforded them protection before the Lord caused the parting of the RED SEA (Exodus 14). During the forty years that the Hebrews were in the WILDERNESS, the Lord led and protected them by means of the cloud (Numbers 9). During the day it rested over the tent of meeting (the SACRED tent where MOSES met with the Lord). At night the cloud appeared to be of fire. When the pillar of cloud moved, the people also moved. When it stayed, they stayed.

The Ten Plagues of Egypt

The Ten Plagues of Egypt
1. The water of the Nile River was turned to blood.
2. Frogs covered the entire land.
3. There were gnats everywhere.
4. There were flies everywhere.
5. All the livestock died of a disease.
6. Boils broke out on all the people and animals.
7. A hailstorm ravaged the land.
8. Clouds of locusts covered the land.
9. Darkness covered the land for three days.
10. The firstborn son and firstborn of the livestock in every household in Egypt were killed.

pillar of salt *See* LOT *and* LOT'S WIFE.

plagues of Egypt When MOSES and AARON told the PHARAOH, "LET MY PEOPLE GO," Pharaoh refused. The Lord then sent a series of plagues upon the land of EGYPT to convince Pharaoh to accede to Moses' request (Exodus 7–11). Pharaoh's magicians were able to duplicate some of the plagues, so Pharaoh wasn't impressed. The tenth and final plague was the death of the oldest son in each family in Egypt. At this, the ISRAELITES were finally able to leave Egypt (*see* PASSOVER).

Potiphar's wife When JOSEPH (the son of JACOB) was overseer in the house of Potiphar, Potiphar's wife tried to seduce him (Genesis 39). Joseph continually resisted her advances, saying it would be wrong for him to sleep with her. She was offended by his rebuffs, so one day she framed Joseph. She screamed that she was being raped, and she pulled Joseph's shirt off him as he ran away from her. The shirt was used as evidence against him, and he was thrown in prison.

priest In both the Old Testament and the New Testament, the priests of ISRAEL were men who performed religious roles in the community. The priests were descendants of AARON in the TRIBE of LEVI. They officiated in the offering of SACRIFICES. *See also* HIGH PRIEST.

The priests and chief priests were generally antagonistic toward Jesus and toward the early Christians. *See also* PRIEST *under "Church Life and Theology" and* SANHEDRIN *under "People and Events in the New Testament."*

Promised Land A name for the land of ISRAEL. God promised ABRAM that his descendants would inherit the entire land of CANAAN (Genesis 13:15). Later, when MOSES led the people of ISRAEL out of EGYPT, they looked forward to returning to the land of the PATRIARCHS—the Promised Land.

prophecy The term *prophecy* is often used to refer to a prediction of future events. It can also mean any message from God. The role of the Old Testament PROPHETS was to proclaim God's messages to his people. Many of these messages included predictions of the judgment that would fall upon God's people or the surrounding nations because of their SINS. The prophets also foretold the coming of a future MESSIAH who would save his people. Christians see Jesus as the fulfillment of those prophecies.

prophet In the Old Testament, the prophets were spokesmen who proclaimed God's messages to the people of ISRAEL. MOSES, SAMUEL, ELIJAH, ELISHA, ISAIAH, and JEREMIAH were a few of the important prophets of ISRAEL. The prophets con-

stantly called the people to repentance and reminded them of the blessings they would receive if they obeyed God's commands. But they also reminded the people that God would judge them for their disobedience. The prophets were frequently rejected and ridiculed by the people.

In the New Testament, JOHN THE BAPTIST was received as a prophet. Many people also saw Jesus as a prophet, as evidenced by his statement that "a PROPHET IS NOT WITHOUT HONOR, SAVE IN HIS OWN COUNTRY." There are many references in the New Testament to "the Prophets" or "the Law and the Prophets." "The Prophets" were the Old Testament Books of PROPHECY and history.

❦ Muslims do not accept Jesus as the SON OF GOD, but they do see him as an important prophet.

Queen of Sheba A wealthy queen who visited King SOLOMON to see if he was as wise as he was reputed to be. When he answered her hardest questions and she saw all his wealth, she said, "In wisdom and wealth you have far exceeded the report I heard" (1 Kings 10:7, NIV).

❦ Scholars believe Sheba was at the southern end of the Arabian peninsula. Ethiopian legend says the Queen of Sheba became one of Solomon's wives and that she bore a son who became the first king of Ethiopia. King Haile Selassie of Ethiopia

(1892–1975) claimed to be a direct descendant of Solomon and the Queen of Sheba.

Rachel Jacob's favorite wife, and the mother of Joseph and Benjamin. (Jacob's ten other sons were from other wives.) When Jacob fled from his brother, Esau, he went to live with Laban, his mother's brother. Laban had two daughters, Leah and Rachel (Genesis 29). Jacob asked if he could marry Rachel, and Laban said he could marry her if he worked for seven years. He faithfully fulfilled his seven years of work, but Laban tricked Jacob and gave him the elder sister, Leah, as a wife. When Jacob objected, Laban said he could also marry Rachel if he promised to work another seven years! Rachel died as she was giving birth to Benjamin.

Rahab A prostitute who lived in the city of Jericho at the time of Joshua's conquest of the Promised Land (Joshua 2–6). Joshua sent two spies into Jericho, and Rahab hid them under piles of flax on her roof when soldiers came to look for them. Then she told the soldiers the spies had already left. She asked for safety from the Israelite army in exchange for saving the spies, and they assured her she would be safe if she hung a red rope in her window for identification. She then helped the spies escape by letting them down by a rope through a window in the city wall. She and her family were the only residents of Jericho who were allowed to live after the Battle of Jericho.

Apparently Rahab later married a man of the tribe of Judah, for the genealogy in the first chapter of Matthew lists Rahab as the mother of Boaz and an ancestor of David and of Jesus.

Rebekah Isaac's wife, and the mother of twin sons, Esau and Jacob. Rebekah was selected as Isaac's wife when Abraham sent his servant to Haran (the city in northwestern Mesopotamia where Abraham had once lived) to find a wife from among Abraham's relatives (Genesis 24). When the servant arrived in the vicinity, he prayed that the Lord would show him the right girl by having her offer to water his camels when he asked for a drink. Rebekah came out to the well and did offer to water his camels, so the servant identified himself and asked her father if he could take her to be Isaac's wife.

REBEKAH'S WELL The well from which Rebekah drew water for Abraham's servant may have looked like this well in Haran.

After her twins were born, Rebekah was more fond of Jacob than of Esau. When it came time for the aged Isaac to bless his eldest son (*see* BLESSINGS AND CURSES), Rebekah helped Jacob deceive Isaac, thereby stealing the blessing that should have gone to Esau.

Red Sea, parting of the When MOSES led the ISRAELITES out of EGYPT, they were pursued by PHARAOH's army. With the Red Sea in front of them and the Egyptian army behind them, the people were trapped! Then the Lord sent a PILLAR OF CLOUD to come between the Egyptians and the Israelites so the Egyptians could not attack. God told Moses to stretch his rod over the sea. He did so, and God opened a path through the sea so the people could cross through on dry land. The Egyptian army pursued them, but as soon as the Israelites were safely through, God caused the water to cascade back into place, drowning Pharaoh's entire army (Exodus 14). This was just one of a series of miracles God performed as the Israelites moved from Egypt back to CANAAN.

❦ Some TRANSLATIONS and COMMENTAR-IES point out that the Hebrew words traditionally translated 'Red Sea' actually mean 'Sea of Reeds'. The exact location of the crossing—and even which body of water was crossed—is uncertain, but God's miraculous protection for his CHOSEN PEOPLE is evident.

PARTING OF THE RED SEA The Israelites cross safely through the Red Sea after leaving Egypt.

Rehoboam SOLOMON's son who succeeded him as king (1 Kings 12). Rehoboam followed bad advice and was very hard on his people. The people of the TRIBES of JUDAH and BENJAMIN stayed loyal to him, but the other ten tribes rebelled and selected JEROBOAM as their king. This was the beginning of the DIVIDED KINGDOM. The SOUTHERN KINGDOM, consisting of only the tribes of Judah and Benjamin, came to be known as the Kingdom of JUDAH. The NORTHERN KINGDOM, representing the other ten tribes, continued to be known as the Kingdom of ISRAEL. Rehoboam was a wicked king, although his grandfather, King DAVID, had been "a man after [God's] own heart."

Ruth The story of Ruth, told in the book of RUTH, is one of the great love stories in the Bible. Ruth was a poor widow from the land of Moab whose husband had been an ISRAELITE. When her mother-in-law, NAOMI, decided to return to ISRAEL, she encouraged Ruth to stay in Moab. But Ruth responded, "WHITHER THOU GOEST, I WILL GO; and where thou lodgest, I will lodge: thy people shall be my people, and thy God my God." When they arrived in Naomi's hometown, Ruth went to the fields of BOAZ, a wealthy relative of her late husband's. There she collected stalks of grain that the harvesters dropped. Because of Ruth's generosity to her mother-in-law, Boaz instructed his workers to drop grain on purpose so Ruth could pick up enough. At the end of the story, Boaz marries Ruth. Their great-grandson was DAVID, the great king of Israel.

RUTH Ruth gathers grain in the field of Boaz.

Sabbath The weekly day of rest. According to the GENESIS account of the CREATION, God created the world in six days, and then he rested on the seventh day. One of the TEN COMMANDMENTS is "REMEMBER THE SABBATH DAY, TO KEEP IT HOLY." The ISRAELITES were to do no work on the Sabbath day, which was the last day of the week.

By the time of Jesus, the PHARISEES had added hundreds of regulations to the laws of the Old Testament, including laws that defined exactly what one could or could not do on the Sabbath. Jesus pointed out that God had never intended the Sabbath law to be burdensome for his people. Jesus made the Pharisees angry when he said, "The Sabbath was made to benefit man, and not man to benefit the Sabbath" (Mark 2:27, TLB).

Saturday is the Jewish Sabbath, but the EARLY CHURCH evidently met on Sunday (Acts 20:7) in commemoration of the RESURRECTION, which took place on the first day of the week. Most Christians follow this pattern and observe Sunday as their day of rest.

sackcloth and ashes As a sign of mourning, people in the Old Testament wore clothes made of sackcloth, a coarse and uncomfortable fabric, and put ashes on their heads.

sacrifice Under the MOSAIC LAW the system of sacrifices and offerings was spelled out in great detail (e.g., in Leviticus 1–7), including both "thank offerings" and sacrifices for ATONE-

MENT. For atonement, each ISRAELITE was to take a DOVE or a SHEEP or a GOAT to the TABERNACLE (later to the TEMPLE), kill it, and give it to the PRIEST, who would sprinkle the blood on the ALTAR, burn part of the sacrifice, and set the remainder aside for eating. Since the penalty for SIN was death, the animal's blood was shed to atone for the sins of the person making the sacrifice. The JEWS practiced the system of sacrifices until A.D. 70, when the temple and the altar were destroyed with the rest of JERUSALEM.

Jesus, the LAMB OF GOD, was the ultimate sacrifice. He was sinless, so he did not have to die. His death on the CROSS, therefore, was an acceptable sacrifice on behalf of all who believe in him.

Samson   One of the judges of IS-RAEL during the period of the JUDGES, Samson is better known as the strong man who was deceived by his lover, DELILAH (Judges 13–16). The Lord gave Samson an unusual measure of strength. Once he killed a lion with his bare hands. Another time he single-handedly removed the doors and doorposts of a city wall and carried them to a distant hillside. Yet another time he killed 1,000 PHILISTINES with the jawbone of a donkey. Samson loved Delilah, a Philistine woman. Delilah tricked Samson into telling her the source of his strength. He admitted that if his long hair were cut (he was a NAZ-IRITE) he would lose his strength. She arranged for it to be cut while he was sleeping, and the Philistines captured him and gouged out his eyes. While in captivity, Samson prayed that the Lord would give him his strength one last time. Samson then caused a large hall to collapse by pushing out the supporting pillars. In his death he caused the deaths of more Philistines than he had killed in his life.

SAMSON Samson pushes out the columns supporting the roof, killing more Philistines in his death than he had killed in his life.

Samuel   One of the great PROPHETS of ISRAEL (1 Samuel 1–16). When he was a child his mother, HANNAH, took him to the TABERNACLE at Shiloh, where he became an assistant to ELI, the HIGH PRIEST. There he heard a message from God in the middle of the night. He thought it was Eli calling him, but Eli recognized that God was calling the boy. Eli told him to say, "Speak, Lord, for thy servant heareth." When Samuel was an old man, the ISRAELITES wanted a king. Samuel objected, but the people insisted, so Samuel anointed SAUL to be the king. Later, when King Saul disobeyed the Lord's commands, Samuel anointed DAVID as the next king.

Sarah or **Sarai** ABRAHAM's wife (Genesis 12–23), and the mother of ISAAC. The Lord had promised Abraham that his descendants would be as numerous as the stars of the sky, but he and Sarah had no children. Sarah took matters into her own hands and gave her servant HAGAR to Abraham so Hagar could bear him a son. Hagar did have a son, ISHMAEL, but he was not the child of the promise. Finally, when Sarah was ninety, Isaac was born.

Saul The first king of ISRAEL (1 Samuel 9–31). Saul was a handsome man, and he stood head and shoulders above his countrymen. The Lord selected him to be king when the ISRAELITES demanded that they have a king like the nations around them. Saul did not fully obey the Lord, however, so the Lord said he would take Saul's throne and give it to DAVID rather than to Saul's son, JONATHAN. Saul was king at the time young David defeated GOLIATH, and shortly thereafter David married

Saul's daughter Michal. David was very popular with the people, and on several occasions Saul tried to kill David, whom he saw as a great threat. David had several opportunities to kill Saul, but he was careful not to harm the one who had been appointed king over Israel. Saul and his son Jonathan were killed in a battle with the PHILISTINES, and David took the throne.

SAUL "Saul had a spear in his hand and he hurled it, saying to himself, 'I'll pin David to the wall.' But David eluded him twice" (1 Samuel 18:10-11, NIV).

scapegoat On the DAY OF ATONEMENT the HIGH PRIEST offered a special SACRIFICE as an ATONEMENT for all the SINS of the people of ISRAEL. Then he placed his hands on the head of a GOAT, confessing the sins of the people. The people's sins were symbolically transferred to the goat, which was then taken out to a lonely place in the desert. This goat was called the scapegoat (Leviticus 16).

❦ The term *scapegoat* has come to mean a person or group that bears blame in place of others.

selah   A notation found primarily in the PSALMS. It may have indicated that the musicians or the congregation were to pause and lift up their hands or instruments, or it may have been comparable to the expression AMEN.

seraphim   *See* CHERUBIM AND SERAPHIM.

serpent   In the Garden of EDEN, EVE was tempted by a serpent to eat the FORBIDDEN FRUIT (Genesis 3). She succumbed to the temptation and also gave some of the fruit to ADAM. In this way SIN entered the world. The GENESIS account of the FALL OF MAN does not give us many details about the serpent, but we need not assume that it was just a common garden snake. It may have been a beautiful creature. It is assumed that the serpent was actually SATAN, the chief of the forces of EVIL. In REVELATION 12:9, the great dragon who fights against MICHAEL and HEAVEN's armies is identified as "that ancient serpent called the DEVIL, or SATAN, who leads the whole world astray" (NIV).

Shadrach, Meshach, and Abednego   These three ISRAELITE men were friends of DANIEL's (Daniel 1–3). Like Daniel, they were captives in BABYLON, and they were made advisers to King NEBUCHADNEZZAR because of their great wisdom. They stayed true to their faith in God, however, so they refused to obey the king's command that everyone in the kingdom was to bow down and worship a huge golden image constructed by Nebuchadnezzar (Daniel 3). Anyone who defied the king's order was to be thrown into a FIERY FURNACE. Before Shadrach, Meshach, and Abednego were sent to the furnace, however, they assured the king that their God was capable of keeping them safe. The king ordered that the furnace be heated seven times hotter than usual, then the three men were bound and thrown in. But when Nebuchadnezzar looked in, he saw four men walking around in the fire, unbound and unharmed. Nebuchadnezzar said that the fourth man looked "like a son of the gods" (NIV). The king then called Shadrach, Meshach, and Abednego out of the furnace and declared that no one in the kingdom was to speak against their powerful God.

Sheba, Queen of   *See* QUEEN OF SHEBA.

sheep   The primary domestic animal in both Old Testament and New Testament times. They were used to provide food and wool, and they were often a measure of personal wealth. Sheep were frequently used as SACRIFICES.

Because sheep need the care and protection of a SHEPHERD, biblical writers often used sheep to symbolize people in need of God's care and protection. ISAIAH wrote, "ALL WE LIKE SHEEP HAVE GONE ASTRAY; we have turned every one to his own way" (Isaiah 53:6).

shepherd Shepherds care for SHEEP. Many well-known persons in the Old Testament worked as shepherds. Among them are JACOB, JOSEPH, MOSES, and DAVID.

Jesus called himself the GOOD SHEPHERD. He meant that he cares for people as tenderly and as vigilantly as a shepherd cares for his sheep. Jesus told the PARABLE of the LOST SHEEP, in which the shepherd leaves the ninety-nine sheep that are safe in the sheepfold to look for the one sheep that is missing.

shibboleth A password used by Jephthah (one of the judges of ISRAEL during the period of the JUDGES) when he was attacking the TRIBE of Ephraim (Judges 12). The people of Ephraim gave away their identity when they were asked to pronounce the word *shibboleth*, for they pronounced it *sibboleth*.

🐌 The word *shibboleth* is now used to refer to any belief or position a person must hold in order to belong to a particular group. For example, "Some Senators feel that support of abortion is a shibboleth for a Supreme Court nominee."

MOUNT SINAI This rugged mountain on the Sinai Peninsula may be the place where Moses received the Ten Commandments.

Sinai, Mount The mountain where the Lord gave MOSES the TEN COMMANDMENTS (Exodus 19–20). The exact site of the biblical Sinai is disputed, but the traditional location is on the Sinai

SHEPHERD The role of the shepherd has not changed significantly since the days of Moses and David and the shepherds of Bethlehem.

Peninsula, the desolate region between ISRAEL and EGYPT.

JOURNEY TO MOUNT SINAI When the Israelites left Egypt in the Exodus, they moved into the Sinai Peninsula. The Lord gave Moses the Ten Commandments at Mount Sinai. The exact location of the mountain where Moses met the Lord is uncertain, but the traditional site is shown here.

Sodom and Gomorrah, destruction of During the time of ABRAHAM and his nephew LOT, the cities of Sodom and Gomorrah, near the DEAD SEA, were renowned for their wickedness. Lot lived in Sodom, and the Lord warned Abraham that he was going to destroy the cities (Genesis 18–19).

Two ANGELS who had appeared to Abraham in human form went to Lot's home in Sodom. The men of the city came to Lot's home and demanded that Lot send his guests out to be raped. Lot pleaded with the crowd, and the angels then helped Lot and his wife and daughters escape. The angels told them not to look back as the cities were being destroyed with FIRE AND BRIMSTONE that rained down from the skies, but LOT'S WIFE did look back and was turned into a pillar of salt.

☙ The term *sodomy* is derived from *Sodom*, because the men of Sodom wanted to homosexually rape Lot's guests.

Solomon The son of DAVID and BATHSHEBA. He succeeded David as king of ISRAEL (1 Kings 1–11), and he built the first TEMPLE in JERUSALEM. He is renowned for his wisdom, his wealth, and his wives (he had more than 700 of them!). Solomon wrote many of the sayings in the book of PROVERBS, and he is traditionally said to have written ECCLESIASTES and the SONG OF SOLOMON, though many scholars dispute this.

The dedication of the temple was a high point in Israel's history. Unfortunately, Solomon started well but finished poorly. His foreign wives influenced him to worship their pagan gods. As a result of this SIN, the kingdom was divided after Solomon's death. His son REHOBOAM succeeded him as king, but only the TRIBES of JUDAH and BENJAMIN accepted Rehoboam as their king. The other ten tribes, under JEROBOAM, rebelled and set up their own kingdom. This was the start of the DIVIDED KINGDOM.

southern kingdom When the Kingdom of ISRAEL split in two after the death of SOLOMON (1 Kings 12), the two southern TRIBES, JUDAH and BENJAMIN, became the Kingdom of JUDAH. It is sometimes called the southern kingdom, in contrast to the NORTHERN KINGDOM of Israel.

still, small voice After ELIJAH's mighty victory over the prophets of BAAL (*see* FIRE FROM HEAVEN), he was spiritually exhausted and discouraged. He went to Mount SINAI, and the Lord spoke to him there. The Lord caused a mighty wind, then an earthquake, then a fire to pass before Elijah, but the Lord was not in these natural phenomena. Then came a still, small voice, and Elijah recognized it as the voice of God (1 Kings 19:12). Today the expression is used to denote the inner promptings of the HOLY SPIRIT in the life of the BELIEVER.

tabernacle The tent-sanctuary where the Lord resided among the people of ISRAEL from the time MOSES received the TEN COMMANDMENTS until SOLOMON built the TEMPLE nearly 500 years later (Exodus 25–27). The tabernacle was very ornate, but it was also portable. The ISRAELITES disassembled it and carried it with them as they traveled through the WILDERNESS. The innermost room was called the HOLY OF HOLIES, just as in the later temple. The ARK OF THE COVENANT was kept in the Holy of Holies.

temple The ornate building that was the center of WORSHIP for the ISRAELITES from the time of SOLOMON till the destruction of JERUSALEM in A.D. 70. Solomon built the first temple in Jerusalem on the mountain where ABRAHAM had nearly sacrificed ISAAC. Solomon's temple was destroyed

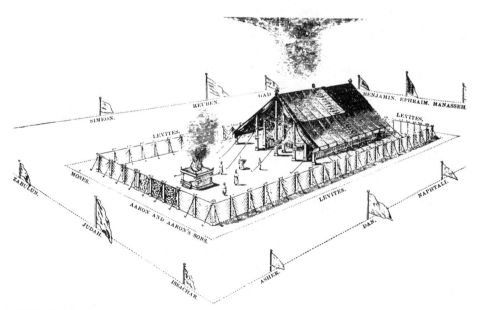

TABERNACLE The tabernacle—a portable tent—was the place where the Lord's presence dwelt among his people.

when the BABYLONIANS captured Jerusalem in 586 B.C. The temple was rebuilt by ZERUBBABEL when the Israelites first returned to their own land after the EXILE. This second temple, not as glorious as Solomon's, survived until the first century B.C. King HEROD the Great then built a third temple. This was the temple of the New Testament period. It was destroyed in A.D. 70 by the armies of the Roman general Titus.

By the time of Jesus, the temple had become quite a place of commerce. Since SACRIFICES were offered at the temple, there were many merchants selling DOVES, SHEEP, and GOATS. JEWS came from many countries to worship at the temple, so there were MONEY CHANGERS to exchange secular money for temple money. Jesus cleansed the temple by throwing out the money changers and merchants. Needless to say, this did not make him very popular with the religious establishment.

TEMPLE This model, located in Jerusalem, shows in incredible detail the temple as it looked in the time of Jesus.

❦ Today there is a Muslim mosque, the Dome of the Rock, on or near the site of the temple. All that remains of Herod's temple is the western wall of the courtyard. It is often called the Wailing Wall, as for centuries the JEWS have lamented the destruction of the temple.

Temptation, the   When ADAM and EVE were in the Garden of EDEN, God told them they could eat the fruit from any tree except the TREE OF THE KNOWLEDGE OF GOOD AND EVIL. Then the SERPENT came to Eve and tempted her to eat the FORBIDDEN FRUIT. He said if she ate it she would be like God, knowing good from EVIL. This is sometimes called the Temptation. Eve ate the fruit and gave some to Adam, who also ate it. The entire event is traditionally called the FALL OF MAN.

Sometimes the TEMPTATION OF JESUS in the WILDERNESS is called the Temptation.

Ten Commandments The law that MOSES received from the Lord at Mount SINAI (Exodus 19–20). The Lord inscribed the commandments on two stone tablets for Moses. When Moses came down from the mountain and saw the GOLDEN CALF AARON had made, he threw down and broke the tablets the Lord had given him. The Lord then gave him the law a second time on new tablets. The Ten Commandments were the

The Ten Commandments

Traditional Protestant numbering. This wording is from the New International Version. Each of the Ten Commandments, in the traditional "Thou shalt not" wording of the King James Version, is listed under "Quotations from the Bible."

1. You shall have no other gods before me.
2. You shall not make for yourself an idol in the form of anything in heaven above or on the earth beneath or in the waters below . . .
3. You shall not misuse the name of the Lord your God, for the Lord will not hold anyone guiltless who misuses his name.
4. Remember the Sabbath day by keeping it holy . . .
5. Honor your father and your mother, so that you may live long in the land the Lord your God is giving you.
6. You shall not murder.
7. You shall not commit adultery.
8. You shall not steal.
9. You shall not give false testimony against your neighbor.
10. You shall not covet your neighbor's house. You shall not covet your neighbor's wife, or his manservant or maidservant, his ox or donkey, or anything that belongs to your neighbor. (Exodus 20:3-17, NIV)

Traditional Catholic numbering. The commandments are not actually numbered in the Bible, so the division into ten separate commandments is traditional. This wording, from the New American Bible, is similar to the wording in Protestant Translations, but Catholics and Lutherans have traditionally combined two commandments at the beginning and divided two commandments at the end of the list.

1. You shall not have other gods besides me. You shall not carve idols for yourselves in the shape of anything in the sky above or on the earth below or in the waters beneath the earth . . .
2. You shall not take the name of the Lord, your God, in vain. For the Lord will not leave unpunished him who takes his name in vain.
3. Remember to keep holy the Sabbath day . . .
4. Honor your father and your mother, that you may have a long life in the land which the Lord, your God, is giving you.
5. You shall not kill.
6. You shall not commit adultery.
7. You shall not steal.
8. You shall not bear false witness against your neighbor.
9. You shall not covet your neighbor's house.
10. You shall not covet your neighbor's wife, nor his male or female slave, nor his ox or ass, nor anything else that belongs him. (Exodus 20:3-17, NAB)

central element in the larger structure of the MOSAIC LAW.

Jesus summarized the Ten Commandments into two simple commands when he said, "THOU SHALT LOVE THE LORD THY GOD WITH ALL THY HEART, AND WITH ALL THY SOUL, AND WITH ALL THY MIND. This is the first and greatest commandment. The second is like unto it, Thou shalt LOVE THY NEIGHBOR AS THYSELF. On these two commandments hang all the LAW and the PROPHETS" (Matthew 22:37-40).

Tigris River One of the great rivers of the Near East, it runs from present-day Turkey through present-day Iraq. It joins the EUPHRATES River shortly before they empty together into the Persian Gulf. The basins of the Euphrates River and Tigris River formed part of the Fertile Crescent of the ancient world. The region of the Tigris and the Euphrates was called Mesopotamia in the Bible (the name comes from the GREEK for 'between the two rivers').

tithe A gift to the Lord equal to one-tenth of one's income. The MOSAIC LAW required that the people of ISRAEL give a tithe (Deuteronomy 14:22-29; Malachi 3:10), partly as a means of supporting the PRIESTS and other LEVITES. Many Christians observe the principle of tithing by giving a tenth of their income to their church and/or other Christian organizations.

tree of life In the very center of the Garden of EDEN stood the tree of life and the TREE OF THE KNOWLEDGE OF GOOD AND EVIL. God told ADAM he could freely eat from all the trees in the Garden except the tree of the knowledge of good and evil. After Adam and EVE ate the fruit of that tree (*see* FALL OF MAN), God banished them from the Garden so they would not also eat from the tree of life "and live forever." The CHERUBIM that guarded the entrance to the Garden were placed there "to guard the way to the tree of life." In the book of REVELATION we find the tree of life in the NEW JERUSALEM.

tree of the knowledge of good and evil The tree in the Garden of EDEN from which EVE took the FORBIDDEN FRUIT. ADAM had been told he could eat from the fruit of any tree *except* this one. When they did eat its fruit, "their eyes were opened, and they saw that they were naked." This is called the FALL OF MAN. *See also* TREE OF LIFE.

tribes of Israel JACOB, one of the PATRIARCHS of the people of ISRAEL, had twelve sons. The descendants of each of these sons became a tribe (extended family) within the nation of Israel. The names of the tribes are: Asher, BENJAMIN, Dan, Ephraim, Gad, JUDAH, Issachar, Levi, Manasseh, Naphtali, Reuben, Simeon, and Zebulun. (The tribes of Ephraim and Manasseh are named for the two sons of JOSEPH.)

Each of the tribes (except the tribe of Levi) was allotted a certain portion of land when the ISRAELITES entered the PROMISED LAND after the EXODUS and after wandering in the WILDERNESS. The LEVITES, who were responsible for the TABERNACLE (and later the TEMPLE), did not get a territory of their own. They were supported by the TITHES that the rest of the people brought to the Lord.

THE TRIBES OF ISRAEL
Each of the twelve tribes of Israel (except Levi) received a territory of its own in the Promised Land. The Levites were supported by the other tribes. The tribes in the north (plus Simeon) eventually became the northern kingdom of Israel. Judah and Benjamin became the southern kingdom of Judah.

unclean animals According to the MOSAIC LAW, certain animals could be eaten and all other animals could not be eaten (Leviticus 11). Those that could not be eaten, including pigs, were said to be unclean. This is part of the basis of the kosher laws still observed by many JEWS.

United Kingdom *See* ISRAEL, KINGDOM OF.

unleavened bread Since it is made without LEAVEN (yeast), unleavened bread does not rise. On the night before the EXODUS, the ISRAEL-ITES were told to bake unleavened bread, as they would not have time to wait for the dough to rise. Ever since, unleavened bread has played an important role in the celebration of the PASSOVER.

Since Jesus and his DISCIPLES ate unleavened bread at the LAST SUPPER (they were celebrating the Passover), unleavened bread is often used by Christians for the COMMUNION service.

vision A dream or dreamlike experience in which a person receives a message from God or an ANGEL. Many people in both the Old Testament and the New Testament had visions. JACOB had a vision in which he saw angels ascending and descending a stairway that stretched between HEAVEN and earth (*see* JACOB'S LADDER). The PROPHETS often received messages in visions. An example is ISAIAH's vision in the TEMPLE: "In the year that king Uzziah died, I saw also the Lord" (Isaiah 6:1).

ZECHARIAH (father of JOHN THE BAPTIST) also had a vision in the temple, when the angel GABRIEL announced that Zechariah and ELIZABETH would have a son. The WISE MEN received instructions in a dream not to tell King HEROD that they had found the infant Jesus. PAUL had a vision in which he was taken up into heaven, and JOHN had an extensive vision that is recorded in the book of REVELATION.

wheat An important grain grown for use in bread. It was also used as a SACRIFICE and in commercial trade. Jesus compared himself to a grain of wheat, which must die in order to produce fruit. He also used wheat and wheat fields to symbolize the people of the world.

wilderness The untamed regions in and around ISRAEL were called the wilderness (sometimes translated 'desert'). It was a dry, rocky area without much vegetation. The wilderness is an image that suggests a time of testing and learning patience. MOSES lived in the wilderness for forty years before leading the ISRAELITES out of EGYPT. After the EXODUS, the Israelites themselves were in the wilderness for forty years before entering the PROMISED LAND. Centuries later, JOHN THE BAPTIST lived and preached in the wilderness near the JORDAN RIVER. Jesus went into the wilderness where he was tempted by SATAN. The APOSTLE PAUL lived in the wilderness for a number of years after his DAMASCUS ROAD experience and before he started his active ministry.

wine The references to wine in the Bible are both positive and negative. In the PSALMS, wine is listed along with many other good gifts from the Lord. Jesus' first MIRACLE was TURNING WATER INTO WINE at a marriage feast, and he and his DISCIPLES drank wine at the LAST SUPPER. PAUL exhorts TIMOTHY to "use a little wine because of your stomach and your frequent illnesses" (1 Timothy 5:23, NIV). But in both Old Testament and New Testament there are warnings about the dangers of wine and of drunkenness (e.g., Proverbs 23:29-35).

Zerubbabel In 538 B.C., Zerubbabel led the first group of about 42,000 JEWS from EXILE in BABYLON back to JERUSALEM (Ezra 1–6). They began rebuilding the TEMPLE, though it was not completed until 516 B.C. under the prompting of the PROPHET Haggai. The story of Zerubbabel is told in EZRA 1–6.

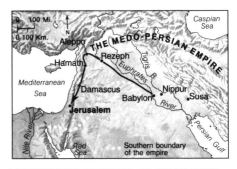

ZERUBBABEL RETURNS TO JERUSALEM
The vast Medo-Persian empire included all the area on this map and more. A group of exiles, under the leadership of Zerubbabel, began the long trip back to their homeland. Many exiles, however, preferred the comfort and security they had in Babylon to the dangerous trip back to Jerusalem, and so they stayed in Babylon.

100 KEY EVENTS IN THE NEW TESTAMENT

1. The ANGEL GABRIEL announces to ZECHARIAH that he and ELIZABETH will have a son
2. The ANNUNCIATION: the angel Gabriel tells the VIRGIN MARY she will have a son
3. An angel appears to JOSEPH, telling him to marry Mary
4. Mary visits Elizabeth
5. JOHN THE BAPTIST is born to Zechariah and Elizabeth
6. Joseph and Mary travel from NAZARETH to BETHLEHEM to enroll in the census
7. The NATIVITY: JESUS is born in a stable in Bethlehem
8. Angels announce Jesus' birth to the SHEPHERDS
9. ANNA and SIMEON bless Jesus in the TEMPLE
10. The WISE MEN arrive from the East and worship Jesus
11. Joseph and Mary flee to EGYPT to keep Jesus safe
12. King HEROD the Great kills all male infants in Bethlehem
13. Joseph and Mary, with Jesus, return from Egypt to Nazareth
14. Jesus, age twelve, teaches the elders in the temple
15. John the Baptist preaches and BAPTIZES in the WILDERNESS
16. John baptizes Jesus in the JORDAN RIVER
17. Jesus is tempted by SATAN in the wilderness
18. John the Baptist proclaims Jesus to be the MESSIAH
19. The first DISCIPLES follow Jesus
20. Jesus performs his first miracle: TURNING WATER INTO WINE
21. Jesus chases the MONEY CHANGERS out of the temple
22. NICODEMUS visits Jesus at night
23. Jesus talks to the WOMAN AT THE WELL
24. Jesus is rejected in his hometown of Nazareth
25. Jesus heals many people in GALILEE
26. Jesus tells the Jewish leaders that he is the SON OF GOD
27. Jesus teaches many truths in the SERMON ON THE MOUNT
28. Jesus forgives the woman caught in the act of ADULTERY
29. Jesus teaches his disciples how to pray—the LORD'S PRAYER
30. Jesus teaches in PARABLES
31. Jesus calms a storm on the SEA OF GALILEE
32. HEROD Antipas kills John the Baptist
33. Jesus feeds a crowd of 5,000 with a few LOAVES AND FISHES
34. Jesus appears to his disciples—WALKING ON WATER
35. MOSES and ELIJAH appear with Jesus at the TRANSFIGURATION
36. Jesus raises LAZARUS from the dead
37. Jesus blesses the little children
38. Jesus enters JERUSALEM—the TRIUMPHAL ENTRY
39. Jesus overturns the money changers' tables
40. Jesus predicts his own death and RESURRECTION
41. Religious leaders plot to kill Jesus
42. Jesus and his disciples observe the PASSOVER—the LAST SUPPER
43. Jesus washes his disciples' feet
44. Jesus prays in the Garden of GETHSEMANE
45. JUDAS ISCARIOT betrays Jesus
46. The SANHEDRIN holds the TRIAL OF JESUS
47. PETER denies knowing Jesus

48. Jesus is taken to Pontius PILATE for questioning
49. Jesus is questioned by Herod Antipas
50. Jesus is mocked by Herod and the Roman soldiers
51. Jesus is again questioned by Pilate
52. Pilate releases BARABBAS
53. Pilate sentences Jesus to death by CRUCIFIXION
54. Jesus is flogged by Roman soldiers
55. Judas Iscariot commits suicide
56. SIMON OF CYRENE carries Jesus' CROSS to GOLGOTHA
57. Jesus dies on the cross—The CRUCIFIXION
58. The curtain in the temple is torn in two
59. Jesus is buried in a tomb donated by JOSEPH OF ARIMATHEA
60. Jesus comes back to life again—the Resurrection
61. MARY MAGDALENE and the other women go to Jesus' tomb
62. Mary sees Jesus near the tomb
63. Jesus appears to the disciples in the Upper Room
64. Jesus appears to two disciples on the road to Emmaus
65. Jesus appears to the disciples again, including THOMAS
66. Jesus appears to the disciples at the Sea of Galilee
67. Jesus gives the GREAT COMMISSION
68. Forty days after the Resurrection, Jesus ascends to HEAVEN— the ASCENSION
69. MATTHIAS is selected to replace Judas Iscariot as an APOSTLE
70. The HOLY SPIRIT comes upon the BELIEVERS at PENTECOST
71. Peter preaches and 3,000 believers are baptized
72. Peter and JOHN heal a crippled man
73. ANANIAS AND SAPPHIRA die after lying to Peter
74. The EARLY CHURCH appoints seven DEACONS
75. STEPHEN is the first CHRISTIAN MARTYR

76. SAUL and other Jewish leaders persecute believers
77. Many people in SAMARIA are converted when PHILIP (the evangelist) preaches there
78. Philip (the evangelist) explains the GOSPEL to the Ethiopian eunuch
79. Saul has a CONVERSION experience on the DAMASCUS ROAD
80. DORCAS is raised back to life when Peter prays for her
81. Peter is called to preach to the GENTILES; CORNELIUS becomes a Christian
82. Believers flee Jerusalem, taking the gospel to other lands
83. An angel rescues Peter from prison
84. PAUL and BARNABAS go on first MISSIONARY JOURNEY
85. The first CHURCH COUNCIL convenes at Jerusalem
86. Paul and Barnabas go on second missionary journey
87. Paul and Barnabas separate; SILAS joins Paul
88. The Philippian jailer is converted
89. Paul preaches on Mars Hill in Athens
90. Paul goes on third missionary journey
91. Paul provokes a riot in Ephesus
92. Paul writes his EPISTLE to the ROMANS
93. Paul returns to Jerusalem and is arrested
94. Paul appears before Felix, the Roman governor of JUDEA
95. Paul appears before Festus, Felix's successor, and appeals to CAESAR
96. Paul appears before King HEROD Agrippa II
97. Paul is shipwrecked while en route to ROME
98. Paul writes "prison epistles" and "pastoral epistles"
99. Jerusalem is destroyed, A.D. 70 (not recorded in the Bible)
100. John writes of his vision of HEAVEN (the book of REVELATION)

PEOPLE AND EVENTS IN THE NEW TESTAMENT

The New Testament is essentially about Jesus Christ. The four GOS-
PELS contain parallel accounts of his life and ministry. They are followed by the book of ACTS, which starts where the Gospels end. It
tells of the activities of Jesus' followers in the first thirty years after
Jesus ascended into HEAVEN.

The EPISTLES contain practical lessons in THEOLOGY and daily living
for Jesus' followers—both in the EARLY CHURCH and today. They were
letters, after all, and what could be more practical than a letter
from a friend? Finally, the book of REVELATION is a look into the future, as the APOSTLE JOHN saw it in a VISION. There we see Jesus
enthroned in glory.

In this chapter you will find key events in the life of Jesus (e.g., the
NATIVITY, the TRANSFIGURATION, the TRIUMPHAL ENTRY, the CRUCIFIXION, the
RESURRECTION) and key places where he traveled. It also includes
some of Jesus' PARABLES, such as the GOOD SAMARITAN and the PRODIGAL
SON. Many other teachings of Jesus are listed under "Quotations
from the Bible." Also included here are some of Jesus' MIRACLES, such
as TURNING WATER INTO WINE. Many of the details of Jesus' ministry are
told in two or more of the Gospels. Nonetheless, I have included only
one Bible reference under most of the entries.

This chapter also contains the names of all the people who play prominent roles in the New Testament, from the WISE MEN to the DISCIPLES to the APOSTLE PAUL. Most people recognize the names of at least a few of Jesus' disciples—perhaps PETER and JOHN. The GOSPEL accounts do not tell us much about some of the disciples, but the names of all twelve of them are included in this chapter. This does not mean that every Christian needs to memorize the names of the disciples, but we should recognize them when we see them.

We also encounter here the villains of the New Testament—King HEROD the Great, JUDAS ISCARIOT, Pontius PILATE, and even HERODIAS and SALOME. Many people are mentioned in the book of Acts, and those whose names are most significant, including Paul, SILAS, BARNABAS, and TIMOTHY are included here.

Alpha and Omega In the GREEK alphabet, alpha is the first letter and omega is the last letter. In Revelation 22:13, Jesus said, "I am Alpha and Omega, the beginning and the end, the first and the last." He meant that he had existed before anything else existed, and he would continue to exist after the heavens and the earth had been destroyed.

Ananias and Sapphira Husband and wife, they were members of the EARLY CHURCH at JERUSALEM. They sold some property and said they were giving the whole sum of money to the church. They actually gave only a part of the price, and they were both struck dead for their duplicity (Acts 5).

Andrew One of the DISCIPLES of Jesus, and the brother of PETER. He was a fisherman, and he had been a disciple of JOHN THE BAPTIST before he met Jesus. Jesus said to Andrew and Peter, "FOLLOW ME, and I will make you FISHERS OF MEN" (Matthew 4:19).

angels Spiritual beings who live in HEAVEN and serve as messengers to earth. Angels were created sinless, but the Bible says that SATAN and his DEMONS are all fallen angels (2 Peter 2:4).

ANGELS "And the angel said unto them, Fear not: for, behold, I bring you good tidings of great joy" (Luke 2:10).

The Bible tells of many instances in which angels interacted with humans. Perhaps the best-known example is when the "multitude of the heavenly host" appeared to the SHEPHERDS outside BETHLEHEM to announce the birth of Jesus (Luke 2:13). The concept of guardian angels comes from Jesus' statement, "See that you do not look down on one of these little ones. For I tell you that their angels in heaven always see the face of my FATHER in heaven" (Matthew 18:10, NIV).

Anna An elderly woman who stayed at the TEMPLE, awaiting the arrival of the MESSIAH. LUKE calls her a prophetess. When JOSEPH and MARY brought the infant Jesus to the temple to be dedicated, Anna recognized Jesus as the Messiah and told everyone that the Messiah had come (Luke 2).

Annunciation, the The announcement by the ANGEL GABRIEL to MARY that she would become the mother of Jesus, even though she was a virgin. After the Annunciation, Mary sang a song that is often called the MAGNIFICAT (Luke 1).

apostle Literally, 'one who is sent', for instance as a MISSIONARY. The term is usually associated with Jesus' twelve DISCIPLES, all of whom (except JUDAS ISCARIOT) went out to spread the GOOD NEWS about Jesus after PENTECOST. PAUL, the greatest missionary in the EARLY CHURCH, was not one of Jesus' twelve disciples, but he is also called an apostle.

Aquila and Priscilla A husband and wife team who were friends and colleagues of the APOSTLE PAUL. They ministered to the young church in Ephesus for a time. Like Paul, they supported themselves by making tents (Acts 18).

THE ANNUNCIATION "The angel said to her, 'Do not be afraid, Mary, you have found favor with God. You will be with child and give birth to a son, and you are to give him the name Jesus'" (Luke 1:30-31, NIV).

archangel A chief among ANGELS. The only archangels named in the Bible are MICHAEL and GABRIEL. LUCIFER (SATAN) has traditionally been identified as a fallen archangel.

Ascension, the After Jesus' CRUCI-FIXION and RESURRECTION, he was on earth forty more days. He appeared to his DISCIPLES on several occasions and gave them various instructions and promised that the HOLY SPIRIT would come to them. One day they went together to the Mount of OLIVES, just outside JERUSALEM, and Jesus rose into the sky and disappeared into a cloud. Then two ANGELS appeared to the disciples and told them that Jesus had gone to HEAVEN (Acts 1). This is called the Ascension.

Augustus The emperor of the RO-MAN EMPIRE at the time of the birth of Jesus. The familiar CHRISTMAS narrative from Luke 2 begins: "And it came to pass in those days, that there went out a decree from CAESAR Augustus, that all the world should be taxed." Because of the census decreed by Augustus, JOSEPH and MARY had to journey from their home in NAZARETH to BETHLEHEM, where Jesus was born.

Barabbas Pontius PILATE had a custom of releasing a Jewish prisoner each year at PASSOVER, as a gesture of goodwill to the Palestinian JEWS. After interrogating Jesus, Pilate was convinced of Jesus' innocence, so he tried to use his annual custom as a means of releasing Jesus. He offered to release either Jesus or Barabbas, a convicted murderer, assuming that the crowd would respond reasonably and ask for Jesus' release. The mob chose Barabbas, and they called for Jesus to be crucified (Luke 23).

Barnabas When PAUL returned to JERUSALEM after his CONVERSION on the DAMASCUS ROAD, the other BELIEVERS were suspicious of him. Barnabas came to Paul's defense, explaining that Paul was now a follower of Christ. Barnabas was not one of the twelve DISCIPLES, but he was an APOSTLE in the EARLY CHURCH (Acts 9–15). He and MARK traveled with PAUL on Paul's first MISSIONARY JOURNEY, though Mark deserted them en route. When Paul and Barnabas were preparing for a second journey, Barnabas again wanted to take Mark with them. Paul refused, so Barnabas and Mark traveled together and Paul traveled with SILAS.

Bartholomew One of the DISCIPLES of Jesus, though the GOSPELS tell us very little about him. He is called NATHANAEL in the Gospel of JOHN.

Behold the man After the TRIAL OF JESUS, the Roman soldiers put a CROWN OF THORNS on Jesus' head, and they put a purple robe on him and mocked him. Pontius PILATE hoped this would satisfy the mob, since he had found Jesus innocent. He brought Jesus out to the mob and said, "Behold the man!" (John 19:5). The Jewish leaders insisted that he be CRUCIFIED, and Pilate eventually gave in to their demands.

❧ The familiar LATIN phrase, as found in the VULGATE, is *Ecce homo.*

BEHOLD THE MAN "Then Jesus came out wearing the crown of thorns and the purple robe. And Pilate said, 'Behold the man'" (John 19:5, TLB).

Bethany   A small village at the foot of the Mount of OLIVES, just outside JERUSALEM. It was the home of Jesus' friends MARY AND MARTHA and their brother LAZARUS. Jesus frequently stayed there.

JESUS VISITS BETHANY
After teaching throughout Galilee, Jesus returned to Jerusalem—walking eighty or more miles. He spoke in Jerusalem and then visited his friends Mary and Martha in the tiny village of Bethany on the slope of the Mount of Olives. It was here that Lazarus was raised back to life.

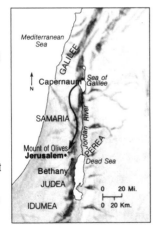

Bethlehem   The small village where Jesus was born—just south of JERUSALEM (see the map at the entry for NAZARETH). A thousand years earlier Bethlehem had been the home of King DAVID, so it was also called the city of David.

When the WISE MEN visited King HEROD the Great to inquire about the newborn KING OF THE JEWS, Herod asked the chief PRIESTS and SCRIBES where the Christ was to be born (Matthew 2). They knew instantly that such a child was to be born in Bethlehem, for Micah 5:2 foretold that a great ruler would be born in Bethlehem.

❧ A favorite CHRISTMAS carol begins, "O little town of Bethlehem, how still we see thee lie."

Bread of Life   Jesus used this expression when he said, "I am the bread of life" (John 6:48, NKJV). Bread was a staple element of daily food in the ancient world, as it is in much of the modern world. Jesus meant that bread sustains physical life, but he himself could provide ETERNAL LIFE.

Caesar   Any of various emperors of the ROMAN EMPIRE. The Caesars mentioned in the New Testament are AUGUSTUS, Tiberius, Claudius, and Nero. Augustus (reigned 30 B.C. to A.D. 14) was emperor at the time of the birth of Jesus (Luke 2:1). Tiberius (A.D. 14–37) was emperor during the time of Jesus' ministry (Luke

3:1). Gaius, or Caligula (A.D. 37–41), is not mentioned in the Bible. Claudius (A.D. 41–54) is mentioned in Acts 18:2 as having forced all JEWS to leave ROME. Nero (A.D. 54–68) is not identified by name, but he was the Caesar to whom PAUL appealed to have his case heard (Acts 25:11).

❦ The German *kaiser* and Russian *czar* or *tsar* are derivatives of *Caesar*.

Caiaphas The HIGH PRIEST who presided at the trial of Jesus. The trial was a mockery, since Caiaphas was one of the leaders who had wanted Jesus arrested (Matthew 26).

calming the storm The Sea of GALILEE is not large, but it lies far below sea level, and storms there can be ferocious. One day Jesus and his DISCIPLES were crossing the Sea of Galilee when a fierce storm arose (Mark 4). Jesus was sleeping in the boat, but the disciples were afraid they were all going to drown. When they awoke Jesus, he said to the wind and the waves, "Quiet! Be still!" And the storm instantly subsided.

Although the disciples had already seen Jesus perform many MIRACLES, they were terrified at this display of power and asked one another, "Who is this? Even the wind and waves obey him!"

Calvary The hill outside the city of JERUSALEM where Jesus was CRUCIFIED. Calvary is also called GOLGOTHA.

BETHLEHEM This photo shows Bethlehem as it appeared a century ago.

❧ The term *Calvary* is often used to refer to the entire event and purpose of Jesus' crucifixion (e.g., there is a GOSPEL SONG called "Calvary Covers It All"). The popular HYMN "The OLD RUGGED CROSS" begins with the words, "On a hill far away stood an old rugged CROSS." The hill is Calvary.

Capernaum A town in GALILEE, on the shore of the SEA OF GALILEE. At the start of Jesus' ministry, after he was rejected by the people in his hometown of NAZARETH, he went to Capernaum and was warmly welcomed (Luke 4). Much of Jesus' public ministry took place in the vicinity of Capernaum.

CAPERNAUM Jesus and his disciples moved on to Capernaum after he was rejected in his hometown of Nazareth. Capernaum was a small village on the shores of the Sea of Galilee. Ruins of an ancient synagogue (perhaps the very building where Jesus taught) can be seen there today.

centurion A Roman military commander who had 100 soldiers under his command. Several centurions are mentioned in the New Testament, including CORNELIUS, who was converted under PETER's teaching.

Christ A title for Jesus. It comes from a GREEK word and is the equivalent of the HEBREW word that means 'MESSIAH', or 'anointed one'.

❧ In contemporary usage, most people use the names Jesus, Christ, and Jesus Christ interchangeably.

CROSS Three styles of Roman crosses.

Cornelius A Roman CENTURION who had a vision in which he was told to send for PETER (Acts 10). After hearing Peter preach, Cornelius became a BELIEVER, and he and everyone in his household were BAPTIZED. His CONVERSION caused a dispute among the church leaders as to whether GENTILES who became believers also had to convert to JUDAISM. The issue was resolved at the Council at JERUSALEM.

cross When Jesus was sentenced to death by Pontius PILATE, he was CRUCIFIED on a cross (Mark 15). A cross consists simply of a wooden crosspiece attached to an upright post. The victim's arms were stretched out on the crosspiece and tied or nailed in place, and the feet were tied or nailed to the upright. The cross was then lifted up and inserted into a hole in the ground, and the victim was left to hang there until he died, usually from suffocation.

The cross of Christ has become a symbol of his death, and particularly of his ATONEMENT for the SINS of mankind. *See also* CRUCIFIX *under "Church Life and Theology."*

crown of thorns After Jesus was betrayed by JUDAS ISCARIOT, he was tried and condemned by the SANHEDRIN and then taken to PILATE for sentencing (*see* TRIAL OF JESUS). Pilate interrogated Jesus but found him not guilty. Nonetheless, to appease the Jewish leaders, Pilate had Jesus scourged. In the process of carrying out this punishment, the soldiers made a crown of thorns and forced it on Jesus' head. They also put a purple robe on him and mocked him as the KING OF THE JEWS.

crucifixion, crucify A form of capital punishment in the ROMAN EMPIRE. The criminal's hands and feet were tied or nailed to a wooden CROSS, which was then lifted up and inserted into a hole in the ground. Crucifixion was excruciatingly painful, and a person could survive on the cross for several days before finally dying. The victim's legs were sometimes broken to keep him from lifting himself up to breathe. This then led to death by suffocation.

After Jesus was betrayed, he was tried by the SANHEDRIN (*see* TRIAL OF JESUS),

which found him guilty of BLASPHEMY. Under the MOSAIC LAW, the penalty for blasphemy was death, so Jesus was taken to Pontius PILATE for formal sentencing. Pilate interrogated Jesus and found him not guilty, but to appease the Jewish leaders he sentenced Jesus to death on a CROSS. The crucifixion of Jesus is an important aspect of Christian DOCTRINE, because Jesus provided ATONEMENT—reconciliation between God and man—by his death.

❦ Tradition tells us that PETER was crucified, but that he asked to be crucified head downward because he felt unworthy to die as Jesus had died.

THE CRUCIFIXION "The people stood watching, and the rulers even sneered at him. They said, 'He saved others; let him save himself'" (Luke 23:35, NIV).

Damascus road SAUL, later known as the APOSTLE PAUL, was traveling from JERUSALEM to Damascus (the capital of Syria) to persecute Christians when he had his CONVERSION experience.

❧ A "Damascus road experience" is a conversion experience.

demons Evil SPIRITS. Demons are probably fallen ANGELS who joined SATAN in his rebellion against God. They help Satan tempt people to SIN, and they have great destructive power. The New Testament contains numerous accounts of people who were demon-possessed. Jesus, however, was always stronger than the demons. Exorcism, the act of casting the demon(s) out of a person who is demon-possessed, involves calling upon the name and power of Jesus against the demon. The GREEK word translated 'demon' in modern TRANSLATIONS was translated 'devil' in the KING JAMES VERSION.

❧ Liberal THEOLOGY tends to discount the existence of demons and of Satan, but the recent increase in spiritism and the occult would seem to validate the traditional understanding that demons are indeed real.

disciples Any follower or learner can be called a disciple, but the term is used specifically for Jesus' twelve closest followers. They are sometimes called The Twelve. Their names were Simon PETER, JAMES and JOHN (sons of Zebedee), ANDREW, BARTHOLOMEW (also called Nathanael), JAMES (son of Alphaeus), JUDAS ISCARIOT, MATTHEW (also called Levi), PHILIP, SIMON THE ZEALOT, THADDAEUS (also called Judas, son of James), and THOMAS.

The disciples are also called the APOSTLES (persons who are sent out to proclaim the GOSPEL), because after Jesus' RESURRECTION and ASCENSION they went throughout the known world to tell others the GOOD NEWS about Jesus. The Bible does not give any details about their deaths (except for James, son of Zebedee, who was put to death by King HEROD Agrippa), but tradition says that most of the disciples died as MARTYRS.

Dorcas A Christian woman known for her acts of MERCY who was brought back to life when PETER prayed for her (Acts 9). Many believed in the Lord as a result of this MIRACLE.

Doubting Thomas *See* THOMAS (the disciple).

dove A bird mentioned in both the Old Testament and the New Testament. It was used as food and also as an acceptable SACRIFICE. The HOLY SPIRIT came down in the form of a dove at the BAPTISM of Jesus. In CHURCH HISTORY, up to the present, the dove has come to symbolize peace, love, and the church.

Ecce homo *See* BEHOLD THE MAN.

Elizabeth (also spelled Elisabeth) The wife of ZECHARIAH and mother of JOHN THE BAPTIST (Luke 1). She was a cousin of MARY, the mother of Jesus. John's birth was foretold by an ANGEL who appeared to Zechariah while he was carrying out his priestly duties in the TEMPLE. While Mary was pregnant, she visited Elizabeth, who was also pregnant. When Elizabeth heard Mary's greeting, "the babe leaped in her womb." She greeted Mary by saying, "Blessed art thou among women, and blessed is the fruit of thy womb."

Emmanuel *See* IMMANUEL.

THE EMPTY TOMB This is the Garden Tomb in Jerusalem. It is similar to the tomb in which Jesus' body was buried.

empty tomb A reference to the RESURRECTION. Roman guards had been posted at Jesus' tomb to make sure no one stole his body (Matthew 27). When the women went to Jesus' tomb early on Sunday morning, however, they found the tomb was empty. Jesus had come back to life!

Eutychus A young man who fell asleep and fell out a window while PAUL was preaching. He died, but Paul prayed for him and he came back to life (Acts 20).

feeding the five thousand *See* LOAVES AND FISHES, MIRACLE OF THE.

flight to Egypt King HEROD the Great was furious when he discovered that the WISE MEN had gone home without telling him where to find the newborn king (Matthew 2). In order to kill the child, he ordered the death of all the boys in BETHLEHEM who were two years of age or younger. An ANGEL appeared to JOSEPH in a dream and told him to take MARY and Jesus to EGYPT, where they would be safe. They left immediately and stayed there until Herod's death about two years later. The HOLY FAMILY then returned to NAZARETH, the village in GALILEE where Joseph and Mary had grown up.

THE FLIGHT TO EGYPT Herod planned to kill the baby Jesus, whom he perceived to be a future threat to his position. Warned of this treachery in a dream, Joseph took his family to Egypt until Herod's death, which occurred a year or two later. They then planned to return to Judea, but God led them instead to Nazareth in Galilee.

Gabriel An ARCHANGEL who served as a messenger from God. He appeared to DANIEL, ZECHARIAH (father of JOHN THE BAPTIST), the VIRGIN MARY, and JOSEPH (husband of Mary). His announcement to Mary (*see* ANNUNCIATION) was that she would have a son who would be the SON OF GOD, even though she was a virgin. Gabriel and MICHAEL are the only ANGELS mentioned by name in the Bible.

Galilee The northern region of the land of PALESTINE, between the MEDITERRANEAN SEA and the Sea of GALILEE. Jesus grew up in NAZARETH, which is in Galilee, and much of his public ministry took place in Galilee. The region of SAMARIA was south of Galilee and lay between Galilee and JUDEA.

SEA OF GALILEE The Sea of Galilee looks much the same today as it did in Jesus' day.

Galilee, Sea of A medium-sized lake (about seven miles across) on the eastern border of GALILEE. PETER, ANDREW, JAMES, and JOHN were all fishermen on the Sea of Galilee, and much of Jesus' ministry took place

in that region. Jesus' MIRACLES of WALKING ON WATER and CALMING THE STORM both took place on the Sea of Galilee. The JORDAN RIVER flows from the Sea of Galilee to the DEAD SEA.

genealogy A listing of ancestors or descendants. The ISRAELITES took great care to preserve their genealogies to show their standing as descendants of ABRAHAM, thus their participation in God's COVENANT to Abraham. There are many genealogies in the Bible, including genealogies of Jesus in MATTHEW 1 and LUKE 3.

🐦 In the KING JAMES VERSION, the genealogies make repeated use of the word *begat*, which means 'became the father of'. The genealogy of Jesus in Matthew 1 begins, "Abraham begat ISAAC; and Isaac begat JACOB; and Jacob begat JUDAH and his brethren."

Gethsemane, Garden of A garden at the foot of the Mount of OLIVES, just outside JERUSALEM. After the LAST SUPPER, Jesus and his DISCIPLES went to Gethsemane to pray, as they frequently did. Jesus prayed, "FATHER, if you are willing, take this cup from me; yet not my will, but yours be done" (Luke 22:42, NIV). As a man, he preferred not to go through with the suffering that lay just ahead, but as the SON OF GOD he wanted God's will to be done. It was immediately after this that

JUDAS ISCARIOT came to Gethsemane and betrayed Jesus to the Jewish leaders.

GARDEN OF GETHSEMANE The Garden of Gethsemane, located at the foot of the Mount of Olives, still contains olive trees that may date back to the first century.

gold, frankincense, and myrrh The three precious gifts that the WISE MEN brought to the baby Jesus (Matthew 2). As in our world today, GOLD was a precious commodity. Frankincense and myrrh were both aromatic substances used as perfumes. The gifts of the wise men were valuable, as befits gifts for a king. JOSEPH and MARY may have used the gold to finance their unexpected FLIGHT TO EGYPT.

Golden Rule A teaching of Jesus from the SERMON ON THE MOUNT (Matthew 7:12). A popular rendition is DO UNTO OTHERS AS YOU WOULD HAVE THEM DO UNTO YOU. Much of civilized behavior falls under the rubric of the Golden Rule. Many religions other than Christianity also have teachings similar to the Golden Rule.

Golgotha The hill outside JERUSALEM where Jesus was CRUCIFIED. It means 'the place of the skull'. In the KING JAMES VERSION it is called CALVARY (Luke 23:33).

❦ Today there are two locations in Jerusalem that are identified as possible sites of Golgotha and the EMPTY TOMB: the Church of the Holy Sepulcher and the Garden Tomb.

Good Samaritan, parable of the When Jesus told a lawyer to LOVE THY NEIGHBOR AS THYSELF, the lawyer asked, "Who is my neighbor?" Jesus responded by telling the PARABLE of the Good Samaritan (Luke 10):

A JEW was traveling along the road to JERICHO and was attacked by bandits who beat him up and robbed him. A Jewish PRIEST came by but did nothing to help the man. Then a LEVITE (a TEMPLE worker) came by and also did nothing to help the man. Finally, a SAMARITAN, who was despised by the Jews, came along and helped the man. He dressed his wounds, took him to an inn, and paid the innkeeper to care for the man.

Jesus asked the lawyer, "Which of the three was a neighbor to the man?" The lawyer answered, "The one who showed pity." Jesus responded, "Go and do likewise."

❦ Today, a Good Samaritan is anyone who goes out of his way to help someone in distress.

Good Shepherd Jesus called himself the Good Shepherd (John 10). He meant that he loves and cares for his followers, just as a SHEPHERD cares for his SHEEP. *See also* LOST SHEEP, PARABLE OF THE.

THE GOOD SHEPHERD "I am the Good Shepherd. The Good Shepherd lays down his life for the sheep" (John 10:11, TLB).

great commission Jesus' instruction to his DISCIPLES to preach the GOSPEL throughout the world: "Therefore go and make disciples of all nations, BAPTIZING them in the name of the FATHER and of the SON and of the HOLY SPIRIT, and teaching them to obey everything I have commanded you" (Matthew 28:19-20, NIV). A slightly different version is recorded in Mark 16:15: "GO YE INTO ALL THE WORLD, and preach the gospel to every creature."

Greece A country in southeastern Europe on the major peninsula that juts into the MEDITERRANEAN SEA east of Italy. It was the center of the Greek Empire, which flourished during the period between the Old Testament and the New Testament. By the first century A.D., Greece was part of the ROMAN EMPIRE. The APOSTLE PAUL visited Greece several times and started several churches there (e.g., in Corinth and Philippi). GREEK was the trade language of the portions of the Roman Empire that had previously been conquered by Alexander the Great, and the New Testament was written in KOINĒ ('common') Greek.

Herod There were four generations of rulers in PALESTINE, all named Herod. They are confusing to many Bible readers, because in most instances the text simply refers to "Herod."

Herod the Great, a ruthless ruler, was king of the entire region of Palestine, 37–4 B.C. He was responsible for many building projects, including the third TEMPLE in JERUSALEM. He was king at the time of the birth of Jesus. The WISE MEN naturally went to see King Herod to inquire about the newborn KING OF THE JEWS (Matthew 2). Herod was insanely jealous of anyone who might try to usurp his throne, so he told the wise men to let him know when they found this new king. When they returned home without reporting back to him, Herod was furious and ordered the death of all the boys in BETHLEHEM under the age of two. (This event is sometimes called the Slaughter of the Holy Innocents.) JOSEPH was warned of this danger in a dream, so he and MARY made a hasty FLIGHT TO EGYPT to protect their baby son. Herod the Great died in 4 B.C., so Jesus' birth may have been as early as 6 B.C.

HEROD Herod the Great was king in Palestine at the time Jesus was born.

When Herod the Great died, his kingdom was divided among three of his sons. JUDEA and SAMARIA went to Archelaus, GALILEE and the region east of the JORDAN RIVER went to Herod Antipas, and the northeastern portions of the kingdom went to Herod Philip I.

When Joseph and Mary and Jesus returned from Egypt, they bypassed Judea and went to Galilee when they heard that the wicked Archelaus had succeeded Herod the Great in Judea (Matthew 2).

Herod Antipas (also called Herod the Tetrarch), the ruler in Galilee, participated in the trial of Jesus (Luke 23). He was visiting in JERUSALEM at the time, so PILATE sent Jesus to him. Herod asked Jesus many questions to which Jesus gave no reply. Herod and his soldiers then mocked Jesus, put a kingly robe on him, and sent him back to Pilate. Herod Antipas was also responsible for the death of JOHN THE BAPTIST (*see* SALOME).

Herod Agrippa, a grandson of Herod the Great, is mentioned briefly in Acts 12, where he is called Herod the king. As his grandfather had been, Herod Agrippa was king over the entire region of Palestine. He was responsible for the death of the APOSTLE JAMES (son of Zebedee), and he imprisoned PETER. He died suddenly after receiving the acclamation of the people of the cities of Tyre and Sidon, who said of him,

"This is the voice of a god, and not of a man." HERODIAS was his sister.

Herod Agrippa II, the son of Herod Agrippa and great-grandson of Herod the Great, is mentioned in Acts 25, where he is called King Agrippa. He was king over northern and eastern Palestine. He interrogated PAUL after Paul's appeal to CAESAR. Secular history tells us that his sister Bernice was his mistress. Another sister, Drusilla, married Felix, the Roman governor of Judea who heard Paul's case (Acts 24).

Herodias A granddaughter of HEROD the Great and sister of HEROD Agrippa I. She married her uncle, HEROD Philip I. Later she married another uncle, HEROD Antipas. JOHN THE BAPTIST kept saying it was wrong for Herod Antipas to marry the wife of Herod Philip, and Herodias got revenge by arranging for John's death. At a wild birthday party for Herod Antipas, Herodias's daughter, SALOME, danced and pleased the king and his guests (Mark 6). Herod told her she could have anything she requested. She consulted with her mother, then asked for the head of John the Baptist on a platter.

holy family JOSEPH, MARY, and Jesus are called the holy family.

Hosanna During Jesus' TRIUMPHAL ENTRY into JERUSALEM, the crowds shouted, "Hosanna to the SON OF DAVID" (Matthew 21:9). *Hosanna* is a HEBREW expression meaning 'Save!' It became an expression of praise.

Immanuel The PROPHET ISAIAH said, "Behold, a virgin shall conceive, and bear a son, and shall call his name Immanuel" (Isaiah 7:14). Matthew 1:23 quotes this PROPHECY and shows that it was fulfilled by Jesus' birth. MATTHEW also tells us what the HEBREW name means—'God with us'. The name is spelled Emmanuel in the KING JAMES VERSION.

THE HOLY FAMILY This painting by Michelangelo shows Joseph, Mary, and the infant Jesus.

James (brother of Jesus) During Jesus' ministry, his brothers did not believe he was the MESSIAH. After Jesus' death, RESURRECTION, and ASCENSION, however, his brother James became one of the leaders of the church in JERUSALEM (Acts 15). Many scholars believe he wrote the letter that we know as the book of JAMES.

❦ There are several references in the New Testament to Jesus' brothers and sisters. Matthew 13:55 lists four brothers: James, Joseph (Joses), Simon, and Jude (Judas). Some people prefer to call them half brothers of Jesus, since God was Jesus' father. The tradition in the ROMAN CATHOLIC CHURCH, which holds that MARY was a virgin her whole life, is that they were cousins of Jesus. Another possibility is that they were JOSEPH's children from an earlier marriage.

James (son of Alphaeus) One of Jesus' DISCIPLES. The Bible gives us no other details about him.

James (son of Zebedee) A fisherman who became one of Jesus' DISCIPLES. James, his brother JOHN, and PETER were the three disciples who were closest to Jesus. James was present at the TRANSFIGURATION and was also with Jesus in the Garden of GETHSEMANE. He was the first of the disciples to be MARTYRED when he was put to death by King HEROD Agrippa (Acts 12).

Jerusalem, Council at The first CHURCH COUNCIL was held in JERUSALEM in about A.D. 50 to decide whether GENTILE converts had to become converts to JUDAISM in order to become Christians. PETER told the church leaders in Jerusalem about the CONVERSION of CORNELIUS, and that the HOLY SPIRIT had come upon Cornelius and the other Gentile believers. The conclusion of the Council was that Gentiles did not have to be CIRCUMCISED in order to be Christians.

Jesus Also called Jesus Christ, he is the central figure in the New Testament. His life and ministry are the subject of each of the four GOSPELS. The name *Jesus* means 'YAHWEH IS SALVATION' and is the same name as the HEBREW *Joshua*. Jesus is often referred to as the founder of the Christian religion. Actually, it was his DISCIPLES and the other APOSTLES who spread the GOSPEL (the GOOD NEWS) and started churches after Jesus' ASCENSION to HEAVEN.

Jesus' mother, MARY, was a virgin, and his birth was announced to SHEPHERDS by ANGELS. He was born in BETHLEHEM, was taken to EGYPT to escape the wrath of a king, and grew up in GALILEE as a carpenter's son. He performed many MIRACLES during his public ministry, was betrayed by one of his DISCIPLES, was CRUCIFIED by the ROMAN government, came back to life again in three days, and ascended into heaven.

The exact years of Jesus' birth and death are uncertain. Scholars believe he was born no later than 4 B.C., which is the year HEROD the Great died. Luke 3:23 tells us that Jesus "was about thirty years old when he began his ministry" (NIV). The events recorded in the GOSPELS suggest that his earthly ministry lasted three or four years, so he might have been about thirty-four when he was crucified. He died during the period that PILATE was governor of JUDEA, which was A.D. 26–36.

Christians accept Jesus as the SON OF GOD, the MESSIAH promised to the people of ISRAEL in the Old Testament. Most JEWS do not accept Jesus as their Messiah, viewing him instead as simply a good teacher. To Muslims, Jesus is an important PROPHET.

John (the disciple) One of Jesus' closest DISCIPLES. John refers to himself as "the disciple whom Jesus loved" (John 13:23). Before meeting Jesus, he was already a disciple of JOHN THE BAPTIST. He wrote the GOSPEL of JOHN, which is an eyewitness account of the life and ministry of Jesus. After the ASCENSION, PETER and John became leaders of the EARLY CHURCH. John wrote the EPISTLES we call 1 JOHN, 2 JOHN, and 3 JOHN. He may also have written the book of REVELATION.

John the Baptist John's role was to announce the coming of the MESSIAH, as ISAIAH had predicted he would. John was the son of ZECHARIAH and ELIZABETH. He lived in the WILDERNESS and ate locusts and wild honey. When he preached, great crowds came out to hear him, and he BAPTIZED them in the JORDAN RIVER. When Jesus came to be baptized, John said, "Behold! The LAMB OF GOD who

takes away the sin of the world!" (John 1:29, NKJV). John was beheaded by HEROD Antipas (*see* HERODIAS *and* SALOME).

Joseph (husband of Mary) The earthly father of Jesus. Very little is known about Joseph, except that he was a carpenter and was a descendant of King DAVID. He was a man of upright principles, as evidenced by his plan not to marry MARY when he found out she was pregnant. An ANGEL told him in a dream that Mary's child had been conceived by the HOLY SPIRIT and that he should marry her (Matthew 1). Presumably he died before Jesus began his public ministry.

Joseph of Arimathea After Jesus died on the CROSS, Joseph of Arimathea asked PILATE for permission to bury the body (John 19). Joseph and NICODEMUS then embalmed Jesus' body and laid it in Joseph's own rock-hewn tomb. Joseph was a member of the SANHEDRIN and had become a follower of Jesus.

Judas (son of James) Another name for THADDAEUS, one of Jesus' DISCIPLES. The Bible tells us very little about him.

Judas Iscariot One of Jesus' DISCIPLES—the one who betrayed him to the Jewish leaders. Judas received THIRTY PIECES OF SILVER for betraying Jesus (Matthew 26). After Jesus' last PASSOVER meal with the disciples (the

Names for Jesus

NAME	MEANING
ALPHA AND OMEGA	The beginning and the end
BREAD OF LIFE	The ultimate sustenance—that which gives ETERNAL LIFE
CHRIST	GREEK: 'Anointed one' (*see* MESSIAH)
GOOD SHEPHERD	One who cares for his SHEEP in the best possible manner
IMMANUEL	GOD with us
JESUS	YAHWEH IS SALVATION
King of ISRAEL	By implication, *the* king (MESSIAH) who had been foretold in the OLD TESTAMENT
KING OF THE JEWS	A facetious title given him by PILATE
LAMB OF GOD	The one whom God accepted as a suitable SACRIFICE
LORD	Master
Master	A person with authority
MESSIAH	HEBREW: 'Anointed one' (*see* CHRIST)
Nazarene	A person from NAZARETH
PRINCE OF PEACE	One who embodies peace and brings peace
PROPHET	A person who speaks with divinely inspired revelations
RABBI	My master; a term of respect used for great teachers
REDEEMER	The one who redeems (buys back)
SAVIOR	One who saves; specifically, the one who can save people from the punishment their SIN deserves
SON OF DAVID	A descendant of King DAVID, but specifically the descendant who would be the promised Messiah
SON OF GOD	Jesus was the "only-begotten" or unique son whose father is God; the second person of the TRINITY
SON OF MAN	A representative of mankind, but Jesus used the term as a claim to divinity
Teacher	One who teaches
WORD	The personification of the message revealed from God

LAST SUPPER), Judas led the Jewish leaders to the Garden of GETHSEMANE and betrayed Jesus there by greeting him with a kiss. When he saw that Jesus was actually condemned to death, Judas committed suicide.

Judea   During the New Testament period, the term was used both for PALESTINE as a whole and specifically for the Roman province of Judea, which was south of SAMARIA. JERUSALEM was the capital of Judea. Pontius PILATE was the Roman governor of Judea during the years of Jesus' public ministry.

King of Kings   In Revelation 19, Jesus is described as a great warrior on a white horse who destroys the beast (the ANTICHRIST) and the kings and nations that follow the beast. On Jesus' robe and on his thigh is written this title: KING OF KINGS, AND LORD OF LORDS. It means that Jesus is more powerful than all other kings, no matter how powerful they may appear.

❦ One of the epic motion pictures built around the life of Jesus was *King of Kings* (1961). The "HALLELUJAH CHORUS" from HANDEL's *MESSIAH* includes the refrain, "King of Kings and Lord of Lords."

king of the Jews   When the WISE MEN visited King HEROD the Great, they asked where they could find the newborn "King of the Jews"

(Matthew 2). They expected to find the infant king in the royal palace.

After PILATE condemned Jesus to death by CRUCIFIXION, the Roman soldiers flogged Jesus. Then they put a purple robe on him and put a CROWN OF THORNS on his head. They knelt down in mockery and said, "Hail, King of the Jews." When Jesus was nailed to the CROSS, the soldiers put a sign above his head that said, in ARAMAIC, LATIN, and GREEK: JESUS OF NAZARETH, THE KING OF THE JEWS (John 19:19). The chief PRIESTS objected to the wording of the sign and asked Pilate to change it to "He said, I am King of the Jews," but Pilate refused to change it.

KING OF THE JEWS The sign above the cross says INRI, an abbreviation for the Latin inscription that means 'Jesus of Nazareth, King of the Jews'.

❦ CRUCIFIXES often show a sign above Jesus' head that says INRI. This is an abbreviation for the Latin words *Iesus Nazarenus Rex Iudaeorum* ('Jesus of Nazareth, King of the Jews').

Lamb of God Once when JOHN THE BAPTIST saw Jesus approaching, John said, "Behold! The Lamb of God who takes away the SIN of the world!" John meant that Jesus was like a sacrificial lamb. He was the perfect SACRIFICE sent by God to atone for the sins of mankind. John went on to say, "I have seen and testified that this is the SON OF GOD" (John 1:29, 34, NKJV).

Last Supper, the At the end of Jesus' public ministry, he and his DISCIPLES celebrated the PASSOVER together (Luke 22). When Jesus broke and blessed the bread he said, "THIS IS MY BODY given for you; DO THIS IN REMEMBRANCE OF ME." Then he took the cup and said, "This cup is the NEW COVENANT in my blood, which is poured out for you" (NIV). While they were eating, JUDAS ISCARIOT left to betray Jesus to the chief PRIESTS. After supper Jesus and the other disciples went to the Garden of GETHSEMANE to pray.

In accordance with Jesus' command, Christians celebrate the LORD'S SUPPER, or COMMUNION, to commemorate his death.

❦ One of the most famous works of Renaissance art is LEONARDO DA VINCI's painting called *The LAST SUPPER* (see p. 358).

THE LAST SUPPER Jesus and his disciples celebrate the Passover on the night he was later betrayed; that meal is now called the Last Supper.

Lazarus The brother of MARY AND MARTHA, and one of Jesus' close friends (John 11). When Lazarus died, Jesus waited several days before going to BETHANY, where Lazarus had lived. When Jesus finally arrived, he asked Mary and Martha to take him to the tomb and to roll the stone away from the opening. Martha responded, "By this time he stinketh, for he hath been dead four days." But when they opened the tomb, Jesus prayed and called out to Lazarus. Lazarus then came back to life and came out of the grave, still wrapped in his grave clothes.

Levi *See* MATTHEW.

loaves and fishes, miracle of the On two different occasions Jesus miraculously provided food for a huge crowd of people who had been listening to him teach (Mark 6,

Mark 8). Once there were 5,000 men (not to mention the women and children), and another time there were 4,000 men. In the first instance, a boy in the crowd gave the DISCIPLES five small loaves of bread and two dried fishes. Jesus took the loaves and fishes, blessed them, and began dividing them. They were miraculously multiplied, and the entire crowd was fed. The feeding of the 5,000 is the only MIRACLE of Jesus that is reported in each of the four GOSPELS.

lost sheep, parable of the Jesus told this PARABLE to show that God cares for and seeks out each person (Luke 15). If a SHEPHERD had 100 SHEEP and lost one of them, he would leave the ninety-nine and search for the one that was lost. In the same way, God searches for each of us, even for notorious sinners. *See also* GOOD SHEPHERD.

Luke The writer of the GOSPEL of LUKE and of the book of ACTS. He was a physician who wanted to write an orderly account of all he had learned about Jesus and about the activities of the APOSTLES and the growth of the EARLY CHURCH. He was a close companion of PAUL's and undoubtedly observed firsthand much of what is recorded in the book of Acts.

Magi *See* WISE MEN.

Magnificat The song the VIRGIN MARY sang after the ANGEL GABRIEL an-nounced to her that she would be the mother of Jesus, the MESSIAH (Luke 1:46-55). *Magnificat* is LATIN for 'magnifies' and is the first word in the Latin text of the Magnificat. It has been repeated by Christians for centuries, both in LATIN and in vernacular languages such as English. It has been set to music in many variations. As translated in the NEW INTERNATIONAL VERSION, it begins:

My soul magnifies the Lord,
My spirit rejoices in God my savior;
For he has been mindful of the humble
    estate of his servant.
Now all generations will call me blessed.

mammon Jesus said in the SERMON ON THE MOUNT, "NO MAN CAN SERVE TWO MASTERS. . . . YE CANNOT SERVE GOD AND MAMMON" (Matthew 6:24). Mammon means money or wealth.

manger A simple wood structure that holds hay for livestock to eat. Jesus was born in a stable because his parents arrived in BETHLEHEM and found that there was NO ROOM IN THE INN (Luke 2). His mother wrapped him in SWADDLING CLOTHES and laid him in the manger. Perhaps the manger was the cleanest spot she could find.

Mark The writer of the GOSPEL of MARK. Also called John Mark, he traveled with PAUL and BARNABAS on their first MISSIONARY JOURNEY, but he deserted them and returned to JERUSALEM. When Barnabas recommended that they again take Mark on their second journey, Paul flatly refused (Acts 15), so Barnabas took Mark, and Paul traveled with SILAS.

Martha *See* MARY AND MARTHA.

Mary (mother of Jesus) She is often called the VIRGIN MARY, because she was a virgin when Jesus was born. She was a young woman, perhaps about fourteen at the time of her engagement to JOSEPH. While she was still engaged, the ANGEL GABRIEL told her (*see* ANNUNCIATION) that she would have a son, and that she was to name him Jesus (Luke 1). She asked how this could be, since she was a virgin, but the angel said, "The HOLY SPIRIT will come upon you, and the power of the Most High will overshadow you. So the holy one to be born will be called the SON OF GOD." Joseph wanted to break their engagement when he found out that Mary was pregnant, but the angel appeared to him in a dream and told him to marry her. We do not know much about Mary after the birth of Jesus, though she was still living at the time of Jesus' death.

The DOCTRINE of the ROMAN CATHOLIC CHURCH is that Mary remained a virgin for her entire life. Many PROTESTANTS do not accept this doctrine, since the GOSPELS name several of Jesus' brothers and refer to his sisters. For a comment about varying interpretations of who "Jesus' broth-

ers" were, see the entry for JAMES (brother of Jesus).

Other DOGMAS of the Roman Catholic church include the IMMACULATE CONCEPTION (the doctrine that Mary was conceived without ORIGINAL SIN) and the Assumption of Mary (the doctrine that she was taken bodily to HEAVEN without dying). She is often called the Mother of God by CATHOLICS (*see* HAIL MARY *under "Church Life and Theology"*).

MARY "The angel said to her, 'Do not be afraid, Mary, you have found favor with God. You will be with child and give birth to a son, and you are to give him the name Jesus'" (Luke 1:30-31, NIV).

Mary and Martha With their brother, LAZARUS, these sisters were Jesus' close friends. Once when

Jesus visited in their home, Mary sat at Jesus' feet and listened to his teaching while Martha worked in the kitchen, preparing the meal (Luke 10). Martha complained that Mary was not doing her share of the work, but Jesus responded, "Mary has chosen what is better" (NIV). Shortly before Jesus was betrayed and killed, Mary anointed his feet with costly perfume and wiped his feet with her hair as an act of devotion.

Mary Magdalene A follower of Jesus, she was present at the CRUCIFIXION and was one of the women who first found out that Jesus had been raised back to life (Luke 24). Tradition says that she had been a prostitute before meeting Jesus, but the GOSPELS do not say so. It is clear, however, that Jesus cast seven DEMONS out of her.

Matthew One of Jesus' DISCIPLES. He had been a TAX COLLECTOR, a despised occupation, before Jesus called him to follow him (Matthew 9). Matthew is traditionally regarded as the writer of the book of MATTHEW. He is also called LEVI in the GOSPEL accounts.

Matthias After the suicide of JUDAS ISCARIOT, the remaining DISCIPLES selected Matthias to take Judas' place as a witness of the RESURRECTION of Jesus. He is described as a person who had been with Jesus and the disciples throughout Jesus' ministry (Acts 1), but the actual process of selecting between two candidates was done by casting lots (like throwing dice) so God would direct the decision.

Messiah Late in the period of the Old Testament the ISRAELITES began looking for Messiah, 'the anointed one', the great king who would be their liberator and SAVIOR (Daniel 9:25-26). His coming had been foreshadowed as early as the time of ADAM and EVE. In the New Testament era, the term *Christ* is equivalent to *Messiah*. Jesus was accepted by many as the Messiah in DAVID's royal line, but others chose not to believe that he was the REDEEMER God had promised. Christians accept Jesus as the Messiah, the one anointed by God as the Savior; most JEWS do not accept Jesus as the Messiah.

❦ One of the great works of SACRED MUSIC is *MESSIAH*, by George Frederick HANDEL. It presents great prophetic passages from the Old Testament, then uses New Testament texts to present the birth, death, and resurrection of Jesus the Messiah.

Michael Michael and GABRIEL are ARCHANGELS and are the only ANGELS mentioned by name in the Bible. Michael is seen in the tenth chapter of DANIEL engaged in warfare against "the prince of PERSIA," which was evidently an evil spirit power. In Revelation 12, Michael and his angels defeat the dragon (SATAN) in a great battle in HEAVEN.

miracles Supernatural events caused by the power of God, often functioning as a sign from God. The Bible is filled with miracles, from the parting of the RED SEA to FIRE FROM HEAVEN to WALKING ON WATER. In a sense, of course, any interaction between God and man is miraculous. Some of the key miracles in the life of Christ are the VIRGIN BIRTH, the RESURRECTION, and the ASCENSION.

Ten Miracles Performed by Jesus

1. TURNING WATER INTO WINE (John 2:1-11)
2. A lame man is healed (John 5:1-16)
3. CALMING THE STORM on the Sea of GALILEE (Mark 4:35-41)
4. Many DEMONS are cast out of a man (Mark 5:1-20)
5. Jairus's daughter is raised from the dead (Mark 5:21-43)
6. Feeding 5,000 people with a few LOAVES AND FISHES (Mark 6:35-44)
7. WALKING ON WATER (Mark 6:45-52)
8. LAZARUS is raised from the dead (John 11:1-45)
9. A blind man receives his sight (Mark 10:46-52)
10. A miraculous catch of fish for the DISCIPLES (John 21:1-14)

Though only one reference is indicated for each miracle, most of these miracles are mentioned in more than one GOSPEL.

EVANGELICALS tend to take at face value the accounts of miracles in the Bible. Christians of a more liberal persuasion are often uncomfortable with the concept of miracles, looking instead for natural explanations for events that are presented in the Bible as miracles.

missionary journeys of Paul The APOSTLE PAUL took three extended trips through the areas that are in present-day Turkey and Greece. His ministry was "both to the JEWS, and also to the Greeks" (Acts 20:21), and he shared the GOOD NEWS about Jesus Christ everywhere he went. Fellowships of BELIEVERS (churches) sprang up in many of the cities he visited, including Ephesus and Galatia (in present-day Turkey) and Philippi, Thessalonica, and Corinth (in present-day Greece). The EPISTLES Paul later sent to these churches are the biblical books of EPHESIANS, GALATIANS, PHILIPPIANS, and so on.

BARNABAS traveled with Paul on his first journey, and SILAS traveled with Paul on the second journey. In his second letter to the CORINTHIANS (chapter 11), Paul described his numerous tribulations. Among other hardships, he was imprisoned, flogged, beaten with rods, stoned, and lashed with thirty-nine lashes on five different occasions. He was shipwrecked three times, and he spent a night and a day in the open sea.

Tradition tells us that Paul also made a trip to Spain near the end of his life, but this is not recorded in the book of ACTS.

money changers   At the time of Jesus there were money changers at the TEMPLE to exchange government-issued money for temple currency. Only temple currency, with no image on the coins, could be used at the temple to buy sacrificial animals. The money changers made an unfair profit in the transaction, and on two occasions Jesus cleansed the temple by turning over the tables of the money changers. He said they had turned his FATHER's house into a den of thieves (Matthew 21:13).

Mount of Olives *See* OLIVES, MOUNT OF.

Nathanael   Another name for BARTHOLOMEW, one of Jesus' DISCIPLES. PHILIP told his friend Nathanael he had found the one MOSES and the PROPHETS had written about—Jesus of Nazareth. Nathanael retorted, "NAZARETH! Can anything good come from there?" When Jesus met Nathanael, he called him "a true ISRAELITE, in whom there is nothing false" (John 1:45-46, NIV).

The Nativity (Luke 2)

And it came to pass in those days, that there went out a decree from Caesar Augustus, that all the world should be taxed. . . . And Joseph also went up from Galilee, out of the city of Nazareth, into Judea, unto the city of David, which is called Bethlehem (because he was of the household and lineage of David:) To be taxed with Mary his espoused wife, being great with child. And so it was, that, while they were there, the days were accomplished that she should be delivered. And she brought forth her firstborn son, and wrapped him in swaddling clothes, and laid him in a manger; because there was no room for them in the inn.

And there were in the same country shepherds abiding in the field, keeping watch over their flock by night. And, lo, the angel of the Lord came upon them, and the glory of the Lord shone round about them: and they were sore afraid. And the angel said unto them, Fear not: for, behold, I bring you good tidings of great joy, which shall be to all people. For unto you is born this day in the city of David a Savior, which is Christ the Lord. And this shall be a sign unto you: Ye shall find the babe wrapped in swaddling clothes, lying in a manger.

And suddenly there was with the angel a multitude of the heavenly host praising God, and saying, Glory to God in the highest, and on earth peace, good will toward men.

And it came to pass, as the angels were gone away from them into heaven, the shepherds said one to another, Let us now go even unto Bethlehem, and see this thing which is come to pass, which the Lord hath made known unto us. And they came with haste, and found Mary, and Joseph, and the babe lying in a manger.

THE NATIVITY "And she brought forth her firstborn son, and wrapped him in swaddling clothes, and laid him in a manger; because there was no room for them in the inn" (Luke 2:7).

Nativity, the The birth of Jesus (nativity means birth). The story of the Nativity is one of the best-known stories in the Bible. It begins with the ANNUNCIATION (Luke 1), the ANGEL GABRIEL's message to MARY that she would become pregnant even though she was a virgin, and that her son would be the SON OF GOD. The angel also gave JOSEPH a message, assuring him that Mary's child was the result of a miraculous conception. When Joseph and Mary went to BETHLEHEM to be enrolled in the census, there was no room for

them in the village inn and they had to stay in a stable. It was there that Jesus was born, and Mary laid him in a MANGER. An angel appeared to the SHEPHERDS in the nearby fields to give them the glorious news that the SAVIOR, Christ the Lord, had been born in Bethlehem.

❧ The Nativity has been the subject of thousands of works of art and songs through the centuries. Many familiar CHRISTMAS carols, including "SILENT NIGHT" and "O COME, ALL YE FAITHFUL," take us back to the events in Bethlehem 2,000 years ago.

Nazareth The village where Jesus grew up. It is in GALILEE, about seventy miles north of JERUSALEM and BETHLEHEM. The familiar NATIVITY narrative in Luke 2 says "And JOSEPH also went up from Galilee, out of the city of Nazareth, into JUDEA, unto the city of DAVID, which is called Bethlehem." Although Joseph and MARY were traveling south, they "went up" to Bethlehem, which is in the hill country of Judea and substantially higher in altitude than Nazareth. Jesus was born in Bethlehem, but his family returned to Nazareth after their unexpected FLIGHT TO EGYPT. Since he grew up in Nazareth, he was called a Nazarene.

There was a Roman army garrison in Nazareth, which may have been one reason the residents of Nazareth were looked down on by other JEWS.

When NATHANAEL first heard about Jesus, he said, "Can any good thing come out of Nazareth?" (John 1:46). Jesus returned to Nazareth after he had started his public ministry, but the people there who knew him so well refused to accept him as the MESSIAH. Jesus said, "A PROPHET IS NOT WITHOUT HONOR, SAVE IN HIS OWN COUNTRY, and in his own house" (Matthew 13:57).

FROM NAZARETH TO BETHLEHEM Caesar's decree for a census of the entire Roman Empire made it necessary for Joseph and Mary to leave their hometown, Nazareth. Mary was nine months pregnant, but they walked the seventy miles to the Judean village of Bethlehem. It was there that Jesus was born.

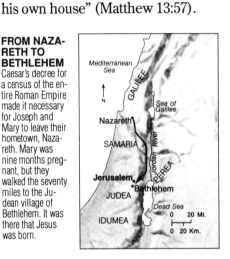

Nicodemus A PHARISEE and a member of the SANHEDRIN. He paid a secret visit to Jesus one night to find out more about Jesus and his teachings. Jesus told him, "No one can see the kingdom of God unless he is BORN AGAIN." Jesus went on to tell Nicodemus, as recorded in JOHN 3:16, "FOR GOD SO LOVED THE WORLD, that he gave his only begotten SON, that whosoever believeth in him should not perish, but have everlasting life."

Nicodemus evidently became a BELIEVER, because he later spoke up in Jesus' defense in the Sanhedrin. Af-

ter the CRUCIFIXION, Nicodemus joined JOSEPH OF ARIMATHEA in asking PILATE for Jesus' body for burial.

no room in the inn When JOSEPH and MARY traveled to BETHLEHEM to register in the census, they found that there was no room available in the village inn (Luke 2). That's why they ended up staying in a stable—where Jesus was born.

Nunc dimittis See SIMEON.

Olives, Mount of The hill immediately to the east of JERUSALEM. The Garden of GETHSEMANE is at the foot of the Mount of Olives. BETHANY, the home of MARY AND MARTHA and LAZARUS, was on the far side of the Mount of Olives. Jesus and his DISCIPLES were on the Mount of Olives when he ascended into HEAVEN. The Mount of Olives is sometimes called Olivet.

Onesimus A slave who ran away from his master, PHILEMON. PAUL befriended Onesimus, who became a BELIEVER under Paul's teaching. Paul sent him back to Philemon with a letter in which Paul asked Philemon to accept Onesimus back as a brother. We know this letter as the book of PHILEMON.

parables Stories with a deeper meaning than is readily apparent. Jesus frequently taught in parables. Sometimes he explained his parables to his DISCIPLES to make sure they understood him (e.g., the parable of the SOWER, Matthew 13:1-23).

The parable of the PRODIGAL SON shows that God continues to love us, no matter how far we roam from fellowship with him. He always awaits our return and welcomes us back. The parable of the LOST SHEEP shows that God loves every one of us. In the parable of the PEARL OF GREAT PRICE, Jesus said the KINGDOM OF HEAVEN is like a pearl that is more valuable than any other possession.

Ten Parables of Jesus

1. The SOWER and the four types of soil (Matthew 13:1-23)
2. The PEARL OF GREAT PRICE (Matthew 13:45-46)
3. The LOST SHEEP (Matthew 18:12-14)
4. The unforgiving debtor (Matthew 18:21-35)
5. The GOOD SAMARITAN (Luke 10:25-37)
6. The rich fool who died (Luke 12:13-21)
7. The PRODIGAL SON (Luke 15:11-32)
8. The obedient and disobedient sons (Matthew 21:28-32)
9. The marriage feast to which no one came (Matthew 22:1-14)
10. The money (TALENTS) loaned for investment (Matthew 25:14-30)

Passion of Christ The events of the last week of Jesus' ministry are called the Passion of Christ. As observed in the church today, Passion Week (also called Holy Week) begins on PALM SUNDAY and ends a week later, before daybreak on EASTER Sunday.

❦ Passion plays are elaborate plays that portray the events in the last week of Jesus' life, culminating in the CRUCIFIXION and RESURRECTION. Perhaps the most famous is the Passion play in Oberammergau, Germany, which is presented every ten years.

Paul Often called St. Paul or the APOSTLE Paul, he was the first great MISSIONARY and THEOLOGIAN in Christian history. He lived in the second half of the first century A.D. and wrote many of the letters that became books of the New Testament. His story is told in the book of ACTS, where he is initially called SAUL (his HEBREW name).

He was a devout JEW—a PHARISEE—who was ferocious in persecuting Christians during the first years of the EARLY CHURCH. Once when he was on his way to Damascus (*see* DAMASCUS ROAD) to persecute the Christians there, he was blinded by a bright light from HEAVEN and heard the voice of Jesus asking, "Saul, Saul, why are you persecuting me?" (Acts 9:4, NKJV). Saul was blind for several days, until Ananias, a Christian leader, was prompted by the HOLY SPIRIT to see him. Ananias laid hands on Saul, and Saul's sight was restored and he received the HOLY

SPIRIT. From that point forward Saul, now called Paul, was a fearless witness of the power of Christ and an intelligent APOLOGIST for the GOSPEL. He was beaten, stoned, flogged, arrested, and thrown in prison because of his faith, but he was not deterred. At the end of his life he was imprisoned in ROME, where, according to tradition, he was MARTYRED under Nero.

pearl of great price, parable of the Jesus said the KINGDOM OF HEAVEN is like a very expensive pearl (Matthew 13). A pearl merchant will sell everything he has to purchase a choice pearl. In the same way, we should be willing to give up all earthly treasures to obtain entrance to the kingdom of heaven.

Pentecost In the Old Testament the Feast of Pentecost was celebrated fifty days after PASSOVER (the word *Pentecost* is derived from the GREEK for 'fiftieth day'). Also called the Feast of Weeks, it was a time to celebrate and praise God for the harvest. By the period of the New Testament, Pentecost also commemorated the giving of the LAW to MOSES. Pentecost is celebrated by JEWS today as Shabuoth.

A week after Jesus' ASCENSION into HEAVEN, at the time of the Feast of Pentecost, Jesus' followers were all together in a room in JERUSALEM. Suddenly a sound like a mighty, rushing wind filled the house, and what seemed to be tongues of fire came and rested on their heads. They were filled with the HOLY SPIRIT, and they began SPEAKING IN TONGUES—speaking languages they had not learned. PETER then gave a great public message, and about 3,000 people became BELIEVERS that day.

In the CHURCH YEAR, Pentecost (also called Whitsunday) is a celebration of the coming of the Holy Spirit. The term *Pentecost* has come to be synonymous with the coming of Holy Spirit. The term *Pentecostal* has been adopted by DENOMINATIONS that emphasize the supernatural GIFTS OF THE HOLY SPIRIT, especially speaking in tongues.

Peter One of Jesus' DISCIPLES, he was also called Simon and Cephas. Both *Peter* (GREEK) and *Cephas* (ARAMAIC) mean 'rock'. Like JAMES and JOHN, Peter was a fisherman, and the three of them were in Jesus' inner circle of followers. Peter was the first of the disciples to recognize that Jesus was the MESSIAH. He said, "THOU ART THE CHRIST, THE SON OF THE LIVING GOD" (Matthew 16:16). After Jesus was betrayed in the Garden of GETHSEMANE, Peter denied knowing him three different times, but then was stricken with grief.

After the ASCENSION, Peter became one of the leaders of the EARLY CHURCH (Acts 1–12). He wrote the books of

1 PETER and 2 PETER. The ROMAN CATH-OLIC CHURCH points to Peter as the first head of the church, with all POPES (i.e., BISHOPS of ROME) being his successors.

❦ St. Peter is popularly said to be the keeper of the keys to HEAVEN, with authority to determine who can enter and who cannot enter.

Pharisees An important party within JUDAISM during the period of the New Testament. They were experts in the MOSAIC LAW and in the hundreds of additional laws devised to ensure that the people kept the laws in the BOOKS OF MOSES. Jesus was very critical of the Pharisees. He called them HYPOCRITES because they were concerned about tiny infractions of their own rules while they themselves did not live by the spirit of the laws of MOSES. NICODEMUS and PAUL were both Pharisees who became followers of Jesus.

Philemon A friend of PAUL's, to whom Paul wrote the letter that we know as the book of PHILEMON. Philemon's slave, ONESIMUS, had run away, but he became a BELIEVER under Paul's teaching. Paul sent Onesimus back to Philemon with a letter in which he asked Philemon to accept Onesimus as a brother.

Philip (the disciple) One of Jesus' DISCIPLES. We do not know much about him except that he introduced NATHANAEL to Jesus. Note

that he is not the same Philip (*see the next entry*) who met the Ethiopian eunuch on the Gaza road.

Philip (the evangelist) One of the seven DEACONS selected by the APOSTLES after the ASCENSION. Philip took the GOOD NEWS to SAMARIA, where many people became BELIEVERS. One day Philip was sent by an ANGEL to the desert road to Gaza (Acts 8). There Philip met an Ethiopian eunuch who was reading PROPHECIES from the book of ISAIAH but without understanding them. Philip helped him understand that Jesus was the person about whom ISAIAH had been prophesying. The Ethiopian was delighted to hear the GOOD NEWS and, when he saw some water, asked Philip to BAPTIZE him.

Pilate, Pontius The ROMAN governor of JUDEA at the time of Jesus' ministry. (Secular history tells us that Pilate was governor during the years A.D. 26–36.) When Jesus was betrayed by JUDAS ISCARIOT and then tried by the Jewish leaders, he was taken to Pilate for sentencing (*see* TRIAL OF JESUS). Pilate questioned him, sent him to HEROD Antipas, questioned him again, and announced that Jesus was not guilty. He had a custom of releasing one Jewish prisoner each PASSOVER, so he offered to set Jesus free, but the people and their leaders asked for the release of the murderer BARABBAS instead. To appease the Jewish leaders, Pilate sentenced Jesus to death by CRUCIFIX-ION. Before doing so, however, he publicly washed his hands as a symbol of his innocence regarding Jesus' death (Matthew 27).

❦ If a person "washes his hands" of a situation, he is disclaiming responsibility for it.

Pontius Pilate *See* PILATE, PONTIUS.

Prince of Peace A title for the MESSIAH, as PROPHESIED in Isaiah 9:6. *See* UNTO US A CHILD IS BORN *under "Quotations from the Bible."*

Priscilla *See* AQUILA AND PRISCILLA.

Prodigal Son, parable of the To illustrate God's love for those who are lost or who reject him, Jesus told this PARABLE (Luke 15):

A man had two sons, the younger of whom demanded his portion of their inheritance. He then left home and squandered his money in riotous living. Finally, penniless and friendless and hungry, he decided to return to his father. He was sure his father would not accept him as a son, but perhaps he could be a servant in his father's household. The father, who had been mourning for him, saw him coming and ran and embraced him. The son apologized and said he was no longer worthy to be called a son, but the father told his servants to kill the FATTED CALF and prepare a celebration feast.

The older brother was angry that the father was celebrating the return of the wayward son. "I've worked hard for you all these years, and you've never put on a celebration for me," he exclaimed. But the father remonstrated, "It is right to celebrate. Your brother was lost, but now he is found."

❦ The word *prodigal* means recklessly extravagant, but by extension from the parable it has come also to mean a person who returns home after a period of rebellion.

THE PRODIGAL SON "While he was still a long distance away, his father saw him coming, and was filled with loving pity and ran and embraced him and kissed him" (Luke 15:20, TLB).

publicans *See* TAX COLLECTORS.

rabbi A Jewish teacher, scholar, and religious leader. Jesus was called a rabbi by some of his followers.

Resurrection, the Resurrection means coming back to life after having died. After Jesus was CRUCIFIED, his body was laid in a rock-hewn tomb donated by JOSEPH OF ARIMATHEA. At the request of the chief PRIESTS, Roman guards were posted to ensure that Jesus' DISCIPLES would not steal his body and claim that he had come back to life. Early on Sunday morning, MARY MAGDALENE and several other women went to the tomb to anoint Jesus' body with spices. They found the tomb was empty, and an ANGEL told them that Jesus had come back to life again (John 20).

Jesus appeared to his disciples and many other followers during the forty days following his resurrection. He was then taken up into HEAVEN (*see* ASCENSION).

Christians around the world celebrate the resurrection of Jesus on EASTER. Also, most Christians observe their day of rest on SUNDAY rather than Saturday (the Jewish SABBATH) because the Resurrection occurred on Sunday.

Roman Empire At its zenith shortly after the New Testament period, the Roman Empire encompassed most of Europe and the lands surrounding the MEDITERRANEAN SEA. It stretched from Spain to PALESTINE, and from England to northern Africa. The Roman Empire consisted of a number of provinces, including JUDEA, SAMARIA, and GALILEE. Christianity spread rapidly through the Roman Empire during the first several centuries after Christ. The Roman government was a very present part of life in Palestine during the time of Jesus. MARY and JOSEPH traveled from NAZARETH to BETHLEHEM because of a census decreed by CAESAR AUGUSTUS. The ZEALOTS were a Jewish party whose aim was to overthrow the rule of ROME in the Jewish territories. Pontius PILATE was the Roman governor of Judea at the time of Jesus' public ministry.

Rome The central city of the ROMAN EMPIRE. The name is sometimes used to refer to the entire Roman Empire or the government of the empire, just as we sometimes use "Washington" and "Tokyo" to refer to the governments of the USA and Japan. PAUL went to Rome to appeal his case to CAESAR (Nero). While he was there under house arrest, he wrote several of his EPISTLES that are now books of the New Testament. *See also* ROME *under "Church History."*

Sadducees An influential priestly party in JUDAISM during the period of the New Testament. The Sadducees accepted only the BOOKS OF MOSES as their SCRIPTURE. The New Testament and JOSEPHUS tell us that the Sadducees did not believe in the supernatural or the resurrection of the dead. The PHARISEES disagreed with the Sadducees on many theological points, but both groups generally rejected Jesus. Jesus, in turn, warned his followers not to be deceived by the teachings of the Pharisees and the Sadducees.

SALOME Salome holds the head of John the Baptist.

Salome Although she is not mentioned by name, she is the daughter of HERODIAS and stepdaughter of King HEROD Antipas whose story is told in the GOSPELS. Salome danced at a wild birthday party for Herod, who was so pleased he offered her anything she requested, up to half his kingdom. She consulted with her mother, who suggested that she ask for the head of JOHN THE BAPTIST on a platter (Mark 6). This saddened Herod, but he felt he could not renege on his promise, so he had John beheaded. Secular history tells us that Salome married Herod Philip II (a son of HEROD the Great). He was her uncle on her father's side and her great-uncle on her mother's side!

Samaria, Samaritans The city of Samaria, about forty miles north of JERUSALEM, was one of the capitals of the NORTHERN KINGDOM of ISRAEL. It was destroyed by the ASSYRIANS in 722 B.C. after a three-year siege. This marked the end of the northern kingdom (2 Kings 17).

During New Testament times, the entire central region of PALESTINE—south of GALILEE and north of JUDEA—was called Samaria. The people of the province of Samaria, the Samaritans, were of mixed ancestry, part Jewish and part GENTILE. As a result of this, the JEWS of Jesus' time considered the Samaritans inferior. Jews would not travel through their land or even speak to them (John 4:9). This provides the context for Jesus' PARABLE of the GOOD SAMARITAN (Luke 10). In the parable, neither the PRIEST nor the LEVITE (a TEMPLE worker) stopped to help the man who had been beaten, but a despised Samaritan stopped and helped him. Jesus told his listeners to emulate the Samaritan, the one who had acted in a neighborly manner.

Jesus shocked his DISCIPLES by traveling through Samaria and by speaking with the WOMAN AT THE WELL, who was a Samaritan (John 4).

Sanhedrin The supreme religious and legal council of the JEWS during the New Testament period. The Sanhedrin had a great deal of civil authority under the rule of the ROMAN EMPIRE, but it did not have the authority to give the death sentence. For that reason, Jesus was taken to PILATE for sentencing after he was tried and found guilty by the Sanhedrin. The members of the Sanhedrin were PRIESTS, PHARISEES, and SCRIBES, and the HIGH PRIEST served as president. The term *chief priests* is frequently used in the GOSPELS to refer to the priests who served in the Sanhedrin as well as other members of prominent priestly families.

Sapphira *See* ANANIAS AND SAPPHIRA.

Saul The HEBREW name of PAUL. In the book of ACTS he is referred to first as Saul of Tarsus, then as Paul.

Savior Jesus is called the Savior because his death paid the penalty for our SINS (*see* ATONEMENT *under "Church Life and Theology"*). In this way he *saves* us from eternal punishment.

scribes The professional interpreters of the LAW during the period of the New Testament. Many of the scribes were PHARISEES. Like the Pharisees and the Sadducees, most of the scribes rejected Jesus. Jesus called them HYPOCRITES, for they insisted that the people follow every detail of the Law, but they themselves missed the spirit of the Law.

Sea of Galilee *See* GALILEE, SEA OF.

sepulcher A tomb. The KING JAMES VERSION uses the word *sepulcher* for the tomb in which Jesus' body was laid after the CRUCIFIXION, but modern TRANSLATIONS tend to use the word *tomb*. It was a small chamber carved in a hillside with a large rock to cover the entrance. *See also* EMPTY TOMB.

Sermon on the Mount Many of Jesus' key teachings are contained in the Sermon on the Mount. It is recorded in chapters 5–7 of the GOSPEL of MATTHEW. The Sermon on the Mount includes the BEATITUDES, the LORD'S PRAYER, the GOLDEN RULE, and phrases such as "ASK, AND IT SHALL BE GIVEN YOU" and "Go the SECOND MILE."

One of the hallmarks of the Sermon on the Mount is the way Jesus reinterprets and applies key teachings from the MOSAIC LAW. For instance, Jesus said, "You have heard that it was said, 'Love your neighbor and hate your enemy.' But I tell you: Love your enemies and pray for those who persecute you" (Matthew 5:43-44, NIV).

seven last words of Christ The term *words* is confusing, for the expression actually refers to the seven *statements* of Jesus while he was on the CROSS. The seven statements have been compiled from the GOS-

PELS, since none of the Gospels records all seven of them. They have been put to music in numerous settings, and GOOD FRIDAY services often include a meditation on this aspect of the PASSION OF CHRIST.

The Seven Last Words of Christ

1. Father, forgive them; for they know not what they do. (Luke 23:34)
2. *To the thief on the cross:* Verily I say unto thee, To day shalt thou be with me in paradise. (Luke 23:43)
3. *To Mary:* Woman, behold thy son! *To John:* Behold thy mother! (John 19:26-27)
4. My God, my God, why hast thou forsaken me? (*Eli, Eli, lama sabachthani?*) (Matthew 27:46, Mark 15:34)
5. I thirst. (John 19:28)
6. Father, into thy hands I commend my spirit. (Luke 23:46)
7. It is finished. (John 19:30)

Silas The APOSTLE PAUL's coworker on his second MISSIONARY JOURNEY. Paul and Silas were thrown into jail in Philippi, and through their ministry the jailer became a BELIEVER (Acts 16).

Simeon An old man who waited expectantly to see the MESSIAH. On the day that MARY and JOSEPH took the infant Jesus to the TEMPLE to present him to the Lord, Simeon went to the temple and recognized Jesus as the Messiah. After holding the child and praising God, Simeon said,

"Lord, now lettest thou thy servant depart in peace . . . for mine eyes have seen thy SALVATION" (Luke 2:29-30). This prayer is called the *Nunc dimittis*, which is how it begins in LATIN.

Simon of Cyrene A visitor in JERUSALEM at the time of Jesus' CRUCIFIXION. Jesus was too weak to carry his own CROSS because he had been flogged by the ROMAN soldiers, so Simon of Cyrene was conscripted to carry it to GOLGOTHA for him (Luke 23).

Simon Peter *See* PETER.

Simon the Zealot One of Jesus' DISCIPLES. Little else is known about him, but the designation "the Zealot" suggests that he may have been a member of the ZEALOTS, a Jewish political group that resisted ROMAN rule.

Son of David When Jesus entered JERUSALEM on a donkey (*see* TRIUMPHAL ENTRY), the crowds shouted, "HOSANNA to the Son of David." When they called him the Son of David, they did not simply mean that he was a direct descendant of King DAVID (which he was). They were hailing him as the MESSIAH, the great deliverer whose coming had been foretold in the Old Testament (Zechariah 9:9).

Son of Man Jesus frequently referred to himself as the Son of Man. While the term seems to emphasize his humanity, Jesus was alluding to the Son of Man mentioned in Daniel 7; he used the term to show that he was the MESSIAH. For instance, MARK 8:31 (NKJV) says, "And he began to teach them that the Son of Man must suffer many things, and be rejected by the elders and chief PRIESTS and SCRIBES, and be killed, and after three days rise again."

sower, parable of the Jesus told this PARABLE (Matthew 13) to illustrate that different people respond differently when they hear the GOSPEL—the GOOD NEWS of God's kingdom:

When a sower (farmer) scattered seed, some fell on the path, and the birds ate it up. Some fell on rocky soil, and it sprouted quickly, but it died in the strong sunshine because its roots had no depth. Some fell among thorns, which grew up and choked out the good plants. And some fell on good soil and grew and yielded an abundant harvest.

Jesus told his DISCIPLES what the parable meant. The seed is the Good News. The path represents the hardened hearts of those who are not receptive to the Good News. The evil one comes and snatches away what has been planted there. The rocky soil is the person who receives the Good News eagerly, but his newly-found faith withers since it has no spiritual roots. The thorny soil is the person who receives the Good News, but the cares of this life spring up and crowd out the spiritual things. Finally, the good soil is the person who is ready to receive the Good News and grow spiritually and yield a harvest of a godly life.

star of Bethlehem *See* WISE MEN.

STEPHEN Stephen is stoned to death—martyred for his faith.

Stephen One of the first group of DEACONS appointed by the APOSTLES after PENTECOST, and the first Christian MARTYR (Acts 7). Stephen performed many miracles, but he was arrested when some Jewish leaders lied about him. He presented a lengthy discourse to the SANHEDRIN, in which he showed that Jesus was the MES-SIAH foretold in the SCRIPTURES. When he accused the Jewish leaders of having murdered the Messiah, they stoned him. The first mention of SAUL of Tarsus is that he was present when Stephen was stoned.

swaddling clothes When Jesus was born his mother wrapped him in swaddling clothes (Luke 2). It's an old-fashioned term, but it simply means strips of cloth that are wrapped around a baby. In the ancient world, the custom of wrapping a baby in swaddling clothes was to ensure that its bones would grow straight.

SYNAGOGUE These ruins are of the synagogue in Capernaum, dating from the fourth century A.D.

synagogue A meeting of JEWS for WORSHIPING God; also, the building where such meetings take place. A synagogue is comparable in function to a Christian church. In New Testament times the synagogue building also functioned as a school. When Jesus traveled around GALILEE and JUDEA, he often taught in synagogues.

talents, parable of the One of Jesus' PARABLES was about a man who gave each of three servants certain sums of money to invest (Matthew 25). To one he gave five talents (a talent was a sum of money, probably more than $1,000), to another two talents, and to another one talent. The servants who received five and two talents invested theirs wisely and doubled their money. The servant who received only one talent buried his in the ground. The master praised the first two as faithful servants, but he called the third one a wicked and lazy servant for not having wisely used what was entrusted to him.

❦ Jesus meant that we are to use wisely all that has been entrusted to us, for we never know when we will be called to account for our life. The use of the word *talent* to mean a special ability or natural aptitude is a figurative extension of *talent* (a monetary value) as it is used in the parable.

tax collectors In the GOSPELS, tax collectors (the KING JAMES VERSION uses the term *publicans*) were at the lowest echelon of Jewish society. They were Jews, but they were hated by their countrymen, both because they often cheated in their tax collecting and because they worked for the oppressive ROMAN government and had frequent contact with GENTILES. Jesus made the PHARISEES furious when he associated with the tax collectors and other sinners. MATTHEW was a tax collector who became one of Jesus' DISCIPLES. ZACCHAEUS was another tax collector who became a follower of Jesus.

temptation of Jesus After Jesus was BAPTIZED by JOHN THE BAPTIST, he went into the WILDERNESS (or desert) for forty days. There he fasted and prayed and was tempted by SATAN. The GOSPEL accounts (e.g., Luke 4) tell of three specific temptations. In each instance Jesus refuted Satan by quoting from the SCRIPTURES.

Jesus was hungry after FASTING so long, and Satan tempted him to turn stones into bread. Jesus quoted from Deuteronomy 8:3 as he responded, "It is written, That MAN SHALL NOT LIVE BY BREAD ALONE, but by every word of God."

Satan then took Jesus to a high mountain and showed him all the kingdoms of the world. Satan said, "If you worship me, it will all be yours" (NIV). Jesus quoted from Deuteronomy 6:13 as he responded, "GET THEE BEHIND ME, SATAN: for it is written, Thou shalt worship the Lord thy God, and him only shalt thou serve."

Finally Satan took Jesus to the high-est point on the TEMPLE and tempted him to jump down and show himself to be the SON OF GOD. Satan quoted from Psalm 91, which says that ANGELS "will lift you up in their hands, so that you will not strike your foot against a stone" (NIV). Jesus responded by quoting from Deuteronomy 6:16, as he said, "It is also written, Do not put the Lord your God to the test."

TEMPTATION OF JESUS "The devil led him up to a high place and showed him in an instant all the kingdoms of the world" (Luke 4:5, NIV).

Thaddaeus One of Jesus' DISCIPLES. Very little is known about him. LUKE called him JUDAS (son of James).

thief on the cross   Jesus was CRU-CIFIED between two thieves. One of them hurled insults at him, "Aren't you the Christ? Save yourself and us." But the other criminal rebuked his fellow. "Don't you fear God? . . . We are getting what our deeds deserve. But this man has done nothing wrong." Then he said, "Jesus, remember me when you come into your kingdom." Jesus answered, "Today you will be with me in PARA-DISE" (Luke 23:39-43, NIV).

thirty pieces of silver   When JUDAS ISCARIOT agreed to betray Jesus to the Jewish leaders, they gave him thirty pieces of silver (Matthew 26). After Jesus was arrested, Judas repented and threw the money onto the floor of the TEMPLE. He then committed suicide. The PRIESTS used the money to buy a field (the Potter's Field) to be used as a cemetery for foreigners.

❦ The term has come to mean any price paid for murder.

Thomas   One of Jesus' DISCIPLES. He is sometimes called Doubting Thomas because of an incident that occurred after Jesus' RESURRECTION (John 20). He had not been present when Jesus appeared to the other disciples, and he did not believe that Jesus was actually alive. He said he would not believe unless he could put his fingers in the holes in Jesus' hands and put his hand in the hole in Jesus' side where he had been pierced by a spear while on the CROSS. A week later, Jesus again appeared to the disciples. He told Thomas, "Put your finger into my hands. Put your hand into my side. Don't be faithless any longer. Believe!" Thomas responded, "My Lord and my God!" (TLB).

❦ A Doubting Thomas is a person who must see something to believe it.

Timothy   A young PASTOR whose mentor in the Christian faith was the APOSTLE PAUL. The books of 1 TIMOTHY and 2 TIMOTHY were letters Paul wrote to Timothy.

Transfiguration, the   One day Jesus took PETER, JAMES, and JOHN with him up a high mountain. While they were there, Jesus' divinity suddenly showed—he was transfigured. The DISCIPLES were allowed to see in advance Jesus' RESURRECTION GLORY. His face shone like the sun, and his clothes became as white as light. Then MOSES and ELIJAH appeared with him. A bright cloud covered them and the voice of God spoke from the cloud: "THIS IS MY BE-LOVED SON, IN WHOM I AM WELL PLEASED" (Matthew 17:5). This event, called the Transfiguration, showed Jesus to be the SON OF GOD.

trial of Jesus   After JUDAS ISCARIOT betrayed Jesus to the Jewish leaders, Jesus was taken to a midnight trial before CAIAPHAS, the HIGH PRIEST. Caiaphas and the SANHEDRIN found

Jesus guilty of BLASPHEMY, a crime punishable by death according to the MOSAIC LAW. Under ROMAN law, however, the Jewish authorities could not impose the death penalty. So the Jewish leaders took Jesus to Pontius PILATE, the Roman governor of JUDEA. He questioned Jesus, but he found him innocent. HEROD Antipas, the king in the region of GALILEE, happened to be in JERUSALEM, so Pilate sent Jesus (who was a Galilean) to Herod for questioning. Herod also found Jesus innocent, and he sent him back to Pilate.

Pilate had Jesus flogged, and the Roman soldiers put a CROWN OF THORNS and a purple robe on him. Pilate then tried to release Jesus, since he had a custom of releasing one Jewish prisoner each year at the time of the PASSOVER, but the Jewish leaders insisted that Jesus be CRUCIFIED. Pilate finally gave in, and he authorized the death sentence, though he publicly washed his hands to show that he was innocent of Jesus' death.

Each of the GOSPELS includes an account of Jesus' trial, though none of them contains all the details. See Matthew 27, Mark 15, Luke 23, and John 18–19.

Triumphal Entry A week before he was CRUCIFIED, Jesus entered JERUSALEM on a donkey (Matthew 21). The crowds recognized this as the fulfillment of an ancient PROPHECY:

"See, your king comes to you, righteous and having SALVATION, gentle and riding on a donkey" (Zechariah 9:9, NIV). In their jubilation, the crowd spread palm branches on the road ahead of him and shouted, "HOSANNA to the SON OF DAVID." They were acclaiming him as the MESSIAH. Just five days later, however, the mob demanded that PILATE crucify Jesus.

Today we commemorate the Triumphal Entry on PALM SUNDAY.

turning water into wine Jesus performed his first MIRACLE at a wedding feast in the village of Cana in GALILEE (John 2). When the master of ceremonies ran out of WINE, Jesus told the servants to fill six large jars with water. Then he told them to draw some out for tasting. The water had become delicious wine, and the master of the feast complimented the bridegroom on serving such good wine.

Via Dolorosa The route Jesus followed as he carried his CROSS from PILATE's residence in JERUSALEM to GOLGOTHA, just outside the city. *Via Dolorosa* is LATIN for 'way of sorrows'. Today, in the "old city" of Jerusalem, the traditional route is marked by fourteen STATIONS OF THE CROSS.

Virgin Birth MARY was still a virgin when Jesus was born, so his birth is called the Virgin Birth. Mary was engaged but not yet married to JOSEPH when the ANGEL GABRIEL appeared to her (see ANNUNCIATION) and told her she would give birth to a son. "How will this be," Mary asked the angel, "since I am a virgin?" The angel answered, "The HOLY SPIRIT will come upon you, and the power of the Most High will overshadow you. So the holy one to be born will be called the SON OF GOD" (Luke 1:26-35, NIV). The fact that Mary was a virgin fulfilled the PROPHECY in Isaiah 7:14 (NIV): "The virgin will be with child and will give birth to a son, and will call him IMMANUEL."

❦ The DOCTRINE of the ROMAN CATHOLIC CHURCH is that Mary remained a virgin throughout her life.

Virgin Mary   *See* MARY (mother of Jesus).

walking on water   Shortly before sunrise on the night after Jesus had performed the miracle of the LOAVES AND FISHES, the DISCIPLES were in a boat in the middle of the Sea of GALILEE. A storm arose, and Jesus saw that they were in trouble and went out to them, walking on the water. They were terrified, thinking he was a ghost, but he told them not to be afraid. PETER then jumped out of the boat and began walking on the water toward Jesus. Suddenly his faith faltered and he began to sink, so Jesus reached out to keep him from sinking. When they got in the boat, the wind died down (Matthew 14).

❦ The term *walking on water* is sometimes used as the epitome of something that is not humanly possible. A person may be very talented, but "he can't walk on water."

WISE MEN "Where is he that is born King of the Jews? for we have seen his star in the east, and are come to worship him" (Matthew 2:2).

wise men   These men, also called Magi, were astrologers (perhaps from BABYLON or PERSIA) who saw a special star in the east and came to JERUSALEM looking for the newborn KING OF THE JEWS (Matthew 2). King HEROD the Great was distraught when he heard of their quest, for he wanted no rival. He inquired of the Jewish teachers and learned that the MESSIAH was to be born in BETHLEHEM. Herod said to the wise men, "Go to Bethlehem and search for the child. And when you find him, come back and tell me so that I can go and worship him too!" (TLB). The wise men went to Bethlehem, found Jesus with his mother, and worshiped him. They gave him precious gifts of GOLD, FRANKINCENSE, AND MYRRH. The wise men were warned in a dream not to return to King Herod, so they returned to their own land by a different way. Herod was furious when he learned that he had been tricked, and he ordered the death of all the boys in Bethlehem under the age of two.

It has traditionally been assumed that there were three wise men, and tradition has even supplied them with names—Caspar, Melchior, and Balthazar—but the Bible does not give us this information.

woman at the well When Jesus was traveling from JUDEA back to GALILEE, he went through SAMARIA. Outside the village of Sychar he stopped at the village well and asked a woman there to give him a drink (John 4). The woman, whose name is not mentioned in the biblical account, expressed surprise that a Jewish man would even speak to a SAMARITAN woman, much less ask for a drink. Jesus responded that she would have asked *him* for *living* water if she had known who he was. Then Jesus told her to get her husband, and she said she was not married. "All too true!" Jesus said. "For you have had five husbands, and you aren't even married to the man you're living with now" (TLB).

After some further conversation, the woman said, "I know that MESSIAH is coming. When he comes, he will explain everything to us." Jesus responded, "I who speak to you am he." She then left her water jug and ran into the village and told everyone, "Come, see a man who told me everything I ever did. Could this be the Christ?" (NIV).

Word, the The GOSPEL of JOHN begins with the words, "IN THE BEGINNING was the Word, and the Word was with God, and the Word was God." The Word was the SON OF GOD, the second person of the TRINITY, who had existed from the very beginning. In the INCARNATION, he was Jesus—the personification of God's message to mankind. But more than that, he was God himself in human form.

Zacchaeus A wealthy TAX COLLECTOR who wanted to see Jesus (Luke 19). Zacchaeus was too short to see over the crowds when Jesus came along the road, so he climbed a sycamore tree. When Jesus came to that spot, he looked up and told Zacchaeus he wanted to have dinner at his house. Like other tax collectors, Zacchaeus charged as much as he could, thereby cheating the public. He was convicted of his SIN because of Jesus' teaching, and he pledged to give half his possessions to the poor.

Zealots A Jewish political party in the first century A.D. They were opposed to paying taxes to ROME, and they sought to free ISRAEL from the yoke of Rome. One of Jesus' DISCIPLES was called SIMON THE ZEALOT, which may indicate an association with that party.

Zechariah (also spelled Zacharias) A PRIEST, he was the husband of ELIZA- BETH and the father of JOHN THE BAPTIST. One day when he was performing his priestly duties in the TEMPLE, the ANGEL GABRIEL appeared to him to tell him that his wife would have a son, and that they were to name him John (Luke 1). Zechariah did not believe the angel, because his wife was too old to have a child. As a result of his disbelief, Zechariah was stricken dumb until the baby was born.

Zion The mountain in JERUSALEM where the TEMPLE was built. By ex- tension, JERUSALEM and all of ISRAEL are sometimes called Zion. By further extension, the worldwide body of Christians is sometimes called Zion.

❦ The Zionist movement of the late nineteenth century was the force behind the migration of JEWS from other lands to PALESTINE, culminating in the establishment of the modern state of Israel.

CHURCH HISTORY

This chapter on CHURCH HISTORY includes the most significant people and events in the history of the church, beginning with the events after those mentioned in the book of Acts. Thus it includes the great CHURCH COUNCILS at NICEA and CHALCEDON, and important movements in church history, such as the REFORMATION, the GREAT AWAKENING, and PENTECOSTALISM. It continues through to the present with terms such as *GLASNOST* and FIRST AMENDMENT RIGHTS, which figure in church history as we see it unfolding in the news each day.

This chapter includes many of the people who have played key roles in church history, including AUGUSTINE OF HIPPO, John WYCLIFFE, Martin LUTHER, IGNATIUS OF LOYOLA, Richard ALLEN, Pope JOHN XXIII, and Billy GRAHAM. Others, such as MICHELANGELO and Johann Sebastian BACH, who are best known as artists and musicians, are listed in the chapter "The Bible and Christianity in the Fine Arts."

Also included are denominational movements such as METHODISM and the ANABAPTIST MOVEMENT, and the largest American DENOMINATIONS.

Church History, 100 B.C. — 1 B.C.

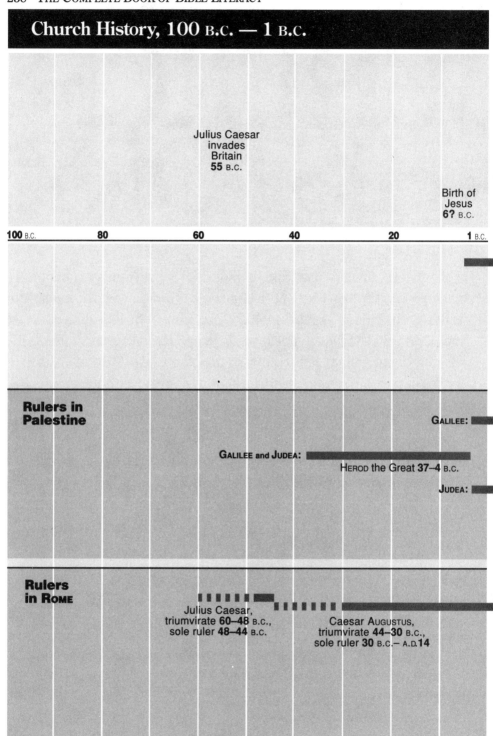

Julius Caesar
invades
Britain
55 B.C.

Birth of
Jesus
6? B.C.

100 B.C.   **80**   **60**   **40**   **20**   **1** B.C.

Rulers in Palestine

GALILEE:

GALILEE and JUDEA:
HEROD the Great **37–4** B.C.

JUDEA:

Rulers in ROME

Julius Caesar,
triumvirate **60–48** B.C.,
sole ruler **48–44** B.C.

Caesar AUGUSTUS,
triumvirate **44–30** B.C.,
sole ruler **30** B.C.– A.D.**14**

A.D. 1— 100

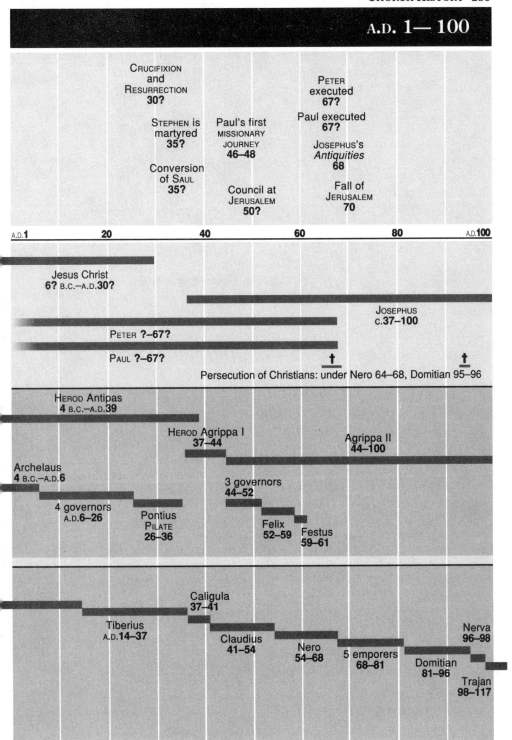

CRUCIFIXION
and
RESURRECTION
30?

STEPHEN is
martyred
35?

Conversion
of SAUL
35?

Paul's first
MISSIONARY
JOURNEY
46–48

Council at
JERUSALEM
50?

PETER
executed
67?

Paul executed
67?

JOSEPHUS's
Antiquities
68

Fall of
JERUSALEM
70

A.D.1   20   40   60   80   A.D.100

Jesus Christ
6? B.C.–A.D.30?

JOSEPHUS
c.37–100

PETER ?–67?

PAUL ?–67?

Persecution of Christians: under Nero 64–68, Domitian 95–96

HEROD Antipas
4 B.C.–A.D.39

HEROD Agrippa I
37–44

Agrippa II
44–100

Archelaus
4 B.C.–A.D.6

3 governors
44–52

4 governors
A.D.6–26

Pontius
PILATE
26–36

Felix
52–59

Festus
59–61

Caligula
37–41

Tiberius
A.D.14–37

Claudius
41–54

Nero
54–68

5 emporers
68–81

Domitian
81–96

Nerva
96–98

Trajan
98–117

Church History, 100 — 300

Plutarch writes *Lives* c.**100**

Marcion rejects Old Testament as part of CANON **150**

Origen compiles Hexapla c.**250**

Hadrian builds wall across England **120**

Ptolemy's concept of earth-centered universe c.**150**

Saint CHRISTOPHER martyred **250?**

Jewish uprising under Bar Kokhba **122–135**

100	120	140	160	180	200	220	240	260	280	300

POLYCARP **? –167**

ORIGEN c.**185–c.254**

EUSEBIUS c.**265–339**

JUSTIN MARTYR c.**100–165**

Tertullian c.**160–230**

Saint Anthony **250–350**

Persecution of Christians:
under Trajan **106–107** †

Aurelius **166–177** †

Severus **211** †

235– 237 †

250– 253 †

257– 260 †

275 †

Rulers in ROME

Commodus **180– 192**

Antoninus Pius **138–161**

Marcus Aurelius **161–180**

Septimius Severus **192–211**

Hadrian **117–138**

17 emperors **211–284**

Diocletian **284– 305**

Trajan **98–117**

ROMAN EMPIRE reaches its greatest extent under Trajan

300 — 500

312 CONVERSION of Constantine

313 Christianity is legalized in ROMAN EMPIRE: Edict of MILAN

Council of NICEA 325

Constantine moves capital from ROME to CONSTANTINOPLE 330

New Testament CANON is final 367

Council of Constantinople 381

Augustine of Hippo converted 386

Augustine's CONFESSIONS 400

Jerome finishes translation of Bible into Latin (VULGATE) 406

Sack of Rome by Visigoths 410

411 Augustine writes The CITY OF GOD

St. Patrick brings the gospel to Ireland 432

Council of CHALCEDON 451

Attila the Hun dies 453

Western Roman Empire conquered by Vandals 476

| 300 | 320 | 340 | 360 | 380 | 400 | 420 | 440 | 460 | 480 | 500 |

Saint PATRICK c.385–c.461

John Chrysostom c.347–407

BENEDICT OF NURSIA c.480–547

JEROME c.347–419

ATHANASIUS c.293–373

CONSTANTINE THE GREAT 280–337

AUGUSTINE OF HIPPO 354–430

Last and worst persecution 303–311
†

End of Western Roman Empire 476

Honorus 395–423

Valentinian III 425–455

9 emperors 455–476

Constantine the Great 306–337

Constantine's sons 337–361

6 emperors 361–395

Roman Empire divided into Eastern and Western Empires 395

Eastern Empire continues to 1453

Church History, 500 — 700

Benedict of Nursia
establishes
monastic Rule
540

Augustine
of Canterbury
brings the
gospel to
England
597

Birth of
Caedmon
in England
671

Gregory the
Great
becomes
pope
590

Mohammed's
hegira to
Medinah
622

Justinian
establishes
legal code
529

Koran is
written
610

500	520	540	560	580	600	620	640	660	680	700

First St.
Paul's
Church in
London
603

BENEDICT OF NURSIA
c.**480–547**

AUGUSTINE OF CANTERBURY
? –604

Mohammed 569–632

Reign of King Arthur
in England
c.**500–c.542**

700 — 900

Lindisfarne Gospels, illustrated manuscripts **700**

731 The Venerable Bede writes *Ecclesiastical History*

Islamic invaders turned back at Tours, France **732**

Charlemagne crowned emperor by Pope Leo III **800**

Controversy over ICONS **726**

Icon controversy settled at Nicea **787**

700	720	740	760	780	800	820	840	860	880	900

CHARLEMAGNE C.**742–814**

The Venerable Bede **672–735**

Alcuin **735–804**

Church History, 900 — 1100

Monastery
at Cluny
founded
909

Viking colony
in Greenland,
Eric the Red
982

Christianization
of Russia
988

Leif Erikson
discovers
North
America
1000

Edward the
Confessor
begins building
WESTMINSTER
ABBEY
1052

GREAT SCHISM
(THE EAST-WEST SPLIT)
1054

First
CRUSADE
1095

900	920	940	960	980	1000	1020	1040	1060	1080	1100

William the Conqueror
invades England,
Battle of Hastings
1066

1100 — 1300

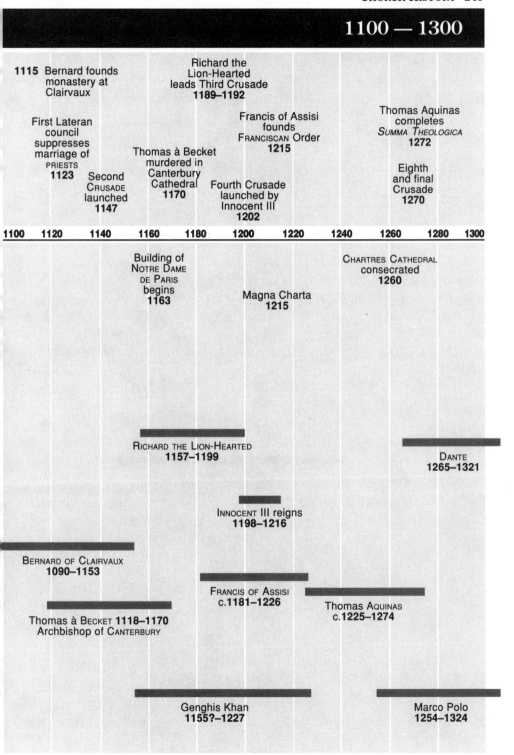

1115 Bernard founds
monastery at
Clairvaux

Richard the
Lion-Hearted
leads Third Crusade
1189–1192

First Lateran
council
suppresses
marriage of
PRIESTS
1123

Francis of Assisi
founds
FRANCISCAN Order
1215

Thomas Aquinas
completes
SUMMA THEOLOGICA
1272

Second
CRUSADE
launched
1147

Thomas à Becket
murdered in
Canterbury
Cathedral
1170

Fourth Crusade
launched by
Innocent III
1202

Eighth
and final
Crusade
1270

| 1100 | 1120 | 1140 | 1160 | 1180 | 1200 | 1220 | 1240 | 1260 | 1280 | 1300 |

Building of
NOTRE DAME
DE PARIS
begins
1163

Magna Charta
1215

CHARTRES CATHEDRAL
consecrated
1260

RICHARD THE LION-HEARTED
1157–1199

DANTE
1265–1321

INNOCENT III reigns
1198–1216

BERNARD OF CLAIRVAUX
1090–1153

FRANCIS OF ASSISI
c.1181–1226

THOMAS AQUINAS
c.1225–1274

Thomas à BECKET **1118–1170**
Archbishop of CANTERBURY

Genghis Khan
1155?–1227

Marco Polo
1254–1324

Church History, 1300 — 1400

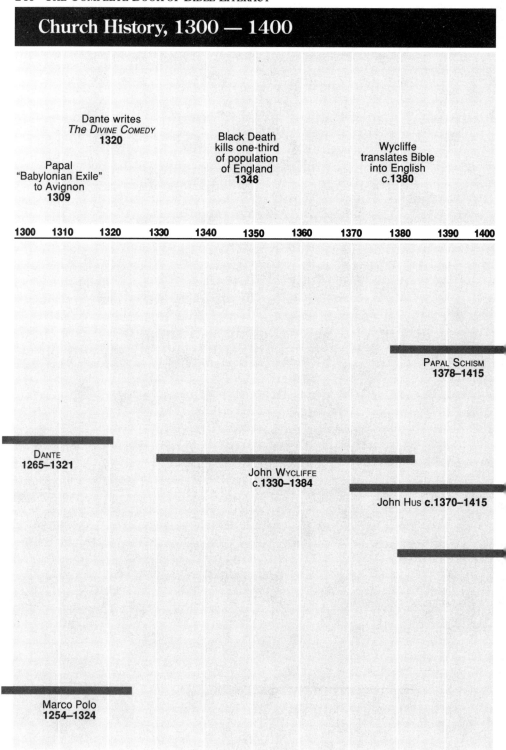

Dante writes
THE DIVINE COMEDY
1320

Papal
"Babylonian Exile"
to Avignon
1309

Black Death
kills one-third
of population
of England
1348

Wycliffe
translates Bible
into English
c.1380

| 1300 | 1310 | 1320 | 1330 | 1340 | 1350 | 1360 | 1370 | 1380 | 1390 | 1400 |

PAPAL SCHISM
1378–1415

DANTE
1265–1321

John WYCLIFFE
c.1330–1384

John HUS **c.1370–1415**

Marco Polo
1254–1324

1400 — 1500

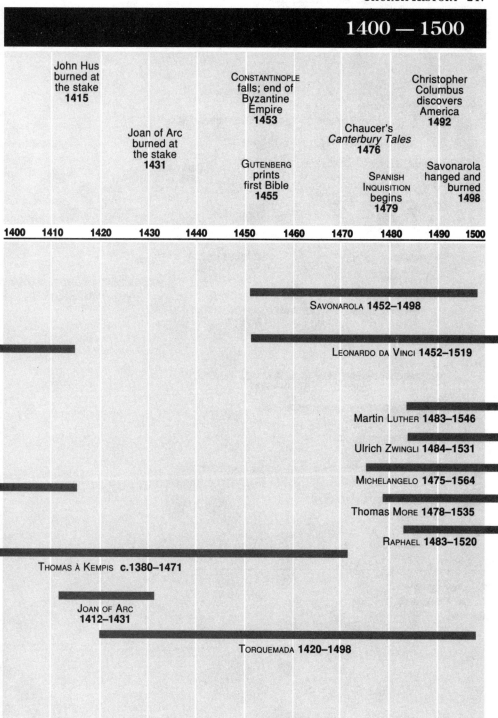

John Hus
burned at
the stake
1415

CONSTANTINOPLE
falls; end of
Byzantine
Empire
1453

Christopher
Columbus
discovers
America
1492

Joan of Arc
burned at
the stake
1431

Chaucer's
Canterbury Tales
1476

GUTENBERG
prints
first Bible
1455

SPANISH
INQUISITION
begins
1479

Savonarola
hanged and
burned
1498

| 1400 | 1410 | 1420 | 1430 | 1440 | 1450 | 1460 | 1470 | 1480 | 1490 | 1500 |

SAVONAROLA **1452–1498**

LEONARDO DA VINCI **1452–1519**

Martin LUTHER **1483–1546**

Ulrich ZWINGLI **1484–1531**

MICHELANGELO **1475–1564**

Thomas MORE **1478–1535**

RAPHAEL **1483–1520**

THOMAS À KEMPIS **c.1380–1471**

JOAN OF ARC
1412–1431

TORQUEMADA **1420–1498**

Church History, 1500 — 1600

ERASMUS publishes GREEK NewTestament **1516**

William TYNDALE'S New Testament published **1526**

1525 ANABAPTIST MOVEMENT begins

1540 IGNATIUS OF LOYOLA founds Society of Jesus (JESUITS)

1534 Henry VIII establishes CHURCH OF ENGLAND

1535 Sir Thomas More beheaded

BOOK OF CONCORD published **1580**

HUGUENOT persecution at its height **1572**

Luther posts NINETY-FIVE THESES **1517**

Luther appears before Diet of WORMS **1521**

Calvin's INSTITUTES published **1536**

The BOOK OF COMMON PRAYER is published **1549**

THIRTY-NINE ARTICLES adopted **1563**

| 1500 | 1510 | 1520 | 1530 | 1540 | 1550 | 1560 | 1570 | 1580 | 1590 | 1600 |

LEO X reigns **1513–1521**

Council of TRENT **1545–1563**

William Shakespeare **1564–1616**

John KNOX **1514–1572**

LEONARDO DA VINCI **1452–1519**

John CALVIN **1509–1564**

Martin LUTHER **1483–1546**

Ulrich ZWINGLI **1484–1531**

MICHELANGELO **1475–1564**

Thomas MORE **1478–1535**

RAPHAEL **1483–1520**

Monarchs of England

Henry VII **1485–1509**

HENRY VIII **1509–1547**

Edward VI **1547–1553**

"Bloody" Mary **1553–1558**

Elizabeth I **1558–1603**

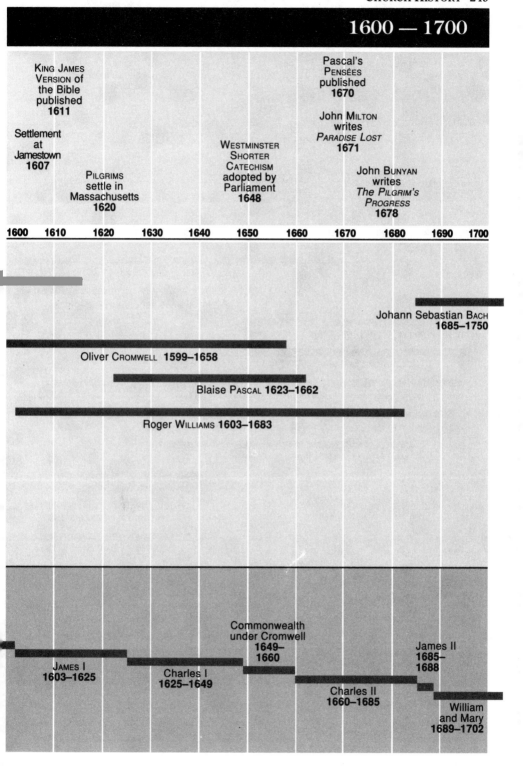

1600 — 1700

KING JAMES
VERSION of
the Bible
published
1611

Settlement
at
Jamestown
1607

PILGRIMS
settle in
Massachusetts
1620

WESTMINSTER
SHORTER
CATECHISM
adopted by
Parliament
1648

Pascal's
PENSÉES
published
1670

John MILTON
writes
PARADISE LOST
1671

John BUNYAN
writes
*The PILGRIM'S
PROGRESS*
1678

| 1600 | 1610 | 1620 | 1630 | 1640 | 1650 | 1660 | 1670 | 1680 | 1690 | 1700 |

Johann Sebastian BACH
1685–1750

Oliver CROMWELL **1599–1658**

Blaise PASCAL **1623–1662**

Roger WILLIAMS **1603–1683**

Commonwealth
under Cromwell
**1649–
1660**

James II
**1685–
1688**

JAMES I
1603–1625

Charles I
1625–1649

Charles II
1660–1685

William
and Mary
1689–1702

Church History, 1700 — 1800

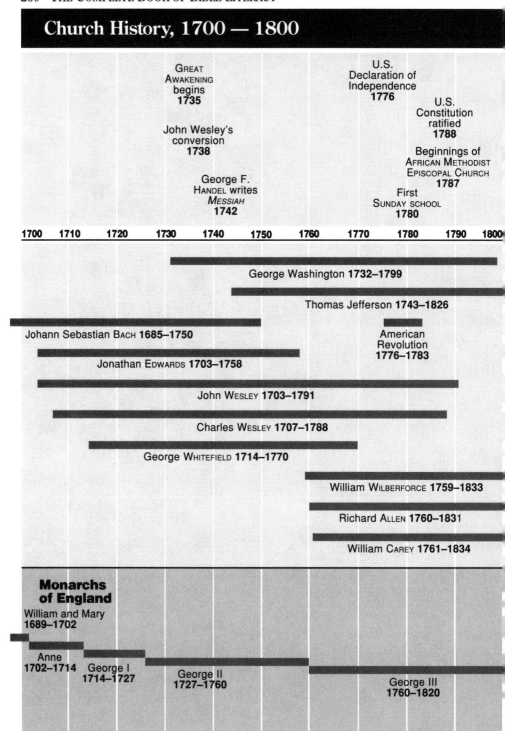

GREAT
AWAKENING
begins
1735

John Wesley's
conversion
1738

George F.
HANDEL writes
MESSIAH
1742

U.S.
Declaration of
Independence
1776

U.S.
Constitution
ratified
1788

Beginnings of
AFRICAN METHODIST
EPISCOPAL CHURCH
1787

First
SUNDAY SCHOOL
1780

| 1700 | 1710 | 1720 | 1730 | 1740 | 1750 | 1760 | 1770 | 1780 | 1790 | 1800 |

George Washington **1732–1799**

Thomas Jefferson **1743–1826**

Johann Sebastian BACH **1685–1750**

American
Revolution
1776–1783

Jonathan EDWARDS **1703–1758**

John WESLEY **1703–1791**

Charles WESLEY **1707–1788**

George WHITEFIELD **1714–1770**

William WILBERFORCE **1759–1833**

Richard ALLEN **1760–1831**

William CAREY **1761–1834**

Monarchs of England

William and Mary
1689–1702

Anne
1702–1714

George I
1714–1727

George II
1727–1760

George III
1760–1820

1800 — 1900

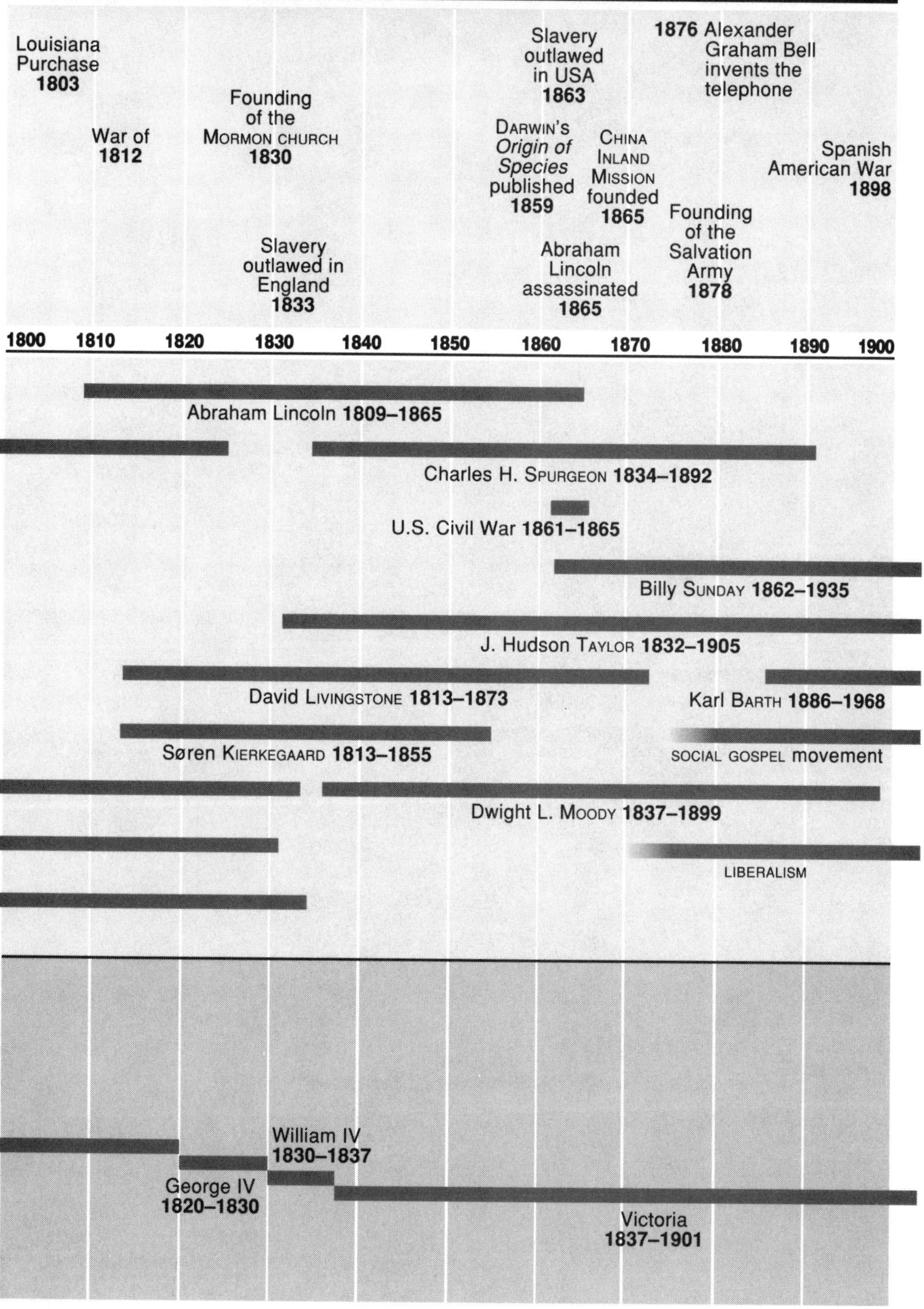

Louisiana
Purchase
1803

War of
1812

Founding
of the
MORMON CHURCH
1830

Slavery
outlawed in
England
1833

Slavery
outlawed
in USA
1863

DARWIN'S
*Origin of
Species*
published
1859

CHINA
INLAND
MISSION
founded
1865

Abraham
Lincoln
assassinated
1865

1876 Alexander
Graham Bell
invents the
telephone

Founding
of the
Salvation
Army
1878

Spanish
American War
1898

| 1800 | 1810 | 1820 | 1830 | 1840 | 1850 | 1860 | 1870 | 1880 | 1890 | 1900 |

Abraham Lincoln **1809–1865**

Charles H. SPURGEON **1834–1892**

U.S. Civil War **1861–1865**

Billy SUNDAY **1862–1935**

J. Hudson TAYLOR **1832–1905**

David LIVINGSTONE **1813–1873**

Karl BARTH **1886–1968**

Søren KIERKEGAARD **1813–1855**

SOCIAL GOSPEL movement

Dwight L. MOODY **1837–1899**

LIBERALISM

William IV
1830–1837

George IV
1820–1830

Victoria
1837–1901

Church History, 1900 — 1950

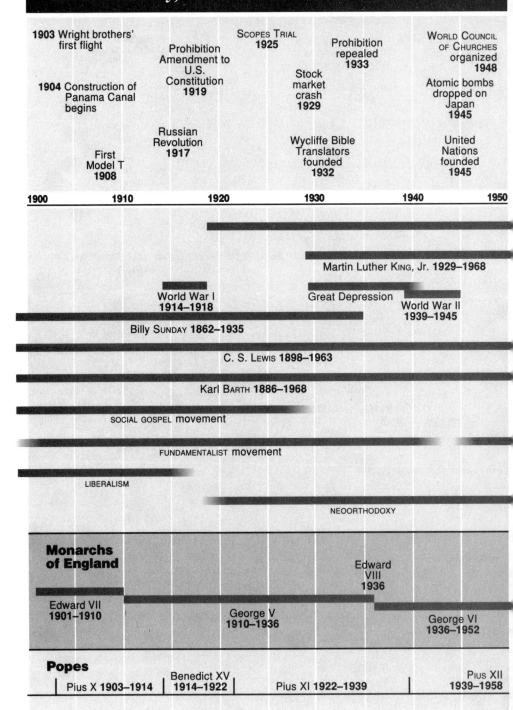

1903 Wright brothers'
first flight

1904 Construction of
Panama Canal
begins

First
Model T
1908

Prohibition
Amendment to
U.S.
Constitution
1919

Russian
Revolution
1917

SCOPES TRIAL
1925

Stock
market
crash
1929

Wycliffe Bible
Translators
founded
1932

Prohibition
repealed
1933

WORLD COUNCIL
OF CHURCHES
organized
1948

Atomic bombs
dropped on
Japan
1945

United
Nations
founded
1945

| 1900 | 1910 | 1920 | 1930 | 1940 | 1950 |

Martin Luther KING, Jr. 1929–1968

World War I
1914–1918

Great Depression

World War II
1939–1945

Billy SUNDAY 1862–1935

C. S. LEWIS 1898–1963

Karl BARTH 1886–1968

SOCIAL GOSPEL movement

FUNDAMENTALIST movement

LIBERALISM

NEOORTHODOXY

**Monarchs
of England**

Edward
VIII
1936

Edward VII
1901–1910

George V
1910–1936

George VI
1936–1952

Popes

Pius X 1903–1914

Benedict XV
1914–1922

Pius XI 1922–1939

PIUS XII
1939–1958

1950 — 2000

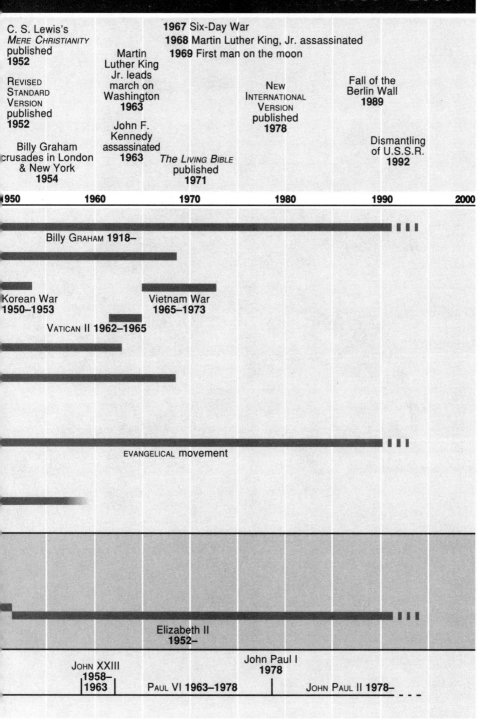

C. S. Lewis's
MERE CHRISTIANITY
published
1952

1967 Six-Day War
1968 Martin Luther King, Jr. assassinated
1969 First man on the moon

Martin
Luther King
Jr. leads
march on
Washington
1963

REVISED
STANDARD
VERSION
published
1952

NEW
INTERNATIONAL
VERSION
published
1978

Fall of the
Berlin Wall
1989

John F.
Kennedy
assassinated
1963

Dismantling
of U.S.S.R.
1992

Billy Graham
crusades in London
& New York
1954

The LIVING BIBLE
published
1971

1950   1960   1970   1980   1990   2000

Billy GRAHAM **1918–**

Korean War
1950–1953

Vietnam War
1965–1973

VATICAN II **1962–1965**

EVANGELICAL movement

Elizabeth II
1952–

JOHN XXIII
1958–
1963

John Paul I
1978

PAUL VI **1963–1978**

JOHN PAUL II **1978–**

CHURCH HISTORY

A.D. In the Western world, history is divided into two eras—the years before Christ (B.C.) and the years after Christ (A.D.). *A.D.* is an abbreviation for the LATIN phrase *anno Domini* ('the year of the Lord'). For those who prefer not to use terms with a specifically Christian connotation, C.E. ('common era') is used instead of A.D.

🐛 The year A.D. 1 is theoretically the first year in the life of Christ, but most historians now agree that Jesus was born no later than 4 B.C., the year in which HEROD the Great died.

African Methodist Episcopal Church The African Methodist Episcopal Church (A.M.E.) and the African Methodist Episcopal Zion Church (A.M.E. Zion) are both African-American DENOMINATIONS with roots in what is now the UNITED METHODIST CHURCH. The A.M.E. Church traces its roots to 1787, when a group of African Americans under the leadership of Richard ALLEN left St. George's Church in Philadelphia, where they had been subject to segregation and humiliation. The A.M.E. Zion Church traces it roots to 1796, when a group of African Americans left the John Street Methodist Episcopal Church in New York City. Many prominent nineteenth-century abolitionists, including Harriet Tubman and Frederick Douglass, were members of the A.M.E. Zion Church. The A.M.E. and A.M.E. Zion Churches are two of the larger denominations in the USA (see the chart at the entry for DENOMINATIONS).

Allen, Richard (1760–1831) An influential African-American church leader in America in the years following the Revolutionary War. He founded the AFRICAN METHODIST EPISCOPAL CHURCH in Philadelphia when he and other African-American Christians were humiliated in white churches.

Amish An ANABAPTIST group that emphasizes peaceful living and community and family values. The Old Order Amish are remarkable because they reject most modern conveniences, including automobiles, televisions, telephones, and mechanized farm equipment. They dress in plain clothing of the style of several centuries ago, and men wear long beards. They try to keep to a minimum any contact with outsiders. They are an offshoot of the MENNONITES, who are less conservative than the Amish. The group originated in Switzerland at the end of

RICHARD ALLEN Founder of the African Methodist Episcopal Church.

the seventeenth century, though most now live in the USA.

Anabaptist movement A movement that began in Switzerland in the 1520s. It emphasized the necessity of the BAPTISM of adult BELIEVERS and opposed INFANT BAPTISM. The members of this movement were called *Anabaptists* (the word means 'baptism again') because they were baptized again as adult believers even if they had been baptized as infants. The Anabaptists were radicals of the REFORMATION period, both for their views on baptism and because they rejected the involvement of the church in government. Church groups today that trace their roots back to the original Anabaptist movement include the MENNONITES and the AMISH.

Anglican churches A term that refers to the CHURCH OF ENGLAND and the various self-governing churches around the world (such as the EPISCOPAL CHURCH) that have ties to the Church of England and share a common heritage in *The BOOK OF COMMON PRAYER* and the EPISCOPAL form of church government.

Aquinas, Thomas (c.1225–1274) A medieval THEOLOGIAN whose writings, including *SUMMA THEOLOGICA* ('a summation of theology'), have influenced theologians and theological thinking over the last 700 years. At a time when the influence of Greek thought was undermining faith in revelation, he synthesized Aristotelian reason and Christian faith. Building on Aristotle's philosophy, Aquinas concluded that God is the first cause—the uncaused cause. His definition of many Christian DOCTRINES (including TRANSUBSTANTIATION) became authoritative in the church. He is generally still viewed as the most authoritative theologian for the ROMAN CATHOLIC CHURCH.

archaeology The study of sites and artifacts from cultures and civilizations of an earlier era. Archaeologists carefully excavate sites of cities, battles, graves, temples, and so on, to understand the culture that created the site. In the Near East, cities were often rebuilt upon the ruins of earlier cities, so some sites contain as many as ten or more levels that might span several thousand years. Today the ruins form mounds called tells. Artifacts at an archaeological site might include tools, jewelry, coins, pottery, religious objects, skeletal remains, or foundations of buildings.

During the past century, archaeologists have found archaeological evidence of many cultural details mentioned in the Bible—including details previously thought by some scholars to be unreliable.

Arianism *See* NICEA, COUNCIL OF.

Arminianism The DOCTRINES based on the teachings of the Dutch THEOLOGIAN Jacob Arminius (1560–1609). In contrast to CALVINISM, with its emphasis on God's sovereign ELECTION, Arminianism sees no conflict between election and man's FREE WILL. Indeed, PREDESTINATION is seen as God's foreknowledge of the way each person will freely choose to accept or reject Christ. METHODIST THEOLOGY is in the Arminian tradition.

ascetic A person who voluntarily abstains from the comforts and pleasures of this life in order to combat vice and cultivate personal holiness. MONASTICISM, with its emphasis on poverty, chastity, and obedience, is an ascetic life-style.

Assemblies of God A DENOMINATION that emphasizes SPEAKING IN TONGUES and affirms BAPTISM IN THE HOLY SPIRIT as a second blessing subsequent to CONVERSION. It is one of the largest PENTECOSTAL denominations in the USA.

Athanasius (c.293–373) BISHOP of Alexandria (EGYPT) and a participant in the Council of NICEA. He was a strong defender of ORTHODOXY, particularly against the HERESY of ARIANISM, which held that Jesus was the SON OF GOD but was a created being and not coeternal with God. A letter written by Athanasius in A.D. 367 contains a list of New Testament books. It is the earliest list that includes only the twenty-seven books that came to be accepted as the New Testament canon (*see* NEW TESTAMENT CANON ESTABLISHED).

Augustine of Canterbury (? – 604) The first archbishop of CANTERBURY. POPE Gregory I sent Augustine from ROME to take the GOSPEL to England. Under his preaching, thousands of people in England were converted, including Ethelbert, the king of Kent.

AUGUSTINE OF HIPPO This picture of Augustine was painted in the fifteenth century.

Augustine of Hippo (354–430) BISHOP of Hippo (in modern-day Algeria). He is often considered the greatest thinker in Christian antiquity and the most important THEOLOGIAN in the Western church during the 1,200 years from PAUL to Thomas AQUINAS. His THEOLOGY was foundational for the sixteenth-century REFORMERS. *CONFESSIONS*, his autobiography, is a classic account of a CONVERSION from paganism to Christianity. His book *The CITY OF GOD* (411) played an important role in establishing Christianity as the major religious power after the fall of ROME.

B.C. In the Western world, history is divided into two eras—the years before Christ (B.C.) and the years after Christ (A.D.). *B.C.* is simply an abbreviation for *before Christ*. For those who prefer not to use terms with a specifically Christian connotation, B.C.E. ('before the common era') is used instead of B.C.

❦ The year 1 B.C. is theoretically the last year before the birth of Jesus, but most historians now agree that Jesus was born no later than 4 B.C., the year in which HEROD the Great died.

Baptist A general term designating the DENOMINATIONS in which adult BELIEVERS are BAPTIZED, but infants are not baptized. Worship in Baptist churches tends to be plain and nonliturgical, with an emphasis on the sermon. *See also* NATIONAL BAPTIST CONVENTION, SOUTHERN BAPTIST CONVENTION.

Baptists, National *See* NATIONAL BAPTIST CONVENTION.

Baptists, Southern *See* SOUTHERN BAPTIST CONVENTION.

Barth, Karl (1886–1968) Barth (pronounced *Bart*) was a Swiss THEOLOGIAN who was a proponent of NEOORTHODOXY, a reaction to the theological LIBERALISM of the early twentieth century. He is considered by many to be the foremost theologian of the twentieth century.

Becket, Thomas à (1118–1170) A twelfth-century archbishop of CANTERBURY. As head of the church in England (this was before the establishment of the CHURCH OF ENGLAND), he opposed King Henry II's attempts to limit the authority of the church. Becket was murdered in the Canterbury CATHEDRAL by four knights who were supporters of the king. He was CANONIZED a few years after his death.

❦ After Becket's death, many pilgrims visited his tomb in Canterbury. The travelers in Chaucer's *Canterbury Tales* were on their way to Canterbury to visit Becket's tomb.

❦ *Murder in the Cathedral* by T. S. Eliot and *Becket* by Jean Anouilh are twentieth-century plays about Becket's murder.

Benedict of Nursia (c.480–547) Founder of the BENEDICTINES, an early MONASTIC order. The Benedictines combine prayer, study, and work as a way of life. Benedict's "Rule" for monastic living gave detailed descriptions of all aspects of life in the monastery. It became the pattern for other monastic orders in the centuries that followed.

Benedictines Members of a RELIGIOUS ORDER founded by BENEDICT OF NURSIA in the sixth century. It was one of the earliest monastic orders (*see* MONASTICISM). The motto of the Benedictines is "Pray and Work." Benedict's "Rule" for his order became the pattern for other monastic orders in the centuries that followed.

Bernard of Clairvaux (1090–1153) A French preacher and THEOLOGIAN who was an adviser to POPES, BISHOPS, and kings, and was instrumental in launching the Second CRUSADE. His emphasis on GRACE was influential four centuries later for LUTHER and CALVIN. His influence reaches us today through several HYMNS, including "O Sacred Head, Now Wounded" and "Jesus, Thou Joy of Loving Hearts."

Bible Belt The areas in the United States, especially in the South, where Christianity and belief in the Bible are more predominant than in other parts of the country. The term is sometimes used disparagingly, and it usually connotes religious and social conservatism.

Bonhoeffer, Dietrich (1906–1945)

A LUTHERAN PASTOR in Germany who was active in the anti-Hitler movement. He was hanged by the Nazis. His major works include *The Cost of Discipleship* (1937) and *Letters and Papers from Prison* (published posthumously in 1951).

Book of Concord Published in 1580, the *Book of Concord* contains all the documents generally accepted by the LUTHERAN church as fundamental to its tradition. It includes the APOSTLES' CREED, LUTHER's Large and Small CATECHISMS, the Augsburg Confession, and the Formula of Concord (developed to settle doctrinal controversies that arose within Lutheranism after Luther's death).

Calvin, John (1509–1564) A great leader of the REFORMATION in Switzerland. He was younger than LUTHER and ZWINGLI and represented the next generation of REFORMERS. His teachings emphasized the SOVEREIGNTY OF GOD and ELECTION. He wrote *INSTITUTES OF THE CHRISTIAN RELIGION*, the most important and influential treatise on PROTESTANT DOCTRINE from the Reformation era. The REFORMED traditions stem from Calvin and CALVINISM.

Calvin was French, but he became the leader of the church in Geneva, which had enormous influence in the affairs of state. Like the other Reformers, Calvin taught that people are saved by GRACE rather than by good works. Nonetheless, he also stressed virtue and the importance of Christian influence in government and public policy. ADULTERY, BLASPHEMY, and HERESY were punishable by death in Geneva.

Calvin had a significant impact on the development of Protestantism. The PRESBYTERIAN form of church government derives from Calvin's teaching. In France, his followers were known as HUGUENOTS. In England, Scotland, and America his followers formed the various PRESBYTERIAN churches.

JOHN CALVIN Leader of the Reformation in Geneva.

Calvinism The DOCTRINES based on the teachings of John CALVIN, one of the great leaders of the PROTESTANT REFORMATION. One of the distinctive features of Calvinism is the SOVER-

EIGNTY OF GOD over the affairs of people, especially in ELECTION, and that JUSTIFICATION and SANCTIFICATION are inseparable in the life of the BELIEVER. The DOCTRINE of election holds that only the elect—those persons chosen by God—will be saved. Churches established by Calvin's followers are known as REFORMED CHURCHES and follow a PRESBYTERIAN form of church government. In America, Calvinist THEOLOGY has also influenced CONGREGATIONAL, BAPTIST, and independent churches.

canon of the New Testament *See* NEW TESTAMENT CANON ESTABLISHED.

Canterbury, archbishop of The ecclesiastical head of the CHURCH OF ENGLAND. In this role, he influences the ANGLICAN CHURCHES around the world. He is appointed by the ruling monarch of Great Britain, who is titular head of the Church of England.

Carey, William (1761–1834) A British MISSIONARY to India in the early nineteenth century. He is known as the "Father of Modern Missions." One of his legacies is the development of mission societies—voluntary societies that send missionaries out to EVANGELIZE in the far corners of the world. Carey was a gifted linguist, and he was personally involved in translating the Bible into thirty-six languages of South Asia.

Catholic When capitalized, *Catholic* means ROMAN CATHOLIC (e.g., Catho-lic schools, Catholic DOCTRINE). When not capitalized, *catholic* means universal, as in the APOSTLES' CREED: "I believe in . . . the holy catholic church . . ."

Catholic church *See* ROMAN CATHOLIC CHURCH.

Catholicism The faith, practice, or system of the ROMAN CATHOLIC CHURCH.

Chalcedon, Council of (*KAL-si-don*) (451) The CHURCH COUNCIL in Chalcedon (in present-day Turkey) addressed the issue of the two natures of Christ. The council affirmed that Christ was both God and man, and that the deity and humanity of Christ exist "without confusion, without change, without division, without separation." The definition accepted by the council has been the measure of ORTHODOXY on this subject ever since.

charismatic movement Also called "charismatic renewal," this movement emphasizes BAPTISM IN THE HOLY SPIRIT and SPEAKING IN TONGUES. Many charismatics (as they are often called) see baptism in the Holy Spirit as a "second blessing"—the coming of the HOLY SPIRIT into a BELIEVER's life at some time subsequent to his or her CONVERSION. Although charismatics share many views in common with those in PENTECOSTAL churches, they tend to be part of non-Pentecostal churches. The movement began about 1960, and now there are several million charismatics in PROTESTANT and CATHOLIC churches throughout the world.

Charlemagne (c.742–814) The first emperor of what came to be known as the Holy Roman Empire, a European empire that existed in name for 1,000 years until it was finally dismantled by Napoleon. Charlemagne was initially king of what is today France and Germany, and he was a friend and defender of Christianity in all his conquered territories. He was crowned emperor as he knelt at the altar in SAINT PETER'S BASILICA on CHRISTMAS Day in the year 800. This surprise coronation by Pope Leo III suggested the supremacy of the church over the state and set the stage for many church-state struggles for centuries to come.

chief end of man *See* WHAT IS THE CHIEF END OF MAN?

China Inland Mission One of the earliest independent mission agencies of the modern MISSIONARY movement. It was founded by J. Hudson TAYLOR in 1865 for the evangelization of China. It is now called Overseas Missionary Fellowship.

Christ is risen/He is risen indeed In the EARLY CHURCH, as in many churches today, BELIEVERS greeted one another on EASTER by saying, "Christ is risen," to which the others would respond, "He is risen indeed."

Christendom The entire Christian church around the world. The word can refer to all Christian people or to all lands in which Christianity predominates.

Christian Science An organization founded by Mary Baker EDDY in 1879. Its official name is the Church of Christ, Scientist. Christian Science does not accept many of the tenets of ORTHODOX Christianity, including the TRINITY. One of the features of Christian Science is the belief that matter and flesh do not really exist. Nothing that is not mind possesses reality. Accordingly, Christian Scientists tend to reject many aspects of modern medicine as inconsequential.

❦ *The Christian Science Monitor* is a widely respected newspaper with national circulation in the USA.

Christopher, Saint (third century) Christopher may have been a MARTYR about A.D. 250. He is the PATRON SAINT of travelers because of the tradition that he once carried the Christ child across a river (the name Christopher means 'Christ-bearer'). Many ROMAN CATHOLICS wear St. Christopher medals for protection as they travel.

❦ In 1969 the ROMAN CATHOLIC CHURCH removed Christopher's feast from the calendar of SAINTS because of a lack of historical evidence as to his existence, but he is still venerated as a saint.

church councils In the EARLY CHURCH, significant theological conflicts were resolved at church councils—gatherings of church leaders from around CHRISTENDOM. The first church council was held in JERUSALEM in about A.D. 50, to decide whether GENTILE converts to Christianity first had to become converts to JUDAISM. Other significant councils were held through the next several centuries: the Council of NICEA (325), called by CONSTANTINE THE GREAT, was the first great ECUMENICAL council, followed by the Council of Constantinople (381) and the Council of CHALCEDON (451).

In response to the PROTESTANT REFORMATION, the ROMAN CATHOLIC CHURCH convened the Council of TRENT (1545–63). Vatican I (1869–70) defined the DOGMA of PAPAL INFALLIBILITY. VATICAN II (1962–65) adopted sweeping changes in the Roman Catholic church.

For PROTESTANTS, DOCTRINES formulated

Most Important Events in Church History

YEAR	EVENT
70	Destruction of JERUSALEM by Titus
313	Edict of MILAN
325	Council of NICEA
367	NEW TESTAMENT CANON in its present form is recognized
386	AUGUSTINE OF HIPPO converted
406	JEROME completes translation of the VULGATE
451	Council of CHALCEDON
540	BENEDICT establishes the monastic Rule
988	Christianization of Russia
1054	The GREAT SCHISM (THE EAST-WEST SPLIT)
1095	CRUSADES launched by Pope Urban II
1272	Thomas AQUINAS completes *SUMMA THEOLOGICA*
1378	The PAPAL SCHISM
1455	GUTENBERG BIBLE printed
1517	LUTHER posts NINETY-FIVE THESES
1525	ANABAPTIST MOVEMENT begins
1534	King HENRY VIII and the Act of Supremacy
1536	CALVIN's *INSTITUTES OF THE CHRISTIAN RELIGION* published
1545	Council of TRENT begins
1611	KING JAMES VERSION of the Bible is published
1735	GREAT AWAKENING begins
1738	John and Charles WESLEY converted
1792	William CAREY helps form Baptist Missionary Society
1906	Azusa Street Revival propels PENTECOSTALISM forward
1962	VATICAN II opens

Source: Adapted from *Christian History* magazine, Fall 1990. Copyright 1990 Christianity Today, Inc. Used by permission.

by ecumenical councils may be true and may unify Christians, but they are not infallible. For Roman Catholics, the decisions of ecumenical councils are infallible and irrevocable.

church fathers The ORTHODOX THEOLOGIANS of the church during the first several centuries after Christ. Included in such a list are JUSTIN MARTYR, ORIGEN, ATHANASIUS, John Chrysostom, JEROME, and AUGUSTINE OF HIPPO.

church history The record of the Christian church from the time of Christ to the present. There are numerous strands, of course, in so complex a subject. The list accompanying this article shows twenty-five of the most important events in church history, as judged by the editors of *Church History* magazine.

Church of England The STATE CHURCH of England, also called the ANGLICAN CHURCH. The Church of England split away from the Western church (*see* ROMAN CATHOLIC CHURCH) in 1534 during the reign of HENRY VIII, since the king would not accept the POPE's ruling that Henry could not divorce his wife. The ruling monarch of England is titular head of the church, though the Archbishop of CANTERBURY is recognized as the ecclesiastical head of the church. The EPISCOPAL CHURCH in the USA and the Anglican Church of Canada are direct descendants of the Church of England.

Church of God in Christ The largest PENTECOSTAL DENOMINATION in the USA. Like other Pentecostal groups, it emphasizes the BAPTISM IN THE HOLY SPIRIT and holiness as the standard for Christian living. Its membership is primarily African American, whereas the ASSEMBLIES OF GOD is primarily white.

Church of Jesus Christ of Latter-day Saints The religious group founded by Joseph SMITH in 1830, also called the MORMONS. Joseph Smith wrote *The Book of Mormon*, which he said was a translation of a text on gold plates that he found in New York. After Smith's death, his followers split into several factions, and Brigham YOUNG became leader of the group that is now the Church of Jesus Christ of Latter-day Saints. Young led his followers to Utah, where they founded Salt Lake City, now the central city of the church. A smaller group called itself the Reorganized Church of Jesus Christ of Latter Day Saints (*see* LATTER DAY SAINTS).

Mormons are known for clean living and a dedication to their families. The DOCTRINES of the Mormon church differ from ORTHODOX Christianity in numerous respects. Mormons deny the TRINITY and believe that mankind's destiny is to evolve to Godhood. Mormon THEOLOGY also says that God continues to give revelations to men, specifically to the leaders of their organization, and that these revelations have a standing equal to or even above that of the Bible.

City of God, The An important book by AUGUSTINE OF HIPPO, in which he interpreted human history as a struggle between God's people, living in the city of God, and the pagans living in the city of the world. Those in the city of God receive ETERNAL LIFE, but those in the city of the world receive eternal DAMNATION. The book was written in A.D. 411 and was motivated by Augustine's reflection upon the significance of the sack of ROME by the Visigoths in 410.

Confessions The autobiography of AUGUSTINE OF HIPPO. It was written about A.D. 400 and tells of Augustine's spiritual struggles and triumphs. He describes his hedonistic life-style as a young man, his struggle with the claims of Christianity, and his CONVERSION to Christianity. It begins with the affirmation, "You made us for yourself, and our hearts are restless until they find their rest in you." Few other books have been as influential in Christian history.

congregational A form of church government that puts ultimate authority in the hands of the CONGREGATION rather than the PASTOR, the ELDERS, or a BISHOP. BAPTIST churches, Congregational churches, and many independent churches have congregational forms of government. For comparison, see EPISCOPAL and PRESBYTERIAN.

Constantine the Great (c.280–337) First emperor of the ROMAN EMPIRE to become a Christian. The story of his conversion is fascinating. When Constantine prayed to the God of the Christians the day before a strategic battle, he had a VISION of a flaming CROSS in the sky and the words "in this sign conquer." His soldiers carried the symbol of the cross on their shields the next day, and they were indeed victorious. Shortly thereafter, in 313, Constantine issued the Edict of MILAN, in which he legalized Christianity and recognized the right of churches to own property. Constantine convened the Council of NICEA in 325 to unite the church against the HERESY of ARIANISM. In 330 he moved the capital of the empire from ROME to Byzantium, which he renamed CONSTANTINOPLE (now Istanbul, Turkey). He was BAPTIZED a Christian on his deathbed.

CONSTANTINE'S ARCH This arch in Rome commemorates Constantine, including his conversion to Christianity. The building in the background is the Colosseum.

Constantinople Present-day Istanbul, the great city on the Bosporus Straits. In A.D. 330, CONSTANTINE THE GREAT moved the capital of the ROMAN EMPIRE from ROME to Byzantium, the city at the crossroads between Europe and Asia. He renamed it Constantinople—the City of Constantine. When the Roman Empire was split into two parts in A.D. 395, Constantinople remained capital of the eastern empire, which came to be known as the Byzantine Empire. Long before the GREAT SCHISM in 1054, Constantinople was the center of the church in the East. It retained this position until the fall of Constantinople to the Muslim Turks in 1453. The Basilica of HAGIA SOPHIA in Constantinople was the central church building of the EASTERN ORTHODOX CHURCH.

The Council of Constantinople was held in 381 to combat numerous HERESIES and to affirm the earlier work of the Council of NICEA.

councils, church See CHURCH COUNCILS.

Counter-Reformation A reform movement in the ROMAN CATHOLIC CHURCH during the period of the PROTESTANT REFORMATION. It included inquisitions (see SPANISH INQUISITION) to rid the church of HERESY and abuses, but it also included elements of theological reform and MISSIONARY zeal. IGNATIUS OF LOYOLA founded the Society of Jesus (see JESUITS) during this time. Much of the Counter-Reformation was based on the reforms established by the Council of TRENT.

Cranmer, Thomas (1489–1556) The CHURCH OF ENGLAND broke with the ROMAN CATHOLIC CHURCH because the POPE would not sanction King HENRY VIII's divorce from his first wife, Catherine of Aragon, but the real architect of ANGLICAN DOCTRINE and LITURGY was Thomas Cranmer. Henry appointed him archbishop of CANTERBURY, and it was Cranmer who urged Henry to authorize distribution of the Bible in English (see TYNDALE, WILLIAM). Cranmer changed the liturgy of the church from LATIN to English when he wrote and compiled *The Book of Common Prayer.* He wrote the Forty-two Articles (later reduced to THIRTY-NINE ARTICLES), the doctrinal anchor for the Church of England. One of the ironies of Henry's divorce from Catherine was played out when Cranmer was burned at the stake as a HERETIC by Mary, the CATHOLIC daughter of Henry and Catherine.

Crusades The Crusades were a series of religious wars in which armies from Christian Europe attempted to take control of the HOLY LAND away from the Muslims. The period of the eight crusades spanned nearly 200 years, from 1095 to 1270. The third Crusade was led by RICHARD THE LION-HEARTED of England. Others were led by kings of France, Germany, and the HOLY ROMAN EMPIRE. The Crusades were largely unsuccessful in dislodging the Muslims from PALESTINE and JERUSALEM, but they expanded trade between Europe and the Middle East.

Darwin, Charles (1809–1882) A British naturalist who first expounded the theory of EVOLUTION. His book *The Origin of Species* (1859) rejects the traditional concept that plants and animals as we know them today were created by a divine act of creation. The emergence and acceptance of the theory of evolution had a profound impact on the religious world, as it caused many biblical scholars to reexamine their understanding of SCRIPTURE. If the story of the CREATION was not literally true, one might also disbelieve many other DOCTRINES that had previously been accepted without question.

☙ Charles Darwin and Abraham Lincoln were born on the same day, February 12, 1809.

denominations Almost from the very beginning of the church there have been differences in THEOLOGY and in church governance between various groups. Today the Christian church is divided into three major branches: ROMAN CATHOLIC, EASTERN ORTHODOX, and PROTESTANT. Within Protestantism, there are

Twenty Largest Religious Bodies in America

Roman Catholic church	57,019,948
Southern Baptist Convention	14,907,826
United Methodist Church	8,979,139
Jews (Orthodox, Conservative, and Reform)	5,944,000
National Baptist Convention, U.S.A., Inc.	5,500,000
Evangelical Lutheran Church in America	5,238,798
Church of Jesus Christ of Latter-Day Saints	4,175,400
The Church of God in Christ	3,709,661
Presbyterian Church (USA)	2,886,482
National Baptist Convention of America	2,668,799
The Lutheran Church, Missouri Synod	2,609,025
The Episcopal Church	2,433,413
African Methodist Episcopal Church	2,210,000
Assemblies of God	2,137,890
Greek Orthodox Archdiocese of North and South America	1,950,000
Churches of Christ	1,626,000
United Church of Christ	1,625,969
American Baptist Churches in the U.S.A.	1,548,573
Baptist Bible Fellowship, International	1,405,900
African Methodist Episcopal Zion Church	1,220,260

Source: *Yearbook of American & Canadian Churches*, 1991 edition, Abingdon Press, Nashville.

hundreds of denominations—groups of churches affiliated with one another by virtue of common beliefs and common governance. While some American denominations are direct descendants of European STATE CHURCHES, others have come into existence when a group within an established denomination becomes disenchanted with the theology or practices of the denomination. They then break away and form a new denomination. Some denominations such as the SOUTHERN BAPTIST CONVENTION include millions of members and thousands of CONGREGATIONS. Other denominations are relatively small, with only dozens of congregations and thousands of members.

dispensationalism A method of biblical interpretation that divides human history into seven ages, or dispensations. People are tested in each dispensation as to their response to God's revelation. SALVATION is always by God's GRACE, but the faith required of humans is different in each dispensation. The present dispensation, the sixth, is the age of the church. Dispensationalists hold to a literal interpretation of the Bible and a premillennial view of the SECOND COMING (*see* MILLENNIUM *under "Church Life and Theology"*). Dispensationalism arose in the nineteenth century and flowered in twentieth-century FUNDAMENTALISM. It was pro-

moted and popularized through the notes in the *Scofield Reference Bible* and is espoused by Dallas Theological Seminary.

Dominicans Members of a RELIGIOUS ORDER that was founded in 1216. The Dominicans were originally itinerant preachers, and their vows include poverty. The order has produced many influential THEOLOGIANS and MISSIONARIES. Thomas AQUINAS and SAVONAROLA were both Dominicans.

early church The Christian Church during the first several hundred years after the life of Christ. As the DISCIPLES and the other early APOSTLES moved out from JERUSALEM after PENTECOST and spread the GOSPEL, the center of Christianity moved westward from Jerusalem to southern Europe, particularly ROME. As the gospel spread, HERESIES quickly arose, and many of the New Testament EPISTLES were written to counter various false teachings. Some key figures in the early church, besides the disciples and PAUL, are Clement, JUSTIN MARTYR, ORIGEN, CONSTANTINE THE GREAT, ATHANASIUS, John Chrysostom, and AUGUSTINE OF HIPPO.

East-West split *See* GREAT SCHISM (THE EAST-WEST SPLIT).

Eastern Orthodox church The family of churches that constitute one of the three great branches of Christianity, along with the ROMAN

CATHOLIC CHURCH and PROTESTANT churches. Historically, there was a natural division in the church. The church in the East, centered in CONSTANTINOPLE, used GREEK as its liturgical language, while the church in the West, centered in ROME, used LATIN. The Eastern Orthodox church split from the Roman Catholic church in the GREAT SCHISM of 1054. It rejects the PAPACY, and its worship is more mystical than that of the Roman Catholic church. The Orthodox churches are the primary churches in Greece (GREEK ORTHODOX CHURCH), Russia (Russian Orthodox church), and several other Eastern European countries.

JONATHAN EDWARDS One of America's greatest preachers.

Eddy, Mary Baker (1821–1910) The founder of CHRISTIAN SCIENCE. She emphasized the use of the mind in healing, claiming that her teachings came by direct revelation of God. Her writings are accepted by Christian Scientists as having equal authority with the Bible.

Edwards, Jonathan (1703–1758) A CONGREGATIONAL MINISTER who became one of the most influential THEOLOGIANS and preachers in American history. His preaching was an important factor in the GREAT AWAKENING in New England. He was the most erudite scholar of his generation, and shortly before his death he became president of the college that later became Princeton University. One of his best-known sermons is "Sinners in the Hands of an Angry God."

episcopal A form of church government with a hierarchy of BISHOPS, in which ultimate authority in the local church resides with the bishop rather than with the PASTOR, representative bodies, or the CONGREGATION. The ROMAN CATHOLIC CHURCH, the EASTERN ORTHODOX CHURCH, the EPISCOPAL CHURCH, and the UNITED METHODIST CHURCH all have episcopal forms of government. For comparison, see CONGREGATIONAL and PRESBYTERIAN.

Episcopal Church A MAINLINE DENOMINATION in the USA that is a direct descendant of the CHURCH OF EN-

GLAND. As an ANGLICAN CHURCH, the governmental structure and LITURGIES of the Episcopal Church are very similar to those of the Church of England. Both churches use *The Book of Common Prayer.*

Erasmus (1466–1536) A Dutch Renaissance scholar who prepared the way for the REFORMERS. His GREEK New Testament, published in 1516, was an important source for Martin LUTHER in his German TRANSLATION and for Stephanus, who prepared the TEXTUS RECEPTUS in 1550.

established church *See* STATE CHURCH.

Eusebius of Caesarea (c.265–339) The "Father of Church History." His histories of the church have provided one of the few windows on the church in ancient times. His great work was *Historia Ecclesiastica.* Eusebius was a contemporary of CONSTANTINE THE GREAT, of whom he wrote a biography, and he participated in the Council of NICEA.

evangelical The evangelical movement arose in the USA after World War II as a refinement of fundamentalism and as an alternative to the trends in established, MAINLINE PROTESTANTISM. Evangelicals uphold the fundamentals of the faith (*see* FUNDAMENTALISM), but they also believe they should be involved with the culture in which they live. Like fundamentalists, evangelicals emphasize the necessity of a personal relationship with Christ as SAVIOR and Lord. They often use the term *BORN AGAIN* to describe their relationship with God.

More broadly, the term *evangelical* refers to REVIVAL movements since the GREAT AWAKENING. The term is also used of a renewal and MISSIONARY movement in the CHURCH OF ENGLAND that began in the late eighteenth century. In Europe, *evangelical* is a synonym for LUTHERAN.

❦ In a survey of adult Americans by the Gallup organization in 1986, 31 percent responded yes to the question, "Would you describe yourself as a born-again Christian?"

Evangelical Lutheran Church in America A MAINLINE DENOMINATION that is the largest of several LUTHERAN DENOMINATIONS in the USA. It is the result of a merger in 1987 of two large Lutheran denominations. All Lutheran churches trace their roots back to the teachings of Martin LUTHER. *See also* LUTHERAN CHURCH, MISSOURI SYNOD.

existentialism A twentieth-century philosophy that emphasizes the individual's freedom and responsibility to find his or her own meaning in life. There is no uniformity to existentialist thought, and those who call themselves existentialists include both Christians and ATHEISTS. The existentialist tends to believe there is no objective truth, or at least that spiritual realities cannot be understood by rational investigation. Søren KIERKEGAARD, a professing Christian, and Friedrich Nietzsche, an atheist, both influenced later existentialist thinkers.

First Amendment rights The First Amendment to the U.S. Constitution provides for FREEDOM OF RELIGION and freedom of speech and of the press. The actual text of the amendment begins, "Congress shall make no law respecting an establishment of religion, or prohibiting the free exercise thereof. . . ." The Supreme Court, particularly since the 1950s, has tended to interpret the First Amendment as calling for a strict SEPARATION OF CHURCH AND STATE. For example, even voluntary prayer in schools has been ruled unconstitutional under the First Amendment. Judicial conservatives tend to think that this interpretation of the First Amendment is incorrect, and that the original intent of the framers of the Constitution was simply that

Congress not institute a STATE CHURCH, as many European countries had at the end of the eighteenth century.

fish, sign of the The initial letters of the GREEK words for *Jesus Christ, Son of God, Savior* spell *ichthus*, the Greek word for 'fish'. The Christians in the EARLY CHURCH used the word *ichthus* and a simple sign of a fish to identify themselves as Christians. This was particularly important when they were being persecuted, as they could identify one another with a sign that looked innocent to those who did not understand it.

FRANCIS OF ASSISI This painting shows Francis contemplating his own mortality.

Francis of Assisi (c.1181–1226) A SAINT, and founder of the FRANCISCAN Order. Francis had a wealthy upbringing, but he left his wealth in order to become a poor itinerant

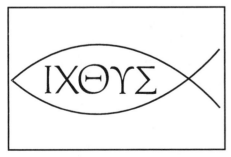

SIGN OF THE FISH The Greek letters spell *ichthus*, which means 'fish'.

preacher. His preaching and life-style included an appreciation of God's CRE-ATION and love of all living things. He initiated the practice of using NATIVITY scenes (crèches) as a way of focusing on CHRISTMAS as a celebration of the birth of Jesus. *See also* SAINT FRANCIS, PRAYER OF *under "The Bible and Christianity in the Fine Arts."*

Franciscans Members of a RELI-GIOUS ORDER founded by FRANCIS OF AS-SISI. It is the largest order in the ROMAN CATHOLIC CHURCH and it includes both men and women. As St. Francis did, Franciscans take a vow of poverty.

Free church tradition Churches formed by breaking away from STATE CHURCHES. Churches stemming from ANABAPTIST, Brethren, and PIETIST traditions, as well as English BAPTISTS and QUAKERS, fall into this broad category.

freedom of religion The freedom to choose a religion (or no religion at all) and to worship freely and openly without fear of reprisal. Many early immigrants, including the PILGRIMS, came to America because there was not sufficient freedom of religion in England or Europe in the seventeenth century. The U.S. Constitution guarantees freedom of religion in the First Amendment (*see* FIRST AMENDMENT RIGHTS).

Friends, Society of Better known as QUAKERS, the Friends include sev-eral groups, all of whom trace their roots to the teachings of George Fox (1624–1691). Seeking religious enlightenment that he did not find in other churches in England, Fox came to rely on "the inner light of the living Christ." Some groups ("meetings") of Friends have no formal ceremonies, CREEDS, or CLERGY. Other groups have PASTORS and conventional WORSHIP services. Friends are PACIFISTS and are known for social action.

fundamentalism A conservative theological movement that arose in the United States at the turn of the twentieth century in reaction to LIB-ERALISM in church and society. Fundamentalists identify certain "fundamentals" of the faith that they feel are required in true BELIEV-ERS. These fundamentals include belief in the deity of Christ, the VIR-GIN BIRTH, the sacrificial death of Christ, the RESURRECTION and ASCEN-SION of Jesus, the INSPIRATION and INER-RANCY OF SCRIPTURE, and the bodily return of Jesus Christ (the SECOND COMING). In contrast to EVANGELICALS, fundamentalists are often separatistic. Many fundamentalists follow a DISPENSATIONALIST interpretation of SCRIPTURE.

❧ Because fundamentalists are often perceived as being reactionary in their conservatism, the term *fundamentalist* is used in the media to describe any conservative and reactionary religious group, including conservative Muslims and conservative Hindus.

glasnost The Russian word for 'openness'. When Mikhail Gorbachev came to power in the Soviet Union in 1985, he introduced a policy of *glasnost,* which opened the way for both FREEDOM OF RELIGION and the demise of the Communist Party in the Soviet Union.

BILLY GRAHAM Twentieth-century evangelist to the world.

Graham, Billy (b.1918) An American EVANGELIST who has held evangelistic crusades and has preached to millions of people in countries around the world. He came to national and international prominence in the early 1950s with successful and long-running crusades in cities such as New York and London. He has been the most prominent and widely respected EVANGELICAL leader in America for many years. He preaches a simple biblical message of REPENTANCE, often punctuating his messages with the statement, "The Bible says . . . "

Grail, Holy The cup used by Jesus at the LAST SUPPER. In medieval legends, the Holy Grail was also used to catch Jesus' blood while he was hanging on the CROSS, and it became the object of quests by King Arthur's knights.

❦ By extension, a grail can be anything that is the object of a long and arduous search.

Great Awakening A REVIVAL that spread across colonial America in the 1730s and 1740s. Its leaders included the popular preachers Jonathan ED-WARDS and George WHITEFIELD. There was a great increase in the establishment of CONGREGATIONAL, PRESBYTERIAN, METHODIST, and BAPTIST churches as a result of the Awakening.

Great Schism (the East-West split) The split between the Eastern and Western churches, which occurred in 1054. From the time of the EARLY CHURCH there were natural divisions between the LATIN-speaking churches in the West, centered in ROME, and the GREEK-speaking churches of the East, centered in CONSTANTINOPLE. The split finally occurred over theological differences. The POPE in Rome EXCOMMUNICATED the patriarch in Constantinople, and vice versa. The Eastern church became the EASTERN ORTHODOX CHURCH, and the Western church eventually came to be known as the ROMAN CATHOLIC CHURCH.

The PAPAL SCHISM that began in 1378 is also sometimes called the Great Schism, or the Great Western Schism.

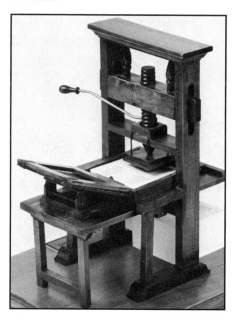

GUTENBERG'S PRESS This is a miniature replica of the press on which Gutenberg first printed the Bible in 1455.

Greek Orthodox Church The Greek Orthodox Church in the USA is actually an ARCHDIOCESE of the Greek Orthodox Church in Greece. It was brought to America by Greek immigrants and is the largest of various EASTERN ORTHODOX CHURCHES in the USA. Church services tend to be elaborate and liturgical.

Gutenberg Bible When Johannes Gutenberg invented movable type in the mid-1400s, one of the first books he printed was the Bible. The text in the Gutenberg Bible was the LATIN VULGATE. There are twenty-one Gutenberg Bibles preserved in museums today.

Henry VIII, King (1491–1547) The king of England who broke with the ROMAN CATHOLIC CHURCH and established the CHURCH OF ENGLAND. His first wife, Catherine of Aragon, was the daughter of Ferdinand and Isabella of Spain (who sponsored Christopher Columbus). Catherine bore a daughter, Mary (later to be known as Bloody Mary for her persecution of PROTESTANTS), but Henry wanted a divorce because he felt he needed a son. His proposed divorce was not sanctioned by POPE Clement VII, so in 1534 Parliament passed the Act of Supremacy, which established the Church of England with the king as head of the church. Henry was eventually married six times.

After a brief reign by Henry's son, Edward VI, Henry's daughter Mary became queen. She was a ROMAN CATHOLIC like her mother and tried to bring England back under the authority of ROME. After Mary's death, Henry's daughter Elizabeth I began her long reign.

Here I stand; I can do no other
When Martin LUTHER was called to recant his teachings at the Diet of WORMS, he refused, saying, "Here I stand; I can do no other. God help me. AMEN."

Holy Grail *See* GRAIL, HOLY.

Holy Roman Empire *See* CHARLE-MAGNE.

HENRY VIII Established the Church of England in 1534.

Huguenots (*HYOO-geh-nots*)
French PROTESTANTS of the sixteenth century who followed John CALVIN's teachings. They were persecuted in their ROMAN CATHOLIC homeland, the worst atrocities being committed in 1572, when thousands of Huguenots were murdered. They received certain freedoms and protection for a time under the Edict of Nantes, but even those freedoms were later rescinded by Louis XIV. Many Huguenots fled to America.

humanism A philosophy that elevates mankind to a preeminent position and celebrates man's freedom. When humanism is non-THEISTIC, dismissing the significance of God, it is often referred to as secular humanism. Secular humanism is a prominent philosophy in America today.

Hus, John (c.1370–1415) A Czech reformer whose attacks on the abuses in the church preceded the PROTESTANT REFORMATION by more than a century. Hus was influenced by John WYCLIFFE, who lived a generation earlier in England. Hus was tried at the Council of Constance (the same CHURCH COUNCIL that ended the PAPAL SCHISM) and was burned at the stake as a HERETIC.

ichthus *See* FISH, SIGN OF THE.

Ignatius of Loyola (1491–1556)
The founder of the Society of Jesus, the RELIGIOUS ORDER commonly called the JESUITS. As a young man, Ignatius was badly wounded in battle. While recuperating, he read about the life of Christ and was inspired to become a soldier for Christ. He was briefly imprisoned by the SPANISH INQUISITION because of his religious views.

indulgences In the ROMAN CATHO-LIC CHURCH, a grant for the remission of part or all of the temporal punishment for SIN. Indulgences are granted both for the living and for those in PURGATORY. Prior to the REFORMATION, indulgences could be obtained in exchange for certain good works, pilgrimages, or donations to the church. The sale of indulgences was one of the practices to which Martin LUTHER objected.

Innocent III, Pope (1160–1216) One of the greatest of the medieval POPES, he reigned 1198–1216. He convened the Fourth Lateran Council, at which the DOGMA of TRANSUBSTANTIATION was defined. Innocent supported the Fourth CRUSADE, and he asserted the power of the PAPACY over kings and emperors. He forced King John of England (of Magna Charta fame) to acknowledge that the English throne was a fief to be granted by the pope.

Inquisition *See* SPANISH INQUISITION.

Institutes of the Christian Religion The classic summary of the Christian faith (1536) by John CALVIN, one of the great leaders of the PROTESTANT REFORMATION. Frequently referred to simply as Calvin's *Institutes*, it is a theological handbook that lays the biblical foundations of REFORMED PROTESTANTISM.

James I, King (1566–1625) The king of England who, under pressure from the PURITANS, authorized the Bible TRANSLATION that came to be known as the Authorized Version or, more popularly, the KING JAMES VER-

SION. It was first published in 1611 and is still widely used today. James became James VI of Scotland when he succeeded his mother, Mary, Queen of Scots, while he was still a boy. He was crowned James I of England in 1603.

JEROME Translated the Bible into Latin in the fifth century.

Jehovah's Witnesses A religious movement that began in the nineteenth century and is still active today. Their founder first predicted that Christ would return to earth in 1914. Jehovah's Witnesses deny the DOCTRINE of the TRINITY, and they practice strict separation from the government and from anyone who is not a member of their church. They do not accept blood transfusions, and they are known for their aggressive door-to-door proselytizing.

Jerome (c.347–419) Translator of the HEBREW Old Testament and the GREEK New Testament into LATIN. His TRANSLATION came to be called the VULGATE (from the Latin for 'common' or 'popular') because it was written in the "vulgar," or common, language. It was the predominant translation in the ROMAN CATHOLIC CHURCH for the next 1,500 years.

DESTRUCTION OF JERUSALEM The Arch of Titus in Rome commemorates the destruction of Jerusalem by the Roman general Titus in A.D. 70. This frieze on the arch shows the temple treasures being carried away.

Jerusalem, destruction of (A.D. 70) JERUSALEM was destroyed by the Roman general Titus in A.D. 70. This forced the dispersion of the young church, which had been centered in Jerusalem, throughout the ROMAN EMPIRE. The destruction of Jerusalem was prophesied by Jesus (Luke 19:41-44), but it is not otherwise mentioned in the Bible.

Jesuits Members of the Society of Jesus, a RELIGIOUS ORDER of men that was founded by IGNATIUS OF LOYOLA in

the sixteenth century. Many Jesuits are teachers or MISSIONARIES. The order operates more than 4,000 schools and colleges around the world.

❦ The term *jesuitical* has a negative connotation—being given to intrigue or deviousness. This is because the Jesuits often wielded power behind the scenes in the governments of Europe.

Joan of Arc (c.1412–1431) A French peasant girl who, at the age of seventeen, led a French army to victory over the English army during the Hundred Years' War. She claimed she received instructions from several SAINTS, which led to her trial as a HERETIC. She was burned at the stake, though the verdict was later overturned. She was CANONIZED by the ROMAN CATHOLIC CHURCH in 1920.

POPE JOHN XXIII He had a short reign (1968–1973), but his influence continues because of Vatican II.

John XXIII, Pope (1881–1963) Although he was POPE for only five years (1958–1963), his influence on the ROMAN CATHOLIC CHURCH has been profound. He convened the Second Vatican Council (*see* VATICAN II), a council that introduced sweeping changes in the church and in the everyday life of Roman Catholics.

POPE JOHN PAUL II His reign began in 1978.

John Paul II, Pope (b.1920) The POPE elected in 1978. Polish by nationality, he was the first non-Italian to be elected pope since the sixteenth century. Like his immediate predecessor, John Paul I (who died a month after his election), John Paul II took a name to honor Pope JOHN XXIII and Pope PAUL VI.

Josephus (c.37–100) A Jewish historian whose writings give tremendous insight into the history and everyday life of first-century JUDAISM. His best-known work is *Antiquities*.

Justin Martyr (c.100–165) An APOLOGIST who defended Christianity against charges of sedition and ATHEISM, frequent charges by the govern-ment of ROME against Christians. He tried to convince the Romans that Christianity was not antithetical to their philosophies, but that their philosophies pointed the way to Christianity. He was martyred under Marcus Aurelius.

Kierkegaard, Søren (1813–1855) A Danish philosopher who believed that the infinite God could only be encountered by exercising a "leap of faith" in the face of objective reasoning. The twentieth-century EXISTENTIALIST movement and Karl BARTH were both influenced by his work.

MARTIN LUTHER KING, JR. American civil rights leader.

King, Martin Luther, Jr. (1929–1968) An African-American BAPTIST

PASTOR who became the preeminent leader of the civil rights movement in America. He was a proponent of nonviolence, and his work was instrumental in the passage of important civil rights legislation. His famous "I Have a Dream" speech was presented at a great civil rights march in Washington, D.C. in 1963. He was assassinated in 1968 at the age of thirty-nine.

❦ Dr. King's birthday is now celebrated as a holiday throughout most of the United States.

JOHN KNOX Leader of the Reformation in Scotland.

Knox, John (c.1514–1572) A reformer and leader of the PROTESTANT REFORMATION in Scotland who founded the (PRESBYTERIAN) Church of Scotland. He was heavily influenced by John CALVIN's teachings.

Latin The official language of the Western church (*see* ROMAN CATHOLIC CHURCH) for most of its history. The Latin VULGATE TRANSLATION of the Bible was completed by JEROME early in the fifth century, and it was the predominant translation of the church for 1,500 years. Until VATICAN II, the Roman Catholic MASS was always in Latin, and official pronouncements of the church are presented in Latin.

Latter Day Saints After Joseph SMITH's death, his MORMON followers split into several groups. The group that called itself the CHURCH OF JESUS CHRIST OF LATTER-DAY SAINTS, under the leadership of Brigham YOUNG, moved to Utah. Another group, which called itself the Reorganized Church of Jesus Christ of Latter Day Saints, moved to Missouri. Members of this smaller group call themselves Latter Day Saints, rather than Mormons.

Leo X, Pope (1475–1521) POPE from 1513 to 1521, the period when the REFORMATION began. Although he EXCOMMUNICATED Martin LUTHER, he never thought Luther was a serious threat to the church. Leo was a great patron of the arts. One of his projects was the rebuilding of SAINT PETER'S BASILICA, a huge job in which

RAPHAEL and MICHELANGELO were both involved.

POPE LEO X He was pope during the early days of the Protestant Reformation. This woodcut was adapted from a portrait by Raphael.

Lewis, Clive Staples (C. S.) (1898–1963) C. S. Lewis was a great Christian writer and APOLOGIST of the twentieth century. He was a professor first at Oxford and then at Cambridge. He wrote fiction for adults (the Space Trilogy, 1938–45) and for children (the Chronicles of NARNIA, 1950–56). His other works include *The Problem of Pain* (1940), *The Screwtape Letters* (1945), *MERE CHRISTIANITY* (1952), and his autobiography, *Surprised by Joy* (1955).

❧ Lewis died on November 22, 1963, the same day President John F. Kennedy was assassinated.

liberalism A theological movement that began in the late nineteenth century. It emphasized freedom, progress, and new ways of thinking, including new ways of looking at the Bible and at Jesus. Liberalism does not accept the traditional view that SCRIPTURE is inspired by God (*see* SCRIPTURE, INSPIRATION OF), and it tends not to accept the deity of Jesus. FUNDAMENTALISM and NEOORTHODOXY were twentieth-century reactions against liberalism.

Livingstone, David (1813–1873) A British MISSIONARY and explorer in Africa in the nineteenth century. When Livingstone had been out of touch with European civilization for some time, the journalist Sir Henry Stanley went to search for him. When they finally met, Stanley gave his famous greeting, "Dr. Livingstone, I presume?"

C. S. LEWIS Scholar, author, apologist.

Luther, Martin (1483–1546) The "Father of the PROTESTANT REFORMATION." Luther was a MONK in Germany who became convinced that the DOC-

TRINES of the church were not consistent with SCRIPTURE. In particular, he felt that the church ignored the biblical teaching of JUSTIFICATION BY GRACE, THROUGH FAITH. In 1517 he posted his NINETY-FIVE THESES on the door of the Wittenberg church. In this document he set forth his disagreements with the Roman authorities in the church, particularly with regard to the sale of INDULGENCES. His rallying cries became *SOLA FIDE* ('by faith alone'), *SOLA GRATIA* ('by grace alone'), and *SOLA SCRIPTURA* ('only the Scriptures'). By *sola fide* he meant that a person could be saved only through faith, not by indulgences granted by the church. In 1520 he was EXCOMMUNICATED by Pope LEO X, and in 1521 he received a hearing before an imperial diet in WORMS. He was asked to recant his teachings, but he refused, saying, "HERE I STAND; I CAN DO NO OTHER. God help me. AMEN."

One of his great contributions to the PROTESTANT movement was his TRANSLATION of the Bible into German. This helped establish a precedent of translating the Bible into the common language of the people. The Luther translation is used to this day in Germany, and it has had an effect on German culture and language similar to that of the KING JAMES VERSION in English.

Luther's followers came to be known as Lutherans, and his teaching formed the foundation for the LUTHERAN churches.

MARTIN LUTHER "Father of the Protestant Reformation." This woodcut was adapted from a 1543 portrait.

Lutheran The church tradition that grew out of the teachings of Martin LUTHER. The Lutherans protested against various DOCTRINES promulgated by the Roman authorities in the church, hence the name PROTESTANT for their movement. Historically, the doctrines of the Lutheran tradition were represented by the terms *SOLA SCRIPTURA* ('only the Scriptures'), *SOLA GRATIA* ('by grace alone'), and *SOLA FIDE* ('by faith alone'). The Lutheran church became the STATE CHURCH of Germany and the Scandinavian countries. *See* *also* BOOK OF CONCORD; LUTHERAN CHURCH, MISSOURI SYNOD; *and* EVANGELICAL LUTHERAN CHURCH IN AMERICA.

Lutheran Church, Missouri Synod A major, theologically conservative LUTHERAN DENOMINATION in the USA. Like all Lutheran churches, it traces its roots to Martin LUTHER. *See also* EVANGELICAL LUTHERAN CHURCH IN AMERICA.

mainline denominations The large established DENOMINATIONS in the USA that historically have played a "culture shaping" role in American society. They include the EPISCOPAL CHURCH, the UNITED METHODIST CHURCH, the PRESBYTERIAN CHURCH (USA), the EVANGELICAL LUTHERAN CHURCH IN AMERICA, and the United Church of Christ. Their leaders tend to be theologically and culturally liberal. Since World War II, EVANGELICALS have tended to distinguish themselves from mainline churches. Membership in mainline denominations has been steadily slipping since the mid-1960s, while membership in evangelical denominations has generally been growing.

martyr A person who is killed because of his or her faith. The first Christian martyr was STEPHEN, and tradition says that most of the APOSTLES suffered martyrdom. Literally millions of Christians have been killed for their faith during the last 2,000 years. During the years of the EARLY CHURCH, many Christians were killed by being THROWN TO THE LIONS.

Mayflower Compact Before the PILGRIMS established their colony in Massachusetts in 1620, they wrote the Mayflower Compact, an agreement that the members of the community would work together and would submit themselves to the laws that were to be adopted "for the general good of the colony." It was the first agreement for self-government in America. Its opening words are, "In the name of God AMEN."

Mennonites A PROTESTANT group that emphasizes peaceful living and community and family values. It dates back to the ANABAPTIST MOVEMENT during the REFORMATION era. The name comes from Menno Simons (c.1496–1561), one of the early leaders. Mennonites are known for their leadership in the peace movement and for their social work in fighting hunger and poverty. The AMISH are a branch of the Mennonite groups.

Methodism, Methodist The REVIVAL movement within the CHURCH OF ENGLAND spearheaded by John and Charles WESLEY in the eighteenth century. The movement was characterized by an emphasis on personal holiness, prayer, good works, and strict discipline. The Methodists eventually broke away from the Church of England but retained an EPISCOPAL form of church structure.

The UNITED METHODIST CHURCH in America is a direct descendant of the early Methodist movement. The AFRICAN METHODIST EPISCOPAL CHURCH (AME) and the AME Zion Church are African-American denominations that are offshoots of the Methodist church.

Milan, Edict of The edict of CONSTANTINE THE GREAT in A.D. 313 that legalized Christianity in the ROMAN EMPIRE. It did not make Christianity the official religion of the empire, but it protected Christians from government persecution and ensured an equal legal footing for Christianity alongside the other religions.

monasticism An ASCETIC way of life in which people (both men and women) live according to a religious rule. Most monastic life is communal and celibate. Some but not all RELIGIOUS ORDERS are monastic. MONKS and NUNS who join a monastic order take vows of poverty, chastity, and obedience.

Moody, Dwight L. (1837–1899) An American EVANGELIST who held great crusades throughout America and England. He was a forerunner in holding the types of crusades later held by Billy SUNDAY and Billy GRAHAM. Moody was also the founder of the Moody Bible Institute in Chicago.

More, Thomas (1478–1535) An English statesman and influential leader of the ROMAN CATHOLIC CHURCH during the reign of King HENRY VIII. Henry elevated More to the position of lord chancellor, but More would not support the king's plan to divorce Catherine of Aragon in defiance of the POPE. More was accused of high treason, and Henry had him beheaded. He is considered by the Roman Catholic church to be a MARTYR, and he was CANONIZED in 1935.

❦ *A Man for All Seasons* is a popular play and movie about Sir Thomas More.

Mormons Members of the CHURCH OF JESUS CHRIST OF LATTER-DAY SAINTS. *See also* SMITH, JOSEPH *and* YOUNG, BRIGHAM.

DWIGHT L. MOODY Nineteenth-century American evangelist.

National Baptist Convention The two largest African-American DENOMINATIONS in the USA are the National Baptist Convention of America and the National Baptist Convention, USA, Inc. Between them they have more than 10 million members. They both trace their history to 1880, and the two groups split in 1915. In THEOLOGY, both groups are similar to other BAPTIST denominations.

National Council of the Churches of Christ in the USA An ECUMENICAL association of Christian churches in the United States. For the most part, the National Council of Churches is made up of PROTESTANT denominations with relatively liberal THEOLOGY, as well as several EASTERN ORTHODOX CHURCHES. A smaller, EVANGELICAL counterpart is the National Association of Evangelicals. *See also* WORLD COUNCIL OF CHURCHES.

neoorthodoxy A theological movement of the twentieth century. Karl BARTH and Reinhold Niebuhr are names particularly associated with neoorthodoxy (*neo* 'new' + ORTHODOXY). It was a reaction against LIBERALISM and was an attempt to regain some of the orthodox truths of the REFORMATION. In contrast to FUNDAMENTALISM, neoorthodoxy did not see the Bible as infallible (*see* SCRIPTURE, INERRANCY OF *under "Church Life and Theology"*), but believed that God speaks through the Bible.

New Testament canon established The CANON is the official list of books included in the Bible. The NEW TESTAMENT contains twenty-seven books—the four GOSPELS, the ACTS OF THE APOSTLES, twenty-one EPISTLES, and the REVELATION. The books of the New Testament were written over a period of about fifty years, from A.D. 40 to 90. The Gospels were written in order to provide an account of the life and ministry of Jesus, and the Epistles were letters that were written (mostly by PAUL) to specific churches or groups of Christians. These letters were widely copied and circulated, and over time the letters written by the APOSTLES or immediate disciples of the apostles were accepted by the church as having divine authority and having been inspired by God.

There was no single point in history when the canon was officially established. Over the first several hundred years of CHURCH HISTORY, various groupings of Gospels and letters were given prominence. The New Testament canon in its present form was largely in place by about A.D. 200, and the first exact listing of the twenty-seven books we now know as the New Testament was included in a letter of ATHANASIUS in A.D. 367. The same list was published shortly thereafter by two different CHURCH COUNCILS.

Nicea, Council of (325) At a CHURCH COUNCIL called by CONSTANTINE in

Nicea (pronounced *ny-SEE-uh*; in present-day Turkey) in A.D. 325, church leaders from around CHRISTENDOM dealt with various HERESIES that had arisen in the 300 years since the time of Christ. In particular, the council was convened to combat Arianism, a heresy that stated that the SON was created by the FATHER and was not of the same essence as the Father. The Council adopted a CREED (later adapted to the form of the Nicene Creed as we know it today) as a universal statement and affirmation of the ORTHODOX beliefs of the Christian church. *See* NICENE CREED *under "Church Life and Theology."*

Nicholas, Saint (fourth century) A BISHOP in Asia Minor (present-day Turkey); he is said to have attended the Council of NICEA. He is the PATRON SAINT of children, and one of the most popular SAINTS of the church. His feast day is December 6, a holiday that is widely celebrated in Europe by giving gifts to children. The Dutch form of Saint Nicholas is *Sinterklaas*, from which we get the contemporary Santa Claus.

Niebuhr, Reinhold *See* NEOORTHODOXY.

Ninety-five Theses The document that Martin LUTHER posted to the door of the Castle Church in Wittenberg in 1517. In it he set forth his various disagreements with the Roman authorities in the church, es-

NINETY-FIVE THESES Luther posts his Ninety-five Theses to the door of the Castle Church in Wittenberg.

pecially regarding the sale of INDUL-GENCES. The document was written in LATIN, but it was soon translated into German and widely distributed. The posting of the Ninety-five Theses is generally considered the start of the PROTESTANT REFORMATION.

Nonconformists Also called dissenters, Nonconformists are persons who do not conform to the practices of a STATE CHURCH. The English BAPTISTS, CONGREGATIONALISTS, and PRESBYTERIANS of the 1600s were Nonconformists, as they rejected certain practices of the CHURCH OF ENGLAND.

Origen (c.185–c.254) A great THEO-LOGIAN and APOLOGIST of the EARLY CHURCH who tried to reconcile Greek philosophy with Christian THEOLOGY. His works of theology laid the foundation for other leaders who followed him.

Orthodox churches *See* EASTERN ORTHODOX CHURCH.

Papal Schism From 1378 to 1415, there were two and then three competing POPES. One pope was in ROME, the traditional seat of the popes, and the other was in Avignon, France, where the PAPACY had been located since 1309. The schism was finally ended by action of the Council of Constance, which deposed all three of the then reigning popes. (The same COUNCIL burned John Hus at the stake as a HERETIC and ordered that John WYCLIFFE's body be exhumed and burned.) The Papal Schism is also known as the Great Western Schism.

Pascal, Blaise (1623–1662) A French mathematician, philosopher, and religious thinker. Much of his religious philosophy is found in *PENSÉES*, a book of collected writings that was published in 1670, after his death. It includes his famous wager on the existence of God.

Patrick, Saint (c.385–c.461) By tradition, Patrick was the MISSIONARY who first took the GOSPEL to Ireland, and under whose preaching Ireland was converted to Christianity. He is the PATRON SAINT of Ireland.

❦ St. Patrick's Day, his feast day, is March 17. It is particularly celebrated by persons with Irish heritage, who wear green on that day.

patron saint A SAINT from whom a person, a group of people, a church, or an institution claims special prayers and protection. For instance, St. CHRISTOPHER is the patron saint of ferrymen and travelers, St. PATRICK is the patron saint of Ireland, etc. A person with the same name as a saint may consider the saint to be his or her patron saint.

Paul VI, Pope (1897–1978) He was POPE from 1963 to 1978, and he continued the reforms begun by his predecessor, Pope JOHN XXIII. He confirmed the ROMAN CATHOLIC CHURCH's ban on contraception in his controversial ENCYCLICAL *Humanae Vitae*. He was the first pope to travel widely around the world.

POPE PAUL VI He reigned from 1973 to 1978.

Peale, Norman Vincent (b.1898) PASTOR and author. His book *The Power of Positive Thinking* (1952) is one of the best-selling books in American publishing history.

Pentecostalism The twentieth-century movement that emphasizes BAPTISM IN THE HOLY SPIRIT as a second blessing, one of the signs of which is SPEAKING IN TONGUES and other charismatic gifts. Pentecostal churches tend to be conservative in THEOLOGY, and there are varying styles of church government. Their churches were among the first to ORDAIN and promote the ministry of women. Two of the largest DENOMINATIONS in America are Pentecostal: the ASSEMBLIES OF GOD and the CHURCH OF GOD IN CHRIST. Beginning in the 1960s, the CHARISMATIC MOVEMENT, which has many similarities to classical Pentecostal teaching and experience, began moving through the ROMAN CATHOLIC CHURCH and MAINLINE PROTESTANT denominations.

Pietism A reform movement within the LUTHERAN church in Germany in the late seventeenth century. The Pietists emphasized fellowship between believers, Bible study, and personal piety. Count von ZINZENDORF and the Moravian church were influenced by the Pietist movement. The Pietist reform in the Lutheran church was taking place at the same time that the PURITANS were trying to bring reform into the CHURCH OF ENGLAND.

NORMAN VINCENT PEALE Beloved pastor and best-selling author.

Pilgrims A small group of English separatists who established the first settlement in Massachusetts (they were heading for Virginia but were blown off course) in 1620. They came to North America in search of FREEDOM OF RELIGION, which they had not experienced in England. They came on a small ship called the *Mayflower*. Their harvest celebration in the fall of 1621 was the first THANKSGIVING.

Pius XII, Pope (1876–1958) POPE from 1939 to 1958, a period that included World War II and the rise of Communism in Eastern Europe after the war. Pius was actively involved in international affairs. During his reign the DOGMA of the bodily assumption of the VIRGIN MARY into HEAVEN was defined.

Polycarp (?–167) BISHOP of Smyrna (in present-day Turkey). Tradition says he was a disciple of the APOSTLE JOHN, and he was burned at the stake because he would not renounce Christ.

presbyterian An ecclesiastical tradition that puts ultimate authority in a hierarchy of representative bodies, starting with duly elected ELDERS in the local church, then a regional group (a presbytery), and a national or international group. The PRESBYTERIAN CHURCH (USA) has a presbyterian form of government. For comparison, see CONGREGATIONAL and EPISCOPAL.

Presbyterian Church (USA) A MAINLINE DENOMINATION that was formed in 1983 as a reunion of the (northern) United Presbyterian Church and the (southern) Presbyterian Church, U.S., which had been separate since the Civil War. The leadership of the PC (USA) is relatively liberal theologically and culturally.

Protestant One of the three great branches of Christianity, along with the ROMAN CATHOLIC CHURCH and the EASTERN ORTHODOX CHURCH. There are literally hundreds of Protestant DENOMINATIONS, all of which come directly or indirectly from the Protestant REFORMATION of the sixteenth century. BAPTIST, EPISCOPAL, CONGREGATIONAL, and PENTECOSTAL churches are all Protestant. There is tremendous theological diversity between Protestant churches, from ultraliberal to ultraconservative.

Puritans A seventeenth-century religious party in England. Their intent was to purify (hence the name Puritan) the CHURCH OF ENGLAND along the lines of CALVINISM. The Puritans emphasized personal piety and upheld the Bible as the sole authority in DOCTRINE and LITURGY and church government. Many Puritans, including the separatist PILGRIMS, emigrated to New England, where their influence was pervasive. The Puritans influenced JAMES I to authorize a new English TRANSLATION of the Bible—the KING JAMES VERSION. The Puritan movement gained such prominence in England that the Puritans, under Oliver Cromwell, engaged in the English Civil War and took control of the government from 1649 to 1660.

❧ Because of the Puritans' stress on personal piety, the term *puritanical* has taken on the pejorative sense of self-righteous adherence to strict moral standards. H. L. Mencken described them as having "the haunting fear that someone, somewhere may be happy."

Quakers *See* FRIENDS, SOCIETY OF.

Reformation There have been two times in CHURCH HISTORY when CHRISTENDOM seemed to be divided all the way to the roots. The first was the GREAT SCHISM (THE EAST-WEST SPLIT) of 1054, when the EASTERN ORTHODOX CHURCH and the ROMAN CATHOLIC CHURCH split apart. The second began in 1517, when Martin LUTHER ignited the PROTESTANT Reformation.

For hundreds of years, individuals and groups within the Western church (e.g., the Waldensians, John WYCLIFFE, and John HUS) had been urging reform of the various abuses that had crept in. Following their example, Luther also cried out for reform—but this time the protest drew wide attention. A movement began that would have a result Luther had never anticipated: the church CATHOLIC would be divided. The sixteenth century was an age of developing nations, and soon German-speaking Switzerland under ZWINGLI, French-speaking Switzerland under CALVIN,

REFORMERS This portion of the Reformers' Wall in Geneva shows Calvin, Farel, Beza, and Knox.

and England under HENRY VIII and Thomas CRANMER took up the banner of reform. Thus was born Protestantism, the third great branch of Christendom. The REFORMERS emphasized the Bible as the supreme authority in matters of faith and practice.

Reformed churches The PROTESTANT churches born out of the REFORMATION that are CALVINIST in THEOLOGY and church government, as opposed to LUTHERAN, ANGLICAN, or ANABAPTIST. Examples would be the PRESBYTERIAN CHURCH (USA), the Christian Reformed Church, and the Reformed Church in America.

Reformers A general reference to the key figures of the REFORMATION. The Reformers include Martin LUTHER, Ulrich ZWINGLI, John CALVIN, and John KNOX.

Richard the Lion-Hearted (1157–1199) A king of England, who led the Third CRUSADE.

Roman Catholic church One of the three great branches of the Christian church, along with the EASTERN ORTHODOX CHURCH and the PROTESTANT churches. For the first thousand years after Christ, the church was catholic (universal) and unified. With the GREAT SCHISM of 1054, the Eastern and Western churches split apart. The Western church, under the BISHOP of ROME, the POPE, was the sole church throughout Western Europe for nearly 500

more years. Then came the Protestant REFORMATION, and Martin LUTHER and others were EXCOMMUNICATED. Various Protestant churches were formed, and the church which continued under the authority of the pope came to be known as the Roman Catholic church.

The Roman Catholic church claims that PETER was the first POPE, with a continuous succession of popes over the past 1,900 years. The pope is the head of the Roman Catholic church, and he is assisted and counseled by CARDINALS. The top CLERGYMEN around the world are the BISHOPS and ARCHBISHOPS. The Roman Catholic church has a long and rich tradition, but significant changes were adopted by VATICAN II, including the celebration of the MASS in the vernacular (rather than the traditional LATIN).

The Roman Catholic church is today the largest body of Christians in the USA, and it is the dominant church throughout Latin America, Southern Europe, and Poland. The Catholic church in the USA tends to be theologically and culturally more conservative than the MAINLINE Protestant churches.

Rome The central city of the ROMAN EMPIRE for centuries, it became one of the centers of the EARLY CHURCH. As the church developed, the BISHOP of Rome, the POPE, played an increasingly dominant role. As a result,

Rome became the central city of the Western church. By the time of the REFORMATION, the term *Rome* was often used to refer to the pope and the entire leadership of the church. *See also* ROME *under "People and Events in the New Testament."*

Salvation Army An international social service organization that also functions as a PROTESTANT DENOMINATION in the Holiness tradition. While it has an emphasis on EVANGELISM, it is best known to the general public for its social work with the poor. During the CHRISTMAS season, representatives of the Army solicit donations for their work by ringing bells in shopping malls and on street corners. The Army was established in 1878. It grew out of a mission work started in 1865 by William Booth, an EVANGELICAL crusader who worked in the slums of London. Salvationists, as members of the Army are called, do not observe any SACRAMENTS.

Savonarola, Girolamo (1452–1498) A DOMINICAN friar and fiery preacher who tried to introduce reforms in the Western church shortly before the PROTESTANT REFORMATION. He was a contemporary of LEONARDO DA VINCI. He was a popular figure in Florence, Italy as he railed against the immorality of Pope Alexander VI and the corruption of the Medici rulers of Florence. He claimed to have special revelation from God, and he was EXCOMMUNI-

CATED when he disregarded the POPE's order that he stop preaching. Shortly thereafter he was hanged and burned as a HERETIC.

Schism, Great *See* GREAT SCHISM (THE EAST-WEST SPLIT). *See also* PAPAL SCHISM.

scholasticism The melding of Aristotelian philosophy and Christian DOCTRINE in the Middle Ages. As a teaching method, it involved argumentation and reconciliation of opposing perspectives. Thomas AQUINAS's *SUMMA THEOLOGICA* is an example of this type of reasoning and teaching.

Scopes trial A famous trial in Tennessee in 1925; it is sometimes called the Monkey Trial. Tennessee law forbade the teaching of EVOLUTION in public schools, and John Scopes, a high-school teacher, purposely broke the law that he felt abridged academic freedom. The prosecuting attorney was William Jennings Bryan, and Scopes was represented by Clarence Darrow. The much-publicized trial highlighted the growing debate between FUNDAMENTALIST Christianity and SECULAR science. Scopes was convicted and fined, but the issue of the appropriateness and constitutionality of the Tennessee law was left unresolved. After the trial, fundamentalists increasingly became outsiders to sophisticated modern culture.

separation of church and state Many immigrants who came to

America in the seventeenth and eighteenth centuries did so to find FREEDOM OF RELIGION. They were escaping the repression of the STATE CHURCHES of Europe. When the U.S. Bill of Rights was adopted, the First Amendment insured both the freedom of religion and that the government would not establish a religion (*see* FIRST AMENDMENT RIGHTS). Over the years, the "establishment clause" of the First Amendment has been interpreted by the Supreme Court to mean that the government at all levels and all governmental agencies (including public schools) must maintain a strict separation from any religious activity, lest they be construed as "establishing" a religion.

Seventh-day Adventists A PROTESTANT DENOMINATION that ascribes special importance to the commandment RE-MEMBER THE SABBATH DAY, TO KEEP IT HOLY. Their name derives from their belief that Saturday, not SUNDAY, is the proper day for observing the SABBATH. Seventh-day Adventists are active in supporting the SEPARATION OF CHURCH AND STATE. Growing out of a movement that predicted Christ's SECOND COMING would occur in 1844, the church was formed in 1863.

Smith, Joseph (1805–1844) Founder of the MORMON church in 1830. He wrote *The Book of Mormon*, which he claimed was a translation of a text on gold plates he found in New York. He was murdered by a mob while he was being held in a jail in Illinois. *See also* CHURCH OF JESUS CHRIST OF LATTER-DAY SAINTS *and* YOUNG, BRIGHAM.

social gospel A movement in PROTESTANT churches from about 1875 to 1930, in which principles from both Old Testament and New Testament were brought to bear on the social problems of the day. Since many of the proponents of this social gospel were influenced by LIBERALISM, conservatives tended to reject the validity of the social gospel. To conservatives, the social gospel was simply a new airing of a "good works" theology. Washington Gladden, a CONGREGATIONALIST MINISTER, has been called the "Father of the Social Gospel." Charles Sheldon's immensely popular book, *In His Steps*, contains many examples of the practical outworking of the social gospel.

sola fide, sola gratia, and ***sola Scriptura*** LATIN: 'by faith alone', 'by grace alone', and 'only the Scriptures'. These were favorite expressions of Martin LUTHER's, since they expressed his belief that a person could be saved only by God's GRACE, not by works or PENANCE or INDULGENCES, and that this grace is appropriated through faith. *Sola Scriptura* expressed Luther's belief that all DOCTRINE had to be validated by holding it against the standard of SCRIPTURE. *See also* JUSTIFICATION BY GRACE,

THROUGH FAITH *under "Church Life and Theology."*

Southern Baptist Convention
The largest PROTESTANT DENOMINATION in the USA. Although they predominate in the South, Southern Baptist churches can be found throughout the country. There are various theological factions within the convention, but in general it is EVANGELICAL in THEOLOGY. Like all BAPTISTS, Southern Baptists BAPTIZE and receive into membership only adults and young people who can articulate a profession of faith (as opposed to INFANT BAPTISM). WORSHIP is nonliturgical, but almost always features a GOSPEL "invitation" after the sermon.

CHARLES SPURGEON One of England's greatest preachers.

Spanish Inquisition A reform movement in Spain at the end of the fifteenth century. Sponsored by Ferdinand and Isabella (who also sponsored Christopher Columbus's voyages), the purpose of the Inquisition was to eliminate HERETICS and to rid the church and society of undesirable elements. The leading inquisitor was Tomás de TORQUEMADA, who burned more than 2,000 heretics and expelled more than 200,000 JEWS from Spain.

❧ The term *inquisition* has come to mean a harsh questioning without regard for an individual's rights.

Spurgeon, Charles Haddon (1834–1892) One of the great BAPTIST preachers of the nineteenth century. He was the PASTOR of the Metropolitan Tabernacle in London. More than 3,000 of his sermons have been published, and he is still frequently quoted by preachers today.

state church A church established by civil authorities; also called an established church. In England, the CHURCH OF ENGLAND is the state church, and the reigning monarch is titular head of the church. In Scandinavian countries the LUTHERAN church is the state church. Citizens are not required to be members of the state church, but in most instances the church is supported financially by the government. In that context, a FREE CHURCH is a church independent of ties to the state or the state church.

The First Amendment to the U.S. Constitution specifically prohibits the United States government or any state from establishing a state church (*see* SEPARATION OF CHURCH AND STATE).

Summa Theologica ('a summation of theology') The great theological work by Thomas AQUINAS. He synthesized Aristotelian philosophy and Christian faith, including an examination of the existence of God. He concluded that God is the uncaused cause. *Summa Theologica* was completed in 1272 and has influenced the development of ROMAN CATHOLIC THEOLOGY over the past 700 years.

Sunday, Billy (1862–1935) A popular EVANGELIST who held great rallies in large cities and small towns across America. He had been a professional baseball player before becoming a REVIVAL preacher. It has been estimated that he preached to 100 million people during his lifetime and had one million converts. His revival ministry can be compared to that of Dwight L. MOODY in the nineteenth century and that of Billy GRAHAM in the second half of the twentieth century.

Taylor, J. Hudson (1832–1905) One of the first MISSIONARIES to China and the founder of the China Inland Mission (now Overseas Missionary Fellowship). Taylor was also an early proponent of "faith missions"—organizations that rely on God to provide financial resources.

Teresa, Mother (b.1910) A ROMAN CATHOLIC NUN who works among the poor in the slums of Calcutta, India. She founded a RELIGIOUS ORDER called the Missionaries of Charity. She is internationally known for her tireless efforts on behalf of the downtrodden. In 1979 she received the Nobel Peace Prize.

MOTHER TERESA Missionary to the poorest of the poor in Calcutta.

Thirty-nine Articles The statement of faith of the CHURCH OF ENGLAND, written in 1563. It was adapted from an earlier document, the Forty-two Articles, written by Thomas CRANMER.

Thomism (*TŌ-mih-zem*) The philosophical system of Thomas AQUINAS, and others whose philosophy derived from his. It is a major foundation in the development of ROMAN CATHOLIC THEOLOGY. *See also* SCHOLASTICISM.

thrown to the lions During the first several centuries after Christ, Christians were persecuted by the ROMAN government. Sometimes they were thrown to hungry lions in the Colosseum as a type of public sport. The Romans did not invent this savagery, however, as we see in the story of DANIEL IN THE LIONS' DEN.

❦ By extension, anyone who feels defenseless against a fierce opponent may say, "I am being thrown to the lions."

Torquemada, Tomás de (1420–1498) A Spanish DOMINICAN who was appointed by Ferdinand and Isabella as inquisitor general (*see* SPANISH INQUISITION). Under his ruthless direction, 2,000 HERETICS were burned, and more than 200,000 JEWS were expelled from Spain.

Tours, Battle of By A.D. 732, Muslim armies had conquered North Africa, had marched across Spain, and had crossed the Pyrenees into southern France. They were turned back by Charles Martel (CHARLEMAGNE's grandfather) at the Battle of Tours. This was an important turning point in the expansion of Islam, as it allowed Europe to maintain its status as a Christian continent.

Trappists Members of a RELIGIOUS ORDER of MONKS. Trappist monks have traditionally been known for taking vows of silence, under which they were rarely allowed to speak to one another.

Trent, Council of (1545–1563) A CHURCH COUNCIL in Trent (northern Italy) called by the POPE in response to the growing influence of the PROTESTANT REFORMATION. The actions of this council substantially defined the ROMAN CATHOLIC CHURCH in the post-Reformation era. Among other subjects, the council decreed that SCRIPTURE and tradition are equal sources of truth, and interpretation of Scripture comes solely through the church.

Tyndale, William (c.1494–1536) A contemporary of Martin LUTHER and, like Luther, a great Bible translator. Tyndale's English TRANSLATION of the New Testament was not the first such translation (he followed John WYCLIFFE by 150 years), but his was the first English translation to be printed (1526) and widely distributed. Tyndale said he wanted to translate the SCRIPTURES so every plowboy could read them in his own language. He lived and worked in exile on the Continent because his translation work was not acceptable to King HENRY VIII and the religious establishment in the days before Henry broke with ROME. Tyndale was tried as a HERETIC and burned at the stake because of his translation. His work was completed by Miles Coverdale, whose complete Bible was printed in 1535 and later widely distributed with King Henry's blessing!

❦ Tyndale House Publishers, the publisher of this book, is named after William Tyndale.

WILLIAM TYNDALE He was burned at the stake because he translated the New Testament into English.

United Methodist Church The second largest PROTESTANT DENOMINATION in the USA, after the SOUTHERN BAPTIST CONVENTION. The United Methodist Church is a MAINLINE DENOMINATION whose leadership is relatively liberal theologically and culturally. It was among the first denominations to allow the ORDINATION of women, and social concerns play a large role in its agenda. The present denomination is the result of various splits and mergers over the years, but its history dates back to the work of John WESLEY and George WHITEFIELD. *See also* METHODISM, METHODIST.

Vatican The administrative center of the ROMAN CATHOLIC CHURCH. The Vatican (or Vatican City) is the world's smallest independent state; it is located inside the city of ROME. The POPE is both head of the Roman Catholic church and head of the government of the Vatican. The Vatican covers substantially less than one square mile in area, and it is dominated by SAINT PETER'S BASILICA. It is home to many art treasures, including the SISTINE CHAPEL and MICHELANGELO'S *PIETÀ*.

The term *Vatican* is often used to refer to the pope and the administration of the Roman Catholic church, just as *Washington* and *Moscow* are used to refer to the governments of the USA and Russia.

Vatican II (Second Vatican Council, 1962–1965) A council of the ROMAN CATHOLIC CHURCH, convened by Pope JOHN XXIII in 1962. Its expressed purpose was to update the church, and it did indeed bring significant changes into the life of the church. There were overtures of reconciliation between the Roman Catholic church and the EASTERN ORTHODOX CHURCH and also with PROTESTANT churches. Personal Bible reading by the laity was encouraged, and the MASS was now to be said in vernacular languages (e.g., English) rather than in LATIN.

Wesley, Charles (1707–1788) Brother of John WESLEY and, with John, one of the founders of METHODISM. Charles was a musician and wrote more than 5,000 hymns, including "CHRIST THE LORD IS RISEN TODAY," "Hark! The Herald Angels Sing," "Soldiers of Christ, Arise," and "Jesus, Lover of My Soul."

JOHN WESLEY This statue of Wesley is very appropriate, since he traveled thousands of miles on horseback.

Wesley, John (1703–1791) One of the founders of METHODISM, and a great EVANGELIST. He was one of the most prominent preachers of the eighteenth century. Wesley was ORDAINED in the ANGLICAN church, but he had a significant CONVERSION experi-

ence at the age of thirty-five while attending a meeting where LUTHER's *Commentary on Romans* was being read. Wesley wrote later that "I felt my heart strangely warmed. I felt I did trust in Christ, Christ alone for SALVATION." John's brother Charles WESLEY worked side by side with him.

Westminster Shorter Catechism A CATECHISM based on the Westminster Confession that was adopted by the English Parliament in 1648 (during the period of PURITAN influence). Its purpose was to provide instruction to children in the essentials of the faith. The first question is, "WHAT IS THE CHIEF END OF MAN?"

What is the chief end of man? The first question in the WESTMINSTER SHORTER CATECHISM. The answer is: "The chief end of man is to GLORIFY God and enjoy him forever."

Whitefield, George (1714–1770) A popular preacher who was influential both in England and in the American colonies. With the WESLEY brothers, he worked for REVIVAL in the church, but he eventually parted with the Wesleys because of his CALVINIST THEOLOGY. His preaching tours in America helped kindle the GREAT AWAKENING.

Wilberforce, William (1759–1833) A brilliant member of Britain's Parliament, and an EVANGELICAL who championed social reform. He was influential in the establishment of numerous

Christian works, including the British and Foreign Bible Society. Perhaps his greatest contribution was his campaign for the abolition of slavery in England and throughout the British Empire. Wilberforce died four days after Parliament passed the Emancipation Act in 1833.

Williams, Roger (c.1603–1683) A PURITAN leader who was expelled from Massachusetts because his separatist views were seen as disruptive. He founded Rhode Island and established it as a colony that guaranteed democracy, FREEDOM OF RELIGION, and SEPARATION OF CHURCH AND STATE.

World Council of Churches An international, ECUMENICAL association of PROTESTANT and ORTHODOX churches seeking to advance Christian unity. Its involvement in and support of liberal, and often radical, causes has tended to overshadow its theological and so-cial contributions. An EVANGELICAL counterpart is the World Evangelical Fellowship. *See also* NATIONAL COUNCIL OF THE CHURCHES OF CHRIST IN THE USA.

Worms, Diet of The diet (a formal assembly of princes) in Worms, Germany (pronounced *Vōrms*) to which Martin LUTHER was called in 1521 to recant his teachings. He responded, "HERE I STAND; I CAN DO NO OTHER. God help me. AMEN."

JOHN WYCLIFFE He translated the Bible into English 140 years before the start of the Protestant Reformation.

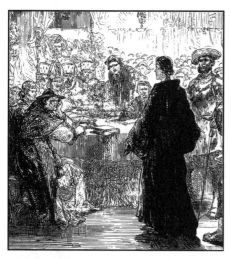

DIET AT WORMS Luther refuses to recant at the Diet at Worms.

Wycliffe, John *(WIH-klihf)* (c.1330–1384) An early English reformer who, like LUTHER 150 years later, rejected many aspects of DOCTRINE in the Western church. His teachings influenced John HUS and laid the foundations for the PROTESTANT REFORMATION on the Continent. His name is associated with a TRANSLATION of the

New Testament from LATIN into English. He started the translation, which was finished after his death by his followers. In 1415, the Council of Constance (the same CHURCH COUNCIL that ended the PAPAL SCHISM and found John Hus guilty of HERESY) ordered that Wycliffe's body be exhumed and burned.

❧ Wycliffe Bible Translators, an organization dedicated to the translation of the Bible into all the languages of the world, was named for John Wycliffe.

Young, Brigham (1801–1877) After Joseph SMITH's death, the MORMONS split into several factions. Brigham Young led his group to Utah, where they founded Salt Lake City in 1847. This group is now known as the CHURCH OF JESUS CHRIST OF LATTER-DAY SAINTS.

❧ Brigham Young University in Salt Lake City is named after him.

Zinzendorf, Count Nikolaus Ludwig von (1700–1760) Founder of the Moravian church, a reform movement that grew out of the LUTHERAN church in the 1720s. Zinzendorf was influenced by the PIETISTS. He was instrumental in sending MISSIONARIES to other lands, and some of those Moravian missionaries played an important role in John WESLEY's spiritual development.

Zwingli, Ulrich (*ZWING-lee* or *TSVING-lee*) (1484–1531) An early leader of the REFORMATION in Switzerland. He was a dynamic Bible expositor and was PASTOR of the largest church in Zurich. He was a contemporary of Martin LUTHER's, but differences in their views of the EUCHARIST kept them from joining forces. John CALVIN, in Geneva, represented the next generation of Reformation leadership in Switzerland.

ULRICH ZWINGLI Leader of the Reformation in Zurich.

CHURCH LIFE AND THEOLOGY

This chapter is about everyday church life—terms that relate to the CHURCH YEAR, to LITURGY, to SACRAMENTS and ORDINANCES, and to offices in the church (e.g., BISHOP, DEACON, ELDER, PASTOR, POPE).

Also included are significant "religious" quotations that are not directly from the Bible but are used in everyday life. These include phrases such as DEARLY BELOVED, WE ARE GATHERED TOGETHER and TO HAVE AND TO HOLD, both of which are taken from the traditional wedding ceremony, and HAIL MARY, FULL OF GRACE, repeated frequently by ROMAN CATHOLICS. Biblical quotations are found in "Quotations from the Bible."

THEOLOGY is the study of God and his relationship to the world. Many people feel that theology is only for MINISTERS and THEOLOGIANS, but theology touches all of us in everyday life. If we believe in God—particularly if we believe in a personal relationship with God—theology helps us define what we believe. The APOSTLES' CREED, which is recited by millions of Christians every week, is a statement of theology. In fact, it contains many theological terms that are directly or indirectly included in this chapter. We can't get away from theology when we describe what we believe.

This chapter contains many familiar terms such as CHRISTIAN, CHURCH, FAITH, and PRAYER that we use in everyday conversation. It also contains technical terms such as ATONEMENT, JUSTIFICATION, REDEMPTION, SALVATION, and SANCTIFICATION. While these are not necessarily terms we use frequently, they describe important aspects of the Christian faith.

Finally, this chapter also includes terms that relate to the book of Revelation—terms such as ANTICHRIST, JUDGMENT DAY, MILLENNIUM, RAPTURE.

Advent The period beginning on the fourth Sunday before CHRISTMAS and ending on Christmas Eve. *Advent* means coming, and it is a time of preparation for Christmas—the celebration of Christ's first coming. Advent also looks ahead to the SECOND COMING. Many Christians commemorate Advent with special devotional readings each day. Many also use an Advent wreath, which contains five candles. One candle is lit on the first Sunday of Advent and each day that week. The next week a second candle is lit, until all four candles are lit during the week before Christmas. Then on Christmas Day the fifth candle, the Christ Candle, is lit.

The first Sunday of Advent is the beginning of the CHURCH YEAR.

agapē There are several different GREEK words that are translated 'love' in English. One of these words, *agapē*, refers to a willful, other-centered love. God's love is *agapē* love, and the Bible exhorts Christians to love God and love one another with this type of love (Matthew 22:37-40). *Agapē* is translated CHARITY in some passages in the KING JAMES VERSION.

agnostic A person who doesn't know if there is a God, and may believe it is impossible ever to know. In contrast, a theist believes there is a God, and an ATHEIST believes there is no God.

All Saints' Day This holy day is celebrated on November 1 by Christians in liturgical churches. It honors all the SAINTS, especially those who are not otherwise honored in the CHURCH YEAR.

❦ Halloween, the night before All Saints' Day, was originally called All Hallows' Eve (the eve of all holy ones' day).

amen An expression of affirmation often spoken at the end of a prayer. It comes from a HEBREW word that means 'it is true'.

Antichrist Anyone who is against Christ is an antichrist, but many Christians believe the book of REVELATION teaches that a final Antichrist will appear in the end times. He will be a magnetic but totally EVIL person who carries out SATAN's plans in the world. He will unite the world under his leadership (see Revelation 13, where he is called the beast). Finally, he will gather all his armies for a battle against Christ, but he will be defeated at the Battle of ARMAGEDDON (Revelation 16, 19) and will be thrown into the lake of fire (*see* HELL).

❦ Christians have identified various evil rulers through the centuries as the Antichrist, but none of them has fulfilled the role described for the Antichrist in Revelation.

apologetics, apologist Apologetics is the logical defense and proof of Christianity. An apologist is a Christian intellectual who specializes in presenting the Christian faith in a way that is understandable to his contemporary culture.

apostasy The deliberate repudiation and abandonment of the faith; a turning away from the faith. A HERETIC rejects some aspect of ORTHODOXY but retains the name Christian. An apostate turns away entirely and rejects identification with the faith.

Apostles' Creed A statement of faith used in both ROMAN CATHOLIC and PROTESTANT churches, dating from about A.D. 150. Although it is an accurate statement of the beliefs of

---

The Apostles' Creed

I believe in God the Father almighty,
Maker of heaven and earth,
And in Jesus Christ, his only Son, our Lord,
Who was conceived by the Holy Ghost,
Born of the Virgin Mary,
Suffered under Pontius Pilate,
Was crucified, dead, and buried;
He descended into hell.
The third day he rose again from the dead.
He ascended into heaven
And sitteth on the right hand of God the Father almighty.
From thence he shall come to judge the quick [living] and the dead.
I believe in the Holy Ghost,
The holy catholic [universal] church,
The communion of saints,
The forgiveness of sins,
The resurrection of the body,
And the life everlasting.

the APOSTLES, it is highly unlikely that any of Jesus' DISCIPLES had any involvement in composing it.

archbishop A high-ranking BISHOP, and the highest-ranking CLERGYMAN in an ARCHDIOCESE. An archbishop has limited authority over the work of the other bishops in his province.

archdiocese The territorial jurisdiction of an ARCHBISHOP. Most archdioceses are major metropolitan areas. *See also* DIOCESE.

Armageddon According to Revelation 16:16, a great battle between good and EVIL will be fought at "the place that in HEBREW is called Armageddon" (NIV). If this is to be a literal battle, the location is uncertain, but it may mean the plains of Megiddo, an area in northern Israel. In the battle, God triumphs over the forces of evil backed by SATAN.

❦ Figuratively, "Armageddon" is any great battle or war, but particularly a battle that is anticipated to have dire or final consequences.

Ash Wednesday The first day of LENT. Christians who observe Ash Wednesday participate in special services, which includes putting ashes on one's forehead as a sign of REPENTANCE for SIN. *See also* MARDI GRAS.

ashes to ashes In the burial service in *The BOOK OF COMMON PRAYER*, the MINISTER says as the earth is put on the casket, "Earth to earth, ashes to ashes, dust to dust." It is a reminder to all present that all of us are mortal. As God said to ADAM, "DUST THOU ART, AND UNTO DUST SHALT THOU RETURN" (Genesis 3:19).

atheist A person who believes there is no God. This is in contrast to a theist, who believes there is a God, and an AGNOSTIC, who does not know if there is a God or believes it is impossible ever to know. Madalyn Murray O'Hair was a prominent American atheist of the late twentieth century who worked to ban religious practices in schools and other public arenas.

atonement One of the central teachings of Christianity, referring to the reconciliation between God and sinners. This reconciliation is brought about through the death of Christ as a substitute for sinful man. Romans 6:23 says, "For the WAGES OF SIN IS DEATH." But God has provided a way for us to be reconciled to him without having to pay the prescribed penalty of death (eternal separation from God). Christ satisfied divine JUSTICE by his suffering and death in the place of sinners. *See also* FORGIVENESS.

Under the old COVENANT of the MOSAIC LAW, the ISRAELITES offered animal SACRIFICES to atone for their SIN. The New Testament points out, however, that "it is not possible that the blood of bulls and of goats should take away sins" (Hebrews 10:4). God applied the benefits and efficacy of the work of Christ to the people in the Old Testament who by faith offered sacrifices that prefigured the final sacrifice of Christ.

Ave Maria   A prayer to the VIRGIN MARY that has been repeated by ROMAN CATHOLICS for centuries. *Ave Maria* is Latin for 'Hail Mary', the salutation given to MARY by the ANGEL GABRIEL when he told her she would be the mother of Jesus, the MESSIAH (*see* ANNUNCIATION *under "People and Events in the New Testament"*). The *Ave Maria* has been set to music in numerous variations. For the English text, see HAIL MARY.

baptism, baptize   The SACRAMENT or ORDINANCE that shows publicly that the individual is a member of the BODY OF CHRIST, the church. As a rite of initiation into the Christian church, baptism binds the candidate to be a responsible follower of Christ. There are two modes of baptism—INFANT BAPTISM and adult (or BELIEVER's) baptism. When an infant is baptized, his parents and/or GODPARENTS pledge to see that the child "is brought up in the Christian faith and life" (*The Book of Common Prayer*). Normally the baptism is then confirmed when the child is old enough to make his or her own affirmation of faith (*see* CONFIRMATION). When older children or adults are bap-

tized, they make their own profession of faith. Infant baptism emphasizes God's electing GRACE and is understood to be the sign of the NEW COVENANT (replacing CIRCUMCISION, the sign of the old COVENANT); believer's baptism emphasizes the human response to God.

Baptism is performed by sprinkling or pouring water on the head or, as done in BAPTIST churches, immersing the candidate completely in water. In most instances the MINISTER or PRIEST says, "I baptize you in the name of the FATHER, and of the SON, and of the HOLY SPIRIT."

baptism in the Holy Spirit   After the RESURRECTION, Jesus told his DISCIPLES, "Wait for the gift my FATHER promised, which you have heard me speak about. For JOHN BAPTIZED with water, but in a few days you will be baptized with the HOLY SPIRIT" (Acts 1:4-5, NIV). The Holy Spirit did indeed come upon and dwell in the disciples—on the day of PENTECOST. With the coming of the Spirit, a new era in the relationship between God and man was initiated. The church—the mystical "BODY OF CHRIST"—was established, and God's Spirit came to live in the minds and hearts of his people (1 Corinthians 3:16). The FRUIT OF THE SPIRIT is evidence of the Spirit that dwells within the BELIEVER.

Christians in the PENTECOSTAL tradition see the baptism in the Holy Spirit as a second blessing that can occur to individuals after CONVERSION. They tend also to expect the miraculous GIFTS OF THE HOLY SPIRIT (particularly SPEAKING IN TONGUES) as a manifestation of the baptism in the Holy Spirit.

believer A Christian; a person who believes in and confesses Jesus as the SON OF GOD who died for him or her.

benediction A blessing, usually pronounced by the MINISTER at the end of a church service.

bishop The highest-ranking clergyman in a DIOCESE or other unit of church government. A bishop oversees the work of other CLERGY in his diocese. *See also* ARCHBISHOP.

blasphemy Insulting or mocking God, or detracting from him in any way. It can include using God's name in vain, which is specifically prohibited in the TEN COMMANDMENTS (THOU SHALT NOT TAKE THE NAME OF THE LORD THY GOD IN VAIN). Blasphemy was punishable by death in the Old Testament. *See also* UNPARDONABLE SIN.

blood of Christ Under the MOSAIC LAW, a system of animal SACRIFICES was established that prefigured the sacrifice of Christ. The blood showed that the animal had died as a provisional ATONEMENT for the SINS of the person making the sacrifice. Under the NEW COVENANT, Jesus was the per-

fect sacrifice that, once for all, secured atonement for sins. As with the Old Testament sacrifices, the *blood* of Christ represented his sacrificial death. In the EUCHARIST, the wine (the CUP) signifies the blood of Christ. *See also* BODY OF CHRIST.

body of Christ In the EUCHARIST, the bread (the HOST) signifies the body of Christ. At the LAST SUPPER, Jesus took bread, gave thanks and broke it, and gave it to his DISCIPLES. He said, "THIS IS MY BODY which is given for you; this do in remembrance of me" (Luke 22:19). *See also* BLOOD OF CHRIST; TRANSUBSTANTIATION; CONSUBSTANTIATION.

In another sense, the church is called the body of Christ (Colossians 1:18). In 1 Corinthians 12, PAUL describes the church as a single body made up of many individual parts, each of which plays an important but different role.

❧ The name of Corpus Christi, Texas, comes from the LATIN phrase *corpus Christi*, 'body of Christ'.

Book of Common Prayer, The The official book containing the LITURGY of the ANGLICAN CHURCHES. It contains the order of worship, including prayers for special occasions, wedding ceremonies, and funeral services. A revised edition was adopted by the EPISCOPAL CHURCH in the USA in 1979. *See also* CRANMER, THOMAS *under "Church History."*

Book of Life A record kept in HEAVEN listing the names of all who have ETERNAL LIFE. In a description of the JUDGMENT DAY, Revelation 20:15 says, "If anyone's name was not found written in the book of life, he was thrown into the lake of fire" (NIV).

born again This term comes from Jesus' conversation with NICODEMUS. Jesus told him, "No one can see the kingdom of God unless he is born again." Nicodemus thought Jesus meant a second *physical* birth, but Jesus meant a *spiritual* rebirth. Jesus went on to say, "FOR GOD SO LOVED THE WORLD that he gave his one and only SON, that whoever believes in him shall not perish but have ETERNAL LIFE" (John 3:16, NIV). Thus, the term means the act in which the HOLY SPIRIT gives eternal life to a person dead in SIN. Through the centuries, most Christians have identified rebirth or regeneration with BAPTISM.

❦ All Christians, by definition, are born again. Many Christians are uncomfortable with the term, however, since it has a connotation of theological conservatism. The media often use the term "born-again Christian" to call attention to a person's own identification as being born again. The term gained prominence during the presidency of Jimmy Carter, who identified himself as a born-again Christian.

canon law The body of ecclesiastical laws governing a church—particularly the ROMAN CATHOLIC CHURCH.

canonization The process by which a person is officially recognized as a SAINT by the ROMAN CATHOLIC CHURCH. To become a saint, a person must have lived an exemplary life, and four MIRACLES must be associated with him or her. Saints are venerated by the Roman Catholic church around the world. In the Catholic tradition, saints go directly to HEAVEN when they die rather than going first to PURGATORY. Saints are then able to intercede in heaven on behalf of the faithful.

The term also refers to the process in which the CHURCH FATHERS recognized the New Testament writings as being the inspired WORD OF GOD (*see* NEW TESTAMENT CANON ESTABLISHED *under "Church History"*).

cardinal A high-ranking BISHOP in the ROMAN CATHOLIC CHURCH. There are 145 cardinals worldwide, and collectively they comprise the Sacred College of Cardinals. Cardinals assist the POPE and rank just below him within the church. Cardinals are appointed by the pope, and the College of Cardinals selects the new pope when a pope dies. Most cardinals serve as heads of ARCHDIOCESES. Others have administrative positions in the VATICAN. There are presently sixteen cardinals in the USA and Canada. Two well-known cardinals of the 1990s are John Cardinal O'Connor of New York and Joseph Cardinal Bernardin of Chicago.

CARDINAL Joseph Cardinal Bernardin, archbishop of Chicago.

catechism A formal series of questions and answers designed to teach children and other Christians the basic beliefs of the Christian faith. In many churches a child must go to catechism classes before being confirmed. One of the historic catechisms is the Westminster Shorter Catechism. *See also* confirmation.

charity The Greek word *AGAPĒ* is sometimes translated 'charity' in the King James Version. In that sense it means self-giving, other-centered love. The thirteenth chapter of 1 Corinthians contains a beautiful description of this type of love. It ends with the statement, "And now abideth faith, hope, charity, these three; but the greatest of these is charity."

❦ Today the more common meaning of charity is simply giving money to those less fortunate than ourselves.

christening The process of naming an infant at the time of its baptism. The minister or priest asks the child's name, and the parents or godparents respond by stating the Christian name (given name) of the child. The minister then baptizes the child, saying, "(Name), I baptize you in the name of the Father, and of the Son, and of the Holy Ghost."

❦ By extension, ships are "christened" when they are first launched.

Christian One who believes in and confesses Jesus as the Son of God who died for him or her. One who is identified with Christ and his church, usually through baptism. As an adjective, *Christian* is used broadly to designate the influence of Christianity in the world, e.g., the Christian West, Christian civilization, Christian culture. More narrowly, it is used by evangelicals to describe their cultural initiatives, e.g., Christian music, Christian books, Christian colleges.

❦ In contemporary usage, *Christian* is often used simply to denote any Western person who is not an adherent of another religion.

Christianity The religion of all those who profess Jesus Christ as the SON OF GOD and the SAVIOR of mankind. It is one of the great faiths in the world today. There are three major branches of Christianity: the ROMAN CATHOLIC CHURCH, the EASTERN ORTHODOX CHURCH, and PROTESTANT churches. The Christian church in its entirety is sometimes called CHRISTENDOM, or simply the church.

Christmas December 25, the celebration of the birth of Jesus. Christians around the world celebrate Christmas by attending special church services and giving gifts to one another. *See also* ADVENT.

❦ The secular celebration of Christmas makes little reference to the birth of Jesus, focusing instead on Santa Claus (Saint NICHOLAS), reindeer, snowmen, and gift giving.

church The word *church* has several related meanings: 1. The body of all Christians, living and dead. Those who are alive are sometimes called the church militant—fighting against SIN and fighting for RIGHTEOUSNESS. Those who are dead and in the presence of God are called the church triumphant. 2. The worldwide body of Christians—all persons in every nation who profess

faith in Christ as the SON OF GOD and SAVIOR (*see* BODY OF CHRIST). 3. A DENOMINATION or major division of the universal church, e.g., the CHURCH OF ENGLAND, the UNITED METHODIST CHURCH, the ROMAN CATHOLIC CHURCH, the EASTERN ORTHODOX CHURCH. 4. A local CONGREGATION of Christians that gathers for service and WORSHIP of God. 5. A building in which a congregation meets for worship.

church year The church year, also called the liturgical year or the Christian year, begins in late November or early December, on the first Sunday of ADVENT. The church year provides a systematic way of celebrating important events in Christian history. Highlights of the church year include CHRISTMAS, EPIPHANY, the Sundays of LENT, EASTER, Ascension Day, PENTECOST (Whitsunday), Trinity Sunday, and ALL SAINTS' DAY. Many days of the year are named in honor of one or more of the SAINTS.

circumcision, circumcise Cutting the foreskin from the penis of a man or, more typically, an infant boy. When the Lord made a COVENANT with ABRAHAM, promising that Abraham would be the father of many nations, he also instituted the ceremony of circumcision (Genesis 17). All the males in Abraham's family and among his descendants were to be circumcised as a sign of the covenant. Boys were to be circumcised when they were eight days old. Ever since then, Jewish males have been circumcised.

In the New Testament, PAUL uses the ceremony of circumcision as a paradigm for the whole system of the LAW. He argues that Christians are no longer bound to the MOSAIC LAW because of the REDEMPTION freely offered through Christ's death. BAPTISM is often seen as the sign of the NEW COVENANT, replacing circumcision, the sign of the old covenant (Colossians 2:11-12).

Although circumcision has no religious significance for Christians, many Christian parents still choose to have their sons circumcised.

clergy Persons who have been ORDAINED for Christian ministry. Clergymen have often been called men of the cloth because of their traditionally distinctive dress.

collect (pronounced *KAH-lekt*) A short prayer used in the LITURGY of many churches.

Communion A SACRAMENT or ORDINANCE in which BELIEVERS eat bread (the HOST) and drink wine (the CUP), according to Jesus' command at the LAST SUPPER, when he said, "DO THIS IN REMEMBRANCE OF ME."

There are various beliefs regarding the meaning of Communion. ROMAN CATHOLICS believe the elements change when they are consecrated by a PRIEST from the substance of bread and wine to the substance of the actual BODY and BLOOD OF CHRIST. This is called TRANSUBSTANTIATION. LUTHERANS traditionally affirm CONSUBSTANTIATION, holding that the body and blood of Christ are present *with* the bread and wine. REFORMED churches affirm that Christ is *spiritually* present with the elements. In the FREE CHURCH TRADITION, the bread and wine are seen as symbolic of the body and blood of Christ (the memorialist view).

Nearly all Christians take Communion occasionally, and in many DENOMINATIONS it is a weekly observance. In the Roman Catholic MASS, the LAYPEOPLE usually receive the HOST but not the CUP. PROTESTANT laypeople receive both the host and the cup. Communion is also called HOLY COMMUNION, the EUCHARIST, the LORD'S SUPPER, or the Lord's Table. *See also* FIRST COMMUNION.

confession In general, the act of stating that one has sinned and is remorseful. The Bible says, "If we confess our sins, God is faithful and just and will forgive us our sins and purify us from all unrighteousness" (1 John 1:9, NIV).

In the ROMAN CATHOLIC CHURCH, as part of the SACRAMENT of PENANCE, individuals confess their SINS to a PRIEST, expressing sorrow for having sinned. The priest may assign an act of penance or restitution; then, as God's representative, the priest extends absolution. Since VATICAN II, confession to a priest has become a less prominent part of everyday life for most Roman Catholics.

confirmation The ceremony in which a child who has been BAPTIZED and has come of age confirms publicly that he or she is a BELIEVER and promises by the GRACE of God to live as a Christian. In many churches a child must go to a confirmation, communicant's, or CATECHISM class prior to confirmation. Confirmation is one of the seven SACRAMENTS in the ROMAN CATHOLIC CHURCH.

congregation A body of people assembled for public WORSHIP.

conscientious objector A person who refuses to serve in the military because of a moral objection to the military and to warfare. Most conscientious objectors claim religious grounds for taking such a stand. The United States recognizes the conscientious objector as having a valid position, though it is difficult to prove conscientious objection if the individual does not belong to a church that is registered as objecting to military service. Many nations with mandatory military service allow conscientious objectors to perform alternate community service.

consubstantiation In LUTHERAN DOCTRINE, there is a real presence of the BODY and BLOOD OF CHRIST *with* the bread and wine in the EUCHARIST. This is in contrast to the ROMAN CATHOLIC DOGMA of TRANSUBSTANTIATION, which asserts that the bread and wine *become* the actual body and blood of Christ. A third view, which CALVIN taught, is that the bread and wine remain actual bread and wine, but the communicant receives the body and blood of Christ in a spiritual manner.

convent A residence for NUNS. The popular image of a convent is of a cloistered and secluded community, but today many convents are modern dwellings in cities.

conversion The act or process of adopting a religion. Conversion sometimes entails switching from one religion to another, as when a Muslim becomes a Christian. The term is also used when a person turns from nonbelief or nominal belief to an active faith. Two famous conversions are those of SAUL of Tarsus on the DAMASCUS ROAD and AUGUSTINE OF HIPPO.

covenant A solemn agreement between two parties, in which one or both promise to perform certain actions. In the Old Testament, God entered into covenants with NOAH, ABRAM, MOSES and the people of IsRAEL, and DAVID. God promised to give Abram descendants as numerous as the stars in the heavens, and he promised to give them the land of CANAAN, from the NILE RIVER to the EUPHRATES RIVER. CIRCUMCISION was instituted as the sign of the covenant.

At Mount SINAI, the Lord said to Moses and Israel, "If you obey me fully and keep my covenant, then out of all nations you will be my treasured possession" (Exodus 19:5, NIV). The Lord then gave Moses the TEN COMMANDMENTS as the standard for the people.

When Christ came, he established the NEW COVENANT, as the Lord had promised in Jeremiah 31:31. This "new covenant" is new in the sense that it is the final and complete revelation of God's covenant with mankind. At the LAST SUPPER Jesus took the cup and said, "This is my blood of the covenant, which is poured out for many for the FORGIVENESS of SINS" (Matthew 26:28, NIV). He meant that his death would provide ATONEMENT for people's sins. Under the new covenant, man's responsibility is to have faith.

The GREEK word translated 'testament', as used in the terms *Old Testament* and *New Testament*, is also commonly translated 'covenant', so the Old Testament is the "old covenant" and the New Testament is the "new covenant."

creation science A modern attempt to merge a literal, biblical understanding of the CREATION with modern science (*see* EVOLUTION). Adherents of creation science attempt to show scientific proof for the Creation as it is described in GENESIS.

creationism The belief that the CREATION took place literally as it is described in the book of GENESIS. This includes the creation of the world and all animals and man as the volitional and deliberate act of God. Creationists do not accept the theory of EVOLUTION as a valid explanation for the development of life and the diversity of species. Many creationists believe the Creation took place in six literal, twenty-four-hour days, and that the earth is relatively young. Many Christians, however, hold to a DOCTRINE of Creation without accepting all aspects of creationism.

creed A formal statement of belief (the word *creed* comes from the LATIN *credo*, 'I believe'). The best-known Christian creeds are the APOSTLES' CREED and the NICENE CREED.

cross, sign of the Making the sign of the cross (also called crossing oneself) is an act of piety. Many Christians cross themselves when they pray. In the Western tradition, the sign of the cross is made by touching the fingers of the right hand to the forehead, then below the breast, then the left shoulder and right shoulder.

crucifix An emblem that shows the body of Jesus hanging on a CROSS. Crucifixes can be large or small. They are often worn on chains as necklaces, and ROMAN CATHOLIC churches often display large crucifixes.

CRUCIFIX This wooden crucifix is about two feet high.

cup In the EUCHARIST, the wine is called the cup. *See also* HOST.

damnation When a person is convicted of an offense, he is punished. The punishment for SIN is damnation—spiritual death, or spiritual separation from God. Christians have traditionally believed that anyone who is not saved by God's GRACE, through faith in Christ, is condemned to eternal damnation in HELL.

deacon In the EARLY CHURCH, deacons were selected by the APOSTLES (Acts 6) to care for the widows and to administer the daily distribution of food. The requirement was that they be wise, full of the HOLY SPIRIT, and well thought of by the rest of the church. Two of the first deacons were STEPHEN and PHILIP (THE EVANGELIST).

Many churches have deacons today. In the ROMAN CATHOLIC and ANGLICAN churches a deacon has taken HOLY ORDERS and often progresses to the priesthood. Deacons in some PROTESTANT churches have spiritual responsibility under the leadership of the PASTOR. In other churches the deacons have responsibility primarily for the physical assets of the church, such as the church building, the parsonage, and the money. *See also* ELDER; TRUSTEE.

Dearly beloved, we are gathered together The opening words of the traditional wedding service, as found in the older editions of *The Book of Common Prayer*.

deism A rationalistic philosophy that includes belief in God as a Supreme Being, but sees him as a master clockmaker who created the universe and then left it to run by itself. He does not intervene in human affairs. Deism (the term comes from the LATIN *deus*, 'god') excludes belief in the TRINITY, the INCARNATION, the ATONEMENT, or MIRACLES. Deism was a prominent religious philosophy among the intelligentsia of the eighteenth century. Benjamin Franklin and Thomas Jefferson considered themselves deists.

depravity, total A DOCTRINE that describes the extent to which human nature is corrupted because of the FALL OF MAN. Total depravity does not mean that there is no goodness in a person or in mankind generally, nor does it mean that an unregenerate person cannot do good. It does mean, however, that every aspect of human nature has been affected by SIN. No one can do anything acceptable to God or claim a right standing with God on his or her own merits. We must rely on God's GRACE to achieve reconciliation with him.

devil SATAN, the angelic being who was the first to rebel against God. He became the chief antagonist of God and God's people. The caricature of the devil as a red-suited person with horns, a pointed tail, and a pitchfork is unfortunate, since it trivializes the existence and superhuman power of the devil and of DEMONS.

diocese The territorial jurisdiction of a BISHOP. *See also* ARCHDIOCESE.

doctrine Teachings of SCRIPTURE; teachings that define and explain various aspects of Scripture, THEOLOGY, and the creeds. A doctrine that has become the official teaching of a church or DENOMINATION may be called DOGMA.

dogma A DOCTRINE officially taught by a church or DENOMINATION. Some dogmas (e.g., the dogma of the TRINITY) are held throughout the church, while others are accepted in only part of the church. The dogma of the IMMACULATE CONCEPTION, for instance, is accepted only by the ROMAN CATHOLIC CHURCH. The PROTESTANT view is that all dogma must be validated by SCRIPTURE. The ROMAN CATHOLIC view is that dogma is God's objective truth defined by the church, and that the dogmas of the church are infallible.

doxology A short HYMN of praise to God. This doxology, written in the seventeenth century, is frequently sung in churches today:

Praise God, from whom all blessings flow;
    Praise him all creatures here below;
Praise him above, ye heavenly host;
    Praise Father, Son, and Holy Ghost.

Easter The Sunday on which Christians celebrate the RESURRECTION of Jesus. It is often considered the most significant event of the CHURCH YEAR because of the APOSTLE PAUL's statement that "if Christ has not been raised, your faith is futile" (1 Corinthians 15:17, NIV). In the Western tradition, Easter is always in late March or early April, on the first Sunday after the first full moon following the spring equinox.

❦ The secular celebration of Easter makes no reference to the Resurrection, focusing instead on the Easter bunny and candy and decorated eggs: symbols of fertility and springtime.

ecumenical, ecumenism An ecumenical movement promotes unity among diverse Christian bodies. Ecumenical movements in recent years have attempted to unite several PROTESTANT DENOMINATIONS, or to reunite the ROMAN CATHOLIC CHURCH and the ANGLICAN CHURCH. The NATIONAL COUNCIL OF THE CHURCHES OF CHRIST IN THE USA and the WORLD COUNCIL OF CHURCHES promote ecumenism.

The great CHURCH COUNCILS of the fourth and fifth centuries are called ecumenical councils because they represented all of CHRISTENDOM. The ROMAN CATHOLIC CHURCH uses the term *ecumenical council* for additional councils (including the Council of TRENT and VATICAN II) that are not accepted by PROTESTANTS or the EASTERN ORTHODOX CHURCH as being ecumenical.

elder A position of leadership for a LAYPERSON in a church. In most churches the elders have some spiritual responsibility for the CONGREGATION, either in their own right or under the leadership of the PASTOR. *See also* DEACON, TRUSTEE.

election The DOCTRINE that God chooses the people who will receive SALVATION. Those who are chosen are called the elect. Two of the great advocates of this doctrine were AUGUSTINE OF HIPPO and John CALVIN. Calvin did not profess to know who had been chosen, but he saw certain actions as indicators that a person was among the elect—a public profession of faith, water BAPTISM, participation in the LORD'S SUPPER, and a moral life. *See also* SOVEREIGNTY OF GOD; PREDESTINATION; *also* CALVINISM *under "Church History."*

encyclical A circular letter from the POPE addressed to the BISHOPS of the ROMAN CATHOLIC CHURCH. Encyclicals set out guidelines for the application of the church's DOGMAS, and CATHOLICS must accept the doctrinal teachings contained in them. Encyclicals are known by the opening words of the LATIN text. For example, Pope PAUL VI's controversial encyclical regarding birth control is known as *Humanae Vitae* ('human lives').

Epiphany January 6, observed to commemorate the coming of the WISE MEN to Jesus in BETHLEHEM. Epiphany also celebrates the coming of Christ for the GENTILES.

eschatology The DOCTRINE of the "last things." The term is often used in relation to events at the end of the world, including the RAPTURE, the TRIBULATION, ARMAGEDDON, the SECOND COMING, and JUDGMENT DAY. There are various and conflicting views of eschatology.

eternal life A phrase used in the Bible to describe the kind of life given by Jesus. It describes more than just the duration of life; it speaks also to the essential quality of life. The Bible tells us in Romans 6:23 that "the WAGES OF SIN IS DEATH, but the gift of God is eternal life through Jesus Christ our Lord." In a prayer recorded in John 17:3, Jesus said, "Now this is eternal life: that they may know you, the only true God, and Jesus Christ, whom you have sent" (NIV).

ethical relativism The theory in ETHICS that there is no fixed standard for right and wrong. Each situation can be judged on its own merits according to the views of the individual and the cultural and historical context. Joseph Fletcher's book *Situation Ethics* (1966) played a key role in establishing this view.

ethics The branch of philosophy that deals with the distinction in human conduct between right or wrong, good or EVIL. Christian DOCTRINES provide an excellent basis for ethics, although Christians often disagree over the morality of such things as war, abortion, and divorce.

Eucharist Another name for COMMUNION. The literal meaning of *Eucharist* is thanksgiving.

euthanasia The act of choosing how and when a person will die, as opposed to letting nature take its course. Assisted suicide and mercy killing are two forms of euthanasia. The issues surrounding euthanasia become increasingly complex as modern medicine is able to prolong life far beyond the point that death would naturally occur. In its most insidious form, as in the Holocaust, euthanasia becomes murder according to an arbitrary standard of who should and should not be allowed to live. The word *euthanasia* comes from GREEK words meaning 'good death'.

evangelism, evangelistic Evangelism is the act of spreading the GOSPEL, the GOOD NEWS about Jesus Christ. The terms *evangel* (of GREEK origin) and *gospel* (of Old English origin) both mean 'good news'. Evangelism can take place on a personal level, or in great evangelistic crusades like those of Billy GRAHAM, or in the form of traditional MISSIONARY work. EVANGELICALS, whether members of MAINLINE or other DENOMINATIONS, tend to be interested in evangelism.

evangelist An evangelist is a person who proclaims the GOSPEL, the GOOD NEWS about Jesus Christ. The term is usually used in reference to someone like Billy GRAHAM, who conducts large public meetings, or crusades. Television evangelists (often called televangelists) have come under substantial criticism in recent years because of their flamboyant life-styles and sometimes exaggerated claims.

The writers of the GOSPELS are sometimes called the EVANGELISTS.

everlasting life *See* ETERNAL LIFE.

evil That which is contrary to the nature and will of God. Wickedness; the opposite of goodness; that which has been tainted by SIN. The Bible does not reveal the origin of evil, except to say that SATAN was the first to commit it. The Bible does affirm, however, that God has it under his control.

evolution The theory that higher life forms evolved over billions of years from lower forms. According to this theory, the first living organism was only a single cell. That organism reproduced and mutated and, through a long sequence of constructive mutations and natural selection, higher life forms (including human beings) evolved. This theory was first made popular by Charles DARWIN in his book *The Origin of Species* (1859).

The theory of evolution is broadly accepted by scientists, and it is taught in public schools as the definitive view of the origin of life on earth. Many Christians believe that this theory contradicts the account of the CREATION presented in the book of GENESIS. Others believe that the Bible explains *who* created life and *why* it was created, and that science explains *how* it was created.

ex cathedra A LATIN phrase that means literally 'from the throne' (i.e., from the BISHOP's throne). When the POPE speaks *ex cathedra*, he is making a pronouncement with the authority of the church. According to ROMAN CATHOLIC DOGMA, the pope is infallible when he speaks *ex cathedra* on matters of faith or morals (*see* PAPAL INFALLIBILITY).

❦ A CATHEDRAL, the principal church within a DIOCESE, is the church that contains the bishop's cathedra ('throne').

excommunication The most severe form of church discipline, in which a person is excluded from the communion of a church because of his or her stubborn sinfulness. In the ROMAN CATHOLIC CHURCH, a person who has been excommunicated is denied the SACRAMENTS and a Christian burial, but is not seen as being outside the GRACE of God. Other forms of church discipline include suspension from the sacraments without excommunication and defrocking (removing from office) an ORDAINED MINISTER.

extreme unction *See* LAST RITES.

faith Confidence or active trust in something that cannot be objectively proven or disproven. In Christian THEOLOGY, faith entails belief in God and in his offer of JUSTIFICATION BY GRACE through Christ. Faith also entails quiet confidence in God as we pray, expecting that he will provide for us as we ask for his will to be done. Faith manifests itself in action, as we see in James 2:20, which says that "faith without works is dead."

The word *faith* also refers to a religion in its entirety (e.g., the Hindu faith, the Christian faith), or to a DE-NOMINATION or other major group within a religion. In this context, a marriage between a ROMAN CATHOLIC and a PROTESTANT might be called an interfaith marriage.

fasting The discipline of going without food for a period of time in order to devote one's time and energy to meditation and prayer. Jesus fasted in the WILDERNESS for forty days and nights.

Father *See* GOD THE FATHER.

First Communion In the ROMAN CATHOLIC CHURCH a child first participates in the EUCHARIST at about age six. This is called the child's First Communion. Parents and friends often celebrate the event with gifts for the child.

for richer for poorer An expression in the traditional wedding vows. *See* TO HAVE AND TO HOLD.

forgiveness Pardon for an offense or a wrong; also called remission of SINS. Because of the FALL OF MAN and our own actions, all humans are sinful. Our SIN separates us spiritually from God, but God forgives us through our faith in the death of Jesus. God continues to forgive us as we continue to confess our sins (1 John 1:9). The Bible tells us that God forgets our sin when he forgives us. It is as far from us as the east is from the west (Psalm 103). We are instructed to forgive one another, as we see in Ephesians 4:32 (NIV): "Be kind and compassionate to one another, forgiving each other, just as in Christ God forgave you."

FOUR HORSEMEN OF THE APOCALYPSE "Behold a pale horse: and his name that sat on him was Death, and Hell followed with him" (Revelation 6:8).

four horsemen of the Apocalypse In Revelation 6, JOHN's VISION includes four horses that represent various aspects of God's future judgment upon mankind. The first horse is white. Its rider is a conqueror and seems to represent a short period of imperial rule. The second horse is red and represents warfare and bloodshed. The third horse is black and represents famine. The fourth is a pale horse and represents death and HELL.

free will   There are differing views among Christians as to the extent to which fallen sinners are free and able to respond to God's GRACE. The ARMINIAN view is that humans are free and able to choose whether or not to obey God's commands and whether or not to accept God's grace. The REFORMED view is that humans can embrace Christ only as God regenerates their hearts.

❦ Whatever the extent of free will, it seems to be contradicted by the SOVEREIGNTY OF GOD. If God already planned and knows everything that will happen, how can people freely do anything, good or bad? Are we not bound to do whatever God has foreordained, whether or not we recognize that we are being guided by his invisible will? One answer is that we have free will as we see things *from our finite human perspective*. From our own vantage point, we can choose whether to obey God and choose whether to accept his grace. Therein lies free will.

fruit of the Spirit   In his letter to the church in Galatia, PAUL writes, "The fruit of the SPIRIT is love, joy, peace, patience, kindness, goodness, faithfulness, gentleness, and self-control" (Galatians 5:22-23, NIV). These virtues are the result of the HOLY SPIRIT's living in and dominating the life of the BELIEVER. The preceding verses contain a list of sinful activities that are the natural result of a person's being dominated by his sinful nature (*see* DEPRAVITY, TOTAL).

gifts of the Holy Spirit   The New Testament teaches that the HOLY SPIRIT gives special gifts or abilities to all Christians. Different gifts are given to different individuals, but all are to be used to strengthen the BODY OF CHRIST, the church. The gifts of the Holy Spirit include faith, healing, working MIRACLES, SPEAKING IN TONGUES, interpreting what has been spoken in tongues, serving, teaching, encouraging, leading, and contributing money. The APOSTLE PAUL is very clear, however, in 1 Corinthians 13 (the LOVE CHAPTER), that we should value LOVE more than any of the spiritual gifts.

"Gloria Patri"   The LATIN name of an ancient Christian HYMN. *Gloria patri* is Latin for 'Glory be to the Father'. It is usually sung in English:

Glory be to the Father,
And to the Son,
And to the Holy Ghost.
As it was in the beginning,
Is now, and ever shall be,
World without end. Amen, amen.

glorification The transformation that will take place when BELIEVERS enter the future KINGDOM OF HEAVEN. We will be given imperishable, glorious, spiritual bodies instead of our present perishable bodies (1 Corinthians 15:35-57).

glorify, glory To glorify God is to honor him, WORSHIP him, and praise him. One aspect of the glory of God is simply the revelation to mankind of his being and his nature, especially in the person and work of Jesus Christ. Hebrews 1:3 says, "The SON is the radiance of God's glory and the exact representation of his being, sustaining all things by his powerful word" (NIV). ADAM was created to reflect the image and glory of God, but he fell short of that destiny, which has been fulfilled in Christ. In another sense, the glory of God is reflected by the church, the BODY OF CHRIST—even though it is very imperfect.

The visible manifestation of God's invisible presence and glory is sometimes called the *Shekinah*. An example is the PILLAR OF CLOUD and PILLAR OF FIRE that protected and led the ISRAELITES in the WILDERNESS.

Glory be to the Father The first line of the "GLORIA PATRI".

God The name most frequently used for the eternal, holy, all-powerful, all-knowing, ever-present personal spirit who created and sustains the universe. To use Thomas AQUINAS's concept, God is the uncaused cause. Christians believe that God exists in three per-

Some of the Names for God in the Bible

NAME	MEANING
Abba	ARAMAIC: 'father', or 'dear father'; Jesus used this term when he was praying in the Garden of GETHSEMANE.
Adonai	HEBREW: 'the Lord, the superior one'
El Shaddai	Hebrew: 'God Almighty'
Elohim	Hebrew: 'The supreme or sovereign God'; it can also mean 'god' in a more generic sense
FATHER	GOD THE FATHER, one of the persons of the TRINITY; this name shows God's fatherly love for us.
JEHOVAH	An alternate form for *Yahweh*.
LORD	Many English TRANSLATIONS use *LORD* (with small capital letters) to translate *Yahweh*.
YAHWEH	The personal name used only of ISRAEL's God; it means 'I AM THAT I AM', or 'I Am the One Who Is'. This name was too HOLY for the Israelites to pronounce, so *Adonai* was substituted in public reading.

sons—GOD THE FATHER, GOD THE SON, and GOD THE HOLY SPIRIT (*see* TRINITY). The WESTMINSTER SHORTER CATECHISM says God is a Spirit who is "infinite, eternal, and unchangeable in his being, wisdom, power, holiness, JUSTICE, goodness, and truth."

The term *god* (not capitalized) is used to refer to any supernatural spirit or power that people WORSHIP. Some religions (e.g., Hinduism) have many gods. The first of the TEN COMMANDMENTS says, "THOU SHALT HAVE NO OTHER GODS BEFORE ME."

God is great, God is good, and we thank him for our food A prayer that many Christians say before a meal. To pray before eating is to "say grace."

God the Father According to the DOCTRINE of the TRINITY, God exists eternally in three persons: God the Father, GOD THE SON, and GOD THE HOLY SPIRIT. God the Father, in eternity past, planned all things, including a wonderful plan of SALVATION because of his great LOVE. This plan involved sending his Son into the world as the REDEEMER for all those who would believe in him.

God the Holy Spirit According to the DOCTRINE of the TRINITY, God exists eternally in three persons: GOD THE FATHER, GOD THE SON, and God the Holy Spirit. God the Holy Spirit is the Helper who came to dwell permanently in the hearts of BELIEVERS after Jesus' ASCENSION into HEAVEN. In this way, God lives in and among us. The Holy Spirit convicts us of SIN, prays for us, and helps us in every way to do God's will.

God the Son According to the DOCTRINE of the TRINITY, God exists eternally in three persons: GOD THE FATHER, God the Son, and GOD THE HOLY SPIRIT. God the Son existed with the Father before the foundations of the world, and he executes his Father's plan of REDEMPTION. God the Son was incarnated as Jesus (*see* INCARNATION). His mother, MARY, was a virgin, and he lived as a perfect man. He was CRUCIFIED, died, and was buried. In his death, he secured ATONEMENT for SIN. Then, after three days, he rose from the dead and later ascended into HEAVEN. There he sits at the right hand of God the Father. Someday he will return to earth in triumph and glory (*see* SECOND COMING).

godfather, godmother, godparents Adults who participate in a child's BAPTISM and pledge to take a role in looking out for the spiritual well-being of the child.

Good Friday The Friday before EASTER, when Christians remember the CRUCIFIXION of Jesus. The name Good Friday seems like a misnomer, since it commemorates Jesus' death. It was a good day, however, in the sense that Christ provided ATONEMENT for our SINS when he died.

Good News When an ANGEL appeared to the SHEPHERDS in the fields outside BETHLEHEM on the night of Jesus' birth (Luke 2), he said, "Fear not: for, behold, I bring you GOOD TIDINGS OF GREAT JOY, which shall be to all people. For unto you is born this day in the city of David a SAVIOR, which is Christ the Lord." The Good News is exactly the news the angels told the shepherds—that God sent a savior to earth to save people from their SIN. The word GOSPEL comes from an Old English word meaning 'good news'.

gospel The GOOD NEWS about Jesus Christ—that he is the SON OF GOD, that he died to secure ATONEMENT for our SIN, and that he rose from the dead, thereby conquering death. The first four books of the New Testament are called the GOSPELS because they contain the Good News about Jesus.

❧ By extension, the word *gospel* has also come to mean anything that is accepted as infallible truth.

❧ The word *gospel* comes from *godspell*, an Old English word meaning 'good news'. *Godspell* was a popular musical in the 1970s. It is a contemporary retelling of the gospel, based on the Gospel of MATTHEW.

grace Something that is freely given, that cannot be earned. In Christian THEOLOGY, grace is the unmerited favor of God bestowed on sinners. Its highest expression is in the REDEMPTION provided by Christ's death. God's grace is extended to us freely because of his great LOVE for us. The APOSTLE PAUL said, "While we were still sinners, Christ died for us" (Romans 5:8, NIV). We receive JUSTIFICATION BY *GRACE*, THROUGH FAITH.

While not all people are recipients of God's *special* grace of personal redemption in Christ, we are all recipients of God's *common* grace—the natural blessings he bestows on all mankind through creation.

Hades In the New Testament, the GREEK word *Hades* refers to the place of the dead. For a fuller explanation, see the entry for HELL.

Hail Mary A popular name for the prayer to the VIRGIN MARY often repeated by ROMAN CATHOLICS. It is also called the *AVE MARIA*.

Hail Mary, full of grace,
The Lord is with thee.
Blessed art thou among women, and
Blessed is the fruit of thy womb, Jesus.
Holy Mary, Mother of God, pray for us
    sinners,
Now and at the hour of our death.

❧ "Hail Mary" has also come to mean a prayer uttered in a moment of desperation. In football, a "hail Mary" pass is a pass thrown in desperation, in hopes that a receiver will be able to catch it.

Hanukkah (also spelled Chanukah; both spellings are pronounced

HAH-nuh-kuh) The Jewish celebration that commemorates the cleansing of the TEMPLE after it was desecrated by the Syrian king Antiochus during the time of the MACCABEES (165 B.C.). Also called the Festival of Lights, it is celebrated in December. Each night for eight nights an additional candle is lit in a special candelabrum called a menorah.

heaven The dwelling place of God. It is very real, but it is not a physical place we can discover with our physical senses. It exists in a spiritual realm. Jesus used the analogy of a house when he told his DISCIPLES, "In my FATHER's house are many rooms; if it were not so, I would have told you. I am going there to prepare a place for you. And if I go and prepare a place for you, I will come back to take you to be with me that you also may be where I am" (John 14:2-3, NIV). Jesus came to earth from heaven, and at the ASCENSION he returned to heaven.

The book of REVELATION contains various descriptions of heaven. We see God seated on a throne, with millions of ANGELS bowing down in WORSHIP before him. Also in Revelation we see JOHN's VISION of a HOLY city, the NEW JERUSALEM, coming down from heaven to be the eternal home of God and of those who have ETERNAL LIFE. It is described as a city with streets of gold and gates made of pearls (*see* PEARLY GATES). It is a glorious place with no crying, no sadness, no death. Many Christians use the word HEAVEN to describe this eternal home.

hell The future dwelling place of SATAN and his DEMONS. Also the place of future punishment for wicked, unredeemed people. It is a place of fire and eternal torment. In Revelation 20:10, 15 it is called the lake of fire. In Mark 9:48, Jesus described hell as a place "where their worm does not die, and the fire is not quenched." In some ways, hell is the antithesis of HEAVEN.

The biblical references to hell are confusing, in part because there are three different words that are all translated 'hell' in the KING JAMES VERSION. The HEBREW word *Sheol* and the GREEK word *Hades* refer to a place where the dead have only a shadowy existence; these words are often translated 'death', 'the grave', or 'Destruction' in modern TRANSLATIONS. The Greek *Gehenna* is usually rendered 'hell' in modern translations and refers to the fires of hell.

heresy Adherence to a religious belief that is contrary to church DOGMA. It is the opposite of ORTHODOXY. There have been and continue to be many heresies that plague the church. Some of the early heresies were Gnosticism, docetism, and Arianism. Gnosticism included the belief that matter is evil and spirit is good, and that SALVATION comes through the acquisition of secret knowledge (gnosis). Docetism included the belief that Jesus was not really a man, but just seemed to be a man. Arianism included the belief that Christ had been created by GOD THE FATHER, so Christ was not coequal and coeternal with the Father. Adherents of heresies are called HERETICS.

heretic A person who adheres to a religious belief contrary to church DOGMA (*see* HERESY). In the history of the church, many heretics have been burned at the stake or otherwise executed. In some cases, people burned as heretics by the rulers of their day were seen by later generations as MARTYRS or even SAINTS. An example is JOAN OF ARC.

hermeneutics The science and art of biblical interpretation. Most Christians affirm the divine inspiration and authority of SCRIPTURE, but they disagree on how the Scriptures should be interpreted. In general, the goal of hermeneutics is to discern the original and authentic meaning of the biblical text. This is done by helping the reader understand the cultural and historical context in which the Bible was written as well as the cultural context in which it is being read.

holy The word *holy* has several related meanings: 1. The HEBREW word for *holy* means 'set apart' or 'separate'. 2. To be without SIN, or separate from sin. 3. SACRED. 4. Christians are said to be holy because they are cleansed by God through the atoning death of Christ. 5. One aspect of SALVATION is SANCTIFICATION, the ongoing development of holiness in the life of the Christian.

❦ The expression "holier than thou" is disdainfully said about people who seem to flaunt their goodness, or "holiness."

Holy Communion Another name for the EUCHARIST, or COMMUNION.

Holy Ghost Another name for the Holy Spirit. *See* GOD THE HOLY SPIRIT.

holy orders A SACRAMENT in the ROMAN CATHOLIC CHURCH by which a man is ordained to special service in the church as a DEACON, PRIEST, or BISHOP.

Holy See The jurisdiction of the POPE; the VATICAN.

Holy Spirit The third person of the TRINITY. *See* GOD THE HOLY SPIRIT.

host In the EUCHARIST, the bread is called the host. The term derives from a LATIN word for 'sacrifice'. *See also* CUP.

hypocrite A person who says one thing but does another. Jesus frequently called the SCRIBES and PHARISEES hypocrites, as when he said they STRAIN AT A GNAT AND SWALLOW A CAMEL.

❦ Many people say they do not want

to follow Christ because of all the hypocrites in the churches. There are indeed many hypocrites, but that simply shows human sinfulness and underscores the need we all have for SANCTIFICATION.

I Am That I Am When MOSES met God at the BURNING BUSH, Moses asked God what his name was. God responded, "I Am That I Am" (Exodus 3:13-14). In HEBREW the name is spelled YHWH, or YAHWEH. In the several centuries before Christ, JEWS were not allowed to pronounce the name because it was HOLY. When they came to the name *Yahweh* in the SCRIPTURE, they said ADONAI ('the Lord'). See the list of names for God at the entry for GOD.

I believe in God the Father almighty The first phrase of the Apostles' Creed. For the complete text, see APOSTLES' CREED.

IHS An ancient Christian symbol that is still frequently seen in churches. It is taken from the first three letters of *IHSOUS*, the GREEK spelling of *Jesus*.

Immaculate Conception The DOGMA of the ROMAN CATHOLIC CHURCH that the VIRGIN MARY was free of ORIGINAL SIN from the moment she was conceived in her mother's womb. This doctrine should not be confused with the VIRGIN BIRTH of Jesus, which means that Mary was a virgin when Jesus was born.

imprimatur The official approval given by a representative of the ROMAN CATHOLIC CHURCH that a book may be printed. *Imprimatur* is LATIN for 'let it be printed'.

❦ More broadly, an *imprimatur* can be any type of endorsement by a person in authority.

in Jesus' name Many Christians end their prayers by saying, "In Jesus' name, AMEN." This tradition comes from Jesus' teaching, as recorded in passages such as John 14:13-14: "And I will do whatever you ask in my name, so that the Son may bring glory to the Father. You may ask me for anything in my name, and I will do it" (NIV).

in sickness and in health An expression in the traditional wedding vows. *See* TO HAVE AND TO HOLD.

Incarnation, the The act whereby the eternal SON OF GOD, the second person of the TRINITY, united himself with human flesh in the person of Jesus (the word *incarnation* means 'in flesh'). Jesus was fully man and fully God simultaneously. Matthew 1:23 says, "Behold, a virgin shall be with child, and shall bring forth a son, and they shall call his name IMMANUEL, which being interpreted is, God with us." Through the Incarnation, God is indeed with us.

The Incarnation is an important aspect of Christian THEOLOGY because GOD THE SON came to earth and became the perfect SACRIFICE on behalf of sinful people to atone for SIN (*see* ATONEMENT). Furthermore, Hebrews 4:15 reminds us that Jesus sympathizes with all our weaknesses, for he has been tempted in every way we are tempted, though he did not sin.

infant baptism *See* BAPTISM.

INRI *See* KING OF THE JEWS *under "People and Events in the New Testament."*

invocation A prayer at the beginning of a WORSHIP service or other public gathering, asking God to be present and to bless the meeting.

Jehovah A name for God. The name *Jehovah* comes from combining two HEBREW names for God—the consonants of YHWH, the name that was too sacred to pronounce, and the vowels of Adonai (see the list of names for God at the entry for GOD). Some English TRANSLATIONS translate YAHWEH as 'Jehovah', while others translate it 'LORD'.

Judgment Day The final day of reckoning, when God settles all accounts, judging EVIL and rewarding faith; also called the Day of the Lord. There are vivid descriptions of the final judgment in the books of DANIEL and REVELATION. Each person will stand before God, the books will be opened, and the individual will be judged according to his deeds recorded in the books. Anyone whose name is not recorded in the BOOK OF LIFE will be thrown into the lake of fire. Some THEOLOGIANS see separate judgments for believers (2 Corinthians 5:10) and unbelievers (Revelation 20:11-15).

justice Doing what is right for another person, or ensuring that what is right takes place. The Old Testament PROPHETS spoke much about the need for justice, and ISRAEL and JUDAH were both criticized for not treating widows and orphans justly. The prophet Micah gave this prescription for right living: "He has showed you, O man, what is good. And what does the Lord require of you? To act justly and to love MERCY and to walk humbly with your God" (Micah 6:8, NIV).

In a stricter sense, justice means giving a person what he deserves as a result of his actions. SCRIPTURE is very clear that "ALL HAVE SINNED AND COME SHORT OF THE GLORY OF GOD," and that "the WAGES OF SIN IS DEATH." According to God's justice, all people deserve DAMNATION. Thankfully, God provided a way of ATONEMENT for those who believe.

justification God's act of forgiving sinners and declaring them RIGHTEOUS, not because they deserve it but because of the righteousness of Christ. Justification is God's free gift for those who accept it (*see* JUSTIFICATION BY GRACE, THROUGH FAITH). God justified sinners in the Old Testament in the same way, though justification was based upon the righteousness of the Christ who had not yet come. The people demonstrated their faith by offering animal SACRIFICES that prefigured the sacrifice of Christ.

justification by grace, through faith A rallying cry of the REFORMERS, who emphasized that God alone saves us (Romans 3:23-24). Nothing we do can make us right with God—not our good works, not our church affiliation, not even faith by itself. As PAUL taught, our SALVATION is God's gift to us: "By GRACE are ye saved through faith; and that not of yourselves: it is the gift of God" (Ephesians 2:8).

kingdom of God or **kingdom of heaven** One of the central themes of Jesus' teaching as recorded in the SYNOPTIC GOSPELS. There are varying views regarding the "kingdom of heaven." It often refers to the sphere in which Christ rules over mankind. In the beginning of his ministry, Jesus preached, "Repent, for the kingdom of heaven is near." Christians see both present and future aspects to that kingdom, as well as spiritual and earthly aspects. In some of his PARABLES, Jesus used everyday situations to describe various aspects of the kingdom of heaven. For instance, he said, "The kingdom of heaven is like a MUSTARD SEED. . . . The kingdom of heaven is like yeast. . . . The kingdom of heaven is like treasure hidden in a field" (Matthew 13, NIV).

last rites The popular name for the anointing of the sick, a SACRAMENT in the ROMAN CATHOLIC CHURCH. It was formerly called extreme unction. When a person is near death a PRIEST anoints him or her with holy oil and prays for the person's physical and spiritual healing.

layman, laywoman, layperson A person in a church who is not ORDAINED. The term *laity* refers generally to the lay people in a church.

Lent A period of penitence and FASTING before EASTER, beginning on ASH WEDNESDAY. Lent lasts for forty days, not counting Sundays. Many Christians observe Lent by giving up some daily food or activity to help them remember Christ's suffering.

limbo In ROMAN CATHOLIC tradition, the final resting place of SOULS (unbaptized infants, for example) who are not sent to HELL but are also not allowed entrance into HEAVEN. The concept of limbo is not held by PROTESTANTS.

❦ By extension, the term *limbo* has come to mean any in-between position, or a state of uncertainty.

litany A repetition of prayers, or a prayer consisting of supplications by the leader and alternate responses by the CONGREGATION. An example is a litany in *The BOOK OF COMMON PRAYER* in which the people repeatedly respond, "Have MERCY upon us."

liturgy The established order or format of public WORSHIP. All churches follow some pattern in public worship. On the "low church" side, PENTECOSTALS favor an unstructured, spontaneous format. On the "high church" side, ROMAN CATHOLICS follow a more highly structured service centered on the EUCHARIST. Worship is often considered "liturgical" to the degree it features the SACRAMENT of COMMUNION.

Lord There are several HEBREW and GREEK words in the Bible that are translated 'Lord' in English. In the New Testament, Jesus was often called Lord, from *kyrios*, a Greek word that could also be translated 'Master'. In the Old Testament, the personal name YAHWEH is also translated 'Lord'. Many English TRANSLATIONS print that particular sense of the Old Testament word LORD in small capitals to show that it is a translation of Yahweh and to distinguish it from *Lord* as a translation of other words.

Lord's Day SUNDAY, the day Christians have traditionally observed as a day of rest.

Lord's Supper Another name for COMMUNION or the EUCHARIST (the term is used by the APOSTLE PAUL in 1 Corinthians 11:20). It is called the Lord's Supper because it commemorates Jesus' death. As Jesus gave his DISCIPLES the bread at the LAST SUP-PER, he said, "THIS IS MY BODY, WHICH IS BROKEN FOR YOU; DO THIS IN REMEMBRANCE OF ME" (1 Corinthians 11:24).

love In the New Testament several different GREEK words are translated 'love'. One of those words, AGAPĒ, means a willful, other-centered love that is unmerited and does not require anything in return. God loves all people with this type of love, and Christians are exhorted also to love one another in this manner. Jesus said, "This is my commandment, that ye love one another, as I have loved you. Greater love hath no man than this, that a man lay down his life for his friends" (John 15:12-13).

Another Greek word in the New Testament is *philia*, which is an emotional love (from which the name *Phil*adelphia is derived—the city of brotherly love). A closely related word means friend.

Lucifer A name sometimes used for SATAN, the DEVIL. It means 'light bearer' and may refer to his attributes before his fall. The name *Lucifer* is used only once in the KING JAMES VERSION (Isaiah 14:12), and it is not used at all in the NEW INTERNATIONAL VERSION.

Mardi Gras The Tuesday before ASH WEDNESDAY. It is also called Shrove Tuesday. *Mardi Gras* is French for 'fat Tuesday'. It was traditionally a celebration of feasting before the beginning of LENT, but it has now become secularized and is simply a day for partying. The most famous celebration of Mardi Gras is in New Orleans. In Latin America the comparable celebration is called *carnival.*

mark of the beast Revelation 13 describes a terrible beast who is given power by SATAN to rule over the entire earth. All except those whose names are written in the BOOK OF LIFE will worship the beast. He will require each person to receive a mark on his or her forehead or right hand in order to buy or sell. The mark of the beast is the number 666. Christians differ in their identification of the beast. Many see him as a political or religious figure of the future.

Mass The celebration of the SACRAMENT of the EUCHARIST. In the ROMAN CATHOLIC CHURCH, the entire service is also called the Mass. It typically includes prayers, readings from SCRIPTURE, a sermon (homily), and the Eucharist. The LITURGY of the Mass can be sung or spoken. Traditionally it included the GREGORIAN CHANTS, sung in LATIN: the *Kyrie* (short for *Kyrie eleison,* 'Lord have mercy'), *Gloria* ('Glory'), *Credo* ('I believe'), *SANCTUS* (short for *Sanctus, sanctus, sanctus,* 'Holy, holy, holy'), and *Agnus Dei* (LAMB OF GOD). The Mass has been celebrated in the vernacular (e.g., English) only since VATICAN II.

matrimony Marriage, in which a man and woman pledge themselves to one another for life. In the ROMAN CATHOLIC and EASTERN ORTHODOX CHURCHES, matrimony is a SACRAMENT.

Maundy Thursday The Thursday before EASTER, when Christians commemorate the LAST SUPPER. Also called Holy Thursday. The name comes from *maundy,* an old English custom in which the king washed the feet of poor people, as Jesus had washed the feet of his DISCIPLES at the Last Supper (John 13).

MAUNDY THURSDAY Jesus washes the disciples' feet at the Last Supper, an event now commemorated on Maundy Thursday.

mercy Kindness, leniency, tender compassion, pardon, pity in action. When the TAX COLLECTOR stood in the TEMPLE and prayed, "God, be merciful to me, a sinner" (Luke 18:13), he was acknowledging his SIN but was asking God to forgive him and view him as though he had no sin.

Millennium, the Revelation 20 says SATAN will be bound and thrown into an abyss for 1,000 years. Because Revelation is not an easy book to interpret, Christians differ as to the precise meaning of the 1,000 years. Premillennialists and postmillennialists both tend to interpret this period of time in a literal sense, with Christ reigning on earth for a millennium (LATIN for 'one thousand years'). The premillennial perspective sees the SECOND COMING as an event immediately *before* Christ establishes his thousand-year reign. The postmillennial perspective sees the Second Coming *after* the thousand-year period. Amillennialists, on the other hand, tend to interpret the time period as a figure of speech that refers to the KINGDOM OF GOD between Christ's first coming and the Second Coming.

minister A PROTESTANT CLERGYMAN. Most ministers are ORDAINED. In most churches, only ordained ministers, often called PASTORS, are authorized to administer the SACRAMENTS or ORDINANCES.

missionary A person commissioned to take the GOSPEL to another culture. The APOSTLE PAUL was one of the first missionaries. He traveled throughout Asia Minor (modern-day Turkey) and GREECE, founding churches. Saint PATRICK was a missionary who took the gospel to Ireland. The JESUITS have a history of missionary work on behalf of the ROMAN CATHOLIC CHURCH. Three great

PROTESTANT missionaries were William CAREY in India, David LIVINGSTONE in Africa, and J. Hudson TAYLOR in China. Today there are hundreds of missionary societies that support thousands of missionaries. One of the great changes in the missionary movement today is that non-Western churches (for instance in Korea) are beginning to send out many missionaries.

monk A man who is a member of a RELIGIOUS ORDER and who lives in a cloistered community called a monastery. The popular image of a monastery is an ancient stone structure in a rural setting, but today some monasteries are modern dwellings in cities.

monotheism The belief in one God. In Deuteronomy 6:4, MOSES proclaims, "HEAR, O ISRAEL: THE LORD OUR GOD IS ONE LORD." JUDAISM, Christianity, and Islam are the three great monotheistic religions. *See also* POLYTHEISM.

mortal sin The DOGMA of the ROMAN CATHOLIC CHURCH traditionally divides SIN into two categories—VENIAL SIN and mortal sin. Mortal sin is more serious than venial sin. It involves a serious sin, undertaken after sufficient reflection and with full consent. It is an act of turning away from God, making the sinner spiritually dead and subject to everlasting punishment. A person who repents and confesses can be forgiven of mortal sin, but one who dies in mortal sin is damned.

new covenant God's COVENANT with mankind is his great and unified plan of FORGIVENESS and SALVATION. Under the Old Testament covenant with MOSES, the people of ISRAEL were to believe God and follow the MOSAIC LAW, including CIRCUMCISION and the system of animal SACRIFICES. In the New Testament, Christ established the new covenant. Instead of animal sacrifices for ATONEMENT, Jesus was the one and only sacrifice whose death could atone for people's SINS once for all. Under the new covenant, God promises to accept those who believe in Jesus as their REDEEMER and SAVIOR.

New Jerusalem According to the

The Nicene Creed

We believe in one God,
  the Father, the Almighty,
  maker of heaven and earth,
  of all that is, seen and unseen.

We believe in one Lord, Jesus Christ,
  the only Son of God,
  eternally begotten of the Father,
  God from God, Light from Light,
  true God from true God,
  begotten, not made,
  of one Being with the Father.
  Through him all things were made.
  For us and for our salvation
    he came down from heaven:
  by the power of the Holy Spirit
    he became incarnate from the Virgin Mary,
    and was made man.
  For our sake he was crucified under Pontius Pilate;
    he suffered death and was buried.
    On the third day he rose again
      in accordance with the Scriptures;
    he ascended into heaven
      and is seated at the right hand of the Father.
  He will come again in glory to judge the living and the dead,
    and his kingdom shall have no end.

We believe in the Holy Spirit, the Lord, the giver of life,
  who proceeds from the Father and the Son.
  With the Father and the Son he is worshiped and glorified.
  He has spoken through the prophets.
  We believe in one holy catholic and apostolic Church.
  We acknowledge one baptism for the forgiveness of sins.
  We look for the resurrection of the dead,
    and the life of the world to come. Amen.

This text of the creed is taken from the 1979 edition of *The BOOK OF COMMON PRAYER.*

book of REVELATION, God will destroy the present HEAVEN and earth and will create a new heaven and a new earth. Part of the new creation will be a HOLY city, the New Jerusalem, that will come down to earth. This will be the dwelling place of God with those who have ETERNAL LIFE. In that place there will be no more crying or death or mourning or pain. The city and its streets will be made of pure GOLD, and the twelve gates of the city will each be made of a single pearl (*see* PEARLY GATES). The New Jerusalem is also identified with the church, which is the bride of Christ.

Nicene Creed An ancient CREED that articulates Christian ORTHODOXY. It was developed from an earlier creed adopted at the Council of NICEA, so it contains language specifically designed to combat the HERESY of Arianism, which held that Jesus was not of the same essence as God. The Nicene Creed is still confessed in many churches today. The version presented on page 332 is taken from the newest edition of *The Book of Common Prayer*.

nun A woman who is a member of a RELIGIOUS ORDER. In many orders nuns live in communities called CONVENTS. Many nuns are teachers, social workers, nurses, etc.

omnipotence of God One of the attributes of God. It means that God is all-powerful.

omnipresence of God One of the attributes of God. It means that God is present everywhere.

omniscience of God One of the attributes of God. It means that God is all-knowing.

ordain, ordination When a person is formally commissioned by a church or DENOMINATION for a particular ministry, he or she is ordained. The individual is usually tested first for knowledge of the SCRIPTURES and the DOCTRINES of the particular church or denomination. In many ordination services, other ordained persons lay hands on and pray for the person being ordained. The ordination of women is not allowed in the ROMAN CATHOLIC CHURCH nor in most conservative PROTESTANT denominations.

ordinance A formal act or rite celebrated by the church. Various churches observe various ordinances, but all include BAPTISM and COMMUNION. Some churches refer not to *ordinances* (commands) but to *sacraments* (holy things).

original sin The DOCTRINE that all persons are inherently guilty of SIN and have a corrupt human nature. Sin entered the human race at the FALL OF MAN, when ADAM disobeyed God and ate the FORBIDDEN FRUIT. The Bible teaches that all people share his guilt and miserable condition. As a result, all people are born in a state of alienation from God. Romans 5:12 says, "Just as sin entered the world through one man, and death through sin, and in this way death came to all men, because all sinned" (NIV).

orthodox, orthodoxy Adherence to the accepted teachings of a religion. Christian orthodoxy is measured both by SCRIPTURE and by the long history of church teaching. The APOSTLES' CREED and the NICENE CREED are both basic guides by which to measure orthodoxy, as they are accepted by both PROTESTANTS and CATHOLICS. If a particular belief (e.g., that Jesus was not really the SON OF GOD) runs counter to one of the ancient creeds, it is not orthodox.

Our Father A popular name for the Lord's Prayer, particularly among ROMAN CATHOLICS. It is also called the PATERNOSTER (from the LATIN for 'our Father'). For the complete text, see LORD'S PRAYER under "Quotations from the Bible."

pacifist A person who believes war is morally wrong. Most pacifists also eschew violence of any kind. MENNONITES and other ANABAPTIST groups, QUAKERS, and JEHOVAH'S WITNESSES are pacifists. *See also* CONSCIENTIOUS OBJECTOR.

Palm Sunday The Sunday before EASTER, when Christians remember Jesus' TRIUMPHAL ENTRY into JERUSALEM. It is called Palm Sunday because the crowd spread palm branches in front of Jesus as he rode into the city on a donkey.

papacy The reign of a POPE; the succession of popes; the administration and function of the pope.

papal infallibility According to ROMAN CATHOLIC DOGMA, the POPE is infallible (without error) when he speaks *EX CATHEDRA* on matters of faith or morals. Papal infallibility was defined in 1870 in a decree of the First Vatican Council. Only two recent papal statements have been presented as infallible: the IMMACULATE CONCEPTION of MARY (defined in 1854) and the bodily assumption of Mary to HEAVEN (defined in 1950).

paradise The word *paradise* has several related meanings, all of which suggest a place of perfection: 1. The Garden of EDEN. 2. The place BELIEVERS go immediately after death (see Jesus' response to the THIEF ON THE CROSS in Luke 23:43). 3. HEAVEN.

❧ Two great works of literature have themes involving paradise: John MILTON's *PARADISE LOST* and DANTE's *DIVINE COMEDY*, one of the major parts of which is called "PARADISO."

parish The local area served by an ANGLICAN or ROMAN CATHOLIC church. A member of a parish is called a parishioner. Roman Catholics are encouraged to participate in their own parish church rather than traveling to a church in another parish.

pastor The spiritual leader of a CONGREGATION. In PROTESTANT churches the pastor is often called the MINISTER. In the ROMAN CATHOLIC CHURCH the pastor is a PRIEST.

Paternoster The LATIN name for the LORD'S PRAYER. *Paternoster* comes from *pater noster* ('our Father'), the first words of the Lord's Prayer in Latin.

pearly gates In Revelation 21:21 each of the gates of the NEW JERU-SALEM is described as being made of a single pearl. The term *pearly gates* has come to mean the entrance into HEAVEN.

penance A SACRAMENT in the ROMAN CATHOLIC CHURCH in which a person is repentant, expresses an intention not to continue sinning, and confesses the SINS to a PRIEST. The priest may require penance (e.g., prayer, FASTING, or abstinence) and/or restitution (making things right), depending on the nature of the sin. Then, as God's representative, the priest extends absolution (FORGIVE-NESS). CATHOLICS are expected to participate in the sacrament of penance (which is also called the Rite of Reconciliation) at least once a year.

polytheism Belief in many gods, in contrast to MONOTHEISM. Hinduism, for example, is a polytheistic religion. The ROMAN EMPIRE at the time of Christ was home to many forms of polytheism.

pontiff Any ROMAN CATHOLIC BISHOP, though the term is usually used specifically for the POPE.

POPE John Paul II was elected in 1978. He is originally from Poland.

pope The head of the ROMAN CATHO-LIC CHURCH. The pope has absolute jurisdiction in the church, though substantial responsibilities are delegated to the CARDINALS and BISHOPS, who are appointed by the pope. Roman Catholics believe that the pope is infallible when he speaks *EX CATHEDRA,* that is, when he speaks for the entire church on matters of faith and morals. The pope lives in and is the head of the government of the VATICAN, an independent principality located in the city of ROME. The pope is acknowledged as a world leader because of his tremendous influence on Roman Catholics around the world.

The Roman Catholic church claims

that PETER was the first pope, and that there is an unbroken line of popes who have succeeded him. Recent popes have been PIUS XII (1939–1958), JOHN XXIII (1958–1963), PAUL VI (1963–1978), John Paul I (1978), and JOHN PAUL II (elected 1978).

pray, prayer Talking with God. Prayer can be very formal, as in reciting a LITANY from a prayer book, or it can be as informal as a quick thought flashed to God while one is stopped at a traffic light. Prayer can be silent or spoken, private or public. The APOSTLE PAUL said, "Pray without ceasing" (1 Thessalonians 5:17).

predestination The DOCTRINE that pertains to God's plans for creation and humankind from before the foundation of the world. Christians hold two different views regarding predestination in SALVATION. The ARMINIAN view understands predestination of certain ones based on God's prior knowledge of who would decide to believe in Christ (*see* FREE WILL). The CALVINIST (or REFORMED) tradition understands predestination as being based upon God's own good will and pleasure, not on human decision (*see* ELECTION).

priest In the ROMAN CATHOLIC CHURCH, EASTERN ORTHODOX CHURCH, and ANGLICAN CHURCH, the PASTOR is called a priest. Roman Catholic priests must follow the rule of celibacy, which means they cannot marry. *See also* PRIEST *under "People and Events in the Old Testament."*

Providence or **Divine Providence** God's general care and provision for all his creatures. In theism, the providence of God regulates the universe.

🌿 Providence, Rhode Island was so named by its founder, Roger WILLIAMS, because of his sense of God's direction and provision.

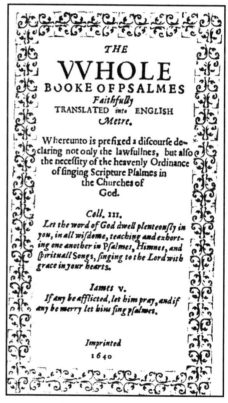

PSALTER The Bay Psalm Book, printed in 1640, was the first book printed in America.

Psalter A book containing the PSALMS arranged for liturgical or devotional use. Some churches read the Psalter responsively; in others, psalms are put to music.

purgatory In ROMAN CATHOLICISM, the place of cleansing after death, usually imagined to involve punishment and suffering. According to this DOCTRINE, Christians go to purgatory to be purified of VENIAL SINS that were unconfessed and unforgiven on earth. After the appropriate cleansing has taken place, the SOUL is ready to be received into HEAVEN. INDULGENCES, MASSES, and prayers for the dead can speed the cleansing process and reduce the time in purgatory. The concept of purgatory is not held by most PROTESTANTS.

A popular misconception is that purgatory is a place where people go who are neither good enough for heaven nor bad enough for HELL.

❦ The second section of DANTE's *DIVINE COMEDY* is "Purgatorio" ('Purgatory').

Purim The contemporary Jewish celebration of the rescue of the JEWS in the time of ESTHER.

R.I.P. These initials stand for *requiescat in pace*, or its English equivalent, 'rest in peace'. The initials are frequently seen on tombstones.

Rapture A phrase used by premillennialists (*see* MILLENNIUM) to describe the event of the members of Christ's body, the church, being "caught up" in the air to meet Christ. They base this upon 1 Thessalonians 4:16-17, which says, "the dead in Christ shall rise first: Then we which are alive and remain shall be caught up together with them in the clouds to meet the Lord in the air: and so shall we ever be with the Lord." Premillennialists are divided over whether the Rapture occurs before, during, or after the TRIBULATION. Not all ESCHATOLOGIES include the Rapture as a distinct event.

redeemer, redemption To redeem something is to buy it back or rescue it. In Christian THEOLOGY, all of creation, including mankind, belonged to God—because he created it all. But with the FALL OF MAN, SIN entered the world, and all people inherit a corrupt nature and are guilty of sin. God, who is HOLY, requires an ATONEMENT for sin. Jesus Christ, through his suffering and death, paid the price of freedom to rescue all who believe. It is in this sense that Jesus is called the Redeemer.

religious order A group of men or women who take religious vows, usually including obedience (to the superior as well as to God), poverty, and chastity (sexual purity). A woman in a religious order is a NUN. A man in a religious order is a MONK if he lives in a monastery. Men in religious orders who are not PRIESTS are called brothers. Most religious orders are ROMAN CATHOLIC or EASTERN ORTHODOX. BENEDIC-

TINES, DOMINICANS, FRANCISCANS, JESUITS, and TRAPPISTS are all members of religious orders. Mother TERESA, who works among the poor in Calcutta, founded an order called the Missionaries of Charity.

repentance Changing one's mind about the wrong one has done and then turning away from it. It is an important concept in Christian THEOLOGY, because we must repent of our sinfulness before we are likely to seek SALVATION. Repentance is an important part of the Christian life—both in the ROMAN CATHOLIC SACRAMENT of PENANCE and in the PROTESTANT view of JUSTIFICATION and SANCTIFICATION. Once Jesus referred to some people who had recently been killed, and he said to his audience, "Unless you repent you will all likewise perish" (Luke 13:5).

revival A religious awakening that sweeps through a CONGREGATION or even an entire nation. A revival is characterized by fervor in WORSHIP, an awareness of personal SIN, an eagerness to seek FORGIVENESS from God and from other people, and an eagerness to share one's experience with others. The GREAT AWAKENING was an important revival in American history. The term is also used, particularly in BAPTIST churches, for any special EVANGELISTIC meeting.

righteous Being and doing what is right in God's sight. Because of

ORIGINAL SIN and DEPRAVITY, no one is truly righteous. But God declares his people righteous because the righteousness of Christ is counted on their behalf (*see* JUSTIFICATION).

rosary A string of fifty beads used by ROMAN CATHOLICS to assist them in repeating a LITANY that includes the APOSTLES' CREED, the OUR FATHER, and the HAIL MARY. To "say the rosary" is to meditate on sacred mysteries from the life of Christ while saying Hail Marys.

sacrament A formal act or rite celebrated by the church. According to the CATECHISM in *The Book of Common Prayer,* "sacraments are outward and visible signs of inward and spiritual GRACE." Various churches observe various sacraments, but all include BAPTISM and COMMUNION. The ROMAN CATHOLIC CHURCH and the EASTERN ORTHODOX CHURCH observe seven sacraments: baptism, the EUCHARIST, CONFIRMATION, PENANCE, MATRIMONY, HOLY ORDERS, and the anointing of the sick (also called holy unction, or extreme unction, or LAST RITES). Some churches refer not to *sacraments* (holy things) but to *ordinances* (commands).

sacred That which is HOLY, or set apart for religious usage. The term is also used in contrast to that which is SECULAR, e.g., SACRED MUSIC.

saints In the ROMAN CATHOLIC CHURCH and the EASTERN ORTHODOX

CHURCH, a saint is a person who has died and has been officially recognized for unusual holiness (*see* CANONIZATION). Several miracles must be attributed to the person before he or she can be made a saint. More broadly, a saint is any holy person. In some contexts, all Christians are called saints.

❧ The Spanish words for saint are *san* (masculine) and *santa* (feminine), as in San Francisco, San Antonio, and Santa Barbara, all of which are cities named for saints. In Portuguese the word is *são*, as in São Paulo, Brazil, which is named for Saint PAUL.

salvation The act or process of being delivered from SIN and its consequences. In Christian THEOLOGY, salvation refers broadly to God's actions in securing deliverance for sinners—including JUSTIFICATION, SANCTIFICATION, and GLORIFICATION. According to the New Testament, we receive salvation as a free gift when we acknowledge our need for God and trust in Jesus' death to pay for our sin.

sanctification The ongoing development of holiness in the life of the Christian. The HOLY SPIRIT dwells within BELIEVERS, convicting them of SIN and changing their character. As we recognize sin, we can call upon the power of God to help us overcome it. The APOSTLE PAUL wrote, "Those who let themselves be controlled by their lower natures live only to please themselves, but those who follow after the Holy Spirit find themselves doing those things that please God (Romans 8:5, TLB).

Satan A name for the DEVIL, the supremely EVIL SPIRIT who is the enemy of God and the enemy of Christians. He is not God's opposite, however, for he was created by God, is under God's control, and will ultimately be defeated by God. Satanism, the cult

---

Bible Verses That Show the Way to Salvation

For all have sinned, and come short of the glory of God. (Romans 3:23)

For the wages of sin is death; but the gift of God is eternal life through Jesus Christ our Lord. (Romans 6:23)

God demonstrates his love for us in this: While we were still sinners, Christ died for us. (Romans 5:8, NIV)

For God so loved the world that he gave his one and only Son, that whoever believes in him shall not perish but have eternal life. (John 3:16, NIV)

If you confess with your mouth, "Jesus is Lord," and believe in your heart that God raised him from the dead, you will be saved. For it is with your heart that you believe and are justified, and it is with your mouth that you confess and are saved. (Romans 10:9-10, NIV)

of Satan WORSHIP, is not a new phenomenon, but it is more visible today than it has often been in the past.

Scripture, inerrancy of The DOCTRINE that the original Bible MANUSCRIPTS were without error. The *original* manuscripts no longer exist, however, and inerrancy does not claim that the early manuscripts we do have are without error. Nor does it claim that any particular TRANSLATION of the Bible is without error.

Scripture, inspiration of The DOCTRINE that the biblical writers were guided by God as they wrote his intended message (2 Peter 1:20-21), although they did not know their writings would later become part of the Bible. A familiar verse that refers to the inspiration of Scripture is 2 Timothy 3:16: "All Scripture is God-breathed and is useful for teaching, rebuking, correcting, and training in RIGHTEOUSNESS" (NIV). The inspiration of Scripture is one of the tenets of FUNDAMENTALISM.

Second Coming The New Testament teaches that Jesus will come to earth a second time. This is called the Second Coming. Jesus himself said he would return: "If I go and prepare a place for you, I will come back and take you to be with me that you also may be where I am" (John 14:3, NIV). At the time of Jesus' ASCENSION into HEAVEN, two heavenly messengers told the DISCIPLES, "This same Jesus, who was taken from you into heaven, will come back in the same way you have seen him go into heaven" (Acts 1:11, NIV).

Jesus did not specify when he would return. Christians in the EARLY CHURCH expected him to return during their lifetime, and believers ever since have hoped that the Second Coming was imminent. For varying views regarding the Second Coming, see MILLENNIUM.

secular Anything that is not SACRED is secular. The term is often used specifically to distinguish between two things, one of which is sacred and the other of which is secular (e.g., SACRED MUSIC and secular music).

seven deadly sins In church tradition, the seven deadly sins are pride, covetousness (greed), lust, envy, gluttony, anger, and sloth (laziness). They are "deadly" because they are so common—and so easy to fall into. They are also called capital sins.

Sheol In the Old Testament, the HEBREW word *Sheol* refers to the place of the dead. For a fuller explanation, see the entry for HELL.

Shrove Tuesday *See* MARDI GRAS.

sin An offense against God; disobedience to God's HOLY standards. According to the Bible, sin entered the world when ADAM and EVE ate the FORBIDDEN FRUIT. As a result, all people are born with innate sin (*see* ORIGINAL SIN). But sin is also a willful disobedience of God's laws, either by not doing what we should do or by doing what we should not do. *See also* MORTAL SIN; VENIAL SIN; SEVEN DEADLY SINS; UNPARDONABLE SIN.

Jesus Christ, the SON OF GOD, secured ATONEMENT for sin through his sacrificial death in place of sinners.

❧ Many actions and attitudes are clearly defined as sin in the Bible, but many people choose to define sin according to contemporary cultural standards rather than according to the standards found in the Bible. For example, the TEN COMMANDMENTS say, "THOU SHALT NOT COMMIT ADULTERY." Yet our contemporary culture chooses not to see ADULTERY as a sin, and even glamorizes it in movies, novels, and television.

sin, unpardonable *See* UNPARDONABLE SIN.

666 In the book of REVELATION, the MARK OF THE BEAST is the number 666. Each person in that day will have to receive the mark on his or her forehead or right hand in order to buy or sell anything.

Son *See* GOD THE SON *or* SON OF GOD.

Son of God A title for Jesus. The New Testament is very clear that Jesus was not just *a* son of God. He was the "only-begotten" or "one and only" Son of God. As GOD THE SON, he is the second person of the TRINITY. *See also* SON OF MAN *under "People and Events in the New Testament."*

soul The terms *soul* and *spirit* are often used interchangeably to refer to the total spiritual (nonphysical) part of a person that lives on after physical death. The Bible does not clearly specify what happens to the soul when the body dies, but a predominant PROTESTANT belief is that the soul of the BELIEVER passes immediately to HEAVEN (2 Corinthians 5:8). The ROMAN CATHOLIC understanding is that most souls destined for heaven go first to PURGATORY. At the time of the resurrection of the dead, the physical body will be raised up and made perfect, enabling the glorified and reunited body and soul to enjoy God forever (1 Corinthians 15:42-44).

sovereignty of God The DOCTRINE that God has absolute authority and control over all things, including the details of human life. The sovereignty of God is an important aspect of CALVINISM. *See also* OMNIPOTENCE OF GOD.

Speak now or forever hold your peace A popular paraphrase of a statement in the traditional wedding ceremony. The actual sentence is, "If any man can show just cause, why [these two persons] may not lawfully be joined together, let him now speak, or else hereafter forever hold his peace."

speaking in tongues One of the GIFTS OF THE HOLY SPIRIT; also called glossolalia. This gift enables a person to speak in a language he or she has not learned. When this ability was first given to the DISCIPLES at PENTECOST, they spoke languages that were understood by visitors in JERUSALEM who came from many different countries.

PENTECOSTAL and CHARISMATIC churches emphasize the gift of speaking in tongues as a sign of BAPTISM IN THE HOLY SPIRIT. The contemporary manifestation tends to be an unknown "prayer language" for the benefit of the individual rather than a known human language for the benefit of others. In some traditions, speaking in tongues is rejected as invalid for the church today.

spirit The vital force that gives life to the physical body. When God created ADAM, God "breathed into his nostrils the breath of life, and the man became a living being" (Genesis 2:7, NIV). When there is no spirit, the body dies. The distinction between SOUL and spirit has been a matter of ongoing debate; many use the terms interchangeably.

The term *spirits* is also used to refer to ANGELS and DEMONS, those supernatural beings who do not have physical bodies. When capitalized, *Spirit* usually refers to the HOLY SPIRIT.

Spirit of the Lord *See* HOLY SPIRIT.

spiritual gifts *See* GIFTS OF THE HOLY SPIRIT.

Stations (Way) of the Cross A devotion commemorating the PASSION and death of Christ. It consists of a series of fourteen meditations (stations) on events in the Passion of Christ. Depictions of these scenes are found in most ROMAN CATHOLIC churches. The Stations of the Cross are also located along the VIA DOLOROSA in JERUSALEM, commemorating the traditional spots where each event actually happened.

Sunday Most Christians treat Sunday as a special day—a day of rest and a day for WORSHIP. Sunday replaces Saturday as the SABBATH because Jesus' RESURRECTION occurred on a Sunday. It is sometimes called the LORD'S DAY.

Sunday school A church program of Christian education for children. The Sunday school movement began in the eighteenth century. In PROTESTANT churches, Sunday school is traditionally held for an hour on SUNDAY morning, before or after the WORSHIP service.

testimony A personal statement of what one has seen or experienced. It is often used by Christians in the sense of recounting a person's

Stations of the Cross

The traditional stations:

1. Jesus' condemnation to death
2. Taking up of the cross
3. The first fall on the way to Calvary
4. Meeting his mother
5. Being assisted by Simon of Cyrene
6. The woman Veronica wipes his face
7. The second fall
8. Meeting the women of Jerusalem
9. The third fall
10. Being stripped
11. Being nailed to the cross
12. Jesus' death
13. The removal of his body from the cross
14. His burial

On Good Friday, 1991, Pope John Paul II made the stations in a different manner, using stations based entirely on the Gospel texts:

1. Jesus in the Garden of Olives (Gethsemane)
2. Jesus is betrayed by Judas and arrested
3. Jesus is condemned by the Sanhedrin
4. Jesus is denied by Peter
5. Jesus is condemned by Pilate
6. Jesus is scourged and crowned with thorns
7. Jesus is made to carry his cross
8. Simon of Cyrene helps Jesus carry his cross
9. Jesus meets the women of Jerusalem
10. Jesus is crucified
11. Jesus promises the kingdom to the repentant thief
12. On the cross Jesus speaks to his mother and his beloved disciple John
13. Jesus dies on the cross
14. Jesus is laid in the tomb

Source: *Catholic Almanac*, 1992 edition

own pilgrimage of faith and God's faithfulness in his or her life.

Thanksgiving An American holiday on which families traditionally gather to celebrate and thank God for all his blessings. The first Thanksgiving was held by the PIL-GRIMS in 1621, when they held a three-day feast to celebrate the successful harvest. Thanksgiving is celebrated in the USA on the fourth Thursday of November (in Canada it is the second Monday of October).

theologian A person who studies THEOLOGY. Great theologians in history include AUGUSTINE OF HIPPO, Thomas AQUINAS and John CALVIN. Twentieth-century theologians include Karl BARTH, Paul Tillich, Carl F. H. Henry (all PROTESTANTS), and Karl Rahner (ROMAN CATHOLIC).

theology The study of God and his relationship to the world. More broadly, theology is a rational interpretation of religious faith. Thousands of books have been written expounding various aspects of Christian theology. The APOSTLES' CREED and the NICENE CREED, however, are very succinct summaries of ORTHODOX theology.

till death us do part An expression in the traditional wedding vows. In the newest edition of *The Book of Common Prayer* the phrase is "until we are parted by death." *See* TO HAVE AND TO HOLD.

to have and to hold A phrase in the bride's and groom's vows in the traditional wedding service. This wording is from the 1979 edition of *The Book of Common Prayer:*

"I, (name), take you, (name), to be my wife [husband], to have and to hold from this day forward, for better for worse, for richer for poorer, in sickness and in health, to love and to cherish, until we are parted by death. This is my solemn vow."

total depravity *See* DEPRAVITY, TOTAL.

transubstantiation In ROMAN CATHOLIC DOCTRINE, the elements of the EUCHARIST, when consecrated, change from the substance of bread and wine to the substance of the actual BODY and BLOOD OF CHRIST. This is in contrast to the LUTHERAN doctrine of CONSUBSTANTIATION, which asserts the real presence of the body of Christ *with* the elements. A third view, which CALVIN taught, is that the bread and wine remain actual bread and wine, but the communicant receives the body and blood of Christ in a spiritual manner.

Tribulation, the The church has experienced tribulation (hardship, persecution) from the earliest days after the RESURRECTION and ASCENSION of Christ. Millions of Christians have been persecuted and even killed because of their faith. According to the books of DANIEL and REVELATION, there will be a terrible period of tribulation in the future. This Great Tribulation will be worse than any before (Matthew 24:21). There are various interpretations as to how long it will last, when it will take place (e.g., before or after the RAPTURE), or whether passages that describe the Tribulation (e.g., Luke 21:5-24) are symbolic or literal.

Trinity Christians believe that God is a Trinity, or three persons in one nature: GOD THE FATHER, GOD THE SON, and GOD THE HOLY SPIRIT. All three are one God, the same in properties and attributes, and equal in power and glory. Although the word *trinity* is not found in the Bible, God progressively revealed himself as a Trinity through the Father's work of creation, the INCARNATION of the Son, and the outpouring of the Holy Spirit at PENTECOST. The New Testament writers reflect a consciousness of the Trinity, as seen in the GREAT COMMISSION: "Therefore go and make disciples of all nations, baptizing them in the name of the Father and of the Son and of the Holy Spirit" (Matthew 28:19, NIV). The DOCTRINE of the Trinity was developed by the EARLY CHURCH and is clearly reflected in the APOSTLES' CREED and the NICENE CREED. Belief in the Trinity is a prime test of Christian ORTHODOXY.

trustee A position of lay leadership in some churches. Trustees are usually responsible for the physical assets of the church.

unpardonable sin Jesus said, "All the SINS and BLASPHEMIES of men will be forgiven them. But whoever blasphemes against the HOLY SPIRIT will never be forgiven; he is guilty of an eternal sin" (Mark 3:28-29, NIV). This unpardonable sin is not a singular event for which a person later feels remorse. It is an ongoing, willful, and active rejection of the testimony of the Holy Spirit concerning the person and truth of Christ, and it can only be committed by an unbeliever. Those who commit it, because of the hardness of their hearts, decisively reject Christ, ridicule that which is HOLY, and are generally unconcerned about their SOULS. Christians who *fear* they have committed the unpardonable sin demonstrate by their REPENTANCE that they have not done so, and the FORGIVENESS of God is freely offered to them.

venial sin The DOGMA of the ROMAN CATHOLIC CHURCH traditionally divides SIN into two categories—venial sin and MORTAL SIN. Venial sin is less serious than mortal sin. It must, however, be confessed and turned from, and PENANCE must be done, either in this life or in PURGATORY. The distinction between mortal and venial sin is not often made today.

We have left undone those things which we ought to have done A statement from the general CONFESSION in *The BOOK OF COMMON PRAYER*. The confession goes on to say, "and we have done those things which we ought not to have done." These SINS are also called sins of omission and sins of commission.

witnessing EVANGELICALS often use the term in the sense of personal EVANGELIZING—sharing the GOOD NEWS about Jesus Christ with another person.

worship To ascribe honor and worth to someone or something. Christians and JEWS are expected to worship God and only God. The worship of God is the essence of the life of the church and the life of the Christian. Many churches call their public gatherings *worship* services.

Yahweh This is the personal name of God in HEBREW. When God spoke to MOSES from the BURNING BUSH, he said his name was Yahweh (Exodus 3:13-14). It means 'I AM THAT I AM', or 'I Will Be What I Will Be'. Because this personal name was so sacred, the JEWS in the centuries before Christ would not even pronounce it. When they came to the name *YHWH* (Yahweh) in the TORAH, they pronounced it *Adonai* (see the list of names at the entry for GOD). *Yahweh* is usually translated 'Lord' in English, and many TRANSLATIONS put *LORD* in small capitals to show that it is a translation of *Yahweh*.

YHWH This is a transliteration of the personal name of God in HEBREW.

It is sometimes called the tetragrammaton ('four letters'). In English it is usually spelled *Yahweh* or *Jehovah*.

Yom Kippur (pronounced *yawm KIP-per*) The contemporary Jewish celebration of the DAY OF ATONEMENT. It is the holiest day in the Jewish calendar.

THE BIBLE & CHRISTIANITY IN THE FINE ARTS

Music has always been an important part of WORSHIP, so music has been associated with the church from the first century to today. SACRED MUSIC encompasses a wide range of styles and forms, including HYMNS, GREGORIAN CHANTS, great ORATORIOS such as HANDEL's *MESSIAH*, GOSPEL MUSIC, and SPIRITUALS. Hundreds of thousands of hymns and GOSPEL SONGS have been written through the ages, and this chapter includes the titles of a few that are most popular, including "AMAZING GRACE," "O COME, ALL YE FAITHFUL," and "HOW GREAT THOU ART." Also included are a few key musicians, such as BACH and HANDEL, who have played an important role in the history of sacred music.

Christianity has also inspired great artists and sculptors, such as MICHELANGELO, whose *DAVID* and *PIETÀ* are masterpieces of the Renaissance. Literally millions of paintings and drawings have been inspired by great biblical themes. Some of the most famous are LEONARDO DA VINCI's *LAST SUPPER* and Michelangelo's frescoes in the SISTINE CHAPEL.

Thousands of new Christian books are published each year, but this chapter includes the most famous books of years gone by—books such as *The PILGRIM'S PROGRESS* by John BUNYAN, *PARADISE LOST* by John MILTON, and *IN HIS STEPS* by Charles Sheldon.

Many motion pictures have been made around great biblical themes. Several are included here, including *The Ten Commandments*, a masterful retelling of an Old Testament story.

Finally, this chapter includes some of the great architectural structures of the Christian world, such as Saint Peter's Basilica, Saint Paul's Cathedral, and Notre Dame de Paris.

a cappella Singing without instrumental accompaniment. The Italian term means, literally, 'in chapel style'.

Abandon hope, all ye who enter here The inscription at the entrance to HELL in DANTE's *DIVINE COMEDY*.

"Adeste Fideles" The original LATIN version of the CHRISTMAS carol we know as "O COME, ALL YE FAITHFUL."

"Amazing Grace" A popular GOSPEL SONG written by John Newton, who as a young man was captain of a slave-trading ship. On one of his voyages Newton read *IMITATION OF CHRIST* by THOMAS À KEMPIS. His ship was nearly sunk by a storm on that same trip, and Newton began thinking about God. John Newton left the sea and slave trading and became a forceful MINISTER in the ANGLICAN church. His background adds meaning to the words of the first verse of "Amazing Grace":

Amazing grace! how sweet the sound,
That saved a wretch like me!
I once was lost, but now am found,
Was blind, but now I see.

"America the Beautiful" A patriotic American HYMN. Katharine Lee Bates wrote it after standing on Pike's Peak, looking out over the Colorado landscape. The first verse ends as a prayer, asking God to shed his GRACE on America.

O beautiful for spacious skies,
For amber waves of grain,
For purple mountain majesties
Above the fruited plain!

America! America!
God shed his grace on thee,
And crown thy good with brotherhood
From sea to shining sea.

Bach, Johann Sebastian (1685–1750) Esteemed by many as the most gifted composer ever to create SACRED MUSIC. Since he was a church organist and director of music, much of his music was written for use in church services. In fact, for many years he produced a new piece of church music each week. He is the best-known musician of the baroque period, and many of his pieces are still used in worship services and in concerts today. The harmonization for the HYMN "O Sacred Head, Now Wounded" is taken from one of Bach's great works. Other well-known sacred works are *Christ Lay in the Bonds of Death, St. Matthew Passion, St. John Passion,* and *Mass in B minor.* Bach and George Frederick HANDEL were both born in 1685.

JOHANN SEBASTIAN BACH This statue of Bach stands outside the Thomaskirche (Leipzig) where Bach served as director of music.

basilica   An early church building with rows of columns running lengthwise down the nave (the main part of the interior of the church) and a semicircular projection at one end of the building. SAINT PETER'S BASILICA in ROME and HAGIA SOPHIA in Istanbul are two of the most famous basilicas in the world.

"Battle Hymn of the Republic"
A HYMN written by Julia Ward Howe after she had visited an army camp during the American Civil War. The words were written to the already-popular tune of "John Brown's Body." In its historical context, it suggested that the war was God's judgment upon the South for their SIN of allowing slavery. The first verse and the refrain are most familiar:

Mine eyes have seen the glory
   of the coming of the Lord;
He is trampling out the vintage
   where the grapes of wrath are stored;
He hath loosed the fateful lightning
   of his terrible swift sword;
His truth is marching on.

Refrain:
Glory! Glory! Hallelujah!
Glory! Glory! Hallelujah!
Glory! Glory! Hallelujah!
His truth is marching on.

Ben-Hur   The book was written in the late 1800s by General Lew Wallace. The motion picture received eleven Academy Awards in 1959, including Best Picture. The story takes place in the first century A.D.—the world in which Jesus lived. The story revolves around Judah Ben-Hur, a JEW, and Massala, a Roman commander in JERUSALEM. Ben-Hur has peripheral contact with Jesus, and when he sees the CRUCIFIXION he becomes a BELIEVER.

"Blessed Assurance" A popular GOSPEL SONG by Fanny CROSBY. She was blind from infancy, and many of her songs include references to seeing, either literally or figuratively. An example is in the second verse of "Blessed Assurance."

Blessed assurance, Jesus is mine!
O what a foretaste of glory divine!
Heir of salvation, purchase of God,
Born of his Spirit, washed in his blood.

Refrain:
This is my story, this is my song,
Praising my Savior all the day long;
This is my story, this is my song,
Praising my Savior all the day long.

Perfect submission, perfect delight,
Visions of rapture now burst on my sight;
Angels descending bring from above
Echoes of mercy, whispers of love.

Books that Have Influenced Contemporary Christian Leaders

R. Kent Hughes, a pastor and author in Wheaton, Illinois, asked twenty-seven distinguished Christian leaders to list the books (other than the Bible) that had influenced them the most. Specifically, he asked:

1. What are the five books, secular or sacred, which have influenced you the most?
2. Of the spiritual/sacred books that have influenced you the most, which is your favorite?
3. What is your favorite novel?
4. What is your favorite biography?

Of all the books listed, these were mentioned more than once:

C. S. LEWIS, *MERE CHRISTIANITY* (6)
John CALVIN, *INSTITUTES OF THE CHRISTIAN RELIGION* (6)
Oswald Chambers, *MY UTMOST FOR HIS HIGHEST* (5)
Fyodor Dostoyevsky, *The Brothers Karamazov* (5)
Leo Tolstoy, *Anna Karenina* (5)
Elisabeth Elliot, *Shadow of the Almighty* (3)
Dr. and Mrs. Howard Taylor, *Hudson Taylor's Spiritual Secret* (3)
A. W. Tozer, *The Pursuit of God* (3)
THOMAS À KEMPIS, *The IMITATION OF CHRIST* (3)
John BUNYAN, *The PILGRIM'S PROGRESS* (3)
Charles Sheldon, *IN HIS STEPS* (2)
James Orr, *The Christian View of God and the World* (2)
C. S. LEWIS, *The Great Divorce* (2)
William Manchester, *American Caesar* (2)
William Manchester, *The Last Lion* (2)
Herman Melville, *Moby Dick* (2)
Leo Tolstoy, *War and Peace* (2)
Charles Colson, *Loving God* (2)
St. AUGUSTINE, *CONFESSIONS* (2)

Taken from *Disciplines of a Godly Man* by R. Kent Hughes, copyright 1992. Used with permission by Good News Publishers/Crossway Books, Wheaton, Illinois.

Book of Martyrs, The Written by John Foxe in 1563, *The Book of Martyrs* is a collection of biographies of PROTESTANT MARTYRS. It was very influential, particularly in the first several centuries after it was written. One reads occasionally of American pioneers who had only a few books—the Bible, *The PILGRIM'S PROGRESS*, and Foxe's *Book of Martyrs*.

Bunyan, John (1628–1688) An English preacher who is best known as the author of *The PILGRIM'S PROGRESS*. He was originally a tinker (a fixer of pots and pans), and after he became a preacher he was twice thrown in jail for preaching without a license. It was while he was in jail that he wrote *The Pilgrim's Progress* (1678), one of the most influential books ever published.

cathedral A church building that contains the official throne of the BISHOP (the word *cathedral* comes from the LATIN word for 'throne'). The ROMAN CATHOLIC CHURCH, the EASTERN ORTHODOX CHURCH, and several PROTESTANT DENOMINATIONS have cathedrals. Most cathedrals are very large and ornate. SAINT PAUL'S CATHEDRAL in London, the Cathedral of NOTRE DAME DE PARIS, and the National Cathedral in Washington, D.C. are some of the better known cathedrals around the world.

Celestial City In *The PILGRIM'S PROG-RESS*, Christian's destination is the Celestial City—HEAVEN.

Chartres, Cathedral of A beautiful thirteenth-century CATHEDRAL in Chartres, France. It is considered to be one of the finest examples of Gothic architecture, with its spires, ornate stonework, pointed arches, high ceilings, stained glass windows, and flying buttresses.

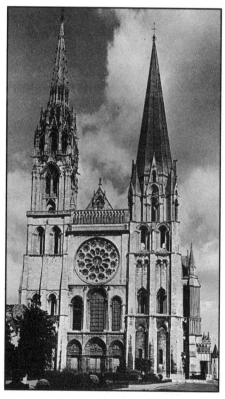

CHARTRES CATHEDRAL One of the most beautiful church buildings in the world.

"Christ the Lord Is Risen Today" A favorite EASTER hymn, the words of which were written by Charles WESLEY. When it was first printed, the printer thought the lines were too short, so he added an *ALLELUIA!* at the end of each line.

Christ the Lord is risen today, Alleluia!
Sons of men and angels say, Alleluia!
Raise your joys and triumphs high, Alleluia!
Sing, ye heavens, and earth reply, Alleluia!

Crosby, Fanny (1820–1915) A beloved writer of HYMNS and GOSPEL SONGS. She was blind from infancy and lived to the age of ninety-five. She wrote more than 8,000 songs! Many of her songs are still sung today, including "BLESSED ASSURANCE," "All the Way My Savior Leads Me," and "Jesus, Keep Me Near the Cross."

Dante (1265–1321) An Italian poet; author of *The DIVINE COMEDY.* He was one of the most learned men and greatest poets of the Middle Ages. His full name was Dante Alighieri.

David A large marble sculpture by MICHELANGELO that depicts DAVID as a young man ready to go to battle against GOLIATH. It is one of the most magnificent sculptures of the Renaissance. It is displayed in Florence, Italy.

Divine Comedy, The A long epic poem by DANTE Alighieri. In the poem, Dante visits HELL, PURGATORY, and HEAVEN. The poem is divided into three parts—"INFERNO" ('hell'), "Purgatorio" ('purgatory'), and "PARADISO" (PARADISE). He finds nine circles in hell where the SOULS of the

damned are being tormented. The sign over the entrance reads, "ABANDON HOPE, ALL YE WHO ENTER HERE." From hell Dante moves to purgatory, where the souls of the dead are looking for forgiveness for their deeds on earth. He finally travels through ten spheres of heaven. *The Divine Comedy* is one of the finest works of literature from the Middle Ages.

❧ It is called a comedy not in the contemporary sense of something that is funny, but in the classical sense that it has a positive ending rather than a tragic ending.

DAVID Michelangelo's *David* is displayed in Florence.

"Fairest Lord Jesus" The first three verses of this popular HYMN were first written in Germany in the seventeenth century. The fourth verse was written two centuries later. The tune is called "Crusaders' Hymn," but the story that it was sung by the CRUSADERS is apocryphal. The first and fourth verses are favorites:

Fairest Lord Jesus,
Ruler of all nature,
O thou of God and man the Son,
Thee will I cherish,
Thee will I honor,
Thou, my soul's glory, joy, and crown!

Beautiful Savior,
Lord of the nations,
Son of God and Son of Man!
Glory and honor,
Praise, adoration,
Now and forevermore be thine!

Faust In a German legend, Faust sells his SOUL to the DEVIL (named Mephistopheles) in exchange for knowledge and pleasure. The story has been the subject of numerous literary works, including Goethe's *Faust*.

"Gonna Lay Down My Burden" An American Negro SPIRITUAL. It starts, "Gonna lay down my burden down by the riverside." The river is the JORDAN RIVER, which is symbolic of the entrance into HEAVEN, just as the Jordan River marked the entrance into the PROMISED LAND for the ISRAELITES after the EXODUS.

gospel music An American style of music that originated with evangelistic meetings in the South. The lyrics of gospel music always have a Christian theme or allusion, but the musical style can be quite varied, having been influenced through the years by jazz, blues, and Negro SPIRITUALS. It has become a style of music used by many famous singers, including Mahalia Jackson, Elvis Presley, the Oak Ridge Boys, and Amy Grant.

gospel songs *See* HYMNS AND GOSPEL SONGS.

Greatest Story Ever Told, The An epic motion picture (1965) that portrays the life of Christ as told in the GOSPELS.

Gregorian chant LATIN chants dating back to the sixth century. They are traditionally used in the MASS of the ROMAN CATHOLIC CHURCH. The chants are sung A CAPELLA and in unison. The various chants include *Kyrie* (short for *Kyrie eleison*, 'Lord have mercy'), *Gloria* ('Glory'), *Credo* ('I believe'), *SANCTUS* (short for *Sanctus, sanctus, sanctus*, 'Holy, holy, holy'), and *Agnus Dei* (LAMB OF GOD).

Hagia Sophia, Basilica of A large and beautiful BASILICA in Istanbul, Turkey. It was once the central church building of the EASTERN ORTHODOX church, but it is now a museum.

"Hallelujah Chorus" The best-known movement from George Frederick HANDEL'S ORATORIO *MESSIAH*.

It is often performed at CHRISTMAS. Audiences traditionally stand when the "Hallelujah Chorus" is sung. The tradition was started when King George II stood, in reverence to God, as it was being sung.

Handel, George Frederick (1685–1769) One of the great composers of the eighteenth century. He wrote many operas as well as ORATORIOS. His most famous work is *MESSIAH* (1742), which was written in only twenty-three days. Numerous HYMN tunes, including "While Shepherds Watch Their Flocks by Night" and "Thine Is the Glory, Risen, Conquering Son," have been adapted from larger works of Handel's. He and Johann Sebastian BACH were contemporaries.

"He Lives" A favorite GOSPEL SONG often sung at EASTER. Both text and music were written by Alfred Ackley after a young JEW asked him, "Why should I worship a dead Jew?" Ackley responded, "But Jesus lives!"

I serve a risen Savior,
He's in the world today;
I know that he is living,
Whatever men may say;
I see his hand of mercy,
I hear his voice of cheer,
And just the time I need him
He's always near.

Refrain:
He lives, he lives,
Christ Jesus lives today!
He walks with me and talks with me
Along life's narrow way.
He lives, he lives,
Salvation to impart!
You ask me how I know he lives?
He lives within my heart.

"He's Got the Whole World in His Hands" An American Negro SPIRITUAL. It evokes the image of God holding the world and everything in it in his hands.

"Holy, Holy, Holy" A stately HYMN that evokes images from the REVELATION and celebrates the TRINITY.

Holy, holy, holy!
Lord God Almighty!
Early in the morning
Our song shall rise to thee;
Holy, holy, holy,
Merciful and mighty!
God in three Persons,
Blessed Trinity!

"How Great Thou Art" A Swedish HYMN made popular by its frequent use in Billy GRAHAM's EVANGELISTIC crusades.

BASILICA OF HAGIA SOPHIA One of the world's great basilicas, it is now a museum.

O Lord my God!
When I in awesome wonder
Consider all the worlds thy hands have
 made,
I see the stars,
I hear the rolling thunder,
Thy power throughout the universe
 displayed.

Refrain:
Then sings my soul,
My Savior God to thee;
How great thou art,
How great thou art!
Then sings my soul,
My Savior God to thee;
How great thou art,
How great thou art!

hymnal A book containing the words and music of HYMNS and GOSPEL SONGS. Hymnals are used in most churches to facilitate congregational singing.

hymns and gospel songs Technically, a hymn is a song of praise sung to God, or a song about the attributes of God. Hymns do not usually have refrains, and they tend to be stately in meter and tempo. More popularly, the term *hymn* is used for any religious song in a Christian church service.

Gospel songs express the Christian's own experiences or feelings about God and the Christian life. Gospel songs often have refrains, and they tend to be less formal in style than hymns. Thousands of gospel songs have been written during the last 200 years. Several of the most popular are "BLESSED ASSUR-

ANCE," "IN THE GARDEN," and "WHAT A FRIEND WE HAVE IN JESUS."

America's Ten Favorite Hymns and Gospel Songs

1. AMAZING GRACE
2. HOW GREAT THOU ART
3. IN THE GARDEN
4. The OLD RUGGED CROSS
5. WHAT A FRIEND WE HAVE IN JESUS
6. A MIGHTY FORTRESS
7. BLESSED ASSURANCE
8. HE LIVES
9. Victory in Jesus
10. HOLY, HOLY, HOLY

Source: Survey of 10,000 newspaper readers by George Plagenz, nationally syndicated columnist, as quoted in *The Almanac of the Christian World*, 1991–1992 edition, Tyndale House Publishers, Inc.

icons Religious images, often of MARY, Jesus, or the SAINTS, used in worship in the various EASTERN ORTHODOX CHURCHES. Icons are often painted on small wooden panels.

❧ An iconoclast is a person who destroys icons or opposes their veneration; by extension, an iconoclast is a person who destroys or attacks any cherished belief or institution.

Imitation of Christ This fifteenth-century book, attributed to THOMAS À KEMPIS, has had a tremendous influence in the church over the last 500 years. Other than the Bible, *Imitation of Christ* may be the most widely read work of Christian literature. Thomas wrote about the importance for the Christian of imitating the spirit and actions of Christ. He stressed the importance of self-discipline, prayer, PENANCE, the SACRAMENTS, and rejection of worldly goods.

In His Steps One of the best-selling books ever published in the USA. Written by Charles Sheldon in 1896, it is about a group of people in a small town who decide to evaluate everything they do by asking what Jesus would have done in that situation. In each instance they find themselves changing their behavior in order to follow "in his steps."

"In the Garden" As we sing this beautiful song, we envision ourselves going into a garden early in the morning and meeting Jesus.

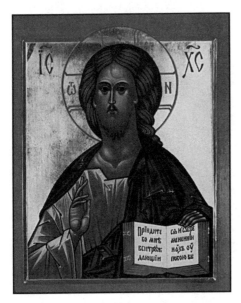

ICONS This is a typical icon.

While it is a very personal song, it is also an allusion to MARY MAGDALENE's encounter with Jesus when she saw him on the morning of the RESURRECTION.

I come to the garden alone,
While the dew is still on the roses;
And the voice I hear, falling on my ear,
The Son of God discloses.

Refrain:
And he walks with me,
And he talks with me,
And he tells me I am his own,
And the joy we share
As we tarry there,
None other has ever known.

"Inferno" The first of three sections in DANTE's epic poem, *The Divine Comedy*. In this section, Dante is led through nine circles of HELL. From hell he moves to PURGATORY, and finally to PARADISE (*see* "PARADISO"). A sign above the entrance to hell reads, "ABANDON HOPE, ALL YE WHO ENTER HERE."

"Jesus Loves Me" A popular children's song known by Christian children around the world:

Jesus loves me, this I know,
For the Bible tells me so.
Little ones to him belong,
They are weak but he is strong.

Refrain:
Yes, Jesus loves me,
Yes, Jesus loves me,
Yes Jesus loves me,
The Bible tells me so.

❦ Karl BARTH was once asked by a sophisticated American student what he thought was the most important concept of Christian thought. Barth, who had written 200 books, had a twinkle in his eye as he responded, "Jesus loves me, this I know, for the Bible tells me so."

"Joshua Fit the Battle of Jericho" An American Negro SPIRITUAL. The allusion is to the Old Testament story of JOSHUA and the Battle of JERICHO (*fit* means *fought*).

"Joy to the World!" A popular CHRISTMAS carol. The text was written by Isaac WATTS, who wrote more than 600 HYMNS. The music was arranged by Lowell Mason, the father of American hymnody, but he indicated that it was adapted from a tune by George Frederick HANDEL.

Joy to the world! The Lord is come;
Let earth receive her king;
Let every heart prepare him room,
And heaven and nature sing.

justify the ways of God to men John MILTON declares that his aim in *PARADISE LOST* is to "justify the ways of God to men." Milton is explaining why God allowed the FALL OF MAN.

Last Supper, The A famous painting by LEONARDO DA VINCI. It portrays Jesus and his DISCIPLES at the LAST SUPPER, moments before JUDAS ISCARIOT goes out to arrange to betray Jesus. The huge painting is on a wall in a monastery in Milan and is in poor condition.

Leonardo da Vinci (1452–1519) An Italian painter, sculptor, architect, and designer of the late fifteenth and early sixteenth century. He was a contemporary of other Renaissance artists, such as MICHELANGELO and RAPHAEL. His best-known religious work is *The LAST SUPPER* (c. 1495). His most famous painting is the *Mona Lisa*.

THE LAST SUPPER This famous fresco by Leonardo da Vinci began deteriorating soon after he painted it.

Lion, the Witch and the Wardrobe, The *See* NARNIA, CHRONICLES OF.

Madonna A name often used for the VIRGIN MARY. The term *Madonna* (Italian for 'my lady') is also used for any artistic depiction of MARY, especially holding the infant Jesus. Many Madonnas were painted during the Renaissance by artists such as MICHELANGELO, RAPHAEL, and LEONARDO DA VINCI.

MADONNA This Madonna is one of many painted by Raphael.

Mere Christianity In this classic book, C. S. LEWIS presents a reasoned approach to belief in the Christian faith. The contents were originally prepared as radio talks for the BBC in the 1940s. The radio talks were revised and published in 1952.

Messiah The most famous ORATORIO (1742) of George Frederick HANDEL. The words are all taken from the Bible. It presents the story of the life of Jesus, beginning with the Old Testament PROPHECIES concerning the MESSIAH, then the NATIVITY, the CRUCIFIXION, and the RESURRECTION of Jesus, and finally his GLORIFICATION in HEAVEN. Two of the best-known movements are the "HALLELUJAH CHORUS" and "Worthy Is the Lamb." It is usually performed at CHRISTMAS, and portions of it are often performed at EASTER. Incredibly, the music was written in a period of only twenty-three days.

Michelangelo (1475–1564) One of the great artists of the Renaissance. His works include the magnificent paintings in the SISTINE CHAPEL and sculptures such as the *PIETÀ*, *DAVID*, and *Moses*. He also designed the great dome on SAINT PETER'S BASILICA in the VATICAN. He was a contemporary of Christopher Columbus and LEONARDO DA VINCI.

"Mighty Fortress, A" Both text and music of this HYMN were written by Martin LUTHER. The music of the REFORMATION came from many sources, including folk tunes and dances. Luther defended this style of music by saying the DEVIL should not have all the good tunes to himself! "A Mighty Fortress" (the German title is "Ein' feste Burg") is perhaps the best known of the hymns of the REFORMATION. Luther wrote it to give his followers courage as they faced a difficult battle in the theological courts. The "ancient foe," of course, is SATAN.

A mighty fortress is our God,
  A bulwark never failing;
Our helper he, amid the flood
  Of mortal ills prevailing:
For still our ancient foe
  Doth seek to work us woe;
His craft and power are great,
  And, armed with cruel hate,
On earth is not his equal.

Milton, John (1608–1674) The great poet of seventeenth-century England. He was appointed as "LATIN secretary" to Oliver Cromwell, a post he held even after he lost his eyesight. His most famous work is the epic PARADISE LOST (1667), one of the masterpieces of the English language. It tells of the revolt of LUCIFER, the CREATION, and the FALL OF MAN.

Mine eyes have seen the glory of the coming of the Lord The first line of the "BATTLE HYMN OF THE REPUBLIC."

My Utmost for His Highest A book of daily devotional readings by Oswald Chambers (1874–1917). It has been loved and appreciated by several generations of Christians.

Narnia, Chronicles of A delightful series of seven children's books (published 1950–56) by the great twentieth-century Christian APOLOGIST, C. S. LEWIS. The Narnia tales contain certain symbolic features. In particular, the first story, *The Lion, the Witch and the Wardrobe*, is filled with symbolism of Jesus' death and RESURRECTION and the ultimate triumph of good over EVIL. Aslan, the lion, is a type of Christ, and the White Witch is a type of SATAN.

"Nearer, My God, to Thee" The words of this HYMN were written by Sarah Adams, a Shakespearean actress. A popular story is that the band on the *Titanic* played "Nearer, My God, to Thee" as the ship was sinking, taking with it 1,500 people who were unable to get into the lifeboats.

Nearer, my God, to thee,
Nearer to thee!
E'en though it be a cross
That raiseth me;
Still all my song shall be,
Nearer, my God, to thee;
Nearer, my God, to thee,
Nearer to thee.

"Nobody Knows the Trouble I've Seen" An American Negro SPIRITUAL. It begins, "Nobody knows the trouble I've seen; nobody knows but Jesus."

Notre Dame de Paris The grand Gothic CATHEDRAL in the heart of Paris. It took 150 years to build and is one of the most famous churches in the world.

Now I lay me down to sleep This prayer is probably the most often quoted prayer used by children at bedtime:

Now I lay me down to sleep,
I pray the Lord my soul to keep.

If I should die before I wake,
I pray the Lord my soul to take.

O beautiful for spacious skies

See "AMERICA THE BEAUTIFUL."

"O Come, All Ye Faithful"

A popular CHRISTMAS carol first written in LATIN in the eighteenth century ("ADESTE FIDELES"). It is sung throughout the English-speaking world:

O come, all ye faithful,
Joyful and triumphant,
O come ye, O come ye
To Bethlehem!
Come and behold him,
Born the king of angels.

Refrain:
O come, let us adore him,
O come, let us adore him,
O come, let us adore him,
Christ the Lord.

"Old Rugged Cross, The"

This popular GOSPEL SONG was written by George Bennard, an American EVANGELIST. He was conducting EVANGELISTIC crusades in Michigan and was meditating on JOHN 3:16. "The Old Rugged Cross" was written to help his listeners better understand the meaning of that verse.

On a hill far away
Stood an old rugged cross,
The emblem of suffering and shame;
And I love that old cross,
Where the dearest and best
For a world of lost sinners was slain.

Refrain:
So I'll cherish the old rugged cross,
Till my trophies at last I lay down;
I will cling to the old rugged cross,
And exchange it someday for a crown.

NOTRE DAME DE PARIS The great Gothic cathedral in Paris.

"Onward, Christian Soldiers" A popular GOSPEL SONG originally written as a marching poem for a group of local schoolchildren. The tune was written by Sir Arthur Sullivan of Gilbert and Sullivan fame.

Onward, Christian soldiers,
Marching as to war,
With the cross of Jesus
Going on before!
Christ, the royal Master,
Leads against the foe;
Forward into battle,
See, his banners go.

Refrain:
Onward, Christian soldiers,
Marching as to war,
With the cross of Jesus
Going on before.

oratorio A musical work on a large scale, usually with a scriptural theme, for soloists, chorus, and orchestra. While it may be very dramatic, it does not use costumes or stage settings. It is presented in concert style in a concert hall or church. George Frederick HANDEL was a prolific writer of oratorios, the most famous of which is *MESSIAH*.

Paradise Lost The seventeenth-century epic poem by John MILTON that is a classic of English literature. It is about the CREATION, the fall of LUCIFER, and the FALL OF MAN. Milton explains that his purpose is to "JUSTIFY THE WAYS OF GOD TO MEN."

"Paradiso" The last section of DANTE's epic poem, *The DIVINE COMEDY*.

After having visited HELL (*see* "INFERNO") and PURGATORY, Dante travels through ten spheres of HEAVEN, or PARADISE.

Pensées A collection of writings (the title means 'Thoughts') by the French philosopher, mathematician, and religious thinker, Blaise PASCAL. The book, which was published after his death, contains random, often mystical thoughts.

Included in *Pensées* is a logical argument regarding the existence of God that has come to be called Pascal's Wager. He postulates logically that God either exists, or he doesn't. If you wager that God exists (and you place your trust in him) and God does indeed exist, you have won ETERNAL LIFE. If God turns out not to exist, you have lost little. If you wager that God does not exist and in fact he does not exist, you have lost nothing. But if you wager that God does not exist and it turns out that he does exist, you have lost eternal life. To Pascal, the logic of the wager inevitably leads one to belief and trust in God.

Pietà A picture or sculpture of the VIRGIN MARY mourning over the body of Jesus after he was taken down from the CROSS (*pietà* is Italian for 'pity'). One of the most famous is MICHELANGELO's stunning sculpture, called simply *Pietà*. He created this larger-than-life marble sculpture in 1498 at the age of twenty-three. It is displayed in one of the chapels of SAINT PETER'S BASILICA in the VATICAN.

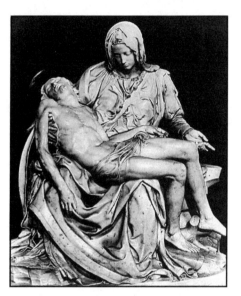

PIETÀ This stunning marble sculpture by Michelangelo was damaged in 1972 by a man who attacked it with a hammer.

Pilgrim's Progress, The One of the most widely-read books ever published. The author, John BUNYAN, was a seventeenth-century English tinker (a mender of pots and pans) who became a NONCONFORMIST preacher. He was imprisoned on two occasions for preaching without a license, and it was in prison that he wrote *The Pilgrim's Progress* (1678). It is an allegory that traces the journey of Christian, the main character, from the City of Destruction to the CELESTIAL CITY (HEAVEN). Along the way he encountered all the temptations and obstacles we experience in our daily lives. Bunyan gave these experiences colorful names such as SLOUGH OF DESPOND, the Hill of Difficulty, Doubting Castle, etc. But Christian was assisted by Evangelist, Faithful, Knowledge, and others who helped him stay on the STRAIGHT AND NARROW path.

Raphael (1483–1520) One of the great Renaissance painters. Like his contemporaries MICHELANGELO and LEONARDO DA VINCI, Raphael painted religious as well as SECULAR themes. Some of his best-known and best-loved works are MADONNAS. Toward the end of his life he supervised the rebuilding of SAINT PETER'S BASILICA for LEO X, the same POPE that EXCOMMUNICATED Martin LUTHER.

Requiem A musical setting for the MASS for the dead, used in funeral services. Some composers, including Mozart and Verdi, wrote very elaborate Requiems. The term is also used more loosely for any music written in honor of the dead. Brahms wrote a Requiem in memory of his mother; it used biblical texts but did not follow the sequence of the Mass for the dead.

sacred music Music used for church services; more broadly, any music with a religious theme. It includes choral and instrumental music. Nearly all of the great composers of the baroque and classical period, including BACH, HANDEL, Mozart, and Beethoven, wrote sacred music.

Saint Francis, Prayer of A prayer written by FRANCIS OF ASSISI. It is often sung in weddings.

The Prayer of Saint Francis

> Lord, make me an instrument of thy peace:
> Where there is hatred, let me sow love;
> Where there is injury, pardon;
> Where there is doubt, faith;
> Where there is despair, hope;
> Where there is darkness, light;
> Where there is sadness, joy.
>
> O divine Master,
> Grant that I may not so much seek
> To be consoled as to console,
> To be understood as to understand,
> To be loved as to love.
> For it is in giving that we receive;
> It is in pardoning that we are pardoned;
> It is in dying that we are born to eternal life.

SAINT PAUL'S CATHEDRAL The earliest church on this site was built in the seventh century.

Saint Paul's Cathedral The huge dome of Saint Paul's, an ANGLICAN CATHEDRAL, dominates the skyline of London. The church was built in the seventeenth century by the great architect Christopher Wren. It was damaged during World War II, but it was rebuilt after the war to Wren's design.

Saint Peter's Basilica Located in the VATICAN in ROME, Saint Peter's Basilica is the largest church building in the world. It is built over the crypt that is believed to contain the body of Saint PETER, one of Jesus' DISCIPLES and the first POPE. The building is in the form of a giant CROSS. MICHELANGELO designed the great dome. The huge plaza in front of the church is the Square of Saint Peter, where a large crowd gathers on CHRISTMAS Day each year to receive a papal blessing.

"Sanctus" An ancient HYMN of praise to God. The LATIN text begins, "Sanctus, sanctus, sanctus" ('Holy, holy, holy').

Serenity Prayer A prayer that has become popular in recent years, particularly in recovery programs such as Alcoholics Anonymous. It has been adapted from a prayer attributed to Reinhold NIEBUHR.

> God, grant me the serenity to accept the things I cannot change,

Courage to change
    the things I can change,
And wisdom to know the difference.

SAINT PETER'S BASILICA The largest and best-known church in the world.

"Silent Night" Of the thousands of CHRISTMAS carols written through the centuries, "Silent Night" is one of the best known and best loved. The words were written in German in 1818 by Father Joseph Mohr, a PRIEST in a tiny Austrian village. The organ in Father Mohr's church was broken, so the music originally prepared for the Christmas Eve service had to be abandoned. Father Mohr wrote the words to "Silent Night" and asked his organist, Franz Gruber, to write music that could be played on guitar. The song might never have traveled beyond the village where it was written, except that the organ repairman heard it and repeated it to others throughout the region.

Silent night, holy night,
All is calm, all is bright
    'Round yon virgin mother and child.

Holy infant so tender and mild,
Sleep in heavenly peace,
    Sleep in heavenly peace.

Sistine Chapel One of several chapels in the VATICAN. It is renowned because its ceiling and walls are decorated with the artwork of Renaissance masters. The entire ceiling and one wall contain frescoes by MICHELANGELO. These paintings portray events from the Bible—the CREATION, the FALL OF MAN, and the history of the ISRAELITE people. One of the best-known illustrations in the ceiling shows God reaching out to touch ADAM's hand and infuse life into him. It took Michelangelo four and a half years to complete the ceiling. The wall above the ALTAR contains Michelangelo's huge masterpiece, *The Last Judgment*, a painting sixty feet high.

SISTINE CHAPEL The ceiling of the Sistine Chapel was painted by Michelangelo. This detail shows God reaching out to infuse life into Adam.

For centuries art critics thought Michelangelo used dark and somber colors in the Sistine Chapel. In recent years, however, the frescoes have been painstakingly cleaned of the soot and wax that had accumulated over 400 years. The frescoes are now seen in colors far more bright and vibrant than anyone had ever imagined.

Slough of Despond In *The PILGRIM'S PROGRESS*, one of Christian's first obstacles on his journey to the CELESTIAL CITY was a swampy area named the Slough of Despond. He got so discouraged he almost returned to the City of Destruction. In BUNYAN's allegory, the Slough of Despond represents any deep discouragement that threatens to sidetrack us from our pursuit of God.

❦ More broadly, a "slough of despond" can be any serious discouragement or depression.

soli Deo gloria Johann Sebastian BACH added this LATIN phrase at the end of many of his compositions. It means 'to God alone be the glory'.

spirituals Songs that originated with the African-American slaves. Spirituals have religious themes, and many of them refer directly or indirectly to freedom from slavery. Another common theme is getting to HEAVEN. Some spirituals that are well known today include "GONNA LAY DOWN MY BURDEN," "JOSHUA FIT THE BATTLE OF JERICHO," "HE'S GOT THE WHOLE WORLD IN HIS HANDS," and "SWING LOW, SWEET CHARIOT."

"Swing Low, Sweet Chariot" An American Negro SPIRITUAL that begins,

"Swing low, sweet chariot, Comin' for to carry me home." The chariot is reminiscent of the CHARIOT OF FIRE that took ELIJAH "home"—to HEAVEN.

"Te Deum" An ancient HYMN of praise to God. As with many LATIN hymns, the name simply comes from the first several words of the Latin text. In this case, the text begins "Te Deum laudamus" ('We praise thee, O God').

We praise thee, O God:
We acknowledge thee to be the Lord.
All the earth doth worship thee,
The Father everlasting.

Ten Commandments, The An epic motion picture directed by Cecil B. DeMille (1956). It is the story of MOSES—his birth, his encounter

WESTMINSTER ABBEY A beautiful Gothic church near the Houses of Parliament.

with the Lord at the BURNING BUSH, the Exodus, receiving the TEN COMMAND-MENTS at Mt. SINAI, and the years of wandering in the WILDERNESS. It is one of the great motion pictures based on a biblical theme.

Thomas à Kempis (c.1380–1471) A medieval MONK, he is generally considered to be the author of *IMITATION OF CHRIST*, one of the most influential Christian books ever written. He emphasized the importance of imitating the spirit and actions of Christ.

Watts, Isaac (1674–1748) One of the great HYMN writers in the history of the church. He wrote more than 600 hymns, including "JOY TO THE WORLD," "When I Survey the Wondrous Cross," "O God, Our Help in Ages Past," and "Am I a Soldier of the Cross."

Westminster Abbey A famous Gothic church located near the Houses of Parliament in London. The present building dates back to 1245. It is the traditional site of royal coronations in England, and many kings, queens, and other famous persons are buried there. The "Poets' Corner" commemorates many of Britain's best-known poets.

"What a Friend We Have in Jesus" The words to this beautiful song were written by Joseph Scriven, an Irishman whose fiancée had accidentally drowned the day before their wedding. He never recovered from his own heartbreak, but he wrote this poem to console his mother in her grief:

What a friend we have in Jesus,
All our sins and griefs to bear!
What a privilege to carry
Everything to God in prayer.
Oh, what peace we often forfeit,
Oh, what needless pain we bear,
All because we do not carry
Everything to God in prayer.

"When the Saints Go Marching In" An American Negro SPIRITUAL. The SAINTS are the Christians who are marching into HEAVEN.

When the saints go marching in,
Oh when the saints go marching in,
O Lord, I want to be in that number,
When the saints go marching in!

HOW TO BECOME MORE BIBLICALLY LITERATE

Do you ever wish you had a better understanding of the Bible? Are you confused by the chronology of events in the Old Testament or in the Gospels? Do you want to learn more about the Minor Prophets—or the Epistles? And what about church history? How can we learn from the past if we don't know the past?

How can we become more literate in all these areas? The most obvious answer to becoming biblically literate is to read the Bible! It's not enough just to read *about* the Bible. Let the Bible itself be your instructor.

Although many of the quotations in this book are taken from the King James Version (since its wording is embedded in our culture), I do not recommend the King James Version for reading. Frankly, it's too difficult for most of us to understand. For pure reading pleasure, I recommend *The Living Bible*. You will find that familiar passages come alive in a new way in its fresh, contemporary language. As Billy Graham once said of *The Living Bible*, "It reads like today's newspaper." If you prefer a version that utilizes more of a word-for-word style of translation, try the New International Version or the New Revised Standard Version. If your church uses the King James Version, you may want to try out the New King James Version. It maintains the stately cadence of the King James Version, but the obscure words and the use of *thee and thou* have been updated.

You may want to try reading straight through the Bible. If so, I suggest that you use an edition such as *The Daily Walk Bible* (Tyndale House), which is available in three different versions—Living Bible, King James Version, and New Revised Standard Version. The Bible text is divided into convenient daily readings, and each day's reading includes a brief devotional introduction.

A more innovative approach to Bible reading is available in *The Daily Bible* (Harvest House), or *The One Year Bible* (Tyndale House). *The Daily Bible*, which uses the New International Version, is arranged in chronological order. Since the traditional order of the BOOKS OF THE BIBLE is not entirely chronological, this arrangement helps the reader understand the flow of history through the Bible. *The One Year Bible* (available in six different translations) is rearranged even more creatively. It is divided into 365 daily readings, and each day's reading includes a portion from the Old Testament, a portion from the New Testament, a PSALM, and a few verses from the PROVERBS. This variety helps you keep going when you hit the portions of the text that most people find difficult to read.

As odd as it may sound, I also recommend Bible story books—even for adults. They give a good overview of the stories from both the Old and New Testaments. They also provide a wonderful introduction to the people of the Bible. There are many good Bible story books. I suggest that you consider one of the following:

The One Year Bible Story Book (Tyndale House)
The Beginner's Bible (Questar)
The Children's Bible in 365 Stories (Lion)
The Children's Bible (Golden)
The Bible in Pictures for Little Eyes (Moody).

In the area of church history, a good introductory book is *Church History in Plain Language*, by Bruce L. Shelley (Word Publishing, 1982). Most Christians are relatively weak in their knowledge and understanding of church history, so I encourage you to read in this area.

In the area of THEOLOGY and Bible DOCTRINE, a good introductory book is *Essential Truths of the Christian Faith* by R. C. Sproul (Tyndale House, 1992).

I hope you'll find some of these resources helpful as you continue on your quest for Bible literacy.

INDEX